Clashing Views on Controversial
Issues in Human Sexuality

NINTH EDITION

Selected, Edited, and with Introductions by

William J. Taverner
Fairleigh Dickinson University

W9-BWB-949

McGraw-Hill/Dushkin
A Division of The McGraw-Hill Companies

To Denise, Robert, and Christopher

Photo Acknowledgment
Cover image: Corbis

Cover Acknowledgment
Maggie Lytle

Manufactured in the United States of America

Ninth Edition

123456789DOCDOC98765

Library of Congress Cataloging-in-Publication Data
Main entry under title:
Taking sides: clashing views on controversial issues in human sexuality/selected, edited, and with introductions by William J. Taverner.—9th ed.
Includes bibliographical references and index.
1. Sex. 2. Sexual ethics. I. Taverner, William J., *comp.*
612.6
0-07-291711-3
ISSN: 1098-5387

Printed on Recycled Paper

Preface

In few areas of American society today are clashing views more evident than in the area of human sexual behavior. Almost daily, in the news media, in congressional hearings, and on the streets, we hear about Americans of all ages taking completely opposite positions on such issues as abortion, contraception, fertility, homosexuality, teenage sexuality, and the like. Given the highly personal, emotional, and sensitive nature of these issues, sorting out the meaning of these controversies and fashioning a coherent position on them can be a difficult proposition. The purpose of this book, therefore, is to encourage meaningful critical thinking about current issues related to human sexuality, and the debates are designed to assist you in the task of clarifying your own personal values in relation to some common, and often polar, perspectives on the issues presented.

This ninth edition of *Taking Sides: Clashing Views on Controversial Issues in Human Sexuality* presents 40 lively and thoughtful statements by articulate advocates on opposite sides of a variety of sexuality related questions. Each issue includes:

- A *question* (e.g., Issue 1 asks, Should sexuality education be comprehensive?);
- An *introduction* that presents background information helpful for understanding the context of the debate and information on the authors who will be contributing to the debate;
- *Essays* by two authors—one who responds yes, and one who responds no to the question; and
- A *postscript* that poses additional questions to help you further examine the issues raised (or not raised) by the authors, including bibliographical resources.

It is important to remember that for the questions debated in this volume, the essays represent only two perspectives on the issue. Remember that the debates do not end there—most issues have many shades of gray, and you may find your own values congruent with neither author. Since this book is a tool to encourage critical thinking, you should not feel confined to the views expressed in the articles. You may see important points on both sides of an issue and may construct for yourself a new and creative approach, which may incorporate the best of both sides or provide an entirely new vantage point for understanding.

As you read this collection of issues, try to respect other people's philosophical worldviews and beliefs and attempt to articulate your own. At the same time, be aware of the authors' potential biases and how they may affect the positions each author articulates. Be aware, too, of your own biases. We all have experiences that may shape the way we look at a controversial issue. Try to come to each issue with an open mind. You may find your values challenged—or strengthened—after reading both views. Although you may disagree with one or even both of the arguments offered for each issue, it is important that you read each statement carefully and critically.

Changes to This Edition

This edition of *Taking Sides/Human Sexuality* includes substantial changes from the previous edition, including 10 brand new issues or issues with updated articles.

Brand New Issues

- Is Masters and Johnson's Model an Accurate Description of Sexual Response? (Issue 3)
- Is Oral Sex Really Sex? (Issue 4)
- Should Emergency Contraception Be Available over the Counter? (Issue 5)
- Is the Testosterone Patch the Right Cure for Low Libido? (Issue 7)
- Should Sexual Content on the Internet Be Restricted? (Issue 10)
- Should the FCC Restrict Broadcast "Indecency"? (Issue 11)

Issues with Updated Articles

Note that some questions have also been rephrased.

- Should Sexuality Education Be Comprehensive? (Issue 1)
- Is the G-Spot a Myth? (Issue 6)
- Is Pedophilia Always Harmful? (Issue 13)
- Should Society Support Cohabitation Before Marriage? (Issue 17)
- Should Same-Sex Marriage Be Legal? (Issue 18)

In all, 19 of the 40 essays are brand new. In addition, introductions and postscripts have been revised and updated where necessary.

A Word to the Instructor

An *Instructor's Manual,* with issue synopses, suggestions for classroom discussions, and test questions (multiple-choice and essay) is available from McGraw-Hill/Dushkin. This resource, authored by Ryan W. McKee, is a very useful accompaniment for this text. A general guidebook, *Using Taking Sides in the Classroom,* which discusses methods and techniques for integrating the pro/con approach into any classroom setting, is also available. An online version of *Using Taking Sides in the Classroom* and a correspondence service for *Taking Sides* adopters can be found at www.dushkin.com/usingts.

Taking Sides: Clashing Views on Controversial Issues in Human Sexuality is one of the many titles in the Taking Sides series. If you are interested in seeing the table of contents for any of the other titles, please visit the Taking Sides Web site at www.dushkin.com/takingsides.

For more information, please contact McGraw-Hill/Dushkin or visit www.dushkin.com, or www.mhhe.com, or by contacting the author at billtaverner@earthlink.net. Ideas for new issues are *always welcome!*

Acknowledgments

First and foremost, I wish to thank my family. Putting together a collection of pro and con essays is no easy task, and the many hours I worked on this book were also hours that my wife spent patiently and graciously watching the kids, letting me bounce ideas off her, reviewing my selections and commentary, helping me to temper my own biases, and being wonderful in every way. Denise, I love you so much. I also thank my children, Robert and Christopher, who always welcomed me with open arms whenever I was done working for the day. I love you all.

I thank my parents and family. As is probably true with many families, visiting with the Taverners for an evening is very much like seeing *Taking Sides* in real life. I love them for their support and for their help in making me think critically about all these issues.

For the hard work that goes into this book, I am indebted to the expert publishing skills of all my colleagues at McGraw-Hill/Dushkin. Thank you, Larry Loeppke, for your patience and support. Thanks to Lori Church for handling all the permissions requests. Thanks to Julie Keck and colleagues for all your efforts in marketing. Most of all, thanks to Jill Peter. Jill advised me on all the new issues, carefully reviewing every article and giving me excellent feedback on what to keep and what to cut. I couldn't have done this edition without Jill.

Many thanks to Ryan W. McKee, author of the Instructor's Manual to *Taking Sides,* who also assisted with editing and researching many of the new issues, and fine-tuning them for publication. Thanks to Elizabeth Schroeder, my coeditor for the *American Journal of Sexuality Education* and the editor of *Taking Sides: Clashing Views on Controversial Issues in Family and Personal Relationships.* Elizabeth is the only colleague I know who truly understands what it takes to put a *Taking Sides* book together! Thanks, Elizabeth, for letting me bounce so many concepts off you.

Thanks to professional colleagues who reviewed parts of the manuscript, or who otherwise shared their expertise generously: Vern Bullough (who gave me a great history lesson on Masters and Johnson), Barbara Huberman (who checked my facts on emergency contraception), Sue Montfort (who is a role model for thoughtful analysis), and Leonore Tiefer (who checked my write-up on Intrinsa for accuracy). Thanks also to Mark Eberle, my high school buddy, now a lawyer, who helped me navigate the legal arguments on sex and the Internet, and explained what "certiorari" means so that I could explain it to my readers.

Thanks to professional colleagues who suggested new issues or pointed me in the direction of great articles: Maggi Boyer, Linda Hendrickson, Barbara Huberman, Lis Maurer, Irene Peters, Erika Pluhar, Deborah Roffman, Martha Roper, Beverly Whipple, and Susie Wilson. Thanks also to my students at Fairleigh Dickinson University who tell me with brutal honesty which issues are interesting, and which are not.

Finally, I wish to thank two colleagues who have been both mentors and friends for many years: Peggy Brick and Robert T. Francoeur. Peggy and I have collaborated on numerous sexuality education manuals, and I value her advice dearly. She is a patient and generous mentor who constantly inspires me to think critically about all matters, not just those related to sexuality education. Bob edited or coedited the first seven editions of *Taking Sides: Clashing Views on Controversial Issues in Human Sexuality.* I have had the pleasure of working with Bob on three previous editions of this book, and was introduced to both *Taking Sides* and Bob when I took his international studies course in Copenhagen, Denmark, 14 years ago. I am grateful for his kind guidance over the years. Every sexuality educator should have the privilege of working with such knowledgeable and caring mentors.

William J. Taverner
Fairleigh Dickinson University

Contents In Brief

Contents

PART 1   SEXUAL HEALTH ISSUES   1

Former United States Surgeon General David Satcher outlines his call to action to promote sexual health and responsible sexual behavior. Dr. Satcher expresses support for a comprehensive approach to sexuality education, inclusive of teaching about abstinence, contraception, and safer sex to help young people avoid unplanned pregnancy and sexually transmitted infections. Editorialist Don Feder argues that comprehensive sexuality education is not effective, and criticizes the methods used to compile the surgeon general's report, which includes interviews with commercial sex workers.

Researchers Sally Guttmacher et al. maintain that their study of New York City high school students who received both condoms and an HIV/AIDS education program versus Chicago high school students who received only HIV/AIDS education proves that distributing condoms in schools does not increase sexual activity but does result in students using condoms more often when they are sexually active. Professor of education Edwin J. Delattre rejects the argument that there is a moral obligation to save lives by distributing condoms in schools. He asserts that distributing condoms in schools promotes morally unacceptable casual sexual relationships.

Stephanie Ann Sanders, a director and scientist with the Kinsey Institute and a contributing author to the *Encarta Online Encyclopedia*, summarizes Masters and Johnson's Human Sexual Response Cycle. Paul Joannides, author of the popular book *The Guide to Getting It On!*, says that the Human Sexual Response Cycle is a "one-size-fits-all" model that does not account for individual variations.

Issue 4.   Is Oral Sex Really Sex?   53

Sexuality educator Rhonda Chittenden says that it is important for young people to expand their narrow definitions of sex and understand that oral sex *is* sex. Chittenden offers additional educational messages about oral sex. Sexuality trainer Nora Gelperin argues that adult definitions of oral sex are out of touch with the meaning the behavior holds for young people. Rather than impose adult definitions of intimacy, educators should be seeking to help young people clarify and understand their own values.

Issue 5.   Should Emergency Contraception Be Available over the Counter?   68

New York Times columnist Jane E. Brody believes that politics, not science, drove the FDA's decision not to allow emergency contraception to be made available over the counter. The Food and Drug Administration, responsible for regulating all drugs dispensed in the United States, says that its decision was not political, and that it would reconsider its decision if presented with evidence that girls under age 16 could take it safely without parental supervision.

Issue 6.   Is the G-Spot a Myth?   79

Psychologist Terence M. Hines says that the widespread acceptance of the G-spot as being real conflicts with available evidence. Hines explains that the existence of the G-spot has never been verified by empirical, objective means and that women may have been misinformed about their bodies and their sexuality. Sexologist Gary Schubach responds to Hines' critique of research on the G-spot. He states that what is commonly referred to as the G-spot is actually the female prostate gland. Renaming the G-spot the "female prostate" may help clear up misconceptions about the location and physiology of this controversial spot.

Loretta M. Kopelman, a professor of medical humanities, argues that certain moral absolutes apply to all cultures and that these, combined with the many serious health and cultural consequences of female circumcision, require that all forms of female genital mutilation be eliminated. P. Masila Mutisya, a professor of multicultural education, contends that we should allow the simplest form of female circumcision, nicking the clitoral hood to draw a couple of drops of blood, as part of the rich heritage of rite of passage for newborn and pubertal girls in those cultures with this tradition.

Janice Weinman, executive director of the American Association of University Women (AAUW), states that, while there has been some progress since the AAUW published its study entitled *How Schools Shortchange Girls* in 1991, its 1998 review of 1,000 research studies entitled *Gender Gaps: Where Schools Still Fail Our Children* found that girls still face a gender gap in math, science, and computer science. Psychologist and author Judith Kleinfeld argues that despite appearances, girls still have an advantage over boys in terms of their future plans, teachers' expectations, and everyday school experiences. Furthermore, minority males in particular are at a disadvantage educationally.

Dorian Solot and Marshall Miller, founders of the Alternatives to Marriage Project (www.unmarried.org), describe some of the challenges faced by people who choose to live together without marrying, and offer practical advice for couples who face discrimination. David Popenoe and Barbara Dafoe Whitehead, directors of the National Marriage Project (marriage.rutgers.edu), contend that living together before marriage is not a good way to prepare for marriage or avoid divorce. They maintain that cohabitation weakens the institution of marriage and poses serious risks for women and children.

The Human Rights Campaign (HRC), America's largest gay and lesbian organization, explains why same-sex couples should be afforded the same legal right to marry as heterosexual couples. John Cornyn, U.S. Senator from Texas, says a constitutional amendment is needed to define marriage as permissible only between a man and a woman. Senator Cornyn contends that the traditional institution of marriage needs to be protected from activist courts that would seek to redefine it.

Author James Bovard asserts that legalizing sex work would help stem the
spread of AIDS and free up the police to focus on controlling violent crime.
Anastasia Volkonsky, founding director of PROMISE, an organization dedicated to combating sexual exploitation, maintains that decriminalizing prostitution would only cause more social harm, particularly to women.

Bernice Sandler, a senior scholar at the National Association for Women in
Education, maintains that schools should pay damages for student-on-student
sexual harassment. She cites several cases in which school authorities
ignored blatant and pervasive sexual harassment of students by other students
until the parents of the harassed students forced action by filing lawsuits seeking compensation for damages. Author Sarah J. McCarthy objects to schools
paying damages for student-on-student sexual harassment, stating that
Congress and lawmakers often jump to legislation as a quick-fix solution. She
asserts that new laws authorizing the filing of lawsuits would empty taxpayers'
pockets, bankrupt school districts, and lead to centralized thought control, an
Americanized version of Chairman Mao's cultural revolution in China.

Introduction

Sexual Attitudes in Perspective

America is one big divided country, with a blue northern and coastal perimeter, and a bright red center! At least that is the picture painted by television and print media's portrayal of American social attitudes. Are you from a "red state," perhaps Florida, or maybe Texas? Then surely you are a Republican who supported George W. Bush in the 2004 presidential election. You also oppose abortion and same-sex marriage, and you probably love hunting and NASCAR. Are you from a "blue state," perhaps California, or maybe Massachusetts? Then surely you are a Democrat who voted for John Kerry in 2004. You support a woman's right to choose, are a staunch civil libertarian, and maybe have plans to attend a friend's same-sex wedding. Oh, and you are also a vegetarian who loves to drink lattes!

If you are scratching your head thinking that neither profile describes you, you are not alone. Texas and Florida may be "red states," but how do we reconcile the fact that more than 6 million Americans in these two states voted for Kerry, who has been called a "bleeding heart liberal"? Or that another 6 million people voted for "redneck conservative" Bush in "blue states" California and Massachusetts? Or that many more millions in other states voted in ways that were inconsistent with their assigned state color? Moreover, what do we know about the 40 percent of eligible voters who did not vote at all in 2004? It's an important question as these non-voters make up almost 100 million Americans! The reality is that our opinions, attitudes, and values on social and sexual issues are as diverse as we are. They are formed by numerous factors that we will explore in this introduction.

As you examine the 20 controversial issues in human sexuality in this volume, you will find yourself unavoidably encountering the values you have absorbed from our society, your ethnic background, your religious heritage and traditions, and your personal experiences. Because these values will influence your decisions, often without being consciously recognized, it is important to actively think about the role these undercurrent themes play in the positions you take on these issues.

Many thanks to Robert T. Francoeur for his insights on this Introduction, parts of which are repeated from previous editions of *Taking Sides* when Francoeur was editor. Dr. Francoeur is the editor of the award-winning *International Encyclopedia of Sexuality,* and there is no greater authority on global cultural differences related to understanding sexuality.

How Social and Ethnic Factors Influence Our Values

American society is not homogeneous, nor is it even red or blue! People who grow up in rural, suburban, and large urban environments sometimes have subtle differences in their values and attitudes when it comes to gender roles, marriage, and sexuality, or trends that may reflect the views of the majority of people in communities. Growing up in different areas of the United States can influence one's views of sex, marriage, and family. This is even more true for men and women who were born, and raised, in another country and culture.

Many studies have shown how values can be affected by one's family income level and socioeconomic status. Studies have also indicated that one's occupation, educational level, and income are closely related to one's values, attitudes, sex-role conceptions, child-rearing practices, and sexual identity. Our values and attitudes about sex are also influenced by whether we are brought up in a rural, suburban, or large urban environment. Our ethnic background can be an important influence on our values and attitudes. In contrast to the vehement debates among white, middle-class Americans about pornography, for instance, Robert Staples, a professor of sociology at the University of California, San Francisco, says that among African Americans, pornography is a trivial issue. "Blacks," Staples explains, "have traditionally had a more naturalistic attitude toward human sexuality, seeing it as the normal expression of sexual attraction between men and women. . . . Rather than seeing the depiction of heterosexual intercourse or nudity as an inherent debasement of women, as a fringe group of [white] feminists claims, the black community would see women as having equal rights to the enjoyment of sexual stimuli. . . . Since the double [moral] standard has never attracted many American blacks, the claim that women are exploited by exhibiting their nude bodies or engaging in heterosexual intercourse lacks credibility" (quoted in Philip Nobile and Eric Nadler, *United States of America vs. Sex* [Minotaur Press, 1986]). While some middle-class whites may be very concerned about pornography promoting sexual promiscuity, many African Americans are far more concerned about issues related to poverty and employment opportunities.

Similarly, attitudes toward homosexuality vary among white, African American, and Latino cultures. In the macho tradition of Latin America, male homosexual behavior may be considered a sign that one cannot find a woman and have sexual relationships like a "real" man. In some African American communities, a similar judgment prevails, and gay and lesbian relationships are often unrecognized. In his book, *On the Down Low: A Journey into the Lives of "Straight" Black Men Who Sleep with Men* (Broadway, 2004), J.L. King explains this cultural ethic, and how "straight" men live secret lives with their same-sex sexual encounters "on the down low," and not impacting their sexual orientation. Understanding this ethnic value becomes very important in appreciating the ways in which African Americans and Latinos respond to the crisis of AIDS and the presence of males with AIDS in their families. The family might deny that a son or husband has AIDS until the very end because others might interpret this admission as a confession that the person is homosexual. Or, a man on the "down low" might receive inadequate treatment from a doctor or health clinic who does not ask the right questions. A clinician who asks him if he is gay, will probably be told no. A clinician who asks a number of questions, including whether he sometimes has sex with men, might be able to get a better picture of his sexuality and needs.

Another example of differing ethnic values is the issue of single motherhood. In ethnic groups with a strong tradition of extended matrilineal families, the concept of an "illegitimate" child born "out-of-wedlock" may not even exist. Unmarried mothers in these cultures do not carry the same stigma often associated with single mothers in other, less-matrilineal cultures. When "outsiders" who do not share the particular ethnic values of a culture enter into such a subculture, they often cannot understand why contraception and sexuality education programs do not produce any substantial change in attitudes. They overlook the basic social scripting that has already taken place. Gender roles also vary from culture to culture. Muslim men and women who grow up in the Middle East and then emigrate to the United States have to adapt to the much greater freedom women have in the States. Similarly, American men and women who have served in the armed forces in Afghanistan, Iraq, Saudi Arabia, and other parts of the Middle East found they had to adapt to very different Muslim cultures that put many restrictions on the movement and dress of women in the military.

A boy who grows up among the East Bay Melanesians in the Southwestern Pacific is taught to avoid any social contact with girls from the age of three or four, even though he may run around naked and masturbate in public. Adolescent Melanesian boys and girls are not allowed to have sex with each other, but boys are expected to have sex both with an older male and with a boy of his own age. Their first heterosexual experiences come with marriage. In the Cook Islands, Mangaian boys are expected to have sex with many girls after an older woman teaches them about the art of sexual play. Mangaians also accept and expect both premarital and extramarital sex.

But one does not have to look to exotic anthropological studies to find evidence of the importance of ethnic values. Even within the United States, subtle but important differences in sexual attitudes and values exist among its diverse population of its native people, and of those who immigrated from all over the world.

Religious Factors in Attitudes Toward Sex

In the Middle Ages, Christian theologians divided sexual behaviors into two categories: behaviors that were "natural" and those that were "unnatural." Since they believed that the natural function and goal of all sexual behavior and relations was reproduction, masturbation was unnatural because it frustrated the natural goal of conception and continuance of the species. Rape was certainly considered illicit because it was not within the marital bond, but since it was procreative, rape was also considered a natural use of sex. The same system of distinction was applied to other sexual relations and behaviors.

Premarital sex, adultery, and incest were natural uses of sexuality, while oral sex, anal sex, and contraception were unnatural. Homosexual relations were both illicit and unnatural. These religious values were based on the view that God created man and woman at the beginning of time and laid down certain rules and guidelines for sexual behavior and relations. This view is still very influential in our culture, even for those who are not active in any religious tradition.

In recent years, several analysts have highlighted two philosophical or religious perspectives that appear throughout Judeo-Christian tradition and Western civilization. Understanding these two perspectives is important in any attempt to debate controversial issues in human sexuality.

Judeo-Christian tradition allows us to examine two distinct worldviews: the *fixed worldview* and the *process worldview*. The fixed worldview says that morality is unchanging. Right and wrong are always right and wrong, regardless of the situation or circumstances. The fixed worldview relies on a literal interpretation of its religious or ethical teachings, without regard for context. The process worldview examines issues of morality in an ever-changing world. What is right or wrong may require a contextual examination, and rules and ethics must constantly be re-examined in light of new information and the world's evolving context.

Take for example the question of masturbation. Where does the Christian prohibition of masturbation come from? If you search the Bible, the word is never mentioned! Yet much of what has been taught in Christianity regarding masturbation comes from the story of Onan:

> Then Judah said to Onan, "Go in to your brother's wife and perform the duty of a brother-in-law to her, and raise up offspring for your brother." But Onan knew that the offspring would not be his. So whenever he went in to his brother's wife he would waste the semen on the ground, so as not to give offspring to his brother. And what he did was wicked in the sight of the Lord, and he put him to death also. (Genesis 38:8–10, English Standard Version)

The passage describes how Judah asked his brother Onan to help him to bear a child, and how Onan would have sexual intercourse with his sister-in-law, but "waste the semen." This phrase has been interpreted literally by fundamentalist Christians to say that semen must never be wasted. Indeed, Catholic theologians in the middle ages even examined whether or not sperm cells had souls![1] This literal interpretation led to prohibitions on masturbation and other sexual behaviors that do not produce pregnancy. The fixed worldview is that God did not want any semen wasted—what Onan did was "wicked," and so masturbation will always be wicked.

---

[1] Under the belief that the sperm cell might have a soul, consider that there are at least 300 million sperm cells in the typical ejaculation. If a male masturbated just one time per month for 10 years, he alone would be responsible for the death of 36 billion ensouled individuals.

Process worldview Christians may read the same passage differently. They might ask, What was the thing Onan did that was 'wicked in the sight of the Lord'? Was it really the wasting of semen? Or was it Onan's intentional failure to produce a child for his brother, as was his traditional obligation at the time? Further, was it his deceit as he apparently enjoyed the sexual interaction with his sister-in-law without fulfilling his obligation? A process worldview Christian might also wonder about the role of female masturbation, since there is no seed released in such an act. Or about the fact that masturbation is such a common behavior, from birth to death, that causes no harm. Or, how masturbation might be a healthy sexual alternative to teen sexual activity[2] or extramarital urges.

This example only serves to illustrate two possible values related to the sometimes controversial issue of masturbation. It may be tempting to stop there and look at only two perspectives, but consider that there are many other reasons people may support or oppose masturbation. The ancient Chinese Tao of love and sex advises that semen should be ejaculated very rarely, for reasons related to mental and physical (not moral) health. Masturbation aside, the Tao advises that males should only ejaculate one time per every 100 acts of inter-course, so that female—not male—pleasure is maximized! Another position on masturbation may be its functionality, as viewed by sex therapists, for treating sexual dysfunction. There are many perspectives on this one topic, and there are similarly many perspectives beyond the two articles presented for every issue in this book.

Consider a non-Western example from recent history—the Islamic cultures of the Middle East and the politics of Islamic fundamentalists. On the fixed worldview side are fundamentalist Muslims who believe that the Muslim world needs to return to the unchanging, literal words of Mohammed and the Koran (the sacred book of the teachings of Allah, or God). Again, there is no gray area in a fixed worldview—what Allah revealed through Mohammed is forever the truth, and the words of the Koran must be taken literally. There is no room for mitigating factors or new or unique circumstances that may arise. The literal interpretation of the Koran calls for purging all Western and modern influences that have assimilated into Islamic society. Consequently, about 25 years ago, Islamic fundamentalists overthrew the shah of Iran and assassinated the president of Egypt, who had encouraged modernization of their countries. More recently, the September 11, 2001, terrorist attacks against the U.S. World Trade Center and the Pentagon represented the rejection of Western influences at its ultimate, deadliest extreme.

On the other side are Muslims who view the world through a process worldview—an ever-changing scene in which they must struggle to reinterpret and apply the basic principles of the Koran to new situations. They consider as progress the new rights that women have earned in recent years, such as the right to education, the right to vote, the right to election of political office, the right to divorce their husbands, the right to contraception, and many other rights.

---

[2] Former U.S. Surgeon General Joycelyn Elders was fired in 1994 for suggesting this.

The fixed and process worldviews are evident throughout the history of American culture. Like Islamic fundamentalists, Christian fundamentalists believe that Americans need to return to traditional values. This worldview often shares a conviction that the sexual revolution, changing attitudes toward masturbation and homosexuality, a tolerance of premarital and extramarital sex, sexuality education in the schools, and the legality of abortion are contributing to a cultural decline and must be rejected. A classic expression of this value system surfaced in the aftermath of the September 11, 2001, terrorist attacks when former presidential candidate Pat Robertson and the Reverend Jerry Falwell agreed that the destruction of the towers of the World Trade Center and the Pentagon were caused by the immoral activism of the American Civil Liberties Union and advocates for abortion and gay rights.

At the same time, other Americans argue for legalized abortion, civil rights for homosexuals, decriminalization of prostitution, androgynous sex roles in child-rearing practices, and the abolition of all laws restricting the right to privacy for sexually active, consenting adults. For a time, the process worldview gained dominance in Western cultures, but renewed influences of such fixed world groups as the Moral Majority and Religious Right have manifested in the recent elections of President George W. Bush and other fundamentalist politicians.

The two worldviews described here characteristically permeate and color the way we look at everything in our lives. One or the other view will influence the way we approach a particular political, economic, or moral issue, and the way we reach decisions about sexual issues and relationships. However, one must keep in mind that no one is ever fully and always on one or the other end of the spectrum. The spectrum of beliefs, attitudes, and values proposed here is an intellectual abstraction. Real life is not that simple. You may find yourself holding fixed worldviews on some issues, and process worldviews on others. Your views may represent neither worldview. Just like there are no pure blue and red states, there are no absolutes when it comes to sexual values. There is a continuum of values, with the fixed worldview on one end, and the process worldview on the other. Your sexual values for each issue presented in this text will likely depend on the issue, your personal experiences with the subject matter, and the values and beliefs that you have accumulated by important sources within your own life.

Personal connection with an issue may be a strong indicator of one's sexual values. If you are among the millions of Americans who have had a sexually transmitted infection, that firsthand experience will likely affect what you believe about condom availability programs or sexuality education. If you are a woman who has experienced female ejaculation, you would be hard-pressed to believe an author's rejection of the G-spot. A family member whom you love and respect, who taught you that pornography is wrong, will make it difficult for you to accept the proposition that it is okay. We are all sexual beings, so many of the issues presented here provide an opportunity for a personal connection to an issue, beyond a simple academic exercise.

As you plunge into the 20 controversial issues selected for this volume, try to be aware of your own predispositions toward certain topics, and try to be sensitive to the kinds of ethnic, religious, social, economic, and other factors that may be influencing the position a particular author takes on an issue. Understanding the roots that support a person's overt position on an issue will help you to decide whether or not you agree with that position. Take time to read a little bit about the authors' biographies, too, as their affiliations may reveal something about their potential biases. Understanding these same factors in your own thinking will help you to articulate more clearly and convincingly your own values and decisions.

On the Internet . . .

The Abstinence Clearinghouse

The Abstinence Clearinghouse is a national, nonprofit organization that promotes the practice of sexual abstinence through the distribution of educational materials and by providing speakers on the topic.

http://www.abstinence.net

Planned Parenthood Federation of America

Planned Parenthood Federation of America, Inc., is the world's largest and most trusted voluntary reproductive health care organization.

http://www.plannedparenthood.org

Food and Drug Administration (FDA)

The FDA is a government body overseen by the U.S. Department of Health and Human Services. Among its many responsibilities is to promote and protect public health by helping safe and effective products reach the market in a timely way.

http://www.fda.gov

Emergency Contraception Web Site

Operated by the Office of Population Research at Princeton University and the Association of Reproductive Health Professionals, this Web site provides accurate information about emergency contraception derived from the medical literature and a directory of local clinicians willing to provide emergency contraceptives.

http://www.not-2-late.com

RESOLVE: The National Infertility Association

RESOLVE: The National Infertility Association provides education, advocacy, and support related to infertility.

http://www.resolve.org

The FGM Education and Networking Project

The FGM Education and Networking Project disseminates on-line and offline material related to female genital mutilation, otherwise known as female circumcision.

http://www.fgmnetwork.org

Sexual Health Issues

*S*exuality has been called a "bio-psycho-socio and cultural phenome-non." *Humans are sexual beings from birth through death, and our sex-ual health is shaped by our physical makeup (biological); our thoughts, feelings, and perceptions of our sexuality (psychological); and the way we interact with our environment (sociological and cultural).*

This section examines nine questions related to how we learn about and experience our sexuality from childhood through our adult years, including how we take care of our reproductive health.

- Should Sexuality Education Be Comprehensive?

- Should Schools Make Condoms Available to Students?

- Is Masters and Johnson's Model an Accurate Description of Sexual Response?

- Is Oral Sex Really Sex?

- Should Emergency Contraception Be Available over the Counter?

- Is the G-Spot a Myth?

- Is the Testosterone Patch the Right Cure for Low Libido?

- Should Health Insurers Be Required to Pay for Infertility Treatments?

- Should Female Circumcision Be Banned?

ISSUE 1

Should Sexuality Education Be Comprehensive?

YES: David Satcher, from *The Surgeon General's Call to Action to Promote Sexual Health and Responsible Sexual Behavior* (United States Department of Health and Human Services, July 9, 2001)

NO: Don Feder, from "Devil Is in the Details of Surgeon General's Sex Report," *Insight on the News* (August 6, 2001)

ISSUE SUMMARY

YES: Former United States Surgeon General David Satcher outlines his call to action to promote sexual health and responsible sexual behavior. Dr. Satcher expresses support for a comprehensive approach to sexuality education, inclusive of teaching about abstinence, contraception, and safer sex to help young people avoid unplanned pregnancy and sexually transmitted infections.

NO: Editorialist Don Feder argues that comprehensive sexuality education is not effective, and criticizes the methods used to compile the surgeon general's report, which includes interviews with commercial sex workers.

In the summer of 2001, United States surgeon general David Satcher released a report titled *The Surgeon General's Call to Action to Promote Sexual Health and Responsible Sexual Behavior*. In his report, Dr. Satcher called for a comprehensive approach to sexuality education for America's children, which includes the teaching of abstinence, as well as other methods for preventing unwanted pregnancy and sexually transmitted infections. By contrast, abstinence-only education forbids any discussion of methods other than sexual abstinence. The surgeon general's report clashed with President George W. Bush's own call for $67 million in new federal spending on abstinence-only education, which would be added to the $250 million abstinence-only education funds already allocated by Congress. Bush's administration immediately distanced itself from the report.

The subject of abstinence-only education versus comprehensive sexuality education has been debated for many years and in many past editions of *Taking Sides*. Abstinence-only education proponents are concerned that any message other than "abstain" is confusing to young people. They fear that teaching other methods for preventing pregnancy and infection gives a mixed message to young people. Many abstinence-only education proponents also believe that sexual behavior outside of marriage is immoral and that young people must be guided strongly to abstain from intercourse until marriage. Abstinence-only education efforts often seek to discredit the reliability of condoms and other methods.

Proponents of comprehensive sexuality education believe that sexuality education should not be limited to discussions of abstinence but should include information about other methods in recognition of the realities young people face. They state that failing to teach all methods does a disservice to the almost 70 percent of young people who will have had intercourse by the time they finish high school. Further, proponents indicate that young people who are *currently* abstaining need information for decisions they may make *later*. Young people, on average, become sexually active eight years before they become married.

The United States is unique in its battle over sexuality education, compared to most other developed nations. Most European nations not only embrace comprehensive sexuality education but also integrate it into government-sponsored pregnancy and sexually transmitted infection prevention campaigns. The resulting teen pregnancy rates are substantially lower than those in the United States, despite similar levels of sexual activity.

In the following selections, David Satcher outlines the steps he believes are necessary to improve the overall sexual health of the United States, including education that is "developmentally and culturally appropriate" and comprehensive in its approach. Don Feder argues that Satcher's conclusions were formed long before the report was developed, as they are congruent with Satcher's prior work heading the Centers for Disease Control (CDC). Feder criticizes the report for its methodologies and conclusions about sexuality education.

David Satcher  **YES**

The Surgeon General's Call to Action to Promote Sexual Health and Responsible Sexual Behavior

I. Introduction

Sexuality is an integral part of human life. It carries the awesome potential to create new life. It can foster intimacy and bonding as well as shared pleasure in our relationships. It fulfills a number of personal and social needs, and we value the sexual part of our being for the pleasures and benefits it affords us. Yet when exercised irresponsibly it can also have negative aspects such as sexually transmitted diseases—including HIV/AIDS—unintended pregnancy, and coercive or violent behavior. To enjoy the important benefits of sexuality, while avoiding negative consequences, some of which may have long term or even life time implications, it is necessary for individuals to be sexually healthy, to behave responsibly, and to have a supportive environment—to protect their own sexual health, as well as that of others.

Sexual health is inextricably bound to both physical and mental health. Just as physical and mental health problems can contribute to sexual dysfunction and diseases, those dysfunctions and diseases can contribute to physical and mental health problems. Sexual health is not limited to the absence of disease or dysfunction, nor is its importance confined to just the reproductive years. It includes the ability to understand and weigh the risks, responsibilities, outcomes and impacts of sexual actions and to practice abstinence when appropriate. It includes freedom from sexual abuse and discrimination and the ability of individuals to integrate their sexuality into their lives, derive pleasure from it, and to reproduce if they so choose.

Sexual responsibility should be understood in its broadest sense. While personal responsibility is crucial to any individual's health status, communities also have important responsibilities. Individual responsibility includes: understanding and awareness of one's sexuality and sexual development; respect for oneself and one's partner; avoidance of physical or emotional harm to either oneself or one's partner; ensuring that pregnancy occurs only when welcomed; and recognition and tolerance of the diversity of sexual

From the *Surgeon General's Call to Action to Promote Sexual Health and Responsible Sexual Behavior,* July 9, 2001. Published by the United States Department of Health and Human Services. References omitted.

values within any community. Community responsibility includes assurance that its members have: access to developmentally and culturally appropriate sexuality education, as well as sexual and reproductive health care and counseling; the latitude to make appropriate sexual and reproductive choices; respect for diversity; and freedom from stigmatization and violence on the basis of gender, race, ethnicity, religion, or sexual orientation.

Sexual health and responsible sexual behavior are both linked to the Surgeon General's Public Health Priorities and the Department of Health and Human Services' *Healthy People 2010* initiative and the *Guide to Community Preventive Services*. These are, in turn, based on the scientific evidence and on principles of health promotion and disease prevention, and provide a basis for approaching these challenges.

The Surgeon General's Public Health Priorities include: (1) a balanced community health system, grounded at the community level and encompassing the promotion of healthy lifestyles, including responsible sexual behavior, and provision of equitable access to health care services; (2) the elimination of racial and ethnic disparities in health; and (3) a global approach to public health and the exchange of information and technology with other nations to improve world health.

Healthy People 2010 identifies national public health priorities and objectives to be achieved over the next decade. Its two overarching goals are to improve years and quality of healthy life and to eliminate disparities in health including those related to HIV/AIDS, sexually transmitted diseases, domestic violence and unintended pregnancy. The document also includes a set of 10 Leading Health Indicators for the nation, one of which is responsible sexual behavior. Two other leading health indicators are also relevant to this *Call to Action*-reducing substance abuse and improving access to health care.

The *Guide to Community Preventive Services: Systematic Reviews and Evidence-Based Recommendations* represents a significant national effort in encouraging evidence-based public health practice. It is being developed to make recommendations regarding public health interventions in a variety of areas, including mental health, violence prevention and sexual behavior. It is intended to provide an independent and scientifically rigorous road map to help reach the goals of improved health envisioned in *Healthy People 2010*.

This *Call to Action* focuses on the need to promote sexual health and responsible sexual behavior throughout the lifespan. Its primary goal is to stimulate respectful, thoughtful, and mature discussion in our communities and in our homes. While sexuality may be difficult to discuss for some, and there are certainly many different views and beliefs regarding it, we cannot afford the consequences of continued or selective silence. It is necessary to find common ground—balancing diversity of opinion with the best available scientific evidence and best practice models—to improve the health of our nation. This *Call to Action* is also the first step toward the development of guidelines to assist parents, clergy, teachers, and others in their work of improving sexual health and responsible sexual behavior.

II. The Public Health Approach

Use of a public health approach is requisite to promoting sexual health and responsible sexual behavior. This approach has four central components: 1) identifying the problem; 2) identifying risk and protective factors; 3) developing and testing interventions; and 4) implementing, and further evaluating, those interventions that have demonstrated effectiveness. In the present case, public health responds to the problem-sexually transmitted diseases, unintended pregnancies, and sexual violence-by asking what is known about its distribution and rates, what factors can be modified, if those modifications are acceptable to the community, and if they are likely to address the problem. Such approaches can range from provision of information about responsible sexuality and interventions designed to promote healthy behavior—such as sexuality education that starts from within the family, where educated and informed adults can also serve as positive role models—to developing vaccines against sexually transmitted diseases (STDs) and AIDS, and to making sexual health care more available and accessible. Additionally, public health focuses on involving communities in their own health and tailoring health promotion programs to the needs and cultures of the communities involved. Because sexuality is one of the human attributes most endowed with meaning and symbolism, it is of particular importance that addressing sexual health issues involve community wide discussion, consultation, and implementation.

This *Call to Action* provides an evidence based foundation for developing a public health approach to sexual health and responsible sexual behavior. It identifies the problems and then discusses risk and protective factors. Numerous intervention models that have been evaluated and shown to be effective, as well as some that are promising but not yet adequately evaluated, are also presented. The last step, implementation of effective interventions, will depend heavily on individual communities and their members.

III. The Public Health Problem

The United States faces a significant challenge related to the sexual health of its citizens. Concerns include: STDs; infertility and cancer resulting from STDs; HIV/AIDS; sexual abuse, coercion and prejudice; unintended pregnancy; and abortion.

Five of the ten most commonly reported infectious diseases in the U.S. are STDs; and, in 1995, STDs accounted for 87 percent of cases reported among those ten. Nevertheless, public awareness regarding STDs is not widespread, nor is their disproportionate impact on women, adolescents, and racial and ethnic minorities well known:

- Chlamydia infection is the most commonly reported STD. While reported rates of infection in women greatly exceed those in men, largely because screening programs have been primarily directed toward women, the rates for both women and men are probably similar. Chlamydia rates for women are highest among those aged

15–19 years and rates for Black and Hispanic women are also considerably higher than those for White women.

- Rates for gonorrhea are highest among women aged 15–19 years and Blacks.
- It is estimated that 45 million persons in the U.S. are infected with genital herpes and that one million new cases occur per year.
- Sexually transmitted infections in both women and men contribute to infertility, which affects approximately 14 percent of all couples in the United States at some time. For example, chlamydia and gonorrhea infections account for 15 percent of cases of infertility in women.
- Human Papillomavirus (HPV) is a sexually transmissible virus that causes genital warts. An estimated 5.5 million persons become infected with HPV each year in the U.S. and an estimated 20 million are currently infected. There are many different types of HPV. While most women who have HPV do not develop cervical cancer, four HPV subtypes are responsible for an estimated 80 percent of cervical cancer cases, with approximately 14,000 new cervical cancer cases occurring per year.

Currently, there are an estimated 800,000 to 900,000 persons living with HIV in the United States, with approximately 40,000 new HIV infections occurring every year. Among those who are currently positive for HIV, an estimated one-third are aware of their status and in treatment, one-third are aware of their status but not in treatment, and one-third have not been tested and are unaware of their status.

Since 1981, a total of more than 774,467 AIDS cases had been reported to the U.S. Centers for Disease Control and Prevention (CDC). The disease has disproportionately affected men who have sex with men—47 percent of reported cases—and minority men who have sex with men have now emerged as the population most affected. A recently released seven city survey indicates that new HIV infection was substantially higher for young Black gay and bisexual men than for their White or Hispanic counterparts. During the 1990s, the epidemic also shifted toward women. While women account for 28 percent of HIV cases reported since 1981, they accounted for 32 percent of those reported between July 1999 and June 2000. Similarly, women account for 17 percent of AIDS cases reported since 1981, but 24 percent of those reported between July 1999 and June 2000.

Sexual abuse contributes to sexual dysfunction and other public health problems such as substance abuse and mental health problems. There are an estimated 104,000 child victims of sexual abuse per year, and the proportion of women in current relationships who are subject to sexual violence is estimated at eight percent. While it is estimated that only a relatively small proportion of rapes are reported, a major national study found that 22 percent of women and approximately two percent of men had been victims of a forced sexual act.

Sexual orientation is usually determined by adolescence, if not earlier, and there is no valid scientific evidence that sexual orientation can be changed. Nonetheless, our culture often stigmatizes homosexual behavior, identity and relationships. These anti-homosexual attitudes are associated with psychological distress for homosexual persons and may have a negative impact on mental health, including a greater incidence of depression and suicide, lower self-acceptance and a greater likelihood of hiding sexual orientation. Although the research is limited, transgendered persons are reported to experience similar problems. In their extreme form, these negative attitudes lead to antigay violence. Averaged over two dozen studies, 80 percent of gay men and lesbians had experienced verbal or physical harassment on the basis of their orientation, 45 percent had been threatened with violence, and 17 percent had experienced a physical attack.

There are also persons who are challenged with developmental, physical or mental disabilities whose sexuality and sexual needs have often been ignored, or at worst, exploited and abused. Although appropriate assistance has been developed for these vulnerable populations, it is seriously under-utilized. Additional materials and programs, as well as further research, are needed.

It is estimated that nearly one-half of all pregnancies in the U.S. are unintended. While women in all age, income, race and ethnicity categories experience unintended pregnancies, the highest rates occur among adolescents, lower-income women and Black women. Unintended pregnancy is medically costly in terms of the precluded opportunity for preconception care and counseling, as well as increased likelihood of late or no prenatal care, increased risk for low birthweight, and increased risk for infant mortality. It is also socially costly in terms of out-of-wedlock births, reduced educational attainment and employment opportunity, increased welfare dependency, and later child abuse and neglect—and economically in terms of health care costs.

An estimated 1,366,000 induced abortions occurred in the U.S. in 1996, a slight increase from the 1,364,000 in 1995, but a 15 percent decrease from the 1,609,000 in 1990. A similar pattern of decrease has been observed in abortion rates with 22.9 abortions per 1000 women aged 15–44 years in 1996 compared to 27.4 in 1990. Moreover, surveillance data indicate that for those States that report previous induced abortions, nearly 45 percent of abortions reported in 1996 were obtained by women who had already had at least one abortion.

The belief that adolescents obtain the majority of abortions in the U.S. is inaccurate. Abortion rates are substantially higher for women in their twenties than for adolescents. Rates in 1996 were 50.7 abortions per 1000 for women aged 20–24 years and 33.6 per 1000 for women aged 25–29 years, compared with a rate of 29.2 abortions per 1000 women aged 15–19 years. Moreover, women over 20 years of age account for 80 percent of total induced abortions. Nonetheless, a higher proportion of adolescent pregnancies end in abortion (29 percent) than do pregnancies for women over 20 years of age (21 percent).

Significant differences of opinion exist regarding the morality of abortion. In general, U.S. courts have ruled that the procedure is legal and health care technology has made abortion relatively safe. However, there is broad accord that abortion should be a rare procedure and that improvements in sexual health and an emphasis on a reduction in the number of unintended pregnancies will clearly move this objective forward. The underpinning of the public health approach to this issue is to apply a variety of interventions at key points to prevent unintended pregnancy from occurring, and thus, ensure that all pregnancies are welcomed.

IV. Risk and Protective Factors for Sexual Health

Human beings are sexual beings throughout their lives and human sexual development involves many other aspects of development- physical, behavioral, intellectual, emotional, and interpersonal. Human sexual development follows a progression that, within certain ranges, applies to most persons. The challenge of achieving sexual health begins early in life and continues throughout the lifespan. The actions communities and health care professionals must take to support healthy sexual development vary from one stage of development to the next. Children need stable environments, parenting that promotes healthy social and emotional development, and protection from abuse. Adolescents need education, skills training, self-esteem promoting experiences, and appropriate services related to sexuality, along with positive expectations and sound preparation for their future roles as partners in committed relationships and as parents. Adults need continuing education as they achieve sexual maturity—to learn to communicate effectively with their children and partners and to accept continued responsibility for their sexuality, as well as necessary sexual and reproductive health care services.

There are also a number of more variable risk and protective factors that shape human sexual behavior and can have an impact on sexual health and the practice of responsible sexual behavior. These include biological factors, parents and other family members, schools, friends, the community, the media, religion, health care professionals, the law, and the availability of reproductive and sexual health services.

Biological Factors

Although human sexuality has come to serve many functions in addition to reproduction, its biological basis remains fundamental to the sexual experience. Sexual response involves psychological processing of information, which is influenced by learning, physiological responses and brain mechanisms which link the information processing to the physiological response. Although there is much that is not well understood about this complex sequence, it is understood that individuals vary considerably in their capacity for physical sexual response. This variability can be explained only in part by cultural factors. The role of early learning or genetic factors, or an interaction between the two, remains to be determined by further research.

Reproductive hormones are clearly important. However, their role is best understood and most predictable for men-and much more complex for women. For example, apart from the fact that women may experience a variety of reproduction-related experiences—the menstrual cycle, pregnancy, lactation, the menopause, and hormonal contraception-all of which can influence their sexual lives, there does appear to be greater variability among women in the impact of reproductive hormones on their sexuality. In addition, variations in the onset of puberty and menstruation can represent special challenges for girls in some populations.

Parents and Other Family Members

A number of family factors are known to be associated with adolescent sexual behavior and the risk of pregnancy. Adolescents living with a single parent are more likely to have had sexual intercourse than those living with both biological parents. Having older siblings may also influence the risk of adolescent pregnancy, particularly if the older siblings have had sexual intercourse, and if an older sister has experienced an adolescent pregnancy or birth. For girls, the experience of sexual abuse in the family as a child or adolescent is linked to increased risk of adolescent pregnancy. In addition, adolescents whose parents have higher education and income are more likely both to postpone sexual intercourse and to use contraception if they do engage in sexual intercourse.

The quality of the parent-child relationship is also significant. Close, warm parent-child relationships are associated with both postponement of sexual intercourse and more consistent contraceptive use by sexually active adolescents. Parental supervision and monitoring of children are also associated with adolescents postponing sexual activity or having fewer sexual partners if they are sexually active. However, parental control can be associated with negative effects if it is excessive or coercive.

Schools

Evidence suggests that school attendance reduces adolescent sexual risk-taking behavior. Around the world, as the percentage of girls completing elementary school has increased, adolescent birth rates have decreased. In the United States, youth who have dropped out of school are more likely to initiate sexual activity earlier, fail to use contraception, become pregnant, and give birth. Among youth who are in school, greater involvement with school-including athletics for girls—is related to less sexual risk-taking, including later age of initiation of sex, and lower frequency of sex, pregnancy, and childbearing.

Schools may have these effects on sexual risk-taking behavior for any of several reasons. Schools structure students' time; they create an environment which discourages unhealthy risk-taking—particularly by increasing interactions between youth and adults; and they affect selection of friends and larger peer groups. Schools can increase belief in the future and help youth plan for higher education and careers, and they can increase students' sense of competence, as well as their communication and refusal skills.

Schools often have access to training and communications technology that is frequently not available to families or clergy. This is important because parents vary widely in their own knowledge about sexuality, as well as their emotional capacity to explain essential sexual health issues to their children. Schools also provide an opportunity for the kind of positive peer learning that can influence social norms.

The Community

Community can be defined in several ways: through its geographic boundaries; through the predominant racial or ethnic makeup of its members; or through the shared values and practices of its members. Most persons are part of several communities, including neighborhood, school or work, religious affiliation, social groups, or athletic teams. Whatever the definition, community influence on the sexual health of those who comprise it is considerable, as is its role in determining what responsible sexual behavior is, how it is practiced and how it is enforced.

The measurable physical characteristics of neighborhoods and communities, such as economic conditions, racial and ethnic composition, residential stability, level of social disorganization, and service availability have demonstrated associations with the sexual behavior of their residents-initiation of sexual activity, contraceptive use, out-of-wedlock childbearing and risk of STD infection. An understanding of these characteristics and their impact on individuals is important in planning and developing services and other interventions to improve the sexual health and promote the responsible sexual behavior of community residents.

A shared culture, based either on heritage or on beliefs and practices, is another form of community. Each of these communities possesses norms and values about sexuality and these norms and values can influence the sexual health and sexual behavior of community members. For example, strong prohibitions against sex outside of marriage can have protective effects with respect to STD/HIV infection and adolescent pregnancy. On the other hand, undue emphasis on sexual restraint and modesty can inhibit family discussion about sexuality and perhaps contribute to reluctance to seek sexual and reproductive health care. Gender roles that accord higher status and more permissiveness for males and passivity for females can have a negative impact on the sexual health of women if they are unable to protect themselves against unintended pregnancy or STD/HIV infection.

When a community—defined by its culture—also has minority status, its members are potential objects of economic or social bias which can have a negative impact on sexual health. Economic inequities, in the form of reduced educational and employment opportunities, and the poverty that often results, has obvious implications for accessing and receiving necessary health education and care. In addition, a history of exploitation has, in some cases, led to distrust and suspicion of public health efforts in some minority communities.

The Media

The media—whether television, movies, music videos, video games, print, or the Internet-are pervasive in today's world and sexual talk and behavior are frequent and increasingly explicit. More than one-half of the programming on television has sexual content. Significant proportions of music videos and Hollywood movies also portray sexuality or eroticism. Among young people, 10–17 years of age, who regularly use the Internet, one-quarter had encountered unwanted pornography in the past year, and one-fifth had been exposed to unwanted sexual solicitations or approaches through the Internet.

Media programming rarely depicts sexual behavior in the context of a long-term relationship, use of contraceptives, or the potentially negative consequences of sexual behavior. The media do, however, have the potential for providing sexuality information and education to the public. For example, more than one-half of the high school boys and girls in a national survey said they had learned about birth control, contraception, or preventing pregnancy from television; almost two-thirds of the girls and 40 percent of the boys said they had learned about these topics from magazines.

While the available research evidence shows a connection between media and information regarding sexuality, it is still inadequate to make the link between media and sexual behavior.

Religion

Simply being affiliated with a religion does not appear to have great effect on sexual behavior; however, the extent of an individual's commitment to a religion or affiliation with certain religious denominations does. For example, an adolescent's frequent attendance at religious services is associated with less permissive attitudes about premarital sexual activity and a greater likelihood of abstinence. On the other hand, for adolescents who are sexually active, frequency of attendance is also associated with decreased use of contraceptive methods among girls and increased use by boys.

Health Care Professionals

Physicians, nurses, pharmacists and other health care professionals, often the first point of contact for individuals with sexual health concerns or problems, can have great influence on the sexual health and behavior of their patients. Yet, both adolescents and adults frequently perceive that health care providers are uncomfortable when discussing sexuality and often lack adequate communication skills on this topic.

Health care providers typically do not receive adequate training in sexual aspects of health and disease and in taking sexual histories. Ideally, curriculum content should seek to decrease anxiety and personal difficulty with the sexual aspects of health care, increase knowledge, increase awareness of personal biases, and increase tolerance and understanding of the diversity of sexual expression. Although such training for physicians has increased-95 percent of North American medical schools offer curriculum material in sexuality-nearly one-third do not address important topics such as taking a sexual history.

The Law

In the United States, the law regulates sexual behavior in complicated ways through criminal, civil, and child welfare law and operates at local, state, and federal levels. Criminal law imposes penalties for certain kinds of sexual activities, considering factors such as age, consent of both parties, the actual act performed, and the location in which it takes place. Civil law complements criminal law and can extend the law's reach. Civil law, for example, provides individuals with protection from sexual harassment and allows legal redress for some victims of sexual violence. It can also have an impact through regulation of relationships such as marriage, divorce, and child custody and support.

The law may also regulate some aspects of the community's influence on sexuality, including the family, schools, and media. While it generally protects parental rights, the law also imposes limits. For example, it protects children from sexual victimization by a family member. The law also regulates access to sexual health services through mechanisms such as parental notification and waiting period requirements. With respect to schools, although states may set certain minimum standards, the law allows individual school systems to determine the content of curriculum, including sexuality education curriculum. In addition, the legal system provides schools with the power to develop and implement programs to address the prevention of sexual harassment, relationship violence, and rape.

Under protection of the First Amendment to the U.S. Constitution, the media have great freedom in the choice of content they portray. At the same time, the law can impose certain restrictions on the media; for example, it may limit minors' access to sexually explicit materials.

Availability of Reproductive Health Services

In the United States, contraceptive and reproductive health services are provided to women and men by a wide range of health care professionals. These services are offered in a variety of settings-private practice offices, publicly funded family planning clinics, private clinics, military clinics, school-based health centers, college and university health centers, and private hospitals. Often, contraceptive services are integrated with other basic preventive health services such as pelvic examinations and pap tests, and screening for sexually transmitted infections. In addition to medical care, counseling or education related to sexual and reproductive health may be provided.

Barriers to obtaining these services can exist if providers are not conveniently located, are not available when needed, do not provide (or are thought not to provide) confidential, respectful, culturally sensitive care, or are not affordable. Federally subsidized family planning services have been an important factor in helping many persons overcome these barriers and avoid an estimated 1.3 million unintended pregnancies per year.

V. Evidence-based Intervention Models

Substantial work has been done in the areas of sexual health and responsible sexual behavior, through public-private partnerships at the national as well as community level, by many researchers and organizations throughout the country. Many of these approaches and programs to improve sexual health have been evaluated and shown to be effective. They include: community based programs, school based programs, clinic based programs, and religion based programs.

Community Based Programs

Youth development programs, although they typically do not specifically address sexuality, have been shown to have a significant impact on sexual health and behavior. Programs that improve education and life options for adolescents have been demonstrated to reduce their pregnancy and birth rates. These programs may increase attachment to school, improve opportunities for careers, increase belief in the future, increase interaction with adults, and structure young people's time.

The CDC has identified a number of effective STD and HIV prevention programs that are curriculum based and presented by peer and health educators in various community settings. Other community interventions have involved changing community norms and the distribution of condoms to reduce unwanted pregnancies and STDs, including HIV. Such interventions have the advantages of reaching large numbers of people at a relatively low cost and engaging the active involvement of community members, including local opinion leaders. They have had considerable success in changing community norms about sexual behavior as evidenced by substantial increases in condom use. It is important to point out that although the correct and consistent use of condoms has been shown to be effective in reducing the risk of pregnancy, HIV infection, and some STDs, more research is needed on the level of effectiveness.

School Based Programs

A majority of Americans favor some form of sexuality education in the public schools and also believe that some sort of birth control information should be available to adolescents. School based sexuality education programs are generally of two types: abstinence-only programs that emphasize sexual abstinence as the most appropriate choice for young people; and sexuality and STD/HIV education programs that also cover abstinence but, in addition, include condoms and other methods of contraception to provide protection against STDs or pregnancy.

To date, there are only a few published evaluations of abstinence-only programs. Due to this limited number of studies it is too early to draw definite conclusions about this approach. Similarly, the value of these programs for adolescents who have initiated sexual activity is not yet understood. More research is clearly needed.

Programs that typically emphasize abstinence, but also cover condoms and other methods of contraception, have a larger body of evaluation evidence that indicates either no effect on initiation of sexual activity or, in some cases, a delay in the initiation of sexual activity. This evidence gives strong support to the conclusion that providing information about contraception does not increase adolescent sexual activity, either by hastening the onset of sexual intercourse, increasing the frequency of sexual intercourse, or increasing the number of sexual partners. In addition, some of these evaluated programs increased condom use or contraceptive use more generally for adolescents who were sexually active.

Despite the available evidence regarding the effectiveness of school-based sexuality education, it remains a controversial issue for many- in terms of whether schools are the most appropriate venue for such education, as well as curriculum content. Few would disagree that parents should be the primary sexuality educators of their children or that sexual abstinence until engaged in a committed and mutually monogamous relationship is an important component in any sexuality education program. It does seem clear, however, that providing sexuality education in the schools is a useful mechanism to ensure that this Nation's youth have a basic understanding of sexuality. Traditionally, schools have had a role in ensuring equity of access to information that is perhaps greater than most other institutions. In addition, given that one-half of adolescents in the United States are already sexually active-and at risk of unintended pregnancy and STD/HIV infection-it also seems clear that adolescents need accurate information about contraceptive methods so that they can reduce those risks.

Clinic Based Programs

Prevention programs based in health clinics that have an impact on sexual health and behavior are of three types: counseling and education; condom or contraceptive distribution; and STD/HIV screening. Successful counseling and education programs have several elements in common: they have a clear scientific basis for their design; they require a commitment of staff time and effort, as well as additional time from clients; they are tailored to the individual; and they include building clients' skills through, for example, exercises in negotiation. Even brief risk-reduction messages have been shown, in some studies, to lead to substantial increases in condom use although other studies have shown little effect. More extensive counseling, either individual or small group, can produce additional increases in consistent condom use.

Most school clinic based condom and contraceptive availability programs include some form of abstinence or risk-reduction counseling to address the concern that increased condom availability could lead to increased sexual behavior. The evidence indicates these programs, while still controversial in some communities, do not increase sexual behavior and that they are generally accepted by adolescents, parents, and school staff.

Because many STDs have no clear symptoms, STD/HIV screening promotes sexual health and responsible sexual behavior by detecting these diseases and preventing their unintentional spread. Routine screening in clinics has also been shown to reduce the incidence of some STDs, particularly chlamydia infection.

Religion Based Programs

Religion based sexuality education programs have been developed and cover a wide spectrum of different belief systems. Taken as a whole, they cover all age ranges, from early elementary school to adults, as well as youth with different sexual orientations and identities. Although it is reasonable to expect that religion based programs would have an impact on sexual behavior, the absence of scientific evaluations precludes arriving at a definitive conclusion on the effectiveness of these programs. More research is needed.

VI. Vision for the Future

Strategies that cover three fundamental areas—increasing awareness, implementing and strengthening interventions, and expanding the research base- could help provide a foundation for promoting sexual health and responsible sexual behavior in a manner that is consistent with the best available science.

1. Increasing Public Awareness of Issues Relating to Sexual Health and Responsible Sexual Behavior

- Begin a national dialogue on sexual health and responsible sexual behavior that is honest, mature and respectful, and has the ultimate goal of developing a national strategy that recognizes the need for common ground.
- Encourage opinion leaders to address issues related to sexual health and responsible sexual behavior in ways that are informed by the best available science and that respect diversity.
- Provide access to education about sexual health and responsible sexual behavior that is thorough, wide-ranging, begins early, and continues throughout the lifespan. Such education should:
  - recognize the special place that sexuality has in our lives;
  - stress the value and benefits of remaining abstinent until involved in a committed, enduring, and mutually monogamous relationship; but
  - assure awareness of optimal protection from sexually transmitted diseases and unintended pregnancy, for those who are sexually active, while also stressing that there are no infallible methods of protection, except abstinence, and that condoms cannot protect against some forms of STDs.
- Recognize that sexuality education can be provided in a number of venues-homes, schools, churches, other community settings-but must always be developmentally and culturally appropriate.
- Recognize that parents are the child's first educators and should help guide other sexuality education efforts so that they are consistent with their values and beliefs.

- Recognize, also, that families differ in their level of knowledge, as well as their emotional capability to discuss sexuality issues. In moving toward equity of access to information for promoting sexual health and responsible sexual behavior, school sexuality education is a vital component of community responsibility.

2. Providing the Health and Social Interventions Necessary to Promote and Enhance Sexual Health and Responsible Sexual Behavior

- Eliminate disparities in sexual health status that arise from social and economic disadvantage, diminished access to information and health care services, and stereotyping and discrimination.
- Target interventions to the most socioeconomically vulnerable communities where community members have less access to health education and services and are, thus, likely to suffer most from sexual health problems.
- Improve access to sexual health and reproductive health care services for all persons in all communities.
- Provide adequate training in sexual health to all professionals who deal with sexual issues in their work, encourage them to use this training, and ensure that they are reflective of the populations they serve.
- Encourage the implementation of health and social interventions to improve sexual health that have been adequately evaluated and shown to be effective.
- Ensure the availability of programs that promote both awareness and prevention of sexual abuse and coercion.
- Strengthen families, whatever their structure, by encouraging stable, committed, and enduring adult relationships, particularly marriage. Recognize, though, that there are times when the health interests of adults and children can be hurt within relationships with sexual health problems, and that sexual health problems within a family can be a concern in and of themselves.

3. Investing in Research Related to Sexual Health and Disseminating Findings Widely

- Promote basic research in human sexual development, sexual health, and reproductive health, as well as social and behavioral research on risk and protective factors for sexual health.
- Expand the research base to cover the entire human life span-children, adolescents, young adults, middle age adults, and the elderly.
- Research, develop, disseminate, and evaluate educational materials and guidelines for sexuality education, covering the full continuum of human sexual development, for use by parents, clergy, teachers, and other community leaders.
- Expand evaluation efforts for community, school and clinic based interventions that address sexual health and responsibility.

VII. Advancing a National Dialogue

The primary purpose of this *Surgeon General's Call to Action* is to initiate a mature national dialogue on issues of sexuality, sexual health, and responsible sexual behavior. As stated so eloquently in the Institute of Medicine report, *No Time to Lose*:

> "Society's reluctance to openly confront issues regarding sexuality results in a number of untoward effects. This social inhibition impedes the development and implementation of effective sexual health and HIV/STD education programs, and it stands in the way of communication between parents and children and between sex partners. It perpetuates misperceptions about individual risk and ignorance about the consequences of sexual activities and may encourage high-risk sexual practices. It also impacts the level of counseling training given to health care providers to assess sexual histories, as well as providers' comfort levels in conducting risk-behavior discussions with clients. In addition, the "code of silence has resulted in missed opportunities to use the mass media (e.g., television, radio, printed media, and the Internet) to encourage healthy sexual behaviors.

The strategies set out above provide a point of reference for a national dialogue. How it will be implemented will be determined by individuals and families, communities, the media, and by government and non-government agencies, institutions, and foundations. We must all share in the responsibility for initiating this dialogue, working at every level of society to promote sexual health and responsible sexual behavior.

Individuals can begin the dialogue—adult with adult, adult with child—by developing their own personal knowledge, attitudes, and skills with respect to sexual health and responsible sexual behavior. Adults can communicate with other adults about their views on responsible sexual behavior, what it is, and how to promote it. Parents can educate their children about sexuality and responsibility, most importantly by being healthy and positive role models.

Communities must necessarily approach a dialogue on sexual health and responsible sexual behavior in different ways, according to their diverse composition and norms. But *all* must participate so that *all* voices are heard. This dialogue can be sponsored by local governments, businesses, churches, schools, youth-serving organizations and other community based organizations and should, at a minimum, include: emphasis on respect for diversity of perspective, opinion and values; assessment of community resources available for educating community members and delivering necessary services; attention to policies and programs that support and strengthen families; and assurance that systems are in place to promote equitable access and respect for all cultural, gender, age, and sexual orientation groups.

Media in all its forms can be engaged, by both public and private entities, in a national dialogue to promote sexual health and responsible sexual behavior. This dialogue should be a long-term effort and should treat sexuality issues responsibly, accurately, and positively. With respect to media programming, the portrayal of sexual relationships should be mature and honest, and responsible sexual behavior should be stressed. Finally, it is also important that young people, as well as adults, be educated to critically examine media messages.

Government, in partnership with foundations and other private organizations, can target support for the research, education, and services necessary to sustain a meaningful campaign to promote sexual health and responsible sexual behavior. Government should continue to develop objective and measurable indicators to monitor progress over time. It can also review policies and laws to ensure that they facilitate—rather than impede—the promotion of sexual health and responsible sexual behavior.

VIII. Conclusion

Based on the scientific evidence, we face a serious public health challenge regarding the sexual health of our nation. Doing nothing is unacceptable. More than anyone, it is our children who will suffer the consequences of our failure to meet these responsibilities.

Solutions are complex but we do have evidence that we can promote sexual health and responsible sexual behavior. Given the diversity of attitudes, beliefs, values and opinions, finding common ground might not be easy but it is attainable. We are more likely to find this common ground through a national dialogue with honest and respectful communication. We need to appreciate and respect the diversity of our culture and be informed by the science that is available to us.

This is a call to all of society to respond to this challenge. These efforts will not only have an impact on the current health status of our nation, but lay the groundwork for a healthier society for future generations.

Don Feder

Devil Is in the Details of Surgeon General's Sex Report

Along with his predecessor, Joycelyn Elders (the mullah of masturbation education), U.S. Surgeon General David Satcher was appointed by President Clinton. It shows, especially in his new report, *A Call to Action to Promote Sexual Health and Responsible Sexual Behavior.*

There's a telling item buried in a *Washington Post* story on the report's release. In compiling his manifesto, he consulted a variety of sources, the surgeon general disclosed, including those who would "qualify as commercial sex workers."

"Now, wait a minute," I said to Damon Thompson, a Satcher spokesman. "Are you telling me the surgeon general asked prostitutes how to teach our children about sex?" After checking with his boss, Thompson assured me that "commercial sex workers" would indeed include ladies of the night. The lunatics haven't just taken over the asylum; they're franchising the operation!

That was not the most incredible aspect of the report. Besides hookers, Satcher received sage advice from their colleagues at Planned Parenthood, the Alan Guttmacher Institute and the Sex Information and Education Council of the United States. Somehow, he overlooked the Penthouse Forum.

Armed with this input, Satcher concluded there is no "scientific evidence" that teaching abstinence until marriage alone is effective. Consequently, he urged schools to adopt curricula that praise self-control and pass out contraceptives.

Imagine a violence-prevention program where kids are given automatic weapons or courses promoting tolerance where students are lectured by white supremacists and Afrocentrists.

Only in the never-never land of sexual pedagogy is "wait until you're married, but here's a condom in case you have an uncontrollable urge in the meantime" considered anything but self-defeating.

Actually, Satcher isn't telling America's youth to wait until marriage. Any old "mutually monogamous" relationship will do. That's because our surgeon general understands that "marriage is not perfect."

So, instead of asking adolescents to exercise restraint (with a pocketful of condoms) until they say, "I do," Satcher wants them to refrain from getting hot and heavy until they achieve a "mutually monogamous" relationship.

How long is this mutuality to exist before couples hop between the sheets? How is a commitment to exclusivity to be manifested, absent vows exchanged before God and man?

Quite coincidentally, Satcher's report endorses conclusions he long has held. In 1994, when Satcher headed the Centers for Disease Control and Prevention (CDC), the agency ran an $800,000 national advertising campaign aimed at America's youth. One ad helpfully advised: "Latex condoms are available in different sizes, colors and textures. Find one that's right for you." And if you have trouble making a selection, consult your friendly, neighborhood commercial sex worker. That's where the surgeon general goes for advice.

Satcher and the rest of the safe-sex crowd neglect to mention that condoms frequently fail. Leslie Unruh of the National Abstinence Clearinghouse says she attended a conference of sex educators where a speaker asked the audience if they would have sex with the man or woman of their dreams knowing that person had HIV/AIDS using only a condom for protection. In a crowd of several hundred, no one raised a hand.

We've had comprehensive sex education (erotic indoctrination, really) for more than 30 years. Children are given instruction in copulation that is comprehensive by the *Kama Sutra's* standards. They've warned continually of the perils of nasty microbes and unwanted pregnancy and are drilled in contraception. Still, each year, there are 1.4 million abortions and 12 million new cases of sexually transmitted diseases. The out-of-wedlock birthrate is 33 percent. Since this carnal explosion parallels the triumph of sexual instruction, could cause and effect be at work here?

Streetwalkers often cruise urban areas with strip clubs and adult bookstores. Might there be a connection between stimulation and gratification? Perhaps Satcher should consult informed sources in the commercial sex industry. No self-respecting parakeet would want the bottom of his cage lined with the pages of the good doctor's report.

POSTSCRIPT

Should Sexuality Education Be Comprehensive?

Research has indicated overwhelming support for comprehensive sexuality education among American parents. A study by the Kaiser Family Foundation, "Sex Education in America: A View from Inside the Nation's Classrooms," revealed that parents thought sexuality education should include how to use condoms (85 percent of parents); how to use other forms of contraception (84 percent of parents); and how to talk about condoms and other methods with partners (88 percent of parents).

Parents also wanted sexuality education to include "real-life" issues, like sexual peer pressure (94 percent), the emotional consequences of becoming sexually active (94 percent), abortion (79 percent), and sexual orientation (76 percent). The report also indicated that most parents (74 percent) wanted these issues to be presented in a balanced way that reflects different views in society.

In researching the impact of education programs, The National Campaign to Prevent Teen Pregnancy, a private, nonpartisan initiative, found no evidence that abstinence-only education delays sexual activity, and no evidence that comprehensive sexuality education increases sexual activity.

Nevertheless, the federal government continues to favor abstinence-until-marriage education programs. Today, in excess of $100 million is available every year for abstinence-only education programs. Federally defined abstinence-only education programs must conform to eight guidelines. They must:

1. Have as its exclusive purpose, teaching the social, physiological, and health gains to be realized from abstaining from sexual activity;
2. Teach that abstinence from sexual activity outside of marriage is the expected standard for all school-age children;
3. Teach that abstinence from sexual activity is the only certain way to avoid out-of-wedlock pregnancy, sexually transmitted diseases, and other associated health problems;
4. Teach that a mutually faithful monogamous relationship in the context of marriage is the expected standard of human sexual activity;
5. Teach that sexual activity outside of the context of marriage may have harmful psychological and physical effects;
6. Teach that bearing children out-of-wedlock is likely to have harmful consequences for the child, the child's parents, and society;
7. Teach young people how to reject sexual advances and how alcohol and drug use increases vulnerability to sexual advances; and
8. Teach the importance of attaining self-sufficiency before engaging in sexual activity.

Concerned with the restrictions of these provisions, members of Congress proposed legislation to require a more comprehensive approach. The Family Life Education Act would require education programs to:

1. Be age-appropriate and medically accurate;
2. Not teach or promote religion;
3. Teach that abstinence is the only sure way to avoid pregnancy or sexually transmitted diseases;
4. Stress the value of abstinence while not ignoring those young people who have had or are having sexual intercourse;
5. Provide information about the health benefits and side effects of all contraceptives and barrier methods as a means to prevent pregnancy;
6. Provide information about the health benefits and side effects of all contraceptives and barrier methods as a means to reduce the risk of contracting sexually transmitted diseases, including HIV/AIDS;
7. Encourage family communication about sexuality between parent and child;
8. Teach young people the skills to make responsible decisions about sexuality, including how to avoid unwanted verbal, physical, and sexual advances and how not to make unwanted verbal, physical, and sexual advances; and
9. Teach young people how alcohol and drug use can affect responsible decision making.

How do these approaches differ? In what ways are they similar? Which approach would you want for yourself, or for your children?

As a contraceptive method, periodic abstinence has been recorded to have a failure rate of 26 percent; that is, of 100 women who begin a given year declaring abstinence as her method, 26 will become pregnant by the end of that year. This statistic led some sexuality educators to comment, "Unfortunately, vows of abstinence break more frequently than condoms do!" What skills are needed to make abstinence "work" effectively? How does one define abstinence? Abstinence is often defined *individually*. One person's abstinence definition may exclude any sexual contact or body touching, while another person's definition may exclude vaginal intercourse only. Furthermore, how does a gay or lesbian person handle the message "abstinence until marriage" in a country that, except for Massachusetts, makes same sex marriages illegal?

Think of the sexuality education that was provided when you attended high school. Was the approach comprehensive, or did it emphasize abstinence as the only option? What characteristics of the program were most or least helpful? How can sexuality education best meet the needs of young people?

Suggested Readings

Advocates for Youth and Sexuality Education Council of the United States, *Toward a Healthy America: Roadblocks Imposed by the Federal Government's Abstinence-Only-Until-Marriage Education Program* (2001).

J. Blake, *Words Can Work: When Talking to Kids about Sexual Health* (Blake Works, 2004).

P. Brick and B. Taverner, *Positive Images: Teaching Abstinence, Contraception, and Sexual Health,* 3rd ed. (Planned Parenthood of Greater Northern New Jersey, 2001).

R. Brown et al., eds., "Opinions in Pediatric and Adolescent Gynecology: Opinions on Abstinence Programs for Adolescents," *Journal of Pediatric and Adolescent Gynecology* (vol. 9, 1996).

J. R. Diggs, "Support of Sex Ed Challenged by Mass. Doctor: John Diggs Disputes Surgeon General's Report," *The Massachusetts News* (August 2001).

D. Haffner, "Abstinence-Only Education Isn't Enough: Teens Need a Wide Range of Information," *Insight on the News* (September 1997).

D. Haffner, "What's Wrong with Abstinence-Only Sexuality Education Programs?" *SIECUS Report* (April 5, 1997).

Human Rights Watch, *Ignorance Only: HIV/AIDS, Human Rights and Federally Funded Abstinence-Only Programs in the United States; Texas: A Case Study* (September 2002).

Kaiser Family Foundation, *Sex Education in America: A View from Inside the Nation's Classrooms* (The Henry J. Kaiser Family Foundation, September 2000).

J. F. Keenan, "Talking about Sex: The Surgeon General's Invitation to a Conversation," *America* (August 13, 2001).

D. Kirby, *Emerging Answers: Research Findings on Programs to Reduce Teen Pregnancy* (National Campaign to Prevent Teen Pregnancy, 2001).

J. McIlhaney, "'Safe Sex' Education Has Failed: It's Time to Give Kids the Good News about Abstinence," *Insight on the News* (September 1997).

K. L. Nelson, "The Conflict Over Sexuality Education: Interviews with Participants on Both Sides of the Debate," *SIECUS Report* (August/September 1996).

N. Seiler, *Is Teen Marriage the Solution?* (Center for Law and Social Policy, April 2002).

J. Stryker, "Abstinence or Else!" *Nation* (June 16, 1997).

W. Taverner, "All Together Now: Combining Pregnancy and STI Prevention Programs," *SIECUS Report* (vol. 31, no. 3, 2003).

W. Taverner, "Sexuality Education 2003 Update," in R.T. Francoeur and R. Noonan, eds., *The International Encyclopedia of Sexuality* (Continuum, 2004, pp. 1176–1178).

W. Taverner, L. Cruz, and J. Oviedo, "Teaching Safer Sex: In English and en Español," *SIECUS Report* (vol. 32, no. 1, 2004).

W. Taverner and S. Montfort, *Making Sense of Abstinence* (Planned Parenthood of Greater Northern New Jersey, 2005).

ISSUE 2

Should Schools Make Condoms Available to Students?

YES: Sally Guttmacher et al., from "Condom Availability in New York City Public High Schools: Relationships to Condom Use and Sexual Behavior," *American Journal of Public Health* (September 1997)

NO: Edwin J. Delattre, from "Condoms and Coercion: The Maturity of Self Determination," *Vital Speeches of the Day* (April 15, 1992)

ISSUE SUMMARY

YES: Researchers Sally Guttmacher et al. maintain that their study of New York City high school students who received both condoms and an HIV/AIDS education program versus Chicago high school students who received only HIV/AIDS education proves that distributing condoms in schools does not increase sexual activity but does result in students using condoms more often when they are sexually active.

NO: Professor of education Edwin J. Delattre rejects the argument that there is a moral obligation to save lives by distributing condoms in schools. He asserts that distributing condoms in schools promotes morally unacceptable casual sexual relationships.

Research shows that nationwide, 70 percent of American high school seniors have engaged in sexual intercourse. In the larger cities and suburbs, the percentage of sexually active students is even higher.

With the highest rate of teenage pregnancy and abortion in North America and Europe, and with young people fast becoming the highest risk group for HIV (human immunodeficiency virus) infection, American parents, educators, and health care professionals have to decide how to deal with these problems. Some advocate teaching abstinence-only sex education and saying nothing about contraceptives and other ways of reducing the risk of contracting sexually transmitted infections (STIs) and HIV infections. Others advocate educating and counseling: "You don't have to be sexually active, but if you are, this is what you can do to protect yourself." Making free condoms available in school takes this one step further. School boards in New York, Baltimore, Chicago, Los Angeles, San Francisco, Philadelphia, Miami, and other cities are convinced that school nurses and school-based health clinics should be allowed to make free condoms available to students, usually without requiring parental notification or permission.

Dr. Alma Rose George, president of the National Medical Association, opposes schools giving condoms to teens without their parents knowing about it. She asserts, "When you give condoms out to teens, you are promoting sexual activity. It's saying that it's all right. We shouldn't make it so easy for them." Faye Wattleton, former president of the Planned Parenthood Federation of America, approves of schools distributing condoms and maintains that requiring the students to obtain written permission from their parents "would be counterproductive and meaningless."

Some detect an overtone of racism in condom availability programs. "When most of the decisions are made, it's by a White majority for schools predominantly Black," says Dolores Grier, noted African American historian and vice chancellor of community relations for the Catholic Archdiocese of New York. "They introduce a lot of Black and Hispanic children to this like they're animals. I consider it racist to give condoms to children." Elijah Mohammed, founder of the Black Nation of Islam, also condemned condom availability programs as racist genocide.

In the following selections, Sally Guttmacher and her colleagues report on their study comparing the sexual activity and condom use of 7,000 students in New York City high schools who received free condoms and 4,000 similar high school students in Chicago who did not have access to condoms at school. Both school systems had similar HIV/AIDS education programs. This study, they maintain, shows that making condoms available in schools does not promote teen sex but does increase condom use by sexually active teens. Edwin J. Delattre opposes condom education because he maintains that it encourages teen sex and does not save lives.

YES

Sally Guttmacher et al.

Condom Availability in New York City Public High Schools

Introduction

Human immunodeficiency virus (HIV) infection is a major threat to the health of adolescents in the United States. Several recent surveys suggest that the majority of today's high school students are sexually active, do not use condoms consistently, and are unaware of their own serostatus, their partners' serostatus, or both. As condoms are the only effective method of preventing HIV transmission among the sexually active, increasing access to condoms and reducing the barriers to condom use may be an effective method for decreasing the risk of HIV transmission among adolescents.

Condoms are readily available at drugstores, but many adolescents may not have the financial resources or self-confidence to purchase them. Although family planning clinics are a cheaper source of condoms, distance and lack of foresight may prevent teens from obtaining them there. School-based condom availability programs reduce financial and psychological barriers and present opportunities for the discussion of condom use and other safer sex practices.

In the few years that school condom availability has become an acceptable public health strategy, more than 400 schools in the United States have implemented such programs. Program variations include differences in where and when condoms are made available, who distributes condoms, who is eligible to receive them, whether counseling is mandatory or voluntary, and the extent of parental involvement. Some of the existing programs are pilot projects that use clinic staff through preexisting school-based clinics, but the majority of schools with condom availability programs do not have school-based clinics. In this [selection] we report on an analysis of data from an evaluation of New York City's systemwide school-based condom availability program.

Condom Availability in New York City

In 1991 the New York City (NYC) Board of Education implemented one of the first non-clinic-based, systemwide school condom availability programs. Each

From Sally Guttmacher, Lisa Lieberman, David Ward, Nick Freudenberg, Alice Radosh, and Don Des Jarlais, "Condom Availability in New York City Public High Schools: Relationships to Condom Use and Sexual Behavior," *American Journal of Public Health*, vol. 87, no. 9 (September 1997). Copyright © 1997 by The American Public Health Association. Reprinted by permission. References omitted.

public high school was mandated to do the following: (1) assemble an HIV/ acquired immunodeficiency syndrome (AIDS) team, composed of the principal, assistant principal, teachers, parents, students, health resource staff, and other interested personnel, to oversee the condom availability program; (2) teach a minimum of six HIV/AIDS lessons in each grade; (3) designate and maintain at least one site at the school as a resource room where condoms and AIDS prevention materials are available; (4) staff this site no less than 10 periods a week and post the hours that the site is open; (5) identify at least one male and one female staff member as condom resource room volunteers and apprise students of the names of these individuals; and (6) arrange for an HIV/ AIDS information session for parents.

To receive condoms, students must give their student identification numbers to the condom resource volunteer. The volunteer is not supposed to distribute condoms to students whose parents have notified the school that they do not want their children to be eligible for the program. (Less than 2% of parents citywide have exercised this option.)

Despite the public health advantages of this program, controversy erupted over its initiation. At the heart of the debate were two recurring issues—the fear that the program would increase adolescent sexual activity, and the role of parents vs schools in matters of teen sexuality. While both proponents and opponents of the program held fast to their beliefs, neither could draw upon the support of empirical evidence. After a lengthy struggle, the program was approved by the school board and, in conjunction with expanded AIDS education, condoms were made available. In spite of the appearance of substantial opposition to condom availability, 69% of parents, 89% of students, and 76% of teachers ultimately supported the program.

Methods

A total of 7119 students from 12 randomly selected NYC schools and 5738 students from 10 Chicago schools participated in a cross-sectional survey in the early fall of 1994. The Chicago public school system, a large, unified urban system that, like the NYC system, is ethnically diverse and has a high dropout rate, provides HIV/AIDS education but does not make condoms available to students. The NYC condom availability program was implemented in every public high school before the evaluation began. Thus, the study was a quasi-experimental design with a post hoc–only comparison.

The 12 schools in the NYC sample were randomly selected after all 120 schools in the system were stratified by type of school (comprehensive, vocational, alternative) and socioeconomic status of the student body, as measured by eligibility for free or reduced-price school lunches. Post-sample selection analysis determined that the sample of 12 schools represented the proportions of the student population in the NYC school system with respect to type of school, family income, and borough location. Ten Chicago public high schools were chosen to match the resulting NYC sample of students on relevant demographic characteristics.

In both NYC and Chicago, students completed self-administered questionnaires during required school classes, such as English or physical education. The required classes were randomly selected, using a quota designed to ensure distribution of students across grades 9 through 12. Students had to be in the classroom at the time the survey was conducted to be included in the sample. Trained data collectors administered the survey in both cities. While teachers remained in the classroom, as required by law, they were not involved in the data collection in any way, nor did they observe the responses of individual students.

The survey was designed to measure students' knowledge, attitudes, and self-reported behavior related to sexual activity, condom use, and HIV risk reduction. Demographic comparisons between the NYC sample and all students in the NYC public high school system revealed that the sample did not differ from the systemwide student population on most characteristics. Girls and Latinos, however, were slightly overrepresented in the sample. The NYC data were then weighted to estimate the age, ethnic, and gender distribution of the NYC public high school system; Chicago data were weighted to approximate the resultant NYC sample; and weighted data were used for all subsequent analyses.

Sexual activity was measured by response to the question, "Have you ever had any form of sex? (Mark all that apply.)" Possible answers were (1) oral intercourse (mouth); (2) vaginal intercourse (vagina); (3) anal intercourse (anus); (4) I have "fooled around" but have not had oral, vaginal, or anal intercourse; (5) I have never had sexual intercourse. Pilot tests focused on ensuring that the students who identified themselves as sexually active would include those who had engaged in nonvaginal (i.e., oral or anal) intercourse. Students who marked choices 1, 2, or 3 were considered sexually active for all subsequent analyses. Condom use was explored for those students who reported having had sex within the past 6 months. Condom use was measured by response (yes or no) to the question, "The *last time* you had sexual intercourse (oral, vaginal, or anal), did you or your partner use a condom?"

Responses to several condom-related questions on the survey were correlated with and supported the validity of the question regarding condom use at last intercourse, for both the NYC and Chicago samples. . . .

We compared NYC students with Chicago students on variables related to sexual behavior and condom use, using weighted and unweighted data and controlling for age, gender, ethnicity, and psycho-social factors. Students who were new to their high school system (i.e., students who had been in an NYC or Chicago public high school for less than 1 year) were categorized as "new students." As new students, they were unlikely to have been exposed to their school's HIV/AIDS prevention strategies prior to participating in the survey and thus served as a proxy baseline measure. In an effort to establish a clean baseline, new students in NYC who had obtained a condom at school . . . , indicating direct exposure to the program, were eliminated from the analyses. (Eliminating these students did not affect any of the subsequent analyses.) Students who had been in an NYC or Chicago public high school for 1 year or more were categorized as "continuing students." Continuing NYC students were then compared with continuing Chicago students.

Multivariate logistic models were used to compare continuing Chicago students with continuing NYC students on condom use at last intercourse, overall sexual activity rates, and other outcome variables. Subgroup analyses were performed to determine the relationship between the program and condom use by gender, ethnic group, and HIV risk status. "High-risk" students were those who reported having had three or more sexual partners within the past 6 months.

For all but the demographic comparisons, logistic regression models were tested on the weighted samples with condom use at last intercourse as the dependent variable. In additional models, sexual behavior, drug use, and HIV risk status were used as the dependent variables. The logistic models controlled for age, gender, ethnicity, age at first intercourse, number of partners, and frequency of sexual intercourse. In addition, the models controlled for a range of other variables that might influence condom use: *salience of HIV/AIDS*, defined as knowing someone who is HIV positive; *self-efficacy*, defined as the degree of confidence students had in their ability to negotiate a series of situations related to sexual activity and condom use . . . ; *assessments of peer risk*, defined as students' perceptions of the proportion of their friends engaging in risky sexual behaviors . . . ; *depression* . . . ; *locus of control*, which measures the extent of control students felt they had over their lives . . . ; and *parental support*, which measures how comfortable students felt talking to their parents about a variety of problems. . . .

Finally, to explore the mechanisms by which condom availability might influence condom use, a series of additional models were tested, to which two predictor variables were added: (1) *use of the condom availability program*, defined as a "yes" response to the question, "In the past 6 months, have you gotten condoms from a teacher or staff person at your school?" and (2) *exposure to HIV/AIDS lessons*, defined as a "yes" response to the question, "In the last semester, were you taught about AIDS/HIV infection in school?" At the time of the survey, only 42% of Chicago students and 53% of NYC students reported having been exposed to the mandatory HIV/AIDS lessons.

For all logistic models, students missing responses on dependent variables were excluded from the analyses. Nonresponses on independent variables showed no correlation with dependent variables and were therefore replaced with appropriate sample means.

Results

. . . The majority of students in the sample were between 15 and 17 years of age. There were slightly more girls than boys. More than a quarter (28%) of the sample were of Hispanic/Latino origin and almost half the sample (47%) were African Americans or Blacks from English-speaking Caribbean countries. These two categories of Blacks are combined because preliminary analyses revealed no differences between the two in sexual activity or other relevant variables.

The two samples were virtually identical with respect to the percentage of students who reported that they had ever had any form of sexual intercourse (new students, 46%; continuing students, 60%). When types of sexual intercourse (vaginal, oral, anal) were compared, the samples were again surprisingly similar. As expected, sexual activity increased with age, and the NYC and Chicago students were remarkably similar in this respect as well as in many other variables related to sexual activity, including age at first intercourse and age of first partner. They were also similar in the percentage of students who reported having had three or more partners in the past 6 months (new students, 23%; continuing students, 19%).

More NYC students than Chicago students (37% vs 25%) . . . reported that they knew someone with HIV infection or AIDS. Because the prevalence of HIV/AIDS is noticeably higher in NYC than in Chicago . . . students' opportunities for interactions with people with HIV/AIDS are significantly greater in NYC. Despite this difference, students in both cities were equally unlikely to feel vulnerable to HIV infection; 91% of students in both cities said it was "unlikely" or "not at all likely" that they would become infected with HIV in the next 5 years. . . .

In both cities a higher proportion of boys than girls were sexually active and a higher proportion of African-American or Caribbean students than students from other ethnic groups reported having had sex. A slightly higher proportion of NYC Hispanic/Latino students than Chicago Hispanic/Latino students reported having had sex. . . . These bivariate analyses are descriptive and present only a preliminary view.

. . . [T]he proportions of new students and continuing students who were sexually active were the same in both NYC and Chicago (47% for new students and 60% for continuing students). For condom use at last intercourse, however, a different pattern emerged. A similar percentage of new students in NYC and Chicago (58% and 60%, respectively) reported using condoms at last intercourse, but among continuing students condom use at last intercourse was significantly higher in NYC.

. . . [R]eported condom use at last intercourse varied by

- age . . . , indicating that older students were less likely to use condoms;
- gender . . . , indicating that girls were less likely than boys to use condoms;
- ethnicity . . . , indicating that African-American and Caribbean students were more likely than White students to use condoms;
- age at first intercourse . . . , indicating that those who became sexually active at a later age were more likely to use condoms;
- number of partners . . . , indicating that those who had more partners were more likely to use condoms;
- frequency of sex . . . , indicating that those who had sex more frequently were less likely to use condoms;
- self-efficacy . . . , indicating that students who felt more confident in their ability to refuse to have sex without a condom were more likely to use condoms;

- peer risk . . . , indicating that students who reported having friends who took a variety of HIV-related risks were less likely to use condoms;
- locus of control . . . , indicating that students who felt they had little control over their lives were less likely to use condoms;
- depression . . . , indicating that students who were more depressed were less likely to use condoms. . . .

Discussion

We used a variety of analytic strategies to examine the relationship between condom availability and sexual behavior. Clearly, making condoms available at school does not lead to increases in sexual activity. New students (the proxy baseline measure for this study) in New York City had the same sexual activity rates as new students in Chicago. In both cities the rate of increase of sexual activity associated with age was the same. A similar study of Latino adolescents in a community-based condom availability program in Boston also found no effect of condom availability on sexual behavior. Thus, the fear that making condoms available will increase sexual activity, a primary political obstacle to making condoms available to high school students, appears to be unfounded.

Additionally, these results suggest that making condoms available in high schools increases condom use. Notably, the impact of exposure to the program on condom use was significantly greater for those students who reported having had three or more partners in the past 6 months (the higher-risk group).

A range of psychosocial, behavioral, and demographic variables also influence condom use at last intercourse, including depression, self-efficacy, age at first intercourse, and gender. For example, although the NYC program is made available to both male and female students, the multiple determinants of condom use vary between males and females. Thus, logistic models, such as those presented in the Results section, were examined separately for males and females and for higher-risk males and higher-risk females. Exposure to the program continued to make an independent, significant contribution to condom use at last intercourse in each of these subgroups, although the relationships between other explanatory variables and condom use differed between males and females.

The major methodological limitation of this study is that there was no baseline measurement of condom use among NYC public high school students prior to the implementation of the condom availability program. Because the program was systemwide, there could be no random assignment to intervention or comparison groups. Thus the comparison group, by definition, had to be another school system. This raised the question of whether some unexplained differences between NYC and Chicago, rather than the condom availability program itself, might account for any observed differences in condom use. A variety of analytic strategies were used to account for these limitations. No singlemethod or analytic strategy could overcome all the limitations, but as others have suggested, these methodologies used together build a case for the overall results.

Conclusions

Other studies have suggested that HIV education alone appears to have little impact on behavior and that most adolescents do not perceive themselves to be at risk for HIV infection, despite the fact that they are engaging in unprotected sex. Classroom-based programs alone have had limited success in delaying the onset of sexual activity, increasing the use of contraceptives and condoms, and decreasing rates of pregnancy and sexually transmitted disease, while programs that include additional enabling or service provisions have been somewhat more successful. The data presented in this [selection] suggest that making condoms available does not encourage students who have never had sex to become sexually active. In addition, adding condom availability to an HIV/AIDS education program has a significant though modest relationship with condom use, particularly among students with multiple partners, whether through direct use of the program or through other, indirect, means.

School may not be the place to reach adolescents at highest risk for HIV infection, yet the school population does include a substantial proportion of students at high risk; nearly 1 in 10 (8.7%) of all NYC public high school students reported that they had had three or more sexual partners in the past 6 months. In fact, while less than one fifth of sexually active NYC students reported actually getting a condom from school, higher-risk students reported getting a condom from school in significantly higher proportions than lower-risk students. Our findings suggest that school-based condom availability, a low-cost, harmless addition to classroom HIV/AIDS prevention education efforts, merits policy consideration because it can lower the risk of HIV infection and other sexually transmitted diseases for urban teens in the United States.

Edwin J. Delattre

NO

Condoms and Coercion:
The Maturity of Self Determination

We [are] told . . . by condom distribution advocates that school distribution of condoms is not a moral issue but rather an issue of life and death. We [are] told, by the same people, that we have a moral obligation to do everything in our power, at all times, to save lives. The incoherence—indeed, contradiction—between these claims reflects the failure of condom distribution advocates to perceive the fact that *all* life-and-death issues are morally consequential; that questions of what schools have the right and the duty to do in the interest of their students are irreducibly moral questions; and that *how* schools should endorse and sustain the honorable conduct of personal life is a moral issue of the most basic and profound sort.

The plain fact is that if our only moral duty were to save lives—at whatever cost to other ideals of life—on statistical grounds, we would have to raise the legal age for acquiring a driver's license to at least twenty-five; we would have to reduce interstate highway speed limits to 35 mph or less; we would have to force everyone in America to undergo an annual physical examination; we would have to outlaw foods that contribute to bad health; we would have to prohibit the use of tobacco and advertisements for it, and spend huge resources to enforce those laws; we would have to eliminate rights of privacy in the home in order to minimize the possibility of domestic violence; we would have to establish laws to determine who can safely bear children, and therefore who is allowed to become pregnant; we would have to make AIDS and drug testing mandatory for all citizens at regular intervals; we would have to do away with the rights of suspects to due process in order to eliminate open-air drug marketplaces in our cities; we would have to incarcerate, on a permanent basis, all prostitutes who test HIV positive; we would have to announce publicly the name of every person who tests HIV positive in order to safeguard others from possible exposure through sexual activity. And so on.

Saving lives is not the only moral concern of human beings. The prevention of needless suffering among adults, youths, children, infants and unborn babies; the avoidance of self-inflicted heartache; and the creation of opportunities for fulfilling work and for happiness in an environment of safety and justice all merit moral attention as well. And even if saving lives were our only moral concern, there is no reason to believe that distributing condoms in schools is the best way to save lives. Certainly, the distribution of condoms is an unreliable substitute for the creation of a school environment that conveys the unequivocal message that abstinence has greater life-saving power than any piece of latex can have.

Furthermore, even if condoms were the best means of saving lives, there would be no compelling reason for schools rather than parents to distribute condoms; no reason for schools to be implicated in the distribution of condoms when others are willing and eager to do so; no reason for schools to assent to the highly questionable claim that *if* they distribute condoms, they will, in fact, save lives.

We have a duty to make clear to our students . . . the implications of sexual involvement with other people who are ignorant of the dangers of sexual transmission of diseases or uncaring about any threat they may pose to the safety of the innocent. Our students need to grasp that if any one of us becomes sexually involved with someone and truly needs a condom or a dental dam because neither we nor the other person knows how much danger of exposure to AIDS that person may be subjecting us to, then we are sleeping with a person who is either staggeringly ignorant of the dangers involved or else is, in principle, willing to kill us. Such a person has not even the decency to wait long enough for informative medical tests to be conducted that would have a chance of disclosing an HIV positive condition; not even the decency to place saving our lives, or anyone else's, above personal gratification. Obviously, if we behave in this way, we, too, are guilty of profound wrongdoing.

This is so inescapably a moral issue—about saving lives—that its omission by condom distribution advocates astounds the imagination. They have said nothing about the kinds of people who are unworthy of romantic love and personal trust, who conceal or ignore the danger they may pose to another's life, even with a condom. These considerations prove yet another fundamental fact of human life: the only things casual about casual sex are its casual indifference to the seriousness of sexual life, its casual dismissal of the need for warranted trust between one individual and another, and its casual disregard and contempt for our personal duty to protect others from harm or death.

We have a duty to explain to students that there is no mystery about discovering and saying what is morally wrong. It is morally wrong to cause needless suffering, and it is morally wrong to be indifferent to the suffering we may cause by our actions. On both counts, sexual promiscuity is conspicuously wrong.

Sexual promiscuity, casual sexual involvement, whether in youth or adulthood, is an affront to all moral seriousness about one's own life and the lives of others. Exposing oneself and others to possible affliction with sexually transmitted diseases is itself morally indefensible, but even where this danger is not present, sexual promiscuity reveals a grave failure of personal character.

A person who is sexually promiscuous inevitably treats other people as mere objects to be *used* for personal gratification, and routinely ignores the possibility of pregnancies that may result in unwanted children whose lot in life will be unfair from the beginning. This is morally wrong; it is an affront to the dignity of human beings, an affront to their right to be treated with concern for their feelings, hopes, and happiness, as well as their safety.

Where promiscuity is shrewdly calculated, it is crudely exploitative and selfish; where promiscuity is impulsive, it is immature and marks a failure of self-control. In either case, promiscuity is incompatible with moral serious-ness, because wherever there is promiscuity, there is necessarily an absence of the emotional and spiritual intimacy that anchor genuine love among human beings, love that is healthfully expressed among morally mature people in nonpromiscuous sexual intimacy.

Those who are sexually promiscuous—or want to become promiscuous by successfully persuading others to gratify their desires—routinely seek to exert peer pressure in favor of sexual indulgence, as surely as drug users seek to impose peer pressure in favor of drug and alcohol consumption. Anyone who believes that such persons will not try to overcome resistance to sexual involvement by insisting that the school distributes condoms; that the Health Center says condoms increase your safety, or at least make sex "less dangerous"; that sexual activity is *only* a health issue and not a moral issue, and that condoms eliminate the health problem—anyone so naive ignores entirely, or does not know, the practices of seduction, the manipulativeness among people who treat others as objects to be used for their own pleasure, or the coercive power of adverse peer pressure.

We also have a duty to describe to our students the very real dangers of promiscuity even with condoms. According to research conducted by Planned Parenthood, condoms have a vastly greater rate of failure in preventing preg-nancy when used by young unmarried women—36.3 percent—than has been reported by condom distribution advocates. The Family Research Council stresses that this figure is probably low where condom failure may involve possible exposure to AIDS, since the HIV virus is 1/450 the size of a sperm and is less than 1/10 the size of open channels that routinely pass entirely through latex products such as gloves.

The behavior of health professionals with respect to "less dangerous" sex ought to be described to students as well. As reported in the Richmond, Virginia. *Times-Dispatch* ten days ago:

> "Dr. Theresa Crenshaw, a member of the national AIDS Commission and past president of the American Association of Sex Education, Counselors, and Therapists, told a Washington conference of having addressed an international meeting of 800 sexologists: 'Most of them,' she said, 'recom-mended condoms to their clients and students. I asked them if they had available the partner of their dreams, and knew that person carried the virus, would they have sex, depending on a condom for protection? No one raised their hand. After a long delay, one timid hand surfaced from the back of the room. I told them that it was irresponsible to give advice to others that they would not follow themselves. The point is, putting a mere balloon between a healthy body and a deadly disease is not safe.'"
> [January 4, 1992, p. A-10]

These reasons of principle and of fact ought to be sufficient to show the hazards. . . . But there is more to the moral dimension of school distribution of condoms, and those who have claimed otherwise deserve a further account with respect to sexual life itself.

In being forced to distribute condoms . . . to children and adolescents whose emotional and intellectual maturity remain, for the most part, in the balance—we are made to convey to the young the false message that we do not know these things about basic decency, about safety, about the high price of putting everything at risk for instant pleasure. And we are also giving youths whose judgment is still being formed the impression that we do not particularly care about the moral dimensions of sexual life, and that there is no particular reason for them to do so either.

Remember: we have been told . . . by adults and youths alike that there *is* no moral issue at stake. The acquiescence of the School . . . in condom distribution tacitly affirms that pronouncement. Their message betrays fidelity to high standards of ethics in education and sensitivity to more comprehensive dimensions of respect for justice, self-control, courage, and regard for persons in the articulation of institutional policy and the conduct of personal life.

Those who have told us that we are not faced with a moral issue transparently lack understanding of the fundamentals of moral maturity and character excellence. Their judgement, shallow as it is, betrays the young to a supposed, but implausible, expediency.

We will be told that all this will be covered by conscientious counseling of youths who request condoms. But, despite the best efforts of our well-intentioned health care professionals, it will not be adequately covered—and it will certainly not be covered for the students, and their former classmates who have dropped out of school, who are subject to peer pressure but never seek condoms themselves.

Condom distribution in the schools, even under the most carefully considered conditions, lends itself to the theme we have heard here: that profound dimensions of moral life, including decent treatment of others, have nothing to do with morality. It is not simply that this position is morally incompetent; it is also cruel in its licensing of peer pressure to become sexually active, peer pressure that can be, and often is, selfish, intolerant, even downright vicious.

The School . . . has sanctioned such peer pressure and has thereby given approval to forms of behavior and manipulation that cause, among the young, enormous suffering. Condom distribution advocates behave as though they know nothing of human nature and nothing of the unfair pressures to which the young are routinely subjected. The School['s] decision has now implicated us in teaching the young that we, too, are ignorant of these facts of life as they apply in youth.

The reply of condom distribution advocates to my reasoning is predictable. Sexual activity among the young is inevitable, they will say, even natural, and for reasons of birth control, avoidance of unwanted teenage pregnancies and protection from sexually transmitted diseases, including AIDS, it is better that students should use condoms than not. They will insist that the availability of condoms does not increase the likelihood of sexual activity and that, in any case, many students who use the condoms will be selectively active rather than promiscuous.

The counterarguments are equally straightforward. If we teach the young that sexual activity is what we expect of them, at least some of them will come to expect it of themselves. We have no right to exhibit, or to have, such low expectations—especially toward those whose decisions about whether to become sexually active remain in the balance or who hope to live in an environment where restraint is not only respected but genuinely admired.

And for those who *are* sexually promiscuous—for whatever motives—whether they act in this way to aggrandize themselves; or to exert power over others; or to gain prestige, or physical pleasure, or peer approval; whether they are sexually active because of a desperate and doomed hope of securing affection and attention; or from failure to grasp alternatives; or from ignorance of consequences of promiscuity; or from a mistaken belief that intercourse and intimacy are the same—for all of them, if it is better that they should use condoms than not, how does it follow that *we* should give them the condoms *in* the High School?

In logic—and in fact—it does *not* follow. Even if it is true that promiscuity with condoms and dental dams is physically less dangerous than promiscuity without them, this ostensible fact in no way suggests or implies that *we* should be in the business of distributing condoms—as surely as the fact that filtered cigarettes are less harmful than unfiltered ones does not imply that we should be distributing free filtered cigarettes in the . . . Public Schools. We should instead be standing on the side of peer pressure against casual sex, and we should be providing resolute support for such peer pressure because it is morally right and because it has a distinctive and irreplaceable power to save lives.

Some condom distribution advocates insist that because we now have a health clinic in the High School, we are obliged to defer to the judgment of experts in health care on this subject. They claim that these experts do not try to tell us what we should do as educators, and we should not tell them what to do in matters of health and health-related services.

This artificial and illusory bifurcation of education and health is based on the false premise that what health officials do in the High School contains no educational lessons and teaches nothing about institutional policy or the decent conduct of personal life.

In this particular matter, health experts have clearly attempted to teach the public—including students—that the High School is an appropriate condom distribution site, while dismissing as irrelevant questions of educational mission and duty; and social service agency leaders have advocated that policy by pandering to and proselytizing for the view naively expressed by the students that there are no moral issues implicit in the policy. They have exceeded their competence in questions of morals.

Furthermore, it is well understood by all of us that condoms are fallible. We have not adequately addressed problems of potential legal liability for . . . the City . . . , the . . . Public Schools, and the School Committee. Yet both health professionals and social service personnel have . . . explicitly dismissed as trivial the prospect of legal liability for our institutions, as though they were qualified not only in matters of ethics but also in matters of law. In both respects, they have acted as educators—miseducators.

In doing so, they have potentially undermined the achievement of healthy levels of self-assertion by students, putting that achievement at risk from dangerous peer pressure. They have likewise jeopardized the achievement of selfrespect among students by teaching them that even a questionable expediency is more important than mature judgment, personal restraint, and respect for the well-being of other people.

These are the facts of our present situation. We have been brought to a moment when we are no longer able to do what we ought to do in the High School, but are forced to do what is educationally wrong. We have been driven to this condition by a collection of flawed arguments about educational policy, about ethical life, and about law.

POSTSCRIPT

Should Schools Make Condoms Available to Students?

The debate over whether or not public schools should make free condoms available to students clearly reflects the opposing philosophical and moral positions of *fixed* versus *process* value systems. The fixed worldview places a top priority on opposing all sexual activity outside marriage. A process worldview maintains that sexual abstinence for teens should be encouraged but that teens should also be provided with the knowledge and ways of reducing the health risk when they do decide to engage in sex.

This debate can be political and heated, especially when the teenagers who are affected by any decision on this issue speak for themselves. In St. Clair Shores, Michigan, five high school students were suspended for wearing buttons promoting condom usage. In Seattle, Washington, activists handing out condoms and risk-reduction pamphlets at local high schools were threatened with arrest for public obscenity.

Approximately one-quarter of all Americans who currently have AIDS were infected during their teen years. In some areas, the rate of HIV infection among teens is doubling every 16 to 18 months. One in four sexually active teens has a sexually transmitted infection.

Despite this debate, which began 10 years ago, a growing number of students in high schools expect to have free condoms available in their schools. For these teenagers the question of whether or not free condoms promote promiscuity is misguided and ignores the reality of their high school lives.

Suggested Readings

D. Kirby et al., "The Impact of Condom Distribution in Seattle Schools on Sexual Behavior and Condom Use," *American Journal of Public Health* (February 1999).

P. O'Campo et al., "Distribution Along a Stages-of-Behavioral-Change Continuum for Condom and Contraceptive Use Among Women Accessed in Different Settings," *Journal of Community Health* (February 1999).

L. Richardson, "When Sex Is Just a Matter of Fact: To High School Students, Free Condoms Seem Normal, Not Debatable," *The New York Times* (October 16, 1997), pp. B1, B6.

ISSUE 3

Is Masters and Johnson's Model an Accurate Description of Sexual Response?

YES: Stephanie Ann Sanders, from "Physiology of Sex," *Microsoft Encarta Online Encyclopedia* (2004)

NO: Paul Joannides, from "The HSRC—Is Everything Better in Black & White?" An Original Essay Written for This Volume (2004)

ISSUE SUMMARY

YES: Stephanie Ann Sanders, a director and scientist with the Kinsey Institute and a contributing author to the *Encarta Online Encyclopedia,* summarizes Masters and Johnson's Human Sexual Response Cycle.

NO: Paul Joannides, author of the popular book *The Guide to Getting It On!,* says that the Human Sexual Response Cycle is a "one-size-fits-all" model that does not account for individual variations.

Scientific interest in the physiological changes that humans experience during sexual activity can be traced to the late nineteenth century. In 1876, the French physician Felix Roubaud wrote about sexual response and described his research on changes in penis size, vaginal lubrication, and other physiological changes. In the 1940s, while renowned sex research Alfred Kinsey was interviewing Americans about their sexual behavior, a lesser-known researcher, Robert Latou Dickinson, studied changes in the vagina when his female subjects masturbated with a glass tube resembling a penis. Dickinson reported his findings in *Human Sex Anatomy* in 1949, and so did others, describing changes that were visible to the naked eye.

William Masters and Virginia Johnson were the first scientists to study sexual response through systematic observation in a laboratory setting. They observed almost 700 subjects who engaged in sexual activity while the researchers measured and recorded their sexual responses with the aid of new technological developments, especially microphotography.

Masters and Johnson's primary interest in studying sexual response was to help therapists identify sources of sexual dysfunction and recommend effective treatment. However, their 1966 book, *Human Sexual Response,* was considered groundbreaking for both its popular insights and its political implications. Their research revealed and emphasized the many similarities in sexual response between men and women. This revelation came to signify equality for women and underscored the importance of regarding women's sexuality as equal to that of men.

Their model of sexual response, the Human Sexual Response Cycle (HSRC) describes four phases of sexual response in men and women—excitement, plateau, orgasm, and resolution. These changes are physiological in nature, as they describe changes in the size and color of sexual organs, as well as changes in blood pressure, heart rate, muscular tension, respiration, and other physical changes. Some researchers have found the focus on physiological changes too limiting. Helen Singer Kaplan added desire as a phase that preceded excitement, describing it as specific sensations that moved a person to seek out (or become receptive to) sexual activity, and suggesting that three phases (desire, excitement, and orgasm) were sufficient to illustrate sexual response.

Others who criticize the HSRC for being too centered on physical changes point to cultures in which sexual experience is intertwined with spirituality. Eastern Tantric traditions of Buddhism, Hinduism, Taoism, and yoga link sexual response with spiritual energy. Critics also charge that the HSRC places a Western emphasis on orgasm as the goal of sex, rather than the intimacy of the couple, or the sensuality of many different behaviors that do not necessarily lead to orgasm. The HSRC has also been criticized for being too medical or for trying to "fit" female sexual response into a mostly male-oriented model.

Despite its many critics, the HSRC remains the one model that can be found in every college text book on sexuality. Even the texts that point out the limitations of the model still describe its four phases of sexual response in great detail.

In the following essays, Stephanie Ann Sanders, writing for the *Encarta Online Encyclopedia,* presents a concise illustration of the HSRC. Paul Joannides challenges the prominence the HSRC is given in sexuality text books, and criticizes it as a "one-size-fits-all" model.

YES ↵

Stephanie Ann Sanders

Physiology of Sex

Understanding the processes and underlying mechanisms of sexual arousal and orgasm is important to help people become more familiar with their bodies and their sexual responses and to assist in the diagnosis and treatment of sexual dysfunctions. Nevertheless, it was not until the work of American gynecologist William H. Masters and American psychologist Virginia Johnson that detailed laboratory studies were conducted on the physiological aspects of sexual arousal and orgasm in a large number of men and women. Based on data from 312 men and 382 women and observations from more than 10,000 cycles of sexual arousal and orgasm, Masters and Johnson described the human sexual response cycle in four stages: excitement, plateau, orgasm, and resolution.

In men who are unaroused, the penis is relaxed, or flaccid. In unaroused women, the labia majora lie close to each other, the labia minora are usually folded over the vaginal opening, and the walls of the vagina lie against each other like an uninflated balloon.

A. Excitement

The excitement stage of sexual arousal is characterized by increased blood flow to blood vessels (vasocongestion), which causes tissues to swell. In men, the tissues in the penis become engorged with blood, causing the penis to become larger and erect. The skin of the scrotum thickens, tension increases in the scrotal sac, and the scrotum is pulled up closer to the body. Men may also experience nipple erection.

In women, vasocongestion occurs in the tissue surrounding the vagina, causing fluids to seep through the vaginal walls to produce vaginal lubrication. In a process similar to male erection, the glans of the clitoris becomes larger and harder than usual. Muscular contraction around the nipples causes them to become erect. However, as the excitement phase continues, vasocongestion causes the breasts to enlarge slightly so that sometimes the nipples may not appear erect. Vasocongestion also causes the labia majora to flatten and spread apart somewhat and the labia minora to swell and open. The upper two-thirds of the vagina expands in a "ballooning" response in which the cervix and the uterus pull up, helping to accommodate the penis during sexual intercourse.

Both women and men may develop "sex flush" during this or later stages of the sexual response cycle, although this reaction appears to be more common among women. Sex flush usually starts on the upper abdomen and spreads to the chest, resembling measles. In addition, pulse rate and blood pressure increase during the excitement phase.

B. Plateau

During the plateau stage, vasocongestion peaks and the processes begun in the excitement stage continue until sufficient tension is built up for orgasm to occur. Breathing rate, pulse rate, and blood pressure increase. The man's penis becomes completely erect and the glans swells. Fluid secreted from the Cowper's gland (located near the urethra, below the prostate) may appear at the tip of the penis. This fluid, which nourishes the sperm, may contain active sperm capable of impregnating a woman. In women, the breasts continue to swell, the lower third of the vagina swells, creating what is called the orgasmic platform, the clitoris retracts into the body, and the uterus enlarges. As the woman approaches orgasm, the labia majora darken.

C. Orgasm

Orgasm, or climax, is an intense and usually pleasurable sensation that occurs at the peak of sexual arousal and is followed by a drop in sexual tension. Not all sexual arousal leads to orgasm, and individuals require different conditions and different types and amounts of stimulation in order to have an orgasm. Orgasm consists of a series of rhythmic contractions in the genital region and pelvic organs. Breathing rate, pulse rate, and blood pressure increase dramatically during orgasm. General muscle contraction may lead to facial contortions and contractions of muscles in the extremities, back, and buttocks.

In men, orgasm occurs in two stages. First, the vas deferens, seminal vesicles, and prostate contract, sending seminal fluid to the bulb at the base of the urethra, and the man feels a sensation of ejaculatory inevitability—a feeling that ejaculation is just about to happen and cannot be stopped. Second, the urethral bulb and penis contract rhythmically, expelling the semen—a process called ejaculation. For most adult men, orgasm and ejaculation are closely linked, but some men experience orgasm separately from ejaculation.

In women, orgasm is characterized by a series of rhythmic muscular contractions of the orgasmic platform and uterus. These contractions can range in number and intensity. The sensation is very intense—more intense than the tingling or pleasure that accompany strong sexual arousal.

D. Resolution

During resolution, the processes of the excitement and plateau stages reverse, and the bodies of both women and men return to the unaroused state. The muscle contractions that occurred during orgasm lead to a reduction in muscular tension and release of blood from the engorged tissues.

The woman's breasts return to normal size during resolution. As they do, the nipples may appear erect as they stand out more than the surrounding breast tissue. Sex flush may disappear soon after orgasm. The clitoris quickly returns to its normal position and more gradually begins to shrink to its normal size, and the orgasmic platform relaxes and starts to shrink. The ballooning of the vagina subsides and the uterus returns to its normal size. Resolution generally takes from 15 to 30 minutes, but it may take longer, especially if orgasm has not occurred.

In men, erection subsides rapidly and the penis returns to its normal size. The scrotum and testes shrink and return to their unaroused position. Men typically enter a refractory period, during which they are incapable of erection and orgasm. The length of the refractory period depends on the individual. It may last for only a few minutes or for as long as 24 hours, and the length generally increases with age. Women do not appear to have a refractory period and, because of this, women can have multiple orgasms within a short period of time. Some men also experience multiple orgasms. This is sometimes related to the ability to have some orgasms without ejaculation.

The HSRC—Is Everything Better in Black & White?

Back in the 1950s and 1960s, there was a famous pair of sex researchers who were working on two charts that were to become the Rosetta Stone of sexual satisfaction. Known as the Human Sexual Response Cycle (HSRC), each chart consisted of "the" four phases of sexual response called excitement, plateau, orgasm, and resolution.

There is not a single college textbook on sex that does not devote several pages to the HSRC charts, and there have been few books written on sex since the 1960s that do not take the HSRC as fact. We regarded this famous pair of sex researchers in the same way that many psychoanalysts did Freud. Rather than viewing them as visionaries, we viewed them as prophets. Rather than looking at their findings through the lens of science, we enshrined them as the Ten Commandments of what human couples do when naked and breathing hard.

In case you weren't aware, the HSRC model is based on the experiences of recruits who were so uninhibited that they were able to get naked, have sex, and pop out easy orgasms in a university laboratory while researchers watched, listened, filmed and measured. As a result, the model is based on only three things: getting hard, getting wet, and coming. Nowhere in this model is there room for how qualities like intimacy, tenderness and even kink can impact, shape and change sex. Nowhere is there concern about desire, anticipation, fantasy, or what happened in the lives of the research subjects before they got naked in the lab and started fucking on command.

When you reduce human sexuality to just three parts—erect penis, lubricated vagina and orgasms—what you get is a mechanistic model of human sexual response. If the three parts are present and accounted for, then your sex life is said to be okay. If one of these "essential" elements is missing, then modern medicine has a pill, patch, or demeaning diagnosis to throw at it.

While the elements that are shown in the two HSRC charts can easily describe the human sexual response of some people, they fall short when describing the sexual response of others.

An original article for this title. Copyright © 2004 by Paul Joannides, author of GUIDE TO GETTING IT ON. Reprinted by permission of the author.

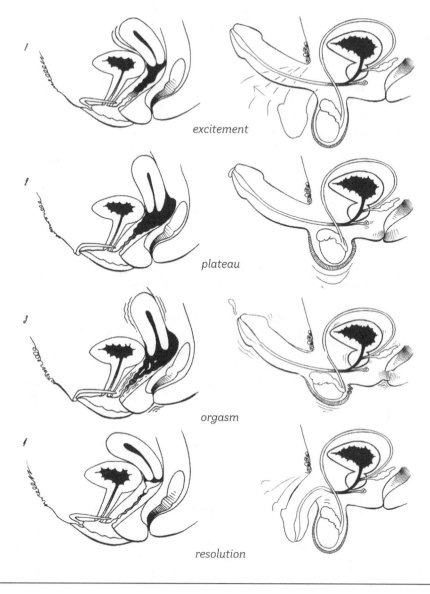

excitement

plateau

orgasm

resolution

Daerick Gross Sr., Illustrator

For instance, consider two situations brought up by Deborah Tolman, followed by three examples of my own:

1. *A young girl is in her gym class and discovers that she enjoys climbing up a rope and sliding down it. Her bare feet are extremely sensitive, so it feels sensual on the bottoms of her feet as the thick cotton rope slides through them. She also finds the feeling of the rope between her legs to be quite nice. She climbs up the rope and slides down several times. She never has an orgasm and was never thinking sexual thoughts.*

Many of us would consider this to be an innocent and delightful sexual experience—totally private and unlabeled. But according to the Human Sexual Response Cycle, there was no orgasm so it was not part of the human sexual response.

> 2. *An adult woman is in a competitive academic situation. She is overwhelmed with nervousness and anxiety. She excuses herself to the rest room and quickly masturbates to orgasm. There was not a sexual thought in her mind when she was masturbating and she had not felt any sexual arousal before going to the rest room to masturbate. For her, the masturbation provided relief from unbearable anxiety. Its effect was similar to downing a shot of whisky or popping a Valium.*

This woman had an orgasm, so it's Bingo according to the HSRC. Motivation and situation are irrelevant to the HSRC, as long as the woman's genitals swelled, quivered and convulsed.

> 3. *One couple makes out passionately for an hour but has no genital contact and no orgasms. Another couple doesn't make out, but has intercourse and orgasms.*

According to the HSRC, the first couple didn't have a complete sexual experience, while the second couple did. But what if you found that the couple who was kissing passionately for an hour had been married for twenty-five years? Even without an orgasm, making out for an hour is a pretty powerful statement about intimacy and sexual satisfaction when a couple has been married for a quarter of a century. Yet they didn't register a blip on the HSRC.

> 4. *A woman seldom has an orgasm with her husband, but looks forward to having intercourse with him.*

According to the HSRC, her husband is the only one who has a complete sexual experience when they are making love.

> 5. *A man who could have been Mr. HSRC hit a patch of black ice while riding his Harley. He is now a quadriplegic who has no feeling below his shoulders, yet he finds that having the top of his head stroked is as blissful and sexually satisfying as his former HSRC marathons.*

The head that this man used to receive was HSRC certified—now that it's lost its metaphorical quality, it's HSRC challenged.

Some therapists would say that the events listed below can be tremendously important elements of a satisfying sex life even if they are not immediately chased by throbbing crotches and pounding orgasms, yet it's difficult to figure where they fit on the charts of the Human Sexual Response Cycle:

- A woman receives a rose and a card saying "Just thinking of you" from her partner while she is at work.

- A woman finds it to be an incredible sexual experience when her lover sucks on her fingers. This is the sum of their sexual activity one night until she is so overwhelmed that she falls asleep in his arms, exhausted but ecstatic.
- A couple talks on the phone during the middle of the day, for no other reason that to connect emotionally.
- One partner lightly tickles, caresses and kisses the other's back for an hour.
- A man opens his briefcase at work and finds a box of condoms with a note from his lover "Hope you'll be ready to use these tonight!"
- One partner licks and kneads the nipples of the other, who then asks to have nipple clamps put on them. This couple never gets around to having orgasms in the traditional sense.
- One partner loves being tickled, so the other ties him up and tickles him mercilessly.
- After talking dirty together, one partner finds it to be a nearly mystical experience when the other probes or fists his or her anus.

The range of orgasmic experience can also be minimized by the HSRC. I know of a woman whose orgasms have unleashed such raw emotional torrents that it left her profoundly sad and sobbing in tears. Another woman wrote to me this week wanting to know if she was strange because after twenty years of having the usual "moaning" kind of orgasms, she now bursts into uncontrollable laughter as she starts to come—with the same husband. But according to the HSRC, an orgasm is an orgasm, who cares about the tears, laughter, moans, silence or whatever.

If you were to accept the HSRC as THE model of human sexual response, it's the sexual equivalent of throwing away color TV and going back fifty years when everything was in black and white. It's calling the smile on the Mona Lisa's face irrelevant, or showing the genitals on the statue of David while covering the rest of him with duct tape or a gunny sack.

The Human Sexuality Response Cycle does not differentiate between love and indifference. It does not explain how the freshly spanked bottom of a lover can be so sexually gratifying for a kinky couple. Forget relationship issues, forget intimacy, forget hopes and dreams. Sexual complexity outside of the three parameters of erection, lubrication and orgasm is irrelevant.

This can be a real problem if one of you is the poster child for the HSRC, but the other is non-compliant and values fun and intimacy more than whether you come.

The HSRC provides a one-size-fits-all approach. Either you wear the male size or the female size. There are no allowances for the way other things in your life shape your sexual experiences. No consideration is given to the influences of your work schedule, the demands of your family, the shadows of your sexual past, the pull of religion and gender roles, the impact of your ethnic background or the dictates of your social class or the demands of the culture you were raised in.

The Human Sexual Response Cycle is about a hard penis going into a very orgasmic and very wet vagina.

There wouldn't be a single thing wrong about the HSRC if it had been proposed as two charts out of ten, or at the very least, if it was layered with other charts. In this way, it could guide modern medicine in providing solutions for men who need help with certain types of erection problems or premature ejaculation, but it wouldn't limit the entirety of human sexual response to that which can be maintained with drugs or surgery. It would recognize that for a lot of people there are many different ways to have a sexual response.

POSTSCRIPT

Is Masters and Johnson's Model an Accurate Description of Sexual Response?

Masters and Johnson's Human Sexual Response Cycle (HSRC) has endured much criticism over the years. Nevertheless, it continues to be described in every college textbook on sexuality. As Paul Joannides says, "There is not a single college textbook on sex that does not devote several pages to the HSRC charts." How does your textbook handle the subject of sexual response? Does it present the HSRC as the *only* model? Is the HSRC model given more prominence than other models of sexual response, or are a variety of models presented with equal validity?

While the HSRC has been criticized for its emphasis on physiological responses, some researchers defend the model precisely for such an emphasis. Upon learning that the HSRC was to be examined in *Taking Sides*, one sexologist tersely commented that the model could not be refuted—it was biological fact. What could be disputed, he said, was how sexual response was "packaged" (e.g., as Kaplan's three-phase model, or with other labels to describe physiological changes that are universal). What do you make of this observation? Does the HSRC present a helpful model of human capacity for physiological sexual response, even if not everyone experiences excitement, plateau, orgasm, or resolution? What do you think of Masters and Johnson's "packaging" of the four phases? Are the physiological changes described in the model universal? Is the model necessary for its detailed descriptions of physiological sexual response?

Interestingly, the work of Masters and Johnson predates much of the research on female ejaculation and the G-spot (see Issue 6 of this *Taking Sides* edition). Do such responses fit into the HSRC?

Joannides illustrates a variety of examples that do not seem to fit within the HSRC, or within traditional understanding of "sexual response" as it is physiologically described. How would you classify the behaviors he described? What do you think about expanding the definition of "sex" beyond being associated with intercourse or orgasm?

Finally, how would you describe the phases of sexual response? Is the HSRC helpful as a model? A baseline? Would your model be entirely different? Would your model include emotional, spiritual, relational, or other characteristics?

Suggested Readings

R. Eisler, *Sacred Pleasure: Sex, Myth, and the Politics of the Body* (Harper-Collins, 1995).

P. Joannides, *The Guide to Getting It On* (Goofyfoot Press, 2004).

G. Kelly, *Sexuality Today: The Human Perspective* (McGraw-Hill, 2005).

G. Kelly, *Sources: Notable Selections in Human Sexuality* (McGraw-Hill/ Dushkin, 1998).

J. Kuriansky, *The Complete Idiot's Guide to Tantric Sex* (Alpha Books, 2002).

W. Masters and V. Johnson, *Human Sexual Response* (Lippincott Williams & Wilkins, 1966).

L. Tiefer, "Historical, Scientific, Clinical, and Feminist Criticisms of 'The Human Sexual Response Cycle' Model," *Annual Review of Sex Research* (vol. 2, 1991).

L. Tiefer, *Sex Is Not a Natural Act and Other Essays* (Westview Press, 2004).

ISSUE 4

Is Oral Sex Really Sex?

YES: Rhonda Chittenden, from "Oral Sex *Is* Sex: Ten Messages about Oral Sex to Communicate to Adolescents," *Sexing the Political* (May 2004)

NO: Nora Gelperin, from "Oral Sex and Young Adolescents: Insights from the 'Oral Sex Lady,'" *Educator's Update* (September 2004)

ISSUE SUMMARY

YES: Sexuality educator Rhonda Chittenden says that it is important for young people to expand their narrow definitions of sex and understand that oral sex *is* sex. Chittenden offers additional educational messages about oral sex.

NO: Sexuality trainer Nora Gelperin argues that adult definitions of oral sex are out of touch with the meaning the behavior holds for young people. Rather than impose adult definitions of intimacy, educators should be seeking to help young people clarify and understand their own values.

In 1998, President Bill Clinton famously stated, "I did not have sexual relations with that woman, Miss Lewinsky." As it later became evident that the president, in fact, did have *oral* sex with intern Monica Lewinsky, a national debate raged over the meaning of sex. What, people asked, does "sexual relations" mean? What about "sex?" Do these terms refer to vaginal intercourse only, or are other sexual behaviors, like oral sex, included?

Some welcomed this unprecedented opportunity to have an open, national discussion about sex in an otherwise erotophobic, sexually repressed culture. Sexuality education professionals lent their expertise, offering suggestions to help parents answer their children's questions about the new term, "oral sex," they might hear on the evening news or at family gatherings. Others feared such openness would inevitably lead to increased sexual activity among teens. Perhaps the media viewed this as a foregone conclusion when they began airing hyped reports indicating a rise in teen oral sex, based on anecdotal, rather than research-based, evidence.

Feature reports, often intended to alarm viewers, have introduced even more new terms into our sexual lexicon. "Friends with benefits" describes a partner pairing based on friendship and casual oral sex. "Rainbow parties" involve events where girls wear different colors of lipstick and boys try to get as many colored rings on their penises as they can. But how much of this is really happening, and how much of this just makes for good television?

Even if *some* of what the reports say is true, many adults—parents, teachers, public health officials, and others—are concerned. Some are worried about the potential rise in sexually transmitted infections that can be passed orally as well as vaginally or anally. Others lament the inequity of oral sex as young people may experience it—with females *giving* oral sex far more than they are *receiving* it. Still others may have religious or other moral reasons that drive their concerns.

The apprehension among many adults is rooted in the very meaning of sex and oral sex. Since many adults hold oral sex to be an intensely intimate act—one that is even more intimate than vaginal intercourse—it is difficult for them to observe what they interpret as casual attitudes toward this behavior.

In the following selections, sexuality education professionals Rhonda Chittenden and Nora Gelperin examine the meaning of sex and oral sex in the context of giving young people helpful educational messages. Chittenden articulates several reasons why it is important for young people to know that oral sex is sex, and offers several other important messages for adults to convey to young people. Gelperin argues that it is not for adults to decide the meaning of such terms for young people. Rather, educators can help young people critically examine the meaning of such words and activities for themselves. She further argues against having overly dramatized media accounts dictate public health approaches.

YES

Rhonda Chittenden

Oral Sex *Is* Sex:
Ten Messages about Oral Sex to
Communicate to Adolescents

As a teen in the early-80s, I was very naïve about oral sex. I thought oral sex meant talking about sex with one's partner in a very sexy way. A friend and I, trying to practice the mechanics, would move our mouths in silent mock-talk as we suggestively switched our hips from left to right and flirted with our best bedroom eyes. We wondered aloud how anyone could engage in oral sex without breaking into hysterical laughter. In our naïveté, oral sex was not only hilarious, it was just plain stupid.

Twenty years later, I doubt most teens are as naïve as my friend and I were. Although the prevalence of oral sex among adolescents has yet to be comprehensively addressed by researchers,[1] any adult who interacts with teens will quickly learn that, far from being stupid or hilarious, oral sex is a common place activity in some adolescent crowds.

Some teens claim, as teens have always claimed about sex, that "everyone is doing it." They tell of parties—which they may or may not have attended—where oral sex is openly available. They describe using oral sex as a way to relieve the pressure to be sexual with a partner yet avoid the risk of pregnancy. Some believe oral sex is an altogether risk-free behavior that eliminates the worry of sexually transmitted infections. There is a casualness in many teens' attitudes towards oral sex revealed in the term "friends with benefits" to describe a non-dating relationship that includes oral sex. In fact, many teens argue that oral sex really isn't sex at all, logic that, try as we might, defies many adults. Most pointedly, teens' anecdotal experiences of oral sex reveal the continuing imbalance of power prevalent in heterosexual relationships where the boys receive most of the pleasure and the girls, predictably, give most of the pleasure.

Not willing to wait until research confirms what many of us already know, concerned adults want to address the issue of adolescent oral sex *now*. We know that young people long for straightforward and honest conversations about the realities and complexities of human sexuality, including the practice of oral sex. But where do we start with such an intimidating topic?

The following ten messages may help caring and concerned adults to initiate authentic conversations about oral sex with young people.

1. Oral sex *is* sex.   Regardless of how casual the behavior is for some young people, giving and receiving oral sex are both sexual behaviors. This is made obvious simply by defining the act of oral sex: oral sex is the stimulation of a person's genitals by another person's mouth to create sexual pleasure and, usually, orgasm for at least one of the partners. It's that straightforward.

Even so, many young people—and even some adults—believe that oral sex is not "real sex." Real sex, they say, is penis-vagina intercourse only. Any other sexual behavior is something "other" and certainly not *real* sex. This narrow definition of sex, rooted in heterosexist attitudes, is problematic for several reasons.

First, such a narrow definition is ahistorical. Art and literature reveal human beings, across human history and culture, consensually engaging their bodies in loving, pleasurable acts of sex beyond penis-vagina intercourse.[2] In Western culture, our notions of sex are still shackled by religious teachings that say the only acceptable sex—in society and the eyes of God—is procreative sex. Of course, the wide accessibility of contraceptives, among other influences, has dramatically shifted our understanding of this.[3] Even still, many people are unaware that across centuries and continents, human beings have enjoyed many kinds of sex and understood those acts to be sex whether or not they involved a penis and a vagina.

Next, by defining sex in such narrow terms, we perpetuate a dangerous ignorance that places people at risk for sexually transmitted infections (STIs), including HIV. Many people, including teens, who define sex in such narrow terms incorrectly reason that they are safe from HIV if they avoid penis-vagina intercourse. Because saliva tends to inhibit HIV, it's true that one's chances of contracting HIV through oral sex with an infected partner are considerably small, compared to the risk of unprotected vaginal or anal sex. Of course, this varies with the presence of other body fluids as well as the oral health of the giver. However, if one chooses to avoid "real sex" and instead has anal sex, the risk for HIV transmission increases.[4] In reality, regardless of what orifice the penis penetrates, all of these sex acts are real sex. In this regard, the narrow definition of sex is troubling because it ignores critical sexual health information that all people deserve, especially those who are sexually active or intend to be in the future.

Finally, this narrow definition of sex invalidates the sexual practices of many people who, for whatever reasons, do not engage in penis-vagina intercourse. Obviously, these people include those who partner with lovers of the same sex. They also include people who, regardless of the sex of their partners, are physically challenged due to illness, accident, or birth anomaly. To suggest to these individuals that oral sex—or any other primary mode of shared sexual expression—is not real sex invalidates the range of accessible and sensual ways they can and do share their bodies with their partners.

Clearly, we must educate young people that there are many ways to enjoy sex, including the sensual placement of one's mouth on another person's genitals. Oral sex may be practiced in casual, emotionally indifferent ways, but this does not disqualify it as a legitimate sex act. Oral sex *is* sex—and, in most states, the law agrees.

2. Without consent, oral sex may be considered sexual assault.   Adults who work with teens know that oral sex often takes place at parties where alcohol and other drugs are consumed. It's imperative, then, that when adults talk to teens about oral sex, we confront the legal realities of such situations. Of course, drinking and drug use are illegal for adolescents. In addition, according to Iowa law, if alcohol or drugs are used by either partner of any age, consent for oral sex (or any sex) cannot be given. Without consent, oral sex may be considered sexual assault.[5] Other states have similar laws.

While giving some adolescents reason to reflect on their substance use, this information may also help them to contextualize their past experiences of oral sex. It may affirm the often uneasy and unspoken feelings of some teens who feel they were pressured into oral sex, either as the giver or receiver. It may also illuminate other risks that often occur when sex and substance use are combined, especially the failure to use protection against pregnancy, and in the case of oral sex, sexually transmitted infections.

3. Practice safer oral sex to reduce the risk of sexually transmitted infections.   Because many young people don't consider oral sex to be real sex, they don't realize that sexually transmitted infections that are typically transmitted through genital-genital contact can also be transmitted through oral-genital contact. Although some are more easily transmitted through oral sex than others, these infections include chlamydia, gonorrhea, herpes, and, in some cases, even pubic lice. The lips, tongue, mouth cavity, and throat, are all vulnerable to various sexually transmitted bacteria and viruses.[6] With pubic lice, facial hair, including mustaches, beards and eyebrows, can be vulnerable.[7]

Aside from abstaining from oral sex, young people can protect themselves and their partners from the inconvenience, embarrassment, treatment costs, and health consequences of sexually transmitted infections by practicing safer oral sex. The correct and consistent use of latex condoms for fellatio (oral sex performed on a penis) and latex dental dams for cunnilingus (oral sex performed on a vulva) should be taught and encouraged. Manufacturers of condoms, dental dams, and pleasure-enhancing lubricants offer these safer sex supplies in a variety of flavors—including mint, mango, and banana—to increase the likelihood that people will practice safer oral sex.[8] Certainly, adolescents who engage in oral sex should be taught about the correct, pleasure-enhancing uses of these products, informed of the location of stores and clinics that carry them, and strongly encouraged to have their own supply at hand.

4. Oral sex is a deeply intimate and sensual way to give sexual pleasure to a partner.   Although casual references to oral sex abound in popular music, movies and culture, many young people have never heard an honest, age-appropriate description of the profoundly intimate and sensual nature of oral sex. Especially for the giver of oral sex, the experience of pleasuring a partner's genitals may be far from casual. Unlike most other sex acts, oral sex acutely engages all five senses of the giver.

As is suggested by the availability of flavored safer sex supplies, for the giver of oral sex, the sense of taste is clearly engaged. If safer sex supplies are not used, the giver experiences the tastes of human body fluids—perhaps semen, vaginal fluids, and/or perspiration. In addition, the tongue and lips feel the varied textures of the partner's genitals, and, depending on the degree of body contact, other touch receptors located elsewhere on the body may be triggered. With the face so close to their partner's genitals, the giver's nose can easily smell intimate odors while the eyes, if opened, get a very cozy view of the partner's body. Lastly, during oral sex the ears not only pick up sounds of voice, moaning, and any music playing in the background, they also hear the delicate sounds of caressing another's body with one's mouth. Obviously, if one is mentally engaged in the experience, it can be quite intense! Honest conversations with adolescents about the intimate and sensual nature of oral sex acknowledge this incredibly unique way human beings share pleasure with one another and elevate it from the casual references of popular culture.

5. Boys do not have to accept oral sex (or any sex) just because it is offered.   As I talked with a group of teenagers at a local alternative high school, it became painfully clear to me that some teen girls offer oral sex to almost any guy they find attractive. As a consequence of such easy availability, these teen boys, although they did not find a girl attractive nor did they desire oral sex from her, felt pressured to accept it simply because it was offered. After all, what real man would turn down sex? Popular music videos, rife with shallow depictions of both men and women, show swaggering males getting play right and left from eager, nearly naked women. These same performances of exaggerated male sexual bravado are mirrored on the streets, in the hallways, and in the homes of many boys who may, for various reasons, lack other more balanced models of male sexuality.

When I told the boys that they were not obligated to accept oral sex from someone to whom they were not attracted, it was clearly a message they had never heard. I saw open expressions of surprise and relief on more than a few young faces. This experience taught me that adults must give young men explicit permission to turn down oral sex—and any sex—they do not want. We must teach them that their manhood is not hinged on the number of sex partners they amass.

6. Making informed decisions that respect others and one's self is a true mark of manhood.   In May 2002, when Oprah Winfrey and Dr. Phil tried to tackle this subject on her afternoon talk show, they not only put the onus of curbing the trend of casual adolescent oral sex on the girls, they threw up their hands and said, "What do the guys have to lose in this situation? Nothing!"

Nothing? I would suggest otherwise. To leave teen boys off the hook in regard to oral sex fails them miserably as they prepare for responsible adult relationships. In doing so, we set up boys to miss out on developing skills that truly define manhood: healthy sexual decision making, setting and respecting personal boundaries, and being accountable for one's actions. We also leave them at risk for contracting sexually transmitted infections. In addition, although our culture rarely communicates this, men who accept oral sex whenever it is offered risk losing the respect of people who do not admire or appreciate men who have indiscriminate sex with large numbers of partners. Clearly, adults—and especially adult men—must be willing to teach boys, through words and actions, that authentic manhood is a complex identity that cannot be so simply attained as through casual sex, oral or otherwise.[9]

7. Giving oral sex is not an effective route to lasting respect, popularity or love.   For some teen girls, giving oral sex is weighted with hopes of further attention, increased likeability, and perhaps even a loving relationship.[10] For them, giving oral sex becomes a deceptively easy, if not short-term, way to feel worthy and loved. Adults who care about girls must empower them to see beyond the present social situation and find other routes to a sense of belonging and love.

One essential route to a sense of belonging and love is the consistent experience of non-sexual, non-exploitive touch. Some adolescent girls seek sex as a way to find the sense of love and belonging conveyed by touch. If a girl's touch needs go unfilled by parents or other caregivers, sex is often the most available means for fulfilling them.[11] Adults who work with girls must acknowledge the deeply human need for touch experienced by some adolescent girls. Although outside the scope of this discussion, girl-serving professionals can provide creative ways for girls to experience safe, non-sexual touch as part of their participation in programs without violating program restrictions on physical touch between staff and clients.

On the other hand, it is possible—and developmentally normal—for teen girls to experience sexual desire. Although our cultural script of adolescent sexuality contradicts this, it may be that some girls, especially older teens, authentically desire the kind of sensual and sexual intimacy oral sex affords. If this is the case, it is essential that adults do not shame girls away from these emergent desires. Instead, they should explore the ways oral sex may increase one's physical and emotional vulnerabilities and strategize ways that girls can stay healthy and safe while acknowledging their own sexual desires.

8. Girls can refuse to give oral sex.   Unlike Oprah and Dr. Phil, I do not believe the onus for curbing casual adolescent oral sex rests solely or even primarily on teen girls. Teen boys can and should assert firmer boundaries around participating in oral sex. The cultural attitudes that make girls and women the gatekeepers of heterosexual male sexual behavior, deciding when and if sex will happen, are unduly biased and burdensome. By perpetuating these attitudes, Oprah and Dr. Phil missed a grand opportunity to teach the value of mutuality in sexual decision-making and relationships, a message many young people—and adults—desperately need to hear.

That said, it is disturbing to hear stories of adolescent girls offering casual oral sex to teen boys. Again, the models of a balanced female sexuality in the media and in the lives of many girls are often few and far between. This, coupled with the troubling rates of sexual abuse perpetrated against girls in childhood and adolescence, makes the establishment of healthy sexual boundaries a problem for many girls.

Therefore, adults must go beyond simply telling girls to avoid giving oral sex for reasons of reputation and health, as was stressed by Dr. Phil. We must empower girls, through encouragement, role plays, and repeated rehearsals, to establish and maintain healthy boundaries for loving touch in their friendships and dating relationships, an experience that may be new to some. Moreover, we must be frank about the sexual double-standards set up against girls and women that make them responsible for male sexual behavior. And, we must create safe spaces where girls can encourage and support each other in refusing to give boys oral sex, thus shifting the perceived norm that "everyone is doing it."

9. Young women may explore their own capacities for sexual pleasure rather than spending their energies pleasuring others.   Some girls will argue that oral sex is just another exchange of friendship, something they do with their male friends as "friends with benefits." I would argue, however, that, in most cases, the benefits are rather one-sided. Rarely do the teen boys give oral sex to the teen girls in exchange. Neither research nor anecdotal evidence indicates a trend of boys offering casual oral sex to girls. It seems that the attention the girls get *en route* to oral sex make it a worthwhile exchange for them, even as they are shortchanged on other "benefits."

If, indeed, girls are fulfilling their valid need for attention and acceptance through giving oral sex, and if they don't consider what they are doing to be "real sex," it stands to reason that many girls engaged in oral sex may not be experiencing genuine sexual desire or pleasure at all. It wouldn't be surprising if they're not. After all, few girls receive a truly comprehensive sexuality education, one that acknowledges the tremendous life-enhancing capacities for desire and pleasure contained in the female body. Our sex education messages are often so consumed by trying to prevent girls from getting pregnant and abused that we fail to notice how we keep them as the objects of other people's sexual behaviors. In doing so, we keep girls mystified about their own bodies and thus fail to empower them as the sexual subjects of their own lives.[12]

Adults can affirm girls' emerging capacities for desire and pleasure by, first, teaching them the names and functions of all of their sexual anatomy, including the pleasure-giving clitoris and G-spot. When discussing the benefits of abstinence, adults can suggest to girls that their growing sexual curiosity and desires may be fulfilled by learning, alone in the privacy of one's room, about one's own body—what touch is pleasing, what is not, how sexual energy builds, and how it is released through their own female bodies. If girls could regard themselves as the sexual subjects of their own lives rather than spending vast energies on being desirable objects of others, perhaps they would make healthier, firmer, more deliberate decisions about the sexual experiences and behaviors they want as adolescents.[13] Not only might girls make better decisions around oral sex, they may feel more empowered to negotiate the use of contraception and safer sex supplies, a skill that would serve them well through their adult years.[14]

10. Seek the support and guidance of adults who have your best interests at heart. Young people do not have to figure it all out on their own. Human sexuality is complicated, and most of us, adults and adolescents, do better by sometimes seeking out the support, guidance, and caring of others who want to see us enjoy our sexualities in healthy, life-enhancing ways. Adults can let young people know we are willing to listen to their concerns around issues of oral sex. We can offer teens support and guidance in their struggles to decide what's right for their lives. We can become skilled and comfortable in addressing risk-reduction and the enhancement of sexual pleasure together, as companion topics. And, finally, adults can use the topic of oral sex as a catalyst to dispel myths, discuss gender roles, and communicate values that affirm the importance of mutuality, personal boundaries, and safety in the context of healthy relationships.

References

1. L. Remez, "Oral Sex Among Adolescents: Is it Sex or Is It Abstinence?" *Family Planning Perspectives*, Nov/Dec 2000, p. 298.

2. R. Tannahill, *Sex in History* (New York: Stein and Day, 1980), pp. 58–346.

3. M. Carrera, *Sex: The Facts, The Acts, and Your Feelings* (New York: Crown, 1981), pp. 49–51.

4. Centers for Disease Control and Prevention, "Preventing the Sexual Transmission of HIV, the Virus that Causes AIDS, What You Should Know about Oral Sex," Dec. 2000. Available at: www.thebody.com/cdc/oralsex.html

5. Iowa Code, Section 709.1, Sexual abuse defined (1999). Available at: www.legis.state.ia.ua/IACODE/1999SUPPLEMENT/709/1.html

6. S. Edwards and C. Carne, "Oral Sex and the Transmission of Viral STIs," *Sexually Transmitted Infections*, April 1998, pp. 95–100.

7. Centers for Disease Control and Prevention, "Fact Sheet: Pubic Lice or 'Crabs'," June 2000. Available at: www.cdc.gov.ncidod/dpd/parasites/lice/factsht_pubic_lice.htm

8. Several online retailers sell safer sex supplies, including flavored condoms and lubricants. Go to www.condomania.com and www.goodvibes.com

9. P. Kivel, *Boys Will Be Men: Raising Our Sons for Courage, Caring and Community.* (Gabriola Island B.C., Canada: New Society, 1999), pp. 177–184.

10. S. Thompson, *Going All the Way: Teenage Girls' Tales of Sex, Romance, and Pregnancy* (New York: Hill & Wang, 1995), pp. 17–46.

11. P. Davis, *The Power of Touch* (Carlsbad, CA: Hay House, 1999), p. 71.

12. M. Fine, "Sexuality, Schooling, and Adolescent Females: The Missing Discourse of Desire," *Disruptive Voices: The Possibilities of Feminist Research*, Ann Arbor: University of Michigan, 1992), pp. 31–59.

13. M. Douglass & L. Douglass, *Are We Having Fun Yet? The Intelligent Woman's Guide to Sex* (New York: Hyperion, 1997), pp. 170–171.

14. TARSHI (Talking About Reproductive and Sexual Health Issues), *Common Ground Sexuality: Principles for Working on Sexuality* (New Dehli, India: TARSHI, 2001), p. 13.

 **NO**

Oral Sex and Young Adolescents: Insights from the "Oral Sex Lady"

A Brief History

I've been the Director of Training at the Network for Family Life Education for three years, but recently I've become known as the "Oral Sex Lady." (My parents are so proud.) It all began when I started receiving more frequent calls from parents, teachers and the media concerning alleged incidents of 11–14 year-olds engaging in oral sex in school buses, empty classrooms or custodial closets, behind the gym bleachers and during "oral sex parties." People were beginning to panic that youth were "sexually out of control." Most people believe young teens should not engage in oral sex, but that's not our current reality. So in response, I developed a workshop about oral sex and young teens, which I have since delivered to hundreds of professionals throughout the country. This process has helped me refine my thinking about this so-called oral sex "problem." Now, when I arrive at a meeting or workshop I smile when I'm greeted with, "Hey, aren't you the Oral Sex Lady?!"

What's the "Problem"?

The 1999 documentary, "The Lost Children of Rockdale County," first chronicled a syphilis outbreak in suburban Conyers, Georgia due to a rash of sex parties. Since then, more anecdotal and media stories about middle school students having oral sex began to surface. Initially, a training participant would tell me about an isolated incident of a young girl caught performing oral sex on a boy in the back of the school bus. During a workshop in Minnesota, I was educated about "Rainbow Parties" in which girls wear different colored lipstick and the goal for guys is to get as many different colored rings on their penises by night's end. In Florida, there were stories of "chicken head" parties where girls supposedly gave oral sex to boys at the same time, thus bobbing their heads up and down like chickens. During a workshop in New Jersey, I learned that oral sex was becoming the ultimate bar mitzvah gift in one community, given under the table during the reception hidden by long tablecloths. (At one synagogue, the caterer was ultimately asked to shorten the tablecloths as a method of prevention!) The media began to pick up on these stories and run cover stories in local and national newspapers and magazines. One could conclude from the media buzz that the majority of early adolescents are frequently having oral sex at sex parties around the country. But what was *really* going on and what can the research tell us?

What is missing from the buzz is any recent scientific data to support or refute the claims of early adolescents having oral sex at higher rates than in previous years. Due to parental rights, research restrictions, and lack of funding, there is no rigorous scientific data conducted on the behavior of early adolescents to establish the frequency or incidence of oral sex. So we are left with anecdotal evidence, research conducted on older adolescents, media reports and cultural hype about this "new" phenomenon. We don't know how frequent this behavior is, at what ages it might begin, how many partners a young teen might have, whether any safer sex techniques are utilized or the reasoning behind a teen's decision to engage in oral sex. What is universal among the anecdotes is that girls are giving oral sex to boys without it generally being reciprocated and it's mostly the adults that find this problematic. But what can we learn from all this?

Major Questions to Consider

Is Oral Sex Really "Sex"?

One of the most common themes I hear during my workshop is that adults want to convince teens that oral sex is really "sex." The adult logic is that if we can just convince teens that oral sex is "really" sex, they will take it more seriously and stop engaging in it so recklessly. This perspective seeks to universally define oral sex from an adult perspective that is out of sync with how many teens may define it. Many teens view oral sex as a way to maintain their "virginity" and reduce their risk for pregnancy and infections. According to a recent Kaiser Family Foundation report, 33 percent of 15–17 year-old girls report having oral sex to avoid having intercourse. In the same report, 47 percent of 15–17 year-old girls and boys believe that oral sex is a form of safer sex. Most people believe that young adolescents should not engage in oral, anal or vaginal sex. As a back up, we should make sure teens understand that if they are going to engage in sexual behaviors, oral sex is less risky for many infections than vaginal or anal sex if latex barriers like flavored condoms and sheer glyde dams[1] are used, and it cannot start a pregnancy.

If You've Only Had Oral Sex, Are You Still a Virgin?

From my experience facilitating workshops on oral sex, professionals really struggle with this question and many of the 32,000 teens per day who come to our *SEX, ETC.* Web site (www.sexetc.org) do too. The concept of virginity, while troublesome to many adults, is still central to the identity of many teens, particularly girls. Many adults and teens define virginity as not having had vaginal intercourse, citing the presence or absence of the hymen. Some adults then wrestle with the idea of what constitutes actual intercourse— penetration of a penis into a vagina, orgasm by one or both partners, oral sex, anal sex, penetration of any body opening? For heterosexual couples, virginity is something girls are often pressured to "keep" and boys are pressured to "lose." The issue also becomes much more volatile when a teen may not have given consent to have intercourse the first time—does this mean that he/she is no longer a virgin? Gay and lesbian teens are also left out when virginity is tied to penis-vagina intercourse, possibly meaning that a gay or lesbian teen might always be a "virgin" if it's defined that way. Educators can help teens think more critically about their definitions of sex, intercourse, and virginity and the meanings of these words in their lives.

How Intimate Is Oral Sex?

Many adults in my workshops express their belief that oral sex is just as intimate as other types of penetrative sexual behaviors. Some adults believe oral sex is even *more* intimate than vaginal or anal intercourse because one partner is considered very vulnerable, it involves all of the senses (smell, taste, touch, sight, and sound) and requires a lot of trust. Many teens, although certainly not all teens, believe oral sex is *less* intimate than vaginal intercourse. Through my experience as an on-line expert for our *SEX, ETC.* Web site, I hear from hundreds of teens every month who submit their most personal sexual health questions. Some of these teens believe oral sex is very intimate and acknowledge the same issues that adults raise while others find it less intimate than vaginal intercourse. From a teen's perspective, it is less intimate because:

- oral sex doesn't require that both partners be nude;
- oral sex can be done in a short amount of time (particularly if performed on adolescent boys);
- oral sex can maintain virginity;
- oral sex doesn't involve eye contact with a partner;
- oral sex doesn't require a method of contraception;
- oral sex doesn't require a trip to the gynecologist; and
- most teens believe oral sex doesn't carry as much of a risk for sexually transmitted infections as vaginal or anal intercourse.

Some girls even feel empowered during oral sex as the only sexual behavior in which they have complete control of their partner's pleasure. Others feel pressured to engage in oral sex and exploited by the experience. So while many adults view oral sex as extremely intimate, some teens do not.

This dichotomy presents challenges for an educator in a group that may assign a different value to oral sex than the educator. Oral sex also requires a conversation about sexual pleasure and sexual response, topics that many educators are not be able to address with young teens. The salient issue is how teens define behaviors, not how adults define behaviors, since we are operating in their world when we deliver sexuality education. I believe our definitions and values should be secondary to those of teens because ultimately teens need to be able to operate in a teen culture, not our adult world.

What Can an Educator Do?

As sexual health educators, our role is to provide medically-accurate information and encourage all adolescents to think critically about decisions relating to their sexuality. We should ask middle school-age adolescents to sift through their own beliefs and hear from their peers, many of whom might not agree about oral sex, virginity, intimacy or the definition of sex. Finding ways to illuminate the variety of teens' opinions about oral sex will more accurately reflect the range of opinions instead of continuing to propagate the stereotype that "all teens are having oral sex." Additionally, instead of focusing exclusively on the ramifications of oral sex and infections, we should address the potential social consequences of having oral sex. Since early adolescents are not developmentally able to engage in long-term planning, focusing on the long-term consequences of untreated sexually transmitted infections (STIs) is not developmentally appropriate. Educators should be cognizant of what is developmentally appropriate for early adolescents and strive to include information about sexual coercion, correct latex condom and sheer glyde dam use, and infection prevention.

So Are They or Aren't They?

Without research, this question will remain unanswered and we must not rely on overly-dramatized media accounts to dictate public health approaches. Instead we should focus on giving young adolescents developmentally appropriate information, consider their reasoning for wanting to engage in oral sex, explore their definitions of sex, virginity and intimacy, and develop programs that incorporate all of these facets. We need to advocate for more research and reasoned media responses to what is likely a minority of early adolescents having oral sex before it becomes overly dramatized by our shock-culture media. Finally, we must not forget that the desire for early adolescents to feel sexual pleasure is normal and natural and should be celebrated, not censored. From my experience as the "Oral Sex Lady," teens are much more savvy than we adults think.

Note

1. Sheer glyde dams are squares of latex that are held in place of the vulva of a female during oral sex to help prevent sexually transmitted infections. They are the only brand of dental dam that is FDA approved for the prevention of infections.

POSTSCRIPT

Is Oral Sex Really Sex?

> **"Sex is more than sexual intercourse.** This means teaching young people that there are many ways to be sexual with a partner besides intercourse and most of these behaviors are safer and healthier than intercourse. The word 'sex' often has a vague meaning. When talking about intercourse, the word 'intercourse' [should be] used."

This statement is taken from a list of principles for sexuality education developed by The Center for Family Life Education, included in the U.S. chapter of the *International Encyclopedia of Sexuality*. Do you agree or disagree with this principle? How does it compare with your own definition of "sex"? Do you agree with Chittenden that young people need to recognize oral sex as "really sex"? Or are you inclined to side with Gelperin as she asserts that adult values and definitions should be secondary, and that young people need to form their own meaning to oral sex?

Chittenden presents specific messages she believes young people need to hear about oral sex. What do you think about these messages? Are they messages you would want to give to a son or daughter, or to a younger sibling? What other advice would you want to give to a loved one who was thinking about having oral sex?

Whereas Chittenden identifies specific messages that need to be articulated to young people, Gelperin seems more inclined to advocate a values clarification process and educational strategies based on the developmental needs of a given audience. What merits do these different approaches have? Would you advocate a combination of these approaches? Or would your own educational approach be very different?

Gelperin expresses great concern about the hype surrounding media reports of oral sex. What do you think about such reports? How do they compare with the social climate in your schools or community as you were growing up?

Since both Chittenden and Gelperin are sexuality education professionals, you may have noticed several overlapping themes, such as the concern both expressed about condom use and protection from sexuality transmitted infections. What other similarities did you observe?

Is it more important to have a uniform definition of "sex," that includes (or does not include) oral sex, or for people to create their own personal definitions that have meaning for themselves and/or their partners? Some reproductive health professionals have ascertained that if you cannot define "sex," then you cannot define its supposed opposite, "abstinence." In other words, one needs to understand what sex is before she or he can determine what it is they are being encouraged to abstain from. How has a culturally vague notion of "sex" and "abstinence" contributed to the widespread failure of abstinence-only education programs?

Suggested Readings

C. Billhartz and C.M. Ostrom, "What's 'Real' Sex? Kids Narrow Definition, Put Themselves at Risk," *Seattle Times* (November 6, 2002).

S. Brown and B. Taverner, "Principles for Sexuality Education," in R.T. Francoeur and R. Noonan, eds., *The International Encyclopedia of Sexuality* (Continuum, 2004).

Centers for Disease Control and Prevention, "Preventing the Sexual Transmission of HIV, the Virus that Causes AIDS, What You Should Know about Oral Sex," (December 2000). Available at www.thebody.com/cdc/oralsex.html

14 and Younger: The Sexual Behaviors of Young Adolescents (National Campaign to Prevent Teen Pregnancy, 2003).

E. Marchetta, "Oral Sex = Safe Sex? No Way!" *SEX, ETC.* (Spring 2001).

National Survey of Adolescents and Young Adults: Sexual Health, Knowledge, Attitudes and Experience (Kaiser Family Foundation, 2003).

L. Remez, "Oral Sex Among Adolescents: Is It Sex or Is It Abstinence?" *Family Planning Perspectives* (November/December 2000).

J. Timpane, "No Big Deal: The Biggest Deal of All—Young Adults and the Oral Sex Code," *Philadelphia Inquirer* (October 28, 2002).

P. Wilson, "Talking with Youth about Oral Sex," *Family Life Matters* (Fall 2000).

ISSUE 5

Should Emergency Contraception Be Available over the Counter?

YES: Jane E. Brody, from "The Politics of Emergency Contraception," *New York Times* (August 24, 2004)

NO: United States Food and Drug Administration, from "FDA's Decision Regarding Plan B: Questions and Answers," www.fda.gov/cder/drug/infopage/planB/planBQandA.htm (2004)

ISSUE SUMMARY

YES: New York Times columnist Jane E. Brody believes that politics, not science, drove the FDA's decision not to allow emergency contraception to be made available over the counter.

NO: The Food and Drug Administration, responsible for regulating all drugs dispensed in the United States, says that its decision was not political, and that it would reconsider its decision if presented with evidence that girls under age 16 could take it safely without parental supervision.

What is emergency contraception? In the past, it was nicknamed "the morning-after pill," indicating that it is a method of postcoital contraception—that is, it can be taken *after* unprotected vaginal intercourse to prevent pregnancy. The term "emergency contraception" is more accurate because it can be taken not just the "morning after," but also *several* mornings after, up to 120 hours (or 5 days) after unprotected intercourse. However, it is *most* effective when begun sooner. If a woman begins taking emergency contraception within one day after unprotected intercourse, she reduces her risk of pregnancy by 95 percent; within three days, pregnancy risk is reduced by 75 percent, and so on.

Emergency contraception is sometimes confused with the "abortion pill," more commonly known as RU-486, mifepristone, or medical abortion. The abortion pill is quite different from emergency contraception. Whereas the abortion pill will induce a non-surgical abortion when taken up to seven weeks after a pregnancy begins, emergency contraception is taken to *prevent* a pregnancy before it begins. Using a high dose of hormones found in the contraceptive pill, it works in multiple ways: (1) it stops a woman from ovulating (releasing an egg) so that the egg does not become fertilized; (2) if ovulation has occurred, it may prevent the egg and sperm from joining; and (3) if fertilization does occur, it may prevent the fertilized egg from implanting in the wall of the uterus so that a pregnancy cannot begin. If a fertilized egg has already implanted, emergency contraception does not work.

For several years now, emergency contraception has been available on a prescription basis. Women who believe they might be at risk for a pregnancy could get a prescription from their doctor or from a family planning center like Planned Parenthood. Sexual health educators have reminded students that the hotline 1-888-NOT-2-LATE will direct them to the nearest provider of emergency contraception. However, some have expressed concern that the requirement to visit a doctor or clinic in order to get a prescription for emergency contraception creates a barrier to young women seeking services. Some women may delay this important decision if they are uncomfortable telling a doctor about their sexual behavior, or may feel embarrassed visiting a family planning center. This may be especially true when a woman is seeking emergency contraception because of a rape or sexual assault.

Health professionals recognize the need to make emergency contraception easily accessible. In the United States, a few states permit trained pharmacists to dispense emergency contraception to women without requiring a clinician's visit. These states include Alaska, California, Hawaii, Maine, New Mexico, New York, and Washington. Several European countries make it available over-the-counter, so that women can get emergency contraception quickly when they need it, without having to consult a doctor or pharmacist.

In the spring of 2004, the U.S. Food and Drug Administration (FDA), the government body that regulates the dispensing of all medications, rejected a proposal to make one type of emergency contraception known as "Plan B" available over-the-counter. This decision surprised many, as the FDA rejected the recommendations and conclusions of its own advisory panel. Some speculated that President George W. Bush's religiously conservative administration was behind the decision. Conservatives generally reject the clinical definition of pregnancy, claiming that life begins when an egg is fertilized, not when the egg implants, as medical organizations and textbooks say. They also believe that increased accessibility of emergency contraception will lead to increased sexual promiscuity.

In the following selections, columnist Jane E. Brody claims that the FDA's decision was politically motivated, while the FDA defends and explains its decision.

 **YES**

The Politics of Emergency Contraception

"Emergency Contraception: Politics Trumps Science at the F.D.A." That is the title of an editorial by Dr. David A. Grimes in the August issue of *Obstetrics & Gynecology,* the journal of the American College of Obstetricians and Gynecologists.

Dr. Grimes is hardly the only one distressed by the Food and Drug Administration's decision in May to refuse to grant over-the-counter access to the morning-after emergency contraceptive known as Plan B. Six months earlier, the agency's advisory committees voted 23 to 4 in favor of removing the requirement that a woman first obtain a prescription from a doctor before she can buy this product. In nearly all cases, the agency abides by the votes of its advisory panels. But not this time. And the reason, Dr. Grimes and other medical leaders have said, is that the agency's "decision-making process is being influenced by political considerations."

The politics in this case involve, indirectly, the Bush administration's advocacy of "abstinence only" to prevent pregnancy in unwed teenagers and, more directly, its objection to abortion, which emergency contraception is not. And Dr. Grimes points out that the rate of unplanned pregnancies in this country "is unparalleled among industrialized nations," and that "each year, nearly 2 percent of all women of reproductive age have an induced abortion."

Women at risk of an unwanted pregnancy deserve to know the reasons that so many leading scientists and organizations have endorsed over-the-counter status for emergency contraception and the reasons that others have objected.

The Need for Intervention

Plan B is a progesterone-based after-the-fact contraceptive meant to be taken as soon as possible after a sexual encounter that places a woman at risk of pregnancy. It is supposed to be used within 72 hours after unprotected intercourse, but it is most effective when taken sooner, within 12 to 24 hours.

There are two other options that can be used when a woman needs post-coital contraception: a drug called Preven that is in effect a high-dose birth control pill, and insertion of a copper IUD, both of which also require a doctor's intervention.

There are many reasons a woman may need postcoital contraception. Condoms can break, diaphragms and cervical caps can become dislodged, IUDs can be expelled unknowingly and birth control pills forgotten. In addition, some women, particularly teenagers, fail to anticipate a sexual encounter or may need to feel "swept away" and are thus unprepared to protect themselves against an unwanted pregnancy. And then there is rape resulting in pregnancy.

As Dr. Fatim H. Lakha and colleagues noted in the July issue of *Women's Health in Primary Care*, "Unprotected sexual intercourse is a fact of life." When that happens, they said, "unintended pregnancy can be prevented" by the use of emergency contraception.

The Objections

Some opponents of emergency contraception confuse it with abortion. But an abortion can occur only after a pregnancy has been established. The National Institutes of Health and the obstetricians group define pregnancy as beginning with the implantation of a fertilized egg in the uterus. Emergency contraception, on the other hand, has no effect once a fertilized egg implants in the womb. It cannot dislodge an established pregnancy or harm a developing embryo. Nor does it appear to work by destroying a fertilized egg or preventing implantation, which would negate the concerns of those who consider fertilization, not implantation, the start of pregnancy.

The mechanism of action of Plan B and Preven is not definitively known, but the evidence indicates that they delay or inhibit ovulation and make the cervical mucus inhospitable to sperm. A woman need not be ovulating at the time of intercourse to become pregnant. Sperm can live for several days in a woman's genital tract waiting for an egg to fertilize. Another objection to emergency contraception is the fear that its ready availability would encourage teenage sexual encounters or foster careless sex among couples who might otherwise have used ordinary contraception. To date, controlled studies have found no evidence that women would neglect to use precoital contraception in favor of an emergency contraceptive, especially since the former is a more reliable way to prevent an unwanted pregnancy.

Nor is there evidence that teenagers would be encouraged to engage in risky sexual behavior. "This is analogous to suggesting that a fire extinguisher beneath the kitchen sink makes one a risky cook," Dr. Grimes wrote.

In fact, one study published this year in *The Journal of Pediatric and Adolescent Gynecology* found no increase in unprotected intercourse when young sexually active teenage girls were given easy access to emergency contraception through an advance prescription. A third objection is that without a doctor to explain the proper use of emergency contraception, women, and especially teenagers, would fail to use it properly. Again, studies have shown that women who were able to self-administer emergency contraception did so correctly and at the proper time and suffered no adverse effects.

An Interim Solution

Any delay in reaching a doctor, getting a prescription for emergency contraception and finding a pharmacy that stocks the drug can render it ineffective. Without any intervention, the average woman's chance of becoming pregnant after one act of unprotected intercourse is 8 percent. When Plan B is used within 24 hours of unprotected intercourse, the pregnancy rate is about four-tenths of 1 percent, or 4 per 1,000, rising to 2.7 percent when treatment begins 48 to 72 hours after. Proper use of emergency contraception, on average, reduces the risk of pregnancy by about 85 percent, and more if the treatment is used within 12 hours. Side effects with Plan B are minor—nausea in about 15 percent of cases, vomiting in 1 percent and a delay in the next menstrual period in 5 percent.

Side effect rates are higher with Preven, which includes an estrogen component as well as a progesterone.

Unless the F.D.A. allows Plan B to be sold without a prescription, advocates for easy access to the drug advise women to get a prescription from their doctors and fill it well before they need it. Unfortunately, few teenagers would be likely to take such a step, unless they are already receiving regular gynecological care. In addition, the added cost of a medical visit can make access to Plan B prohibitive for many women, especially teenagers.

Six states, including California and Washington, have laws that allow a woman to buy emergency contraception from a pharmacist without a prescription. Other states might consider following suit. Still, education must coincide with access. Even in California, only 29 percent of the women most at risk of an unintended pregnancy were aware of emergency contraception, according to a new study in *The American Journal of Obstetrics and Gynecology.*

Finally, every woman must realize that emergency contraception is a backup, not a substitute for more reliable precoital contraception. Emergency contraception is not as effective in preventing pregnancy as, say, oral contraceptives, implants or the copper IUD. And if, after using emergency contraception, a woman fails to menstruate within three or four weeks, she is advised to take a pregnancy test, which is included in the emergency contraceptive packet.

**United States Food and
Drug Administration**

FDA's Decision Regarding Plan B: Questions and Answers

1. What is emergency contraception?

Emergency contraception is a method of preventing pregnancy to be used after a contraceptive fails or after unprotected sex. It is not for routine use. Drugs used for this purpose are called emergency contraceptive pills, post-coital pills, or morning after pills. Emergency contraceptives contain the hormones estrogen and progestin (levonorgestrel), either separately or in combination. FDA has approved two products for prescription use for emergency contraception—Preven (approved in 1998) and Plan B (approved in 1999).

2. What is Plan B?

Plan B is emergency contraception, a backup method to birth control. It is in the form of two levonorgestrel pills (0.75 mg in each pill) that are taken by mouth after unprotected sex. Levonorgestrel is a synthetic hormone used in birth control pills for over 35 years. Plan B can reduce a woman's risk of pregnancy when taken as directed if she has had unprotected sex. Plan B contains only progestin, levonorgestrel, a synthetic hormone used in birth control pills for over 35 years. It is currently available only by prescription.

3. How does Plan B work?

Plan B works like other birth control pills to prevent pregnancy. Plan B acts primarily by stopping the release of an egg from the ovary (ovulation). It may prevent the union of sperm and egg (fertilization). If fertilization does occur, Plan B may prevent a fertilized egg from attaching to the womb (implantation). If a fertilized egg is implanted prior to taking Plan B, Plan B will not work.

4. What steps did FDA take in considering switching Plan B from prescription to nonprescription (over-the-counter (OTC)) status?

From the United States Food and Drug Administration, 2004. www.fda.gov/cder/drug/omfopage/planB/planBQand A.htm

FDA received an application to switch Plan B from prescription to nonprescription status. FDA staff reviewed the scientific data contained in the application which included among other data, an actual use study and a label comprehension study.

On December 16, 2003, we held a public advisory committee meeting with a panel of medical and scientific experts from outside the federal government. The members of the Nonprescription Drugs Advisory Committee and the Advisory Committee for Reproductive Health, met jointly to consider the safety and effectiveness data of nonprescription use of Plan B. Although the joint committee recommended to FDA that this product be sold without a prescription, some members of the committee, including the Chair, raised questions concerning whether the actual use data were generalizable to the overall population of nonprescription users, chiefly because of inadequate sampling of younger age groups.

Following the advisory committee meeting, FDA requested additional information from the sponsor pertaining to adolescent use. The sponsor submitted this additional information to FDA in support of their pending application to change Plan B from a prescription to an over-the-counter product. This additional information was extensive enough to qualify as a major amendment to the NDA. Under the terms of the Prescription Drug User Fee Act (PDUFA) performance goals, major amendments such as this may trigger a 90-day extension of the original PDUFA deadline.

Now FDA has completed its review of the supplemental application and concluded that the application could not be approved at this time because 1) adequate data were not provided to support a conclusion that young adolescent women can safely use Plan B for emergency contraception without the professional supervision of a licensed practitioner and 2) a proposal from the sponsor to change the requested indication to allow for marketing of Plan B as a prescription-only product for women under 16 years of age and a nonprescription product for women 16 years and older was incomplete and inadequate for a full review. Therefore, FDA concluded that the application was not approvable.

5. Why didn't FDA follow the recommendation of the Advisory Committees?

The recommendations of FDA advisory committees are advisory in nature and the Agency is not bound to follow their recommendations. FDA makes a decision on whether a product should be approved after evaluating all data and considering the recommendations of the advisory committee.

6. Why did FDA issue a Not Approvable letter?

The agency issued a Not Approvable letter because the supplemental application did not meet the criteria for approval in that it did not demonstrate that Plan B could be used safely by young adolescent women for emergency contraception without the professional supervision of a licensed practitioner. The issuance of a Not Approvable letter does not mean that a supplemental application cannot be approved. The Not Approvable letter describes what the applicant would need to do to obtain approval for the supplemental application. In this case, the applicant would have to either provide additional data demonstrating that Plan B can be used safely by women under 16 years of age without the professional supervision of a practitioner licensed by law to administer the drug or provide additional support for the revised indication to allow for marketing Plan B as prescription-only for women under the age of 16 and as nonprescription for women 16 years of age and older.

> *7. Was there a difference of opinion within the Center for Drug Evaluation and Research (CDER) regarding the final decision?*

Yes, there was a difference of opinion within CDER. The scientific interchange of ideas is widely encouraged during the review process to ensure a thorough vetting of the issues. However, ultimately, a final decision must be made based on the evaluation of the data, taking into account all of the views expressed.

> *8. Is this FDA's final decision regarding the availability of Plan B for OTC use?*

No. The Not Approvable letter to the sponsor outlines what the sponsor must do to obtain approval of the supplemental application.

Wide availability of safe and effective contraceptives is important to public health. We look forward to working with the sponsor if they decide to pursue making this product available without a prescription.

> *9. Oral contraceptives have been used for four decades, and this product has been approved and used safely since 1999. How could FDA turn it down?*

Oral contraceptives as a class of drugs are only available by prescription. This product has been used safely by prescription only and for the reasons already stated, it is not being made available for OTC use at this time.

> *10. The sponsor has talked about making the product over-the-counter for young women over a certain age and behind-the-counter for younger girls. Is there evidence to support such a scheme? Does FDA have the authority to carry it out?*

The sponsor has submitted a plan and the FDA is examining its regulatory authority to approve a product marketed in this manner.

> *11. Did the FDA bow to political pressure in making this decision?*

No. This decision was made within the Center for Drug Evaluation and Research.

12. Dr. Steven Galson signed the letter FDA sent to the sponsor. Does Dr. Galson usually sign such letters? Why did Dr. Galson sign the letter?

No, Dr. Galson does not usually sign regulatory action letters. However, his opinion of the adequacy of the data in young adolescents differed from that of the review staff. He believes that additional data are needed and for that reason he made the decision to take final action within the Office of the Center Director.

POSTSCRIPT

Should Emergency Contraception Be Available over the Counter?

The *New England Journal of Medicine* immediately criticized the FDA's decision, saying, "The data overwhelmingly demonstrate that emergency contraception is safe and effective when available without a prescription." Forty-one members of Congress also asked the FDA to reconsider its decision. Two members, a Republican and a Democrat, Louise M. Slaughter (D-NY) and Christopher Shays (R-CT), called for an investigation of the FDA's decision-making process and for the resignation of FDA officials responsible for the decision.

In making its decision, the FDA underscored its concern that emergency contraception first be proven safe for adolescent women under age 16. This is not a typical standard for determining the over-the-counter status of other medications. Normally, when considering whether or not a drug is safe, the FDA examines its toxicity, side effects, how it makes its way through a person's system, and whether or not it is addictive. The FDA's response makes reference to Dr. Steven Galson, the acting director of the FDA's Center for Drug Evaluation and Research. At a teleconference, Dr. Galson added that he worried about young women having access to emergency contraception, saying it might make them more likely to have sex without a condom.

A 2004 study by the Alan Guttmacher Institute disproved this assertion, finding that teens who were provided with *advance* doses of emergency contraception did not have more unprotected intercourse. Moreover, these teens were significantly more likely to use emergency contraception sooner, when necessary, than those who had to rely on a provider to dispense it.

About 42 million American women, or seven in 10 women of reproductive age (15 to 45), are sexually active and do not want to become pregnant. Yet about half of America's annual 6.3 million pregnancies are accidental. Researchers believe that widespread use and availability of emergency contraception could prevent an estimated 1.7 million unintended pregnancies and 800,000 abortions every year.

The FDA's decision puts the ball back in the courts of individual states. To date, seven states have decided to make emergency contraception available via trained pharmacists; four other states are considering legislation to expand accessibility of emergency contraception. What is your opinion? What are the benefits (or barriers) to having a doctor examine a patient before dispensing emergency contraception? Do you think there should be age restrictions on access to emergency contraception? Would you recommend the hotline 1-888-NOT-2-LATE to a friend who had unprotected intercourse?

Suggested Readings

H. Boonstra, "FDA Rejects Expert Panel Recommendation, Blocks OTC Switch for Plan B Emergency Contraception," *The Guttmacher Report on Public Policy* (vol. 7, no. 2, June 2004).

H. Boonstra, "Emergency Contraception: Steps Being Taken to Improve Access," *The Guttmacher Report on Public Policy* (vol. 5, no. 5, December 2002).

H. Boonstra, "Emergency Contraception: The Need to Increase Public Awareness," *The Guttmacher Report on Public Policy* (vol. 5, no. 4, October 2002).

P. Brick and B. Taverner, "The Importance of Timing: Knowing the Difference Between Emergency Contraception and Mifepristone," *Educating about Abortion* (Planned Parenthood of Greater Northern New Jersey, 2001).

P. Brick and B. Taverner, "Emergency Contraception: For Emergency Use Only!" *Positive Images: Teaching Abstinence, Contraception, and Sexual Health* (Planned Parenthood of Greater Northern New Jersey, 2001).

J.M. Drazen, M.F. Greene, and A.J.J. Wood, "The FDA, Politics, and Plan B," *The New England Journal of Medicine* (April 8, 2004).

R. MacLean, "Teenagers Given Advance Emergency Contraception Still Use Pill and Condoms," *Perspectives on Sexual and Reproductive Health* (vol. 36, no. 3, May/June 2004).

R.G. Sawyer and E. Thompson, "Knowledge and Attitudes about Emergency Contraception in University Students," *College Student Journal* (vol. 37, no. 4, 2003).

ISSUE 6

Is the G-Spot a Myth?

YES: Terence M. Hines, from "The G-Spot: A Modern Gynecologic Myth," *American Journal of Obstetrics and Gynecology* (August
2001)

NO: Gary Schubach, from "The Human Female Prostate and Its
Relationship to the Popularized Term, G-Spot, *Tools and Education for a
Better Sex Life,* http://www.doctorg.com/gspot-truth.htm (2001)

ISSUE SUMMARY

YES: Psychologist Terence M. Hines says that the widespread
acceptance of the G-spot as being real conflicts with available
research evidence. Hines explains that the existence of the G-spot
has never been verified by empirical, objective means and that
women may have been misinformed about their bodies and their
sexuality.

NO: Sexologist Gary Schubach responds to Hines' critique of
research on the G-spot. He states that what is commonly referred
to as the G-spot is actually the female prostate gland. Renaming the
G-spot the "female prostate" may help clear up misconceptions
about the location and physiology of this controversial spot.

In late 2001, sexnet, an online discussion community of sexologists, was
stirred by the news that the G-spot may not be real. For twenty years, most
sex researchers, educators, counselors, and therapists had accepted the existence of the G-spot, even while they acknowledged there were many unanswered questions. Female ejaculation has also been accepted as factual,
widely documented by the work of Beverly Whipple and others. The article
by Terence M. Hines, from which one of the following selections has been
excerpted, led to much debate and discussion on sexnet about a tenet that
had been largely unchallenged.

The G-spot is named for Dr. Ernest Gräfenberg, who first described it in
a 1950 article in the *International Journal of Sexology*. The term *G-spot* was
coined in 1982 by Alice Kahn Ladas, Beverly Whipple, and John D. Perry in
The G Spot and Other Discoveries About Human Sexuality. The G-spot made its

way into most modern college sexuality textbooks, described as being located on the anterior wall of the vagina, with its stimulation leading to ejaculation in some women.

Before the work of Ladas, Whipple, and Perry (and the research that followed), the expulsion of fluid during orgasm was believed to be the result of urinary stress incontinence. Sex educators and therapists have been concerned that this dysfunctional label might lead women to feel shameful about an experience that is intended to be pleasurable—and unrelated to urination. Research in recent years has focused on the chemical consistency of female ejaculatory fluid to determine that the fluid is not urine. This is an important distinction for many women and their partners, who do not believe themselves to be urinating at the height of orgasm. Many conclude that the fluid comes from the Skene's glands, referred to by some as the female prostate.

In the following selections, Terence Hines critically examines research on the G-spot, highlighting the limitations, methodological flaws, and inability of the research to conclusively determine the existence of the G-spot. Gary Schubach responds to Hines' criticisms by proposing that much of the confusion comes from the misuse of the term "spot." Rather than focusing on a physical patch of tissue on the anterior vaginal wall, the term *female prostate* or *prostata feminina* may provide a more accurate description of both the anatomic source of female ejaculation and the source of pleasure more commonly known as the G-spot.

The G-Spot: A Modern Gynecologic Myth

The G-spot is an allegedly highly erogenous area on the anterior wall of the human vagina. Since the concept first appeared in a popular book on human sexuality in 1982, the existence of the spot has become widely accepted, especially by the general public. This article reviews the behavioral, biochemical, and anatomic evidence for the reality of the G-spot, which includes claims about the nature of female ejaculation. The evidence is far too weak to support the reality of the G-spot. Specifically, anecdotal observations and case studies made on the basis of a tiny number of subjects are not supported by subsequent anatomic and biochemical studies.

— (Am J Obstet Gynecol 2001; 185: 359–62.)

The term *G-spot* or *Grafenberg spot* refers to a small but allegedly highly sensitive area on the anterior wall of the human vagina, about a third of the way up from the vaginal opening. Stimulation of this spot is said to result in high levels of sexual arousal and powerful orgasms.[1] The term *G-spot* was coined by Addiego et al[2] in 1981 to recognize Dr Ernest Grafenberg who, they said, was the first to propose the existence of such an area in a 1950 paper.[3] The G-spot broke into public consciousness in 1982 with the publication of the popular book on human sexuality "The G Spot and Other Recent Discoveries About Human Sexuality."[1] One survey study[4,11] suggests that the reality of the G-spot is widely accepted at least by professional women. A 192-item questionnaire on sexuality was mailed to "a random sample of 2350 professional women in health-related fields in the United States and Canada."[11] The response rate was 55% with a total of 1289 questionnaires being returned. Of this sample, 84% responded that they "believed that a highly sensitive area exists in the vagina."[4] Most popular books on sexuality take it for granted that the G-spot is real. Even a leading college-level sexuality text[5] uncritically reports that the spot is "located within the anterior (or front) wall of the vagina, about one centimeter from the surface and one-third to one-half the way in from the vaginal opening."

Given the widespread acceptance of the reality of the G-spot, one would expect to find a considerable body of research confirming the existence of such a structure. In fact, such supporting evidence is minimal at best. Two types of evidence have been used to argue for the existence of the G-spot and will be reviewed in turn. The first is behavioral, the second is based on claims of female ejaculation. This issue of female ejaculation is relevant to the G-spot for 2 reasons. First, the two are often considered together in the popular literature with the strong implication that the reality of ejaculation supports the reality of the G-spot. Second, some authors[4] mistake the presence of glands that may produce a female ejaculate with the G-spot, a topic discussed in detail later.

Behavioral Evidence

Ladas, Whipple, and Perry[1] reported anecdotes about women who had powerful orgasms when their G-spot was stimulated. Anecdotes aside, there are only 2 published studies of the effects of specific stimulation of this area. The first study[2] reported a single case of a woman who experienced "deeper" orgasms when her G-spot was stimulated. During one session with the subject during which digital stimulation of the anterior vaginal wall was administered, it was reported that the area "grew approximately 50%."

Two years later, Goldberg et al[6] examined 11 women, both to determine whether they had a G-spot and to examine the nature of any fluid they ejaculated during orgasm. The latter aspect of this article will be discussed later. To determine whether the subjects possessed G-spots, 2 gynecologists examined each subject. Both had been given a 3-hour training session on how to examine for the presence of a G-spot. This training consisted of "a special type of bimanual exam as well as a sexological exam where they palpated the entire vagina in a clockwise fashion." Using this technique, they judged that 4 of the 11 women had G-spots.

Even if a G-spot had been found by using techniques such as those described in a much larger sample, this would still have provided little real evidence for the existence of the spot. Almost any gentle, manual stimulation of any part of the vagina can, under the right circumstances, be sexually arousing, even to the level of orgasm.[7,8] The fact that manual stimulation of the putative G-spot resulted in real sexual arousal in no way demonstrates that the stimulated area is anatomically different from other areas in the vagina. The subjects in these studies knew that researchers were searching for an allegedly sexually sensitive area, as did the individuals who performed the stimulation. Under these conditions, it is highly likely that the demand characteristics of the situation played a major role in the responsiveness of the female subjects.

One might think that Grafenberg's original 1950 paper,[3] which is credited with introducing the concept, would contain significant evidence for the spot. It does not. In that paper, Grafenberg discusses no evidence for a G-spot. Rather, he reports anecdotes about some of his female patients. Some he terms *frigid*. Others, he says, derived sexual pleasure from inserting objects, such as hat pins, into their urethras. Just how later writers (ie., 2) transformed these reports into evidence for a G-spot is unclear.

Grafenberg[3] does make some mention of the innervation of the vagina. He cites Hardenbergh[9] whom, he says, "mentions that nerves have been demonstrated only inside the vagina in the anterior wall, proximate to the head of the clitoris." Hardenbergh does indeed make this statement, but provides no citation. Hardenbergh then goes on to rather dismiss claims of vaginal sensitivity in the course of his discussion of his questionnaire study of female sexual experience, the actual topic of his paper.

Female Ejaculation

The second source of evidence for the existence of a G-spot is the claim that women sometimes ejaculate a non-urine fluid during orgasm. Initially, the relationship between female ejaculation and the G-spot was tenuous and nonanatomic. Grafenberg[3] noted the possible existence of such ejaculation. Ladas, Whipple, and Perry[1] devoted an entire chapter to the topic in their book. The chapter consists largely of anecdotes about ejaculation.

Belzer[10] concluded that "female ejaculation . . . is theoretically plausible" based on a brief literature review and interview-generated anecdotes. The interviews were conducted by students taking a graduate level course on sexuality. Six students interviewed "about 5" people each, male or female. Included in the interview was a question about female ejaculation. Of the 6 students, each "found at least 1 person who reported that she herself, or, in the case of a male informant, his female partner, had expelled fluid at orgasm." Three of these women were then interviewed at length about their ejaculation, and their comments are included in the paper in some detail. In the questionnaire study[4,11] discussed above, 40% of the respondents reported experiencing ejaculation.

Anecdotal and interview-generated reports such as those noted above are far from adequate to show that the ejaculated fluid is anything other than urine. Such evidence would be provided by chemical analysis of the ejaculated fluid. Addiego et al[2] were the first to perform such a chemical analysis. They obtained samples of urine and ejaculate from 1 female subject. They reported a higher level of prostatic acid phosphatase in the ejaculate than in the urine. Prostatic acid phosphatase is found in high levels in male ejaculate and originates in the prostate which, of course, produces components of the male ejaculate. This evidence could be taken, indirectly, as support for a "female prostate" and, more indirectly, for the G-spot. However, Belzer[12] later noted that the test used was "not entirely specific for acid phosphatase," citing a review to this effect by Stolorow, Hauncher, and Stuver.[13] In another study[6] of the chemical nature of female ejaculate, 11 subjects were studied. All produced preorgasmic urine samples. All then engaged in "some form of non-coital activity resulting in orgasm" and 6 collected some resulting ejaculate. The urine and ejaculate samples did not differ in levels.

Anatomic Considerations

Other researchers have taken a more anatomic approach to the issue of prostatelike components in female ejaculate. If women ejaculate a fluid that is not urine, or has non-urine constituents, it must be coming from someplace other than the bladder. Following Severly and Bennett,[15] Tepper et al[16] suggested that any non-urine female ejaculate would likely come from the female paraurethral glands, also known as Skene's glands or ducts. On anatomic grounds, these glands were considered analogous with the male prostate by Huffman[17] who also provided a detailed anatomic description and notes on the history of anatomic thought on the nature of these glands. If these glands are analogous to the male prostate, it might be expected that their secretions would be similar to those of the prostate. It was this hypothesis that Tepper et al[16] tested.

Eighteen autopsy specimens and 1 surgical specimen were obtained. These were sectioned and examined for immunologic reactions to prostate-specific acid phosphatase and prostate-specific antigen by using a peroxidase-antiperoxidase method. The results showed that "eighty-three percent (15/18) of the specimens had glands that stained with antibody to prostate-specific antigen and 67% (12/18) with PSAcPh (prostate-specific acid phosphatase)."[16] The authors concluded that "we have clearly demonstrated . . . that cells of the female paraurethral glands and adjacent urethral mucosa contain antigenic substances identical to those found in the prostate." Heath,[18] commenting separately on this finding, stated that the "homology between male and female prostate was shown."

More recent studies[14] have come to similar conclusions and have confirmed the presence of prostate-specific antigen reactivity in the paraurethral tissues. These studies, using immunohistochemical techniques to look for prostate-specific antigen expression, found the market in the "superficial layer of the female secretory (luminal) cells of the female prostatic glands and membranes of secretory and basal cells and membranes of cells of pseudostratified columnar epithelium of ducts."[14] On the basis of these findings, Zaviacic and Ablin[14] argued for dropping the term *Skene's glands* and replacing it with *female prostate*. Whatever term one favors, these results are in line with a view of female ejaculate in which "evacuation of the female prostate induced by orgasmic contractions of the muscles surrounding the female urethra may account for the increased PSA (prostate-specific antigen) values in urine after orgasm."[14]

It was the results of the study by Pepper et al[16] that led Crooks and Baur,[4] in their aforementioned college sexuality text, to confuse the concept of glands that release something with a sensitive area that would have to have a large number of nerve endings to support the reported heightened sensitivity. Specifically, Crooks and Baur stated that the G-spot consists of a "system of glands (Skene's glands) and ducts that surround the urethra."

If the G-spot does exit, it will certainly be more than a "system of glands and ducts." If an area of tissue is highly sensitive, that sensitivity must be mediated by nerve endings, not ducts. One can ask whether, on embryologic grounds, one would expect to find tissue with nerve endings inside the vagina. Heath[18] seems to have been the first to discuss this issue in light of the topics considered in this article. He criticized Kinsey, Pomeroy, and Martin[19] for stating that the entire vagina originates from the mesoderm, which is "poorly supplied with end organs of touch." Rather, Heath[18] cites

Koff's[20] work, which is said to show that the upper 80% of the vagina is of mesodermal origin, but the lower 20% is of ectodermal origin, the ectoderm also giving rise to the skin.

A more modern view of the embryology of the vagina is that the vestibulum, bladder, and urethra are of endodermal origin, whereas the rest of the vagina, and the vulva, are of ectodermal origin.[21] This view leaves open at least the possibility that tissue with nerve endings sufficient for the function of a G-spot could be present in the lower portion of the anterior vaginal wall, where the G-spot is said to be.

There have, of course, been histologic studies of the vagina and surrounding tissue. In 1958, Krantz[22] reviewed the early literature, starting with Tiedman's 1822[23] treatise, and then reported the results of his own microscopic analysis. The various studies Krantz reviewed are difficult to evaluate in terms of the issue at hand because they used various methods and many different species. Krantz himself examined only human tissue. In the vagina itself, what he termed "ganglion cells" were found "along the lateral walls of the vagina adjacent to the vascular supply" that were thought to be "parasympathetic terminal neurons." Regarding the types of nerve cell endings that mediate sensations of touch, pressure, and pain in cutaneous tissue, "no corpuscles were observed in the muscularis tunica propria and epithelial areas" although "a very small number/of fibers/were found to penetrate the tunica propria and occasionally terminate in the epithelium as free nerve endings." As would be expected from their well-known high levels of sensitivity, tissues of the external genitals were rich in the various disks, corpuscles, and nerve endings found in other highly sensitive cutaneous tissue.

No further work on the innervation of the vagina seems to have been done after Krantz[22] until 1995 when Hilliges et al[24] published their results. Anatomic techniques had obviously advanced between 1958 and 1995 and these latter authors used immunohistochemical techniques to search for nerve cells in the vagina. Twenty-four vaginal biopsy specimens, 4 from each of 6 women undergoing operation for "benign gynecological disorders not including the vagina," were obtained. The 4 locations from which biopsy specimens were obtained were the "anterior and posterior fornices, the anterior vaginal wall at the bladder neck level, and the introitus vagina region."

Results generally showed a greater degree of innervation than previously reported by Krantz.[22] There was innervation of the introitus vaginae, with this are showing free nerve endings and a few structures that resembled Merkel's disk. The anterior vaginal wall showed more innervation than the posterior wall, but this was subepithelial, and there was "no evidence for intra-epithelial innervation of this part of the vagina." Such innervation would be expected if a sensitive G-spot existed in the area.

The failure of Hilliges et al[24] to find a richly innervated area on the anterior vaginal wall does not prove that the G-spot does not exist there. The authors did not specifically set out to search for the G-spot and did not sample the entire anterior vaginal wall. Thus, they might have simply missed it. Nonetheless, the existence of such a spot would presume a plexus of nerve fibers, and no trace of such appeared in the results.

Finally, it should be pointed out that the issue of the existence of the G-spot is not just a point of minor anatomic interest. As noted, the G-spot seems to be widely accepted as being real, at least within a sample of American and Canadian women.[4,11] If the G-spot does not exist, then many women have been seriously misinformed about their bodies and their sexuality. Women who fail to "find" their G-spot, because they fail to respond to stimulation as the G-spot myth suggests that they should, may end up feeling inadequate or abnormal.

Two conclusions emerge from this review. First, the widespread acceptance of the reality of the G-spot goes well beyond the available evidence. It is astonishing that examinations of only 12 women, of whom only 5 "had" G-spots, form the basis for the claim that this anatomic structure exists. Second, on the basis of the existing anatomic studies reviewed above, it seems unlikely that a richly innervated patch of tissue would have gone unnoticed for all these years. Until a thorough and careful histologic investigation of the relevant tissue is undertaken, the G-spot will remain a sort of gynecologic UFO: much searched for, much discussed, but unverified by objective means.

References

1. Ladas A.K., Whipple B., Perry J.D. *The G spot and other discoveries about human sexuality.* New York: Holt, Rinehart, and Winston; 1982.

2. Addiego F., Belzer E.G., Comolli J., Moger W., Perry J.D., Whipple B. Female ejaculation: a case study. *J Sex Res 1981;* 17: 1–13.

3. Grafenberg E. The role of the urethra in female orgasm. *Int J Sexology* 1950; 3: 145–8.

4. Davidson J.K., Darling C.A., Conway-Welch C. The role of the Grafenberg spot and female ejaculation in the female orgasmic response: an empirical analysis. *J Sex Marital Ther 1989;* 15: 102–20.

5. Crooks R., Baur K. *Our sexuality.* 7th ed. Pacific Grove (Calif): Brooks/Cole; 1999.

6. Goldberg D.C., Whipple B., Fishkin R.E., Waxman H., Fink P.J., Weisberg M. The Grafenberg spot and female ejaculation: a review of initial hypotheses. *J Sex Marital Ther 1983;* 9: 27–37.

7. Alzate H., Londono M. Vaginal erotic sensitivity. *J Sex Marital Ther 1984;* 14: 529–37.

8. Hardenbergh E.W. Psychology of the feminine sex experience. *Int J Sexology 1949;* 2: 224–8.

9. Belzer E.G. Orgasmic expulsion of females: a review and heuristic inquiry. *J Sex Res 1981;* 17: 1–12.

10. Darling C.A., Davidson J.K., Conway-Welch G. Female ejaculation: perceived origins, the Grafenberg spot/area, and sexual responsiveness. *Arch Sex Behav 1990;* 19: 29–47.

11. Belzer E.G. A review of female ejaculation and the Grafenberg spot. *Women's Health 1984;* 9: 5–16.

12. Stolorow M.D., Hauncher J.D., Stuver W.C. Identification of human seminal acid phosphatase by electrophoresis. *J Assoc Off Anal Chem 1976;* 59: 1352–6.

13. Zaviacic M., Ablin R.J. The female prostate and prostate-specific antigen. Immunohistochemical localization, implications for this prostate marker in women, and reasons for using the term "prostate" in the human female. *Histol Histopathol 2000;* 15: 131–42.

14. Severly J.L., Bennett J.W. Concerning female ejaculation and the female prostate. *J Sex Res 1978;* 14: 1–20.

15. Tepper S.L., Jagirdar J., Heath D., Geller S.A. Homology between the female paraurethral (Skene's) glands and the prostate. *Arch Pathol Lab Med 1984;* 108: 423–5.

16. Huffman J.W. The detailed anatomy of the paraurethral ducts in the adult human female. *Am J Obstet Gynecol 1948;* 55: 86–101.

17. Heath D. An investigation into the origins of a copious vaginal discharge during intercourse: "enough to wet the bed"—that "is not urine." *J Sex Res 1984;* 108: 423–5.

18. Kinsey A.C., Pomeroy W.B., Martin C.E. *Sexual behavior in the human female.* Philadelphia: W.B. Saunders; 1948.

19. Koff A.K. Development of the vagina in the human fetus. *Contrib Embryol 1933;* 24: 59–90.

20. Westrom L.V., Willen R. Vestibular nerve fiber proliferation in vulvar vestibulitis syndrome. *Obstet Gynecol 1998;* 91: 572–6.

21. Krantz K. Innervation of the human vulva and vagina. *Obstet Gynecol 1959;* 12: 382–96. 2fs

22. Tiedman F. *Tabula nervorum utera.* Heidelberg; 1822.

23. Hilliges M., Falconer C., Ekman-Ordeberg G., Johansson O. Innervation of the human vaginal mucosa as revealed by PGP 9.5 immunohistochemistry. *Acta Anat 1995;* 153: 119–26.

Gary Schubach  **NO**

The Human Female Prostate and Its Relationship to the Popularized Term, G-Spot

An interesting controversy has arisen concerning an article by Dr. Terence Hines entitled, "The G-Spot: A Modern Gynecologic Myth." Hines concludes: "the evidence is far too weak to support the reality of the G-spot."[1] I couldn't disagree more.

Part of the trouble with the Hines article, as well as the entire discussion concerning the Gräfenberg Spot, popularly termed the "G-Spot," is the lack of agreement on its definition. In his article, Hines states that Gräfenberg did not provide significant evidence for the existence of the **spot**. Actually, in his writings Gräfenberg (1950) only uses the word **"spot"** twice, and then solely to make the **opposite** point that ". . . there is no **spot** (emphasis added) in the female body from which sexual desire could not be aroused."[2] He states, in fact, that "innumerable erotogenic **spots** (emphasis added) are distributed all over the body, from where sexual satisfaction can be elicited; these are so many that we can almost say that there is no part of the female body which does not give sexual response; the partner has only to find the erotogenic zones."[3]

Gräfenberg **does not** refer to the G-spot as "a small but allegedly highly sensitive area on the anterior wall of the human vagina about a third of the way up from the vaginal opening,"[4] but to the "area" or "zone" on the upper wall of the vagina *through* which the prostate (aka Skene's glands and ducts) can be accessed.[5] In women, the prostate gland, while generally smaller than the male prostate, also surrounds the urethra, close to the urethral opening. The great sensitivity comes not from what is **on** the upper wall of the vagina, but from glands and ducts **behind** the vaginal wall

It should be clear from an unbiased reading of Gräfenberg's paper that he is talking about the prostate (aka Skene's glands) when he writes, "Analogous to the male urethra, the female urethra also seems to be surrounded by erectile tissues like the corpora cavernosa. In the course of sexual stimulation, the female urethra begins to enlarge and can be felt easily. It swells out greatly at the end of orgasm. The most stimulating part is located at the posterior urethra, where it arises from the neck of the bladder."[6]

The biggest problem I have with the Hines article, however, is that he cites relevant articles that support the existence of a female prostate gland as the so-called G-Spot, but ends up concluding that it does not exist. Though he finds the G-spot so hard to locate himself, he promises to discuss Drs. Davidson, Darling and Conway-Welch's acknowledgement that the female prostate gland is indeed the G-Spot[7] and, then, never really does. Instead, he ends up making the statement, "If the G-Spot does exist, it will certainly be more than a system of glands and ducts. If an area of tissue is highly sensitive, that sensitivity must be mediated by nerve endings, not ducts."[8] Hines is correct but, as already noted, **the female prostate is not located on the wall of the vagina, and the nerves that give the prostate its sensation may be in the muscle coat around the glands rather than in the glands themselves.** Recent studies have also suggested that the anterior wall of the vagina could be more densely innervated than the posterior wall.[9,10]

Further, in his evidence against the so called G-Spot, Hines states that the "issue of female ejaculation is relevant to the G-spot for two reasons. First, the two are often considered together in the popular literature with the strong implication that the reality of ejaculation supports the reality of the G-spot. Second, some authors mistake the presence of glands that may produce a female ejaculate with the G-spot, (a topic discussed in detail later)."[11] However, he never discusses it in detail in his article. Contrary to Hines' assumptions, both my own and other studies have shown conclusively that a woman can reach orgasm by stimulation of the prostate though the upper wall of the vagina which may or may not include ejaculation. Similar to men, it is also possible for women to have an ejaculation without prostate (G-Spot) stimulation.[12]

I have no argument with Hines' point, "that manual stimulation of the putative G-spot, resulted in real sexual arousal, in no way demonstrates that the stimulated area is anatomically different from other areas in the vagina."[13] However, while citing various pathological studies, including a 1948 study in the *American Journal of Obstetrics and Gynecology,*[14] Hines omits at least seven authoritative pathological studies[15–21] that support the existence of a female prostate gland. From the research of deGraff in 1672[22] to the recent work of Zaviacic,[23,24] there have been numerous studies that in some way support the conclusion that, what has been called Skene's and/or paraurethral ducts and glands, are a homologue of the male prostate.

Hines opined that there is lack of evidence in support of female ejaculation. Yet, he overlooked Santamaría[25] who showed the presence of PSA in female urethral expulsions, as well as my own doctoral research[26] that showed differences in the chemical composition of fluid obtained by catheterization from the same woman's baseline urine specimen and a specimen that was drained from her bladder prior to ejaculation. His complaint about the insufficiencies of pre-1985 research concerning the presence of acid phosphatase (PAP) also shows a lack of awareness that forensic pathologists, due to PAP occurring naturally in the vagina, long ago discredited PAP detection as a certain prostatic marker.[27,28]

Hines proposes that if women ejaculate a fluid that is not urine or has non-urine constituents, it must be coming from someplace other than the bladder. However, my study showed, for the first time, what had been suggested by Goldberg[29] thirteen years earlier; namely, that ejaculatory fluid possibly originates not from **either** the bladder or the urethral glands, but from **both**.[30]

I'm afraid that I also cannot agree with Dr. Hines' observation that most popular books, and even textbooks, recognize the existence of the G-Spot as the prevailing medical or social paradigm. Such noted experts in the field of human sexuality as Alfred Kinsey and Masters and Johnson, dismissed female ejaculation as being an "erroneous but widespread concept."[31] Masters and Johnson also argued against the existence of the erogenous zone known as the "G-spot" and steadfastly stood for the premise that the clitoris alone was responsible for triggering female orgasm.

Dr. Hines and I, however, **completely** agree that the existence of the G-Spot is not just an issue of minor anatomical interest. It is an area of enormous importance in terms of how millions of women view their sexuality, and the amount of pleasure and intimacy they can experience with their sexual partners. If the evidence demonstrates the G-spot and female ejaculation, as components of natural sexual functioning, women can be freed from guilt and shame about prostate (G-Spot) stimulation and the expulsion of fluid during sex. In addition, Hines' article exposes the need for health professionals to have more education and training in Human Sexuality. Such knowledge will help them better serve their patients. The current debate demonstrates why Dr. Milan Zaviacic's medical school textbook, *The Human Female Prostate: From Vestigial Skene's Glands and Ducts to Woman's Functional Prostate*,[32] should be **required** medical school reading.

In conclusion, this article has demonstrated that the term "spot" is not a useful metaphor to describe the anatomical basis of the female erogenous experience of stimulation of the upper vaginal wall. The term only contributes to the confusion. A more accurate and descriptive term, such as the female prostate or *prostata feminina*, should make it easier for everyone to understand the issues involved and to better serve women's health needs. In fact, the Federative International Committee on Anatomical Terminology has recently agreed to adopt the term female prostate (or prostata feminina), implying function as well as form in its definitive *Histology Terminology*.

It is clear that more research is needed to answer the questions past studies have raised, but it is my hope that the foregoing discussion has illuminated some important issues for further exploration. For example, a noteworthy outcome to this discussion might be the search for scientific consensus concerning whether the female prostate is indeed the illusive G-Spot. Specifically, it would be valuable to analyze urethral expulsions during sexual arousal for the presence of PSA in comparison with baseline and other urine specimens from the same female subject. Additionally, all urethral expulsions could be examined for possible evidence of hormonal alterations as a result of sexual arousal. The physiological process by which the bladder sphincter may involuntarily open as a result of stimulation of the female prostate (G-Spot) also warrants further study.

References

1. Hines, T.M. "The G-spot: A Modern Gynecologic Myth." *American Journal of Obstetrics and Gynecology,* 359, (August, 2001), 185.

2. Gräfenberg, E. "The Role of the Urethra in Female Orgasm." *International Journal of Sexology,* 3, (1950), 145. May be viewed at http:www.DoctorG.com/Grafenberg.htm.

3. Gräfenberg, p. 147.

4. Ibid.

5. Gräfenberg, p. 145–8.

6. Gräfenberg, p. 146.

7. Davidson, J.K., Darling, C.A., and Conway-Welch, C. "The Role of the Grafenberg Spot and Female Ejaculation in the Female Orgasmic Response: An Empirical Analysis." *Journal of Sex and Marital Therapy,* 15, (1989), 102–20.

8. Hines, p. 361.

9. Hilliges, M., Falconer, C., Ekman-Ordeberg, G., and Johansson, O. Innervation of the Human Vaginal Mucosa as revealed by PGP 9.5 Immunohistochemistry." *Acta Anat (Basel),* 153(2), (1995), 119–26.

10. Zaviacic, Milan. *The Human Female Prostate: From Vestigal Skene's Glands and Ducts to Woman's Functional Prostate.* Slovak Academic Press, 1999, p. 83.

11. Hines, p. 359.

12. Schubach, G. "Urethral Expulsions During Sensual Arousal and Bladder Catheterization in Seven Human Females." *Electronic Journal of Human Sexuality,* 4, (August 25, 2001), may be viewed at http://www.ejhs.org/volume4/Schubach/abstract.html

13. Hines, pp. 359–360.

14. Huffman, J.W. "The detailed anatomy of the paraurethral ducts in the adult human female." *American Journal of Obstetrics and Gynecology,* 55, (1948) 86–101.

15. Skene, A.J.C. "The Anatomy and Pathology of Two Important Glands of the Female Urethra." *American Journal of Obstetrics and Diseases of Women and Children,* 13, (1880), 265–270.

16. Caldwell, G.T. "The Glands of the Posterior Female Urethra." *Texas State Journal of Medicine,* 36, (1941), 627–632.

17. Folsom, A.I., and O'Brien, H.A. "The Female Obstructing Prostate." *Journal of the American Medical Association,* 121, (1943), 573–580.

18. Deter, R., Caldwell, C., and Folsom, A. A Clinical and Pathological Study of the Posterior Female Urethra. *Journal of Urology,* 55, (1946), 651–662.

19. Huffman J.W. "Clinical Significance of the Paraurethral Ducts and Glands." *Archives of Surgery,* 62, (1951), 615–626.

20. Johnson, F.P. "The Homologue of the Prostate in the Female." *Journal of Urology,* 8, (1922), 13–33.

21. Ricci, J.V., Lisa, J.R., and Thom, C. H. "The Female Urethra." *American Journal of Surgery,* 79, (1950), 449–506.

22. De Graaf, R. (1672) "New Treatise Concerning the Generative Organs of Women." In *Journal of Reproduction and Fertility,* Supplement No. 17, 77–222. H.B. Jocelyn and B.P. Setchell, Eds. Oxford, England: Blackwell Scientific Publications, 1972.

23. Zaviacic, M., and Whipple, B. "Update on the Female Prostate and the Phenomenon of Female Ejaculation." *The Journal of Sex Research,* (1993), 149.

24. Zaviacic, M., and Ablin, R.J. "The Female Prostate." *Journal of the National Cancer Institute,* 90, No.9 (May 6, 1998), 713–714.

25. Santamaria, F.C. "Female Ejaculation, Myth and Reality." (Proceedings of the 13th World Congress of Sexology, Valencia, Spain, June 1997), 325–332. May be viewed at http://www.DoctorG.com/myth_reality1.htm.

26. Schubach

27. Graves, H.C., Sensabaugh, G.F., and Blake, E.T. "Postcoital Detection of a Male-Specific Semen Protein: Application to the Investigation of Rape." *New England Journal of Medicine,* 312 (6), (Feb 7, 1985), 338–43.

28. Gomez, R.R., Wunsch, C.D., Davis, J.H., and Hicks, D.J. "Qualitative and Quantitative Determinations of Acid Phosphatase Activity in Vaginal Washings." *American Journal of Clinical Pathology,* 64, (1975), 423–432.

29. Goldberg, D.C., Whipple, B., Fishkin, R.E., Waxman, H., Fink, P.J., and Weisberg, M. "The Gräfenberg Spot and Female Ejaculation: A Review of Initial Hypotheses." *The Journal of Sex and Marital Therapy,* 9 (1), (Spring 1983), 31.

30. Schubach, pp. 39–40.

31. Masters, W., and Johnson, V. *Human Sexual Response.* Boston: Little, Brown, 1966. p. 135.

32. Zaviacic, Milan. *The Human Female Prostate: From Vestigal Skene's Glands and Ducts to Woman's Functional Prostate.* Slovak Academic Press, 1999.

POSTSCRIPT

Is the G-Spot a Myth?

Hines concludes his selection by calling the G-spot a "gynecologic UFO"—something that is much searched for and much discussed but unverified by objective means. What do you think about his assessment? Were you impressed by the apparent lack of empirical evidence? What do you make of two decades worth of sexologists acknowledging the existence of the G-spot, as identified anecdotally in their patients and research subjects and as identified in their practice? Schubach suggests that while the G-spot does, in fact, exist, the anatomical and physiological descriptions of it have been misconstrued. Noting that the sensations (and ejaculation) related to the region described may actually involve the Skene's glands, Schubach suggests renaming the area the "female prostate" or "prostate feminine." What do you think of this proposal? Do you think a change in terminology will help women and their partners who may be searching for a single "spot"?

Both authors comment on the importance of women being informed about their bodies and express concern about the inadequacy some women may feel with respect to the G-spot. Schubach is concerned about guilt and shame women may feel when G-spot responses are not acknowledged or understood. Hines is concerned about women who are unable to find their G-spots, when their textbooks are so definitive about saying they have one. What does your textbook say about the G-spot? Do you think information about the G-spot could help alleviate negative feelings? Or does it present sexual performance pressures for women and their partners?

Finally, you may have taken note that the issue of whether or not the G-spot is a myth was debated by two men, Terence Hines and Gary Schubach. As the Introduction notes, the G-spot was named after Ernest Gräfenberg. Further, the Skene's gland was named after a nineteenth-century gynecologist, Alexander Skene. Yet another man, William Taverner, is writing this passage. What thoughts do you have about so many men examining a question of female sexuality and sexual response?

Suggested Readings

E. Grafenberg, "The Role of the Urethra in Female Orgasm," *International Journal of Sexology* (vol. 3, 1950).

D. Heath, "An Investigation into the Origins of a Copious Vaginal Discharge During Intercourse: 'Enough to Wet the Bed,'—That Is 'Not Urine,'" *Journal of Sex Research* (vol. 20, 1984).

S. Reinberg, "The G-Spot: A Gynecological UFO?" *Reuters Health* (August 29, 2001).

D. Sundahl, *Female Ejaculation and the G-Spot* (Hunter House, 2003).

B. Whipple et al, *The G-Spot: And Other Discoveries about Sexuality* (Owl Books, 2005).

C. Winks, *The Good Vibrations Guide: The G-Spot* (Down There Press, 1998).

M. Zaviacic, *The Human Female Prostate: From Vestigal Skene's Glands and Ducts to Woman's Functional Prostate* (Slovak Academic Press, 1999).

ISSUE 7

Is the Testosterone Patch the Right Cure for Low Libido?

YES: Carolyn Susman, from "Look Who's Smiling Now: A New Patch Delivers to Menopausal Women a Dose of What the Guys Have: Sex-Drive-Revving Testosterone," *Palm Beach Post* (October 30, 2004)

NO: Iver Juster, Gary Schubach, and Patricia Taylor, from "Testosterone Patches—The Cure for Low Female Sexual Desire?" http://www.DoctorG.com/intrinsa.htm (2002)

ISSUE SUMMARY

YES: Columnist Carolyn Susman comments favorably on Intrinsa, a testosterone patch intended to treat low female desire in women. Susman outlines research findings that say the patch could improve sexual desire in women.

NO: Iver Juster, a family practitioner, Gary Schubach, a sex researcher and educator, and Patricia Taylor, a sex researcher and sexual enhancement coach, reject the idea that female sexual desire is hormonally driven, and say that the testosterone patch should not be regarded as a cure-all.

Most people have heard of Viagra, the little blue pill designed to treat erectile dysfunction in men. Prescribed to about 16 million men worldwide, Viagra has catapulted pharmaceutical manufacturer Pfizer into a giant in the business. The popularity of the little blue pill continues to soar. Its logo is emblazoned on a NASCAR race car, and it has even received endorsements from former presidential candidate Bob Dole, who has spoken candidly about his erectile dysfunction in Viagra commercials.

Some have hailed Viagra as a miracle pill that has revolutionized the treatment of sexual dysfunction and has improved the sex lives of millions of men. But many health professionals point to the far more common psychogenic causes of sexual dysfunction that cannot be treated by medication. They contend that non-medical treatments (improving partner communication, for example) would be far more effective.

In 2004, Proctor and Gamble announced their application to the U.S. Food and Drug Administration (FDA) seeking approval for Intrinsa, a drug to treat hypoactive sexual desire disorder, or low libido, in women. If approved, Intrinsa would be the first such treatment for women to have FDA approval.

The active ingredient in Intrinsa is testosterone, a hormone that contributes to sex drive in both men and women. After menopause, testosterone production levels drop in women. Supporters of the testosterone patch say that it will improve sexual libido by increasing testosterone levels in the bodies of menopausal and postmenopausal women.

Whereas the Viagra pill increases blood flow to the penis to enhance erection, Intrinsa dispenses a hormone—testosterone—continuously into a woman's body by means of a transdermal patch. This means that while Viagra can be stored in the medicine cabinet and used when the mood strikes, Intrinsa would need to be worn continuously, and could take weeks or even months before any effect is noticed. When sexual libido is enhanced, it could be at times when a woman is not interested in sexual activity.

Some sexologists wondered what took so long for this type of treatment to arrive. Viagra has been FDA approved for treating male erectile dysfunction since 1997, and other testosterone treatments have been available for men since 1953. Critics wonder if sexism might explain why these treatments for men have been available for so long while an estimated 15 million women who struggle with low libido have remained overlooked until now.

Other sexologists respond that this estimated number of cases is inflated, and that the vast majority of real cases of both female and male sexual dysfunction are caused by psychological or interpersonal factors that are better treated with non-medical intervention. They charge that pharmaceutical companies are making their billions through the "medicalization" of sexuality.

In the following essays, columnist Carolyn Susman describes the research findings that led to the FDA's approval of Intrinsa, while also outlining the possible risks and side effects. The team of Iver Juster, Gary Schubach, and Patricia Taylor express their concerns that Intrinsa will follow in Viagra's footsteps, and come to be regarded as a "magic pill" that will not solve underlying, non-hormonal factors related to sexual arousal and dysfunction.

YES

Carolyn Susman

Look Who's Smiling Now: A New Patch Delivers to Menopausal Women a Dose of What the Guys Have: Sex-Drive-Revving Testosterone

Let's be upfront: Sex, for women, takes work.

We have to relax, get in the mood and concentrate on something other than a grocery list or a crazed kid before we can come close to having an orgasm.

When Lynette on the ABC-TV show *Desperate Housewives* rolls her eyes and asks her husband, "Do you mind if I just lay here?," lots of us can relate. The woman has four children under 6 and hardly has time to brush her teeth. Wanting to have sex is a big part of enjoying the experience. But there are many women who can't even get that far. So drug companies have been researching like mad, trying to come up with a product that will put the oomph back.

For some women, the wait may be over.

While only time will heal the libido-deadening effect of a houseful of screaming youngsters, a new testosterone patch is just months from becoming the first federally approved product to treat low desire in menopausal women.

Procter & Gamble's patch, to be called Intrinsa, is expected to be the first product approved by the U.S. Food and Drug Administration to deal with what doctors call hypoactive sexual desire disorder (HSDD.)

Naturally and surgically menopausal women may suffer from low sex drives because their hormone balances have changed. Menopause produces a decline in estrogen and testosterone (women produce small amounts of this "male" hormone nicknamed the "hormone of desire") and that can affect sex drive.

The good news is that studies showed women reported increases in desire, satisfaction with sex, orgasm, responsiveness and self-image while receiving a low, controlled dose of natural testosterone. The hormone is delivered via a thin, transparent patch on either the lower back, abdomen or arm.

Side effects didn't seem to curb their enthusiasm, either. Irritation at the patch site, and even excess facial hair, were reported. But researchers said the women kept using the patch anyway.

The catch is that the patch has been tested in, and will be prescribed for, women who have undergone surgical menopause. But it is expected that doctors will prescribe it also for women who complain of low sex drive and are going through natural menopause. The patch is now being studied on those women.

Younger women—like the exhausted Lynette—might also want it, but there is no data to support its use for them, and the package insert warns the patch shouldn't be used by women who might become pregnant.

The other catch is that the patch was tested while women were taking oral or transdermal estrogen—trials started in 2002—so women may be advised to take this hormone while on the patch.

The Women's Health Initiative concluded last year that estrogen increases the risk for blood clots and strokes, so women advised to use estrogen with the libido patch will have to discuss risk factors with their doctors.

But with no other approved products on the market right now for low libido in women, millions are anxious to give it a go. (There are over-the-counter products available, such as the herbal tablet, Avlimil, but none have undergone the clinical trials required to get FDA approval.)

"This can't be approved soon enough," says Dr. Maureen Whelihan, an obstetrician/gynecologist in West Palm Beach who is a member of Procter & Gamble's Florida Female Sexual Function Advisory Board. "It's extremely safe." And if one approved treatment is good, two must be even better.

Close on the heels of Intrinsa is LibiGel, a testosterone gel for treatment of female sexual dysfunction, being developed by BioSante Pharmaceuticals, also for surgically menopausal women.

How do they feel about the competition?

Stephen Simes, president and chief executive officer of BioSante, says his company is glad that the FDA seems to be taking testosterone seriously as a libido treatment for women and expects his product to apply for approval by the end of 2006.

"By that time we expect the market (demand) to be multibillion dollars."

LibiGel is applied to the upper arm from a metered-dose bottle and rubbed in. It takes about 30–60 seconds to dry with no residue. The dosing is once-per-day, while the Intrinsa patch is changed twice weekly.

Not all doctors are certain these products will break the low-sexual-desire cycle. "It's still premature to say what does or doesn't work in improving women's sexual libido, but researchers are learning more all the time," said Dr. Vivian M. Dickerson, president of the American College of Obstetricians and Gynecologists, in a statement released a month ago.

It's also true that some women may not care a hoot about either product.

After all, not all women consider low sexual desire a problem. And a study sponsored by Procter & Gamble proves the point.

Of 2,000 American women surveyed, one in three naturally menopausal women reported problems with sexual desire. But only one in 10 said it upset them.

NO ⬅

Iver Juster, Gary Schubach,
and Patricia Taylor

Testosterone Patches—The Cure for Low Female Sexual Desire?

Proctor & Gamble is about to release a new drug, Intrinsa™, which is intended for women suffering from a loss of sexual desire as a result of medical or surgical menopause. The drug is being developed as a skin patch containing testosterone, a hormone that affects sexual desire in women. While there is considerable evidence that testosterone can impact sexual desire after menopause[1-3], we don't accept the idea that female sexual desire is totally or—even mostly—about hormones. A growing body of evidence—as well as most people's personal experience—tells us that emotional connection and good communication play key roles. Our fear is that Proctor & Gamble is about to spend $100,000,000 to convince all women that the cure for low sexual desire is Intrinsa™.

We fear that, since most people hope this is true, Intrinsa™ use will lead to preventable disappointments.

Let's start with some hormone science. Studies do show that testosterone can make a big difference for women who have had their ovaries removed. However, it won't do much good for post-menopausal women who don't have low free testosterone levels. While we're sure Procter and Gamble is not deliberately promoting the idea that sexual desire is about hormones and needs drugs to fix it, they are certainly capitalizing on the increasing public hope that sexual desire is basically a medical issue and can be fixed with drugs or surgery, and if not that, then a new partner. Because of this, people will take drugs or get surgery and not deal with issues of turn on, communication, and personal transformation. The most one could hope for is a return to the previous state of affairs, definitely an improvement, but, for most people in long term relationships, the previous state of affairs wasn't all that great.

In terms of using testosterone to stimulate sexual desire in women, the long-term effects are unknown and might prove to be dangerous. After years of promoting HRT (hormone replacement therapy—estrogen or estrogen/progesterone) to millions of women, United States health authorities have stopped

---

Intrinsa™ is a registered trademark of Proctor and Gamble.

From *Testosterone Patches—The Cure for Low Female Sexual Desire?*, 2002. Copyright © 2002 by Dr. Gary Schubach. http://www.doctororg.com/gspottruth.htm, 2002. Reprinted by permission.

clinical trials of various forms of HRT because of the dangerous nature of their findings[4,5] and the North American Menopause Society has recommended that these hormones not be prescribed except for short-term relief of severe symptoms of menopause[6]. In the case of declining levels of testosterone, just because a hormone is declining from levels achieved at age 25 doesn't imply that it should (in terms of healthy outcomes) be replaced back to those levels (or even higher).

The lessons from estrogen and estrogen/progesterone are quite relevant in this regard. It may be years before we know about the safety of testosterone replacement, especially after natural menopause. The first good studies will likely be completed after at least five years of use of the drug. These initial studies will likely be simple case-control studies (find two groups of people; one group of 'cases' has some disease you want to study like heart disease or some kind of cancer; the other group is a 'control' with those who don't have the disease; then you look back to get the odds of 'exposure,' to testosterone.). Early case-control studies of estrogen and estrogen/progesterone suggested that these medications were beneficial or at least not harmful for preventing heart disease[7] and in combination even prevented uterine cancer[8]. Later more rigorous studies called 'retrospective cohort studies' often agreed with the case-control studies[9]. It was only when we had 'randomized prospective trials' that the truth (even though suggested by a few of the earlier studies) emerged[10,11]. It could be at least ten years until we get to that point with testosterone, if indeed anyone even decides to study it.

When Intrinsa™ is released, with its $100 million ad campaign, we strongly suspect that there will be enormous patient pressure on doctors to prescribe Intrinsa™ for all women who perceive themselves to have low sexual desire, regardless of their age or reproductive status. In order to be medically responsible, Intrinsa™ should not be prescribed for any woman until tests have been performed to determine whether she really has low testosterone levels. If the testosterone levels are low, our recommendation would be to replace testosterone at the lowest level of *free* testosterone in range for women in their late 30s; get tested for cancer and liver function as well as blood counts a couple of times a year; get screened for cancer as recommended; and live an extremely healthy lifestyle. And be aware that women using this patch are part of an uncontrolled experiment.

Even for women whose biochemical profile and history make a strong case for the patch, it's only a part of improving her sex life. We believe that the emotional and psychological components are still the most important aspects of female sexual desire. And let's distinguish between *sexual drive* and *sexual desire*. One can have profound levels of desire—for emotional connection, physical contact, and erotic arousal and adventure—with minimal levels of drive. We are not born knowing how to be sublime lovers, but the good news is that that can be learned, as a reflection of love and caring for another human being.

Sadly, in our culture, boys and girls are not given good information about human sexuality so as to be able to craft a rewarding sex life. We are a society full of contradictions about sex and young people are coming to sexual maturity full of fears and confusion and misunderstandings. Men are not taught how to pleasurably stimulate a woman sexually and function with beliefs that intercourse is the ultimate sexual goal and is the way to sexual satisfaction for both partners. Yet study after study shows how dissatisfied women are with intercourse alone as a path to sexual gratification, and how women's sexual response cycles are usually much longer than men's. It would make sense to be teaching men and women lovemaking techniques that will allow for—even celebrate—the differences in male and female physiology.

Just as Viagra has turned out not to be the universal panacea for male sexual issues, Intrinsa™ will not be the "magic pill" that resolves the problem of female low sexual desire, either pre- or post-menopause. The human issues, how to love and care for another human being and be aware of and satisfy their emotional as well as physical needs, are still the most important factors.

Notes

1. Davis SR. The use of testosterone after menopause. *Journal of the British Menopause Society*. 2004;10(2):65–69.

2. Goldstat R, Briganti E, Tran J, Wolfe R, Davis SR. Transdermal testosterone therapy improves well-being, mood, and sexual function in premenopausal women. *Menopause*. 2003;10(5):390–398.

3. Mazer NA, Shifren JL. Transdermal testosterone for women: a new physiological approach for androgen therapy. *Obstetrics and Gynecology Surveys*. 2003; 58(7):489–500.

4. Manson JE, Hsia j, Johnson KC, Women's Health Initiative. Estrogen plus progestin and the risk of coronary heart disease. *New England Journal of Medicine*. 2003;349:523–534.

5. Writing Group for the Women's Health Initiative Investigators. Risks and benefits of estrogen plus progestin in healthy menopausal women: A randomized, controlled trial. *JAMA*. 2002;288:321–333.

6. North American Menopause Society. Amended report from the NAMS Advisory Panel on Postmenopausal Hormone Therapy. *Menopause*. 2003;10:6–12.

7. Grodstein F, Stampfer MJ. The epidemiology of coronary heart disease and estrogen replacement in postmenopausal women. *Progress in Cardiovascular Disease*. 1995;38:199–210.

8. Grady D, Rubin SM, Penn DB. Hormone therapy to prevent disease and prolong life in postmenopausal women. *Archives of Internal Medicine*. 1992;116: 1016–1037.

9. Grodstein F, Stampfer MJ, Manson JE, et al. Postmenopausal Estrogen and Progestin Use and the Risk of Cardiovascular Disease. *N Engl J Med*. August 15, 1996 1996;335(7):453–461.

10. Grady D, Herrington D, Bittner B, The HERS Research Group. Cardiovascular disease outcomes during 6.8 years of hormone therapy. *JAMA*. 2002;288: 49057.

11. Hulley S, Furberg C, Barrett-Conner E, Group THR. Risk factors and secondary prevention in women with heart disease: The Heart and Estrogen/Progestin Replacement Study. *Annals of Internal Medicine*. 2003;138:81–89.

POSTSCRIPT

Is the Testosterone Patch the Right Cure for Low Libido?

The Food and Drug Administration (FDA) convened an advisory committee of independent scientists to give expert advice on whether or not the FDA should approve Intrinsa to treat low libido in women. The 14-member committee voted unanimously against recommending approval, and urged additional research to ensure the safety of the patch. The FDA usually, but not always, follows the expert advice of its panel. (See Issue 5 on the FDA's decision on emergency contraception for a notable exception.) In this case, manufacturer Proctor and Gamble decided to withdraw their application and resubmit a new application to address the concerns the panel raised.

One wonders how the product will be marketed if and when it becomes available. The marketing strategy may reveal a great deal about the traditional views Americans hold regarding male and female sexuality. For example, a prominent marketing campaign for Viagra featured a man standing in front of the word "Viagra," blocking most of the V so that it appears that two horns are protruding from his head. The unmistakable reference to Viagra making a man "horny" is further confirmed by the logo that urges men to "get back to mischief." Might Intrinsa be marketed in the same way? Do you believe society would look favorably upon women as "horny little devils" in the same way male sexual urges are accepted and encouraged? Bob Dole's celebrity rose when he became a spokesman for Viagra. Will the public regard an older woman in the same way when she speaks openly about overcoming her low sex drive? What does this say about our collective social attitudes toward female and male sexuality?

Beyond the marketing of the product, what do you make of the availability of medical treatments for sexual dysfunction? Are they to be championed for expanding choices that individuals are free to accept or reject? Are they to be regarded with skepticism for contributing to the medicalization of sexuality, or for the financial gains of pharmaceutical companies?

Susman refers to potential interest in Intrinsa among younger women who experience low sex drive, although there is no data to support its effectiveness in younger women. What other suggestions would you make to a friend who has a low sex drive? Why might women be unconcerned about low sexual desire, as Susman suggests?

Juster, Schubach, and Taylor state that young people are "coming to sexual maturity full of fears and confusion and misunderstandings," receiving misinformation—or no information—about sexual pleasure and satisfaction for both partners. Do you agree or disagree? How would you recommend that young people learn about sexual pleasure? Juster et al also contend that too much emphasis is placed on vaginal intercourse as the "ultimate sexual goal," and that this may also contribute to lower levels of sexual satisfaction in women. Some sex educators teach about "outercourse" (non-penetrative sexual behaviors) as a way for couples to enjoy pleasurable—and safer—sexual activities that are more mutually satisfying without the performance pressures that are sometimes associated with vaginal intercourse. What do you think of outercourse as a sexual expression for adults? For young people?

The Sexuality Information and Education Council of the United States (SIECUS) published *New Expectations: Sexuality Education for Mid and Later Life,* a sexuality education resource designed to address the changing sexual experiences and needs of adults. Learning about sexuality and developing positive feelings about sexuality may go a long way toward helping adults avoid or overcome sexual difficulties without medication. How would you feel about a loved one participating in a sex ed class for older adults? Would you consider participating in such a class as an older adult?

Suggested Readings

Associated Press, "F.D.A. Panel Says Sex Patch Needs More Testing," *New York Times* (December 2, 2004).

J.R. Berman and J. Bassuk, "Physiology and Pathophysiology of Female Sexual Function and Dysfunction," *World Journal of Urology* (vol. 20, no. 2, 2002).

L. Berman, "Not In the Mood? Now There's a Patch," accessed at www.bermancenter.com (October 29, 2004).

L. Berman, "Women's Sexual Health Deserves Equal Attention," *USA Today* (November 22, 2004).

P. Brick, "Outercourse Is In" *Teaching Safer Sex* (Planned Parenthood of Greater Northern New Jersey, 1998).

P. Brick and J. Lunquist, *New Expectations: Sexuality Education in Mid and Later Life* (SIECUS, 2003).

E. Kaschak and L. Tiefer, *A New View of Women's Sexual Problems* (Haworth Press, 2002).

M. Kaufman, "Safety Tests Urged for Libido Patch," *Washington Post* (December 3, 2004).

J. Lite, "Stuck on the Love Patch," *New York Daily News* (October 2, 2004).

C. Peale, "P&G Poised to Move on Intrinsa," *The Cincinnati Enquirer* (November 28, 2004).

C. Shultz, "Let Us Women Patch It Together," *Cleveland Plain Dealer* (November 8, 2004).

K.E. Walsh and J.R. Berman, "Sexual Dysfunction in the Older Woman: An Overview of the Current Understanding and Management," *Drugs & Aging* (vol. 21, no. 10, 2004, pp. 655–675).

ISSUE 8

Should Health Insurers Be Required to Pay for Infertility Treatments?

YES: Diane D. Aronson, from "Should Health Insurers Be Forced to Pay for Infertility Treatments? Yes," *Insight on the News* (February 8, 1999)

NO: Merrill Matthews, Jr., from "Should Health Insurers Be Forced to Pay for Infertility Treatments? No," *Insight on the News* (February 8, 1999)

ISSUE SUMMARY

YES: Diane D. Aronson, executive director of RESOLVE, the National Infertility Association's consumer-advocacy and patient-support organization, argues that infertility is a disease of the reproductive system that strikes people in all walks of life. She concludes that requiring insurance companies to pay for proven medical treatments for infertility is the right thing to do in a country that places great value on healthy families.

NO: Merrill Matthews, Jr., a medical ethicist and vice president of domestic policy at the National Center for Policy Analysis, maintains that requiring all health insurance plans to pay for infertility treatments could significantly increase insurance costs for everyone.

In 1978, the birth of Louise Joy Brown, the world's first test-tube baby, marked the dawn of high-tech infertility treatments. Only a decade or two ago, reproductive "miracles" made front-page headlines. As we enter the twenty-first century, women are having seven, even eight, babies in one delivery. Infertile couples are paying several thousand dollars for egg donors. A single sperm is microinjected into an egg, which is then implanted in a surrogate mother's uterus. Sisters, mothers, and mothers-in-law serve as surrogates for women who cannot carry a full-term pregnancy. Eggs and sperm, or fertilized eggs, are harvested and inserted in the fallopian tubes of infertile women. Japanese scientists are currently experimenting with an artificial uterus. The possibilities appear unlimited in this brave new world of having babies.

Remedies for infertility can come at a steep price. About 85 percent of infertile couples can eventually have a baby with low-tech treatments that cost under $2,000. For couples under age 35, the average high-tech cost is about $25,000; for older couples, over age 35, the cost rises to an average of $45,000. Achieving a pregnancy with donor sperm can cost about $8,000; donor eggs, $30,000; a surrogatemother, $60,000; and a surrogate mother impregnated with donor eggs, about $90,000. The neonatal costs of the Chukwu octuplets born in Houston, Texas, on December 20, 1998, have been estimated at $2 million. One can add to this base another very conservative $1.6 million in costs to raise these eight infants to age 18.

Compare these costs with a basic fee of $8,000 for adoption, without legal, court, and certificate costs. There is also a waiting period of about a year and a half for adoption. Adopting a child from another country can run about $15,000 for basic costs.

At the same time, the number of reproductive age couples in the United States with infertility problems has been rising, from 8 percent in 1983 to a current 10 percent. One in four couples over age 35 is infertile. These figures are important for this controversial issue. If voters force the states or federal government to require insurance companies to provide coverage for some or all infertility treatments, the average citizen will have to pick up the additional cost. Projecting today's costs ahead five or ten years can be risky for two reasons. First, the number of couples in the high-infertility-rate group, over age 35, is growing rapidly as more and more women and men delay starting a family while they develop their careers and attend college and graduate school. Second, as medical knowledge and skills in treating infertility increase, the success rate increases. Better success rates encourage more couples to try both the low and high-tech solutions. Better success rates also encourage more physicians to train in this financially rewarding specialization. In the past 20 years, the number of board-certified endocrinologists—one of the specializations in infertility technology—has increased from 100 to 500. Hospitals and clinics update their facilities and pass the costs onto their patients and to the taxpayers.

In the following selections, Diane D. Aronson argues that couples who need medical assistance for infertility should not be denied the opportunity to become pregnant and have children. She observes that legislators and employers are beginning to recognize that helping couples who are struggling to build a much-wanted family is the "right thing to do." Merrill Matthews, Jr., does not object to insurance companies paying for modern medical interventions, which is what most infertile couples need. However, he does object to the costs. He is concerned about the rare but multimillion-dollar cost of high profile cases of multiple births, which whet the appetite for more reproductive technology; the complications that come with different state and federal mandates; and the fairness of applying such mandates.

Diane D. Aronson

 **YES**

Should Health Insurers Be Forced to Pay for Infertility Treatments? Yes

What is the most important concern in your life? For many people, the answer would be family. If you are a couple with a vision of building a family, the condition of infertility can interrupt this basic human desire. Infertility is a life-changing crisis that affects more than 10 percent of the reproductive age population in the United States. Having children and raising a family, which comes easily to many couples, can be a heartbreaking challenge for those afflicted with infertility.

Infertility is a disease of the reproductive system which affects both men and women; it is not elective or selective. It strikes people in all walks of life, and it crosses racial, ethnic, religious and socioeconomic boundaries. Couples who experience infertility most often have to pay out of pocket for their diagnoses and treatments. Health-insurance coverage usually either is nonexistent or minimal.

For many couples, only medical treatment can enable them to become pregnant and have children. While adoption is an option for many, the costs can reach $30,000, and there are not enough babies available in the United States to meet the need. Proven medical treatments are available, and insurance coverage should be provided as it is for other diseases. Insurance covers the maternal and neonatal costs for fertile couples who are able to have children. Individuals with infertility pay into the insurance plans that cover those costs, even though they often cannot access care to bear children. Couples who need medical assistance should not be denied the opportunity to become pregnant and have children.

In any given month, a normally fertile couple has a 22 percent chance of becoming pregnant. Nearly two-thirds of couples receiving infertility treatments have successful pregnancies. Most who successfully obtain medical assistance for infertility are able to do so through relatively low-cost ($500 to $2,000) and noninvasive treatments such as medication or intrauterine insemination.

Approximately 5 percent of couples who seek treatment undergo assisted reproductive technology, or ART, such as in vitro fertilization, which costs approximately $12,000 per attempt. When the woman has blocked fallopian tubes or the man has a low sperm count, ART treatment may be the only method by which a couple can become pregnant. Another treatment option is surgery, which usually costs more than ART but often is covered by insurance plans. Because of this coverage, couples may undergo multiple surgical procedures, even if ART would be the best and most cost-effective option. Such partial coverage encourages inefficiency and, at times, incorrect treatment choices. Insurance coverage of the range of treatments would allow for better management of care, as physicians and patients could then better determine the most effective treatment path.

Infertility insurance coverage also would help to manage the rate of multiple births that result from some treatments. The multiple-birth rate among those who obtain infertility treatments is higher than among the general population. The neonatal costs following multiple births are high, as are the health risks to the mother and the babies. (The neonatal costs of the Chukwu octuplet births in Houston on Dec. 20, 1998, are estimated to be more than $2 million.)

When couples are struggling to have a child and do not have insurance coverage, they may be more willing to take risks in treatment that increase their chances of having a pregnancy but also could increase the chances of having a multiple birth. When paying out of pocket, knowing that they will not be able to afford more than a certain number of treatments affects their decisions and their willingness to take risks. Insurance coverage would remove that incentive. Further, insurance coverage would bring about additional oversight and management of care from the insurance company, which could in turn reduce the rate of multiple births. A 1998 study, led by physician David Frankfurter of Beth Israel Deaconess Medical Center in Boston, found that in states with mandated infertility-insurance coverage the average number of embryos transferred in an in vitro fertilization attempt was lower and the multiple-birth rate per attempt was lower than in states without mandates. The study's authors concluded that this lower rate of multiple births may be a result of less pressure from patients to maximize the chance of pregnancy and increased pressure from insurers to minimize the likelihood of multiple births.

Couples who experience infertility ride an emotional roller coaster—from diagnosis through treatment—a very difficult experience. The physical and emotional struggles are further exacerbated when couples face financial hurdles because of a lack of insurance coverage. Alice D. Domar of the Mind/Body Institute at Beth Israel Deaconess Medical Center led a study of women with chronic diseases which found that the psychological effect of experiencing infertility was similar to that of cancer and heart disease. Compounding the emotional distress is the stigma of infertility and the difficulty that many couples have in telling their family and friends.

What is fair when it comes to insurance coverage? The Supreme Court strengthened the arguments in favor of infertility-insurance coverage when it issued a ruling in June 1998 that demonstrated the importance of reproduction and the ability to have children. In *Bragdon vs. Abbott* the high court ruled that reproduction is a major life activity under the Americans with Disabilities Act, or ADA. According to the ADA, an individual is disabled if he or she has a mental or physical impairment that substantially limits one or more major life activities. Therefore, those who are impaired in their ability to reproduce may qualify for protection from discrimination based on that disability. This ruling allows those experiencing infertility to make claims of discrimination when employers specifically exclude infertility treatment from insurance plans. A number of lawsuits have arisen in the wake of that decision.

While Bragdon was not a case involving infertility (the plaintiff was an HIV-positive woman who was denied dental care), lower courts have ruled in cases specific to infertility that it qualifies as a disability under the ADA. In *Bielicki vs. The City of Chicago,* police officers Anita and Vince Bielicki sued the city of Chicago for excluding infertility treatment from their health plans. After the U.S. District Court for the Northern District of Illinois ruled that reproduction is a major life activity and that the Bielickis' lawsuit could go forward, the city decided to settle. Most infertility-treatment costs incurred by employees in the previous 10 years were reimbursed, and city health-insurance plans now include infertility coverage. The precedents set by this case and the Supreme Court ruling, and the prospect of further lawsuits, have brought infertility-insurance coverage to the attention of a growing number of employers and legislators.

William M. Mercer, a benefits consulting firm, published a report in 1997 which disclosed that approximately 25 percent of employers provide some infertility insurance coverage. Another consulting firm, the Segal Co., issued an August 1998 report which found that only 7 percent of employer plans cover infertility treatment, and about 14 percent of plans cover the costs of infertility diagnosis. Most of those plans that cover treatment do not cover all infertility services.

The costs of including infertility coverage in an insurance plan are low. Studies cited by the Mercer report found that the cost of in vitro fertilization coverage is approximately $2.50 per member per year. Another study, by Martha Griffin and William F Panak, published in the July 1998 issue of *Fertility and Sterility,* found that the cost of comprehensive infertility coverage is $1.71 per family plan per month. Isn't it worth the cost of a monthly cup of coffee to ensure that couples who are struggling to build much-wanted families are afforded the option?

Several state legislatures have responded to the needs of their constituents and recognized the importance of supporting couples who are striving to build their families. Thirteen states enacted infertility insurance laws after they determined that such financial assistance is in the best interest of their residents. The mandates are quite different in scope and substance. Ten states have a mandate to provide some level of infertility insurance. Three states have a mandate to offer under which insurance companies must have infertility insurance available for purchase, but employers do not have to choose to provide that coverage to their employees.

A number of state legislatures considered infertility-insurance laws in the 1997–98 legislative session, and new legislation is being drafted for introduction in 1999. Mandates may be introduced in Florida, Indiana, Michigan, Nevada, New Hampshire, New Jersey, New York, Pennsylvania, Tennessee and Texas. Infertility patients, providers and others who understand the need for insurance coverage are working to gather support for mandates, and a number of legislators have committed to assist.

The existing infertility-insurance mandates have allowed many couples to obtain needed medical treatments and to build their families. However, even in states with mandates, many employees still do not have insurance coverage because of the Employee Retirement Income Security Act, or ERISA. Employers who self-insure are exempt from any state health-insurance mandates, including infertility mandates. In some states, more than 50 percent of employees work for exempted employers. Self-insured employers sometimes do choose to follow the state's policy lead and provide infertility coverage to their employees. A federal infertility insurance mandate, a long-term goal of infertility community, would cover all employers and make coverage consistent across states.

Legislators and employers are beginning to recognize that helping couples who are struggling to build much-wanted families is the right thing to do. In a country that places great value in family, it is salutary that insurance coverage for couples with infertility is just around the corner.

← NO

Should Health Insurers Be Forced to Pay for Infertility Treatments? No

When miracles happen on a regular basis, they no longer are miracles—and they may even be seen as problems. That's what has happened with the miracle of multiple births.

Geraldine Brodrick, 29, of Sydney, Australia, performed a miracle in 1971 when she gave birth to nine babies. All died. But 30 years of advances in infertility treatments and neonatology have made multiple births almost common and fairly safe. Bobbi McCaughey of Carlisle, Iowa, also 29, gave birth to septuplets in 1997, all of whom survived. And now Nkem Chukwu of Houston has given birth to octuplets, one of whom died. There also are nonscientific reasons for the increase in the frequency of multiple births. One is that health insurers often are willing or required to pay for infertility treatments. As a result, an increasing number of infertile couples seeks counseling and medical help in having a baby.

According to the Centers for Disease Control and Prevention, 1.2 million women (about 2 percent) of reproductive age visited a medical professional about infertility in 1995. And 9.3 million women (15 percent) had used some kind of fertility service at one time in their lives, compared with 6.8 million (12 percent) who had done so in 1988.

Most women who pursue treatment need only moderate medical intervention, such as counseling or drug therapy. Others need more aggressive or invasive care, such as surgery or assisted reproductive technology, or ART. ART includes such procedures as in vitro fertilization, in which eggs and sperm are taken from the couple, fertilized outside the womb and then implanted in the uterus.

While moderate medical intervention for infertility can be relatively affordable for most couples—$500 to $2,000—more aggressive therapy can cost as much as $12,000. And in vitro fertilization can be expensive—$10,000 to $15,000 per attempt. It often takes several attempts before a prospective mother is successfully impregnated—which can drive up the cost significantly.

According to a 1994 *New England Journal of Medicine* study by Peter J. Neumann et al., the estimated cost per live delivery for in vitro fertilization ranged between $66,667 in the first cycle to $114,286 by the sixth cycle. A July

From Merrill Matthews, Jr., "Should Health Insurers Be Forced to Pay for Infertility Treatments? No," *Insight on the News* (February 8, 1999). Copyright © 1999 by News World Communications, Inc. Reprinted by permission of *Insight on the News*.

1998 study by Martha Griffin and William F. Panak, published in *Fertility and Sterility*, found the cost of ART per live delivery in 1993 was $59,484.

Because some infertility treatments can be prohibitively expensive for middle- and lower-income families, advocacy groups have lobbied legislators to require insurance to cover the treatments—and many have listened. For years state legislatures have passed laws—"mandates"—that require insurers to cover providers such as chiropractors and podiatrists or for services such as drug and alcohol-abuse treatments. In 1965 there were only eight mandates nationwide. Today there are more than 1,000. And one mandate that has been gaining popularity—especially among politicians who want to be perceived as sympathetic to women's needs—requires health insurers to cover infertility treatments.

While these mandates make insurance coverage more comprehensive, they also make it more expensive because people use insurance for services they previously paid for out of pocket. For example, consider a patient who was spending $50 a month out of pocket to visit a chiropractor. If the government requires insurers to cover 80 percent of his cost, the patient then is out only $10 a month. If he believes he benefits from the chiropractic care, he may double the frequency of his visits and still spend less than he spent before the mandate was passed. While the patient's personal health-care costs have gone down, total costs to the system have doubled—from $50 to $100 a month. If many patients do the same, insurers eventually will have to increase their rates to make up for the additional costs.

So while it may be true that chiropractors charge less per service than medical doctors and may in certain circumstances provide better care, the additional utilization increases overall health-care costs. Of course, special interests who push for insurance coverage of their particular specialty may believe that such action will improve the quality of care. But they also know that providers will get more visits and therefore more money. That's one of the reasons they work so hard to get legislators to mandate coverage of their specialty. And that's also why they search for data and justifications that will "prove" their assertions.

For example, Griffin, a doctoral candidate in the College of Nursing at the University of Rhode Island, and Panak, a psychologist at the University of Northern Iowa, believe that insurance should cover infertility treatments and produced a study to justify their beliefs. Their examination of the Massachusetts infertility mandate led them to claim that "limiting the number of ART attempts could motivate clinics to maintain policies of transferring numerous embryos as a way of increasing success rates for couples who cannot afford numerous ART attempts. Thus, limits on ART cycles inadvertently could maintain high rates of multiple births and the associated medical complications and economic costs of these births."

In other words, if cost were not a factor, infertility clinics and patients might be less aggressive in their attempts to ensure pregnancy on the first attempt by implanting numerous embryos. If true, that could decrease the number of multiple births and costs would go down.

The problem is that mandates also increase total utilization of health care. If insurance is required to cover infertility treatments, more women will get the treatments. The attempt to remove or destroy some of the fertilized embryos, a process known as selective reduction, is seen by many couples as abortion, a broader social issue that many people oppose. Chukwu was offered selective reduction and declined for religious reasons. Indeed, because some women are reluctant to have embryos removed, there is a debate within the medical community about whether such women should even be offered fertility drugs. Thus, multiple births will not go down as the authors suggest.

Proponents of infertility mandates also assert that the cost of adding the coverage is minimal and would have little impact on premiums. In support, they cite various studies that project a premium increase of between $0.40 and $2.50 per family per month.

There are several problems with these projections. First, they seldom take into consideration other factors. For example, Chukwu's medical bills for her octuplets will reach an estimated $2 million. She is covered by insurance, so the family will not have to bear most of the cost; the insurer will. But insurance is just a pass-through mechanism. That is, insurers pass expenses on to all the people who pay the premiums. Thus policyholders pay higher premiums for the infertility treatments of others and eventually bear the costs of postnatal care.

Actuaries take these collateral effects into consideration when calculating the costs of mandates. For example, when Milliman & Robertson, one of the leading actuarial firms in the country, did a cost analysis of a typical infertility mandate adopted by state legislatures, it estimated the mandate would increase the cost of a health-insurance policy 3 to 5 percent per year, or $105 to $175 a year for a basic health-insurance policy that had no other mandates included.

Which brings us to a second problem. Even if proponents of insurance coverage for infertility were correct in asserting that a mandate would be relatively inexpensive, the larger problem is the total number of mandates. Most states have adopted 30 to 40 health-insurance mandates. While the Milliman & Robertson study makes it clear that most of these mandates are inexpensive— adding less than 1 percent to the cost of a policy—the sum of their costs can make a health-insurance policy prohibitively expensive, boosting premiums by 40 percent to 50 percent in most states.

A third problem is fairness. Thirteen states have adopted some form of infertility mandate. In some cases the legislation requires insurers to cover infertility treatments; in other cases it requires only that coverage be offered. Some states limit how much money insurers are required to spend on treatments (say, to $15,000), while other states exempt very small employers (those with, say, fewer than 25 employees).

However, state-insurance laws primarily affect only small employers and individuals such as the self-employed who purchase private insurance for themselves and their families. That's because most large employers self-insure under the Employee Retirement Income Security Act, or ERISA, a federal law that supersedes state laws. Companies that insure their employees under ERISA avoid state mandates completely.

Thus state mandates affect only a small segment of those with private insurance, and the costs of those mandates fall on a relatively small number of people. As a result, premium increases in the small group and individual health-insurance markets grow much faster than in the large group market. Ironically, it is in the small group and individual markets where people are least able to afford the premium increases.

Of course, many large companies that self-insure voluntarily cover infertility treatments. But that's a choice the companies have made, not one imposed by government. It's those governmental impositions that can lead a business or a family to decide to cancel coverage. Which leads us to the real question: Do we want to put an increasing number of low-income families at risk of lacking basic health insurance so that infertile couples can have their treatments paid for by somebody else?

At a time when health-insurance premiums are projected to increase significantly during the next few years and demographers are worried about world population growth, it simply makes no sense for the government to force insurers to subsidize infertility treatments. Those who have the income to pay for the treatments or who are disciplined enough to save the money to pay for them should have that option. But since it is their choice, it should be their responsibility, not a financial burden that others must bear.

POSTSCRIPT

Should Health Insurers Be Required to Pay for Infertility Treatments?

The controversy about whether or not insurance companies should be required to pay for infertility treatments available now or in the future raises two questions. The first question is, How do we view infertility? Is it a disease, a disability, or an emotionally draining, psychologically devastating disappointment for some men and women? Unlike a disease, infertility is certainly not life threatening. So where does infertility fit into the priorities of the health care budget? Consider that many insurance companies will not pay for the contraceptive pill for women seeking to avoid unwanted pregnancies, and many will not pay for regular mammograms for women at risk for breast cancer.

The second question is international in scope. Around the world, the fertility rate is dropping. European countries and Japan are well below replacement level, with 1.3 to 1.5 children per fertile woman. Despite the fact that the United States has a total fertility rate slightly above replacement level, America's population is expected to rise from the current 276 million to 338 million in 2025 and over 400 million in 2050. In the same 50 years the world's population is expected to rise from its current 6 billion to almost 8 billion in 2025 and over 10 billion in 2050.

In the early 1960s, America and the world saw the birth of reproductive technologies, which for the first time in human history separated sexual intercourse and intimacy from the baby-making process. Also, for the first time, sex and reproduction became separate issues, each with their own ethic to be worked out within changing social values. On the side of sexual values, many feel that "the pill" and women's liberation have led to a widespread acceptance of premarital sex. On the reproductive side, we are still wrestling with the values we want to hold to in this sometimes frightening new era of test-tube babies, frozen embryos, embryo transplants, surrogate mothers, three mothers and two fathers for a single baby, and future possibilities such as the genetically engineered "designer child."

Suggested Readings

Anonymous, "Baby Business," *The Colorado Business Journal* (February 19, 1999).

L. M. Silver, *Remaking Eden: Cloning and Beyond in a Brave New World* (Avon Books, 1997).

ISSUE 9

Should Female Circumcision Be Banned?

YES: Loretta M. Kopelman, from "Female Circumcision/ Genital Mutilation and Ethical Relativism," *Second Opinion* (October 1994)

NO: P. Masila Mutisya, from "A Symbolic Form of Female Circumcision Should Be Allowed for Those Who Want It," An Original Essay Written for This Volume (November 1997)

ISSUE SUMMARY

YES: Loretta M. Kopelman, a professor of medical humanities, argues that certain moral absolutes apply to all cultures and that these, combined with the many serious health and cultural consequences of female circumcision, require that all forms of female genital mutilation be eliminated.

NO: P. Masila Mutisya, a professor of multicultural education, contends that we should allow the simplest form of female circumcision, nicking the clitoral hood to draw a couple of drops of blood, as part of the rich heritage of rite of passage for newborn and pubertal girls in those cultures with this tradition.

Each year in central and northern Africa and southern Arabia, 4–5 million girls have parts of their external genitals surgically removed in ceremonies intended to honor and welcome the girls into their communities or into womanhood. About 80 million living women have had this surgery performed sometime between infancy and puberty in ancient rituals said to promote chastity, religion, group identity, cleanliness, health, family values, and marriage goals. Female circumcision (FC) is deeply embedded in the cultures of many countries, including Ethiopia, Sudan, Somalia, Sierra Leone, Kenya, Tanzania, Chad, Gambia, Liberia, Mali, Senegal, Eritrea, Ivory Coast, Upper Volta, Mauritania, Nigeria, and Egypt.

Opponents of FC call it female genital mutilation (FGM) because the usual ways of performing FC frequently cause serious health problems, such as hemorrhaging, urinary and pelvic infection, painful intercourse (for both partners), infertility, delivery complications, and even death. Besides denying women orgasm, the health consequences of FC also strain the overburdened, limited health care systems in the developing nations in which it is practiced.

In Type 1 FC, the simplest form, the clitoral hood is pricked or removed. Type 1 FC should not preclude orgasms in later life, but it can when performed on the tiny genitals of infants with the pins, scissors, and knives that traditional practitioners commonly use. In Type 2 (intermediate) FC, the clitoris and most or all of the minor labia are removed. In Type 3 FC, known as pharonic circumcision, or infibulation, the clitoris, minor labia, and parts of the major labia are removed. The vulval wound is stitched closed, leaving only a small opening for passage of urine and menstrual flow. Traditional practitioners often use sharpened or hot stones or unsterilized razors or knives, frequently without anesthesia or antibiotics. Thorns are sometimes used to stitch up the wound, and a twig is often inserted to keep the passage open. Healing can take a month or more. In southern Arabia, Sudan, Somalia, Ethiopia, and other African nations, more than three-quarters of the girls undergo Type 2 or 3 FC.

Impassioned cultural clashes erupt when families migrate from countries where FC is customary to North America and Europe. In their new homes immigrant parents use traditional practitioners or ask local health professionals to perform FC. Some doctors and nurses perform FC for large fees; others do it because they are concerned about the unhygienic techniques of traditional practitioners. In the United Kingdom about 2,000 girls undergo FC each year, even though it is legally considered child abuse. Many international agencies, such as UNICEF, the International Federation of Gynecology and Obstetrics, and the World Health Organization (WHO), openly condemn and try to stop FC. France, Canada, and the United Kingdom have banned FC; the American Medical Association has denounced it; and the U.S. Congress has made all FC illegal.

The question discussed here is whether or not the traditional pluralism and openness of American culture can make some accommodation that would allow thousands of immigrants to maintain the essence of their ancient, traditional rites of passage for young girls in some symbolic way. Some commentators argue that we should prohibit Types 2 and 3 circumcision for health reasons but allow some symbolic ritual nicking of the clitoral hood as a major element in the extensive ceremonies and educational rites of passage that surround a girl's birth into her family and community or her passage to womanhood in these African and Arabic cultures. In the following selections, Loretta M. Kopelman advocates a ban on all female circumcision. P. Masila Mutisya advocates allowing a symbolic female circumcision, similar to the removal of the male foreskin (prepuce), with modern medical safeguards.

YES ←

Loretta M. Kopelman

Female Circumcision/Genital Mutilation and Ethical Relativism

Reasons Given for Female Circumcision/Genital Mutilation

According to four independent series of studies conducted by investigators from countries where female circumcision is widely practiced (El Dareer 1982; Ntiri 1993; Koso-Thomas 1987; Abdalla 1982), the primary reasons given for performing this ritual surgery are that it (1) meets a religious requirement, (2) preserves group identity, (3) helps to maintain cleanliness and health, (4) preserves virginity and family honor and prevents immorality, and (5) furthers marriage goals including greater sexual pleasure for men.

El Dareer conducted her studies in the Sudan, Dr. Olayinka Koso-Thomas in and around Sierra Leone, and Raquiya Haji Dualeh Abdalla and Daphne Williams Ntiri in Somalia. They argue that the reasons for continuing this practice in their respective countries float on a sea of false beliefs, beliefs that thrive because of a lack of education and open discussion about reproduction and sexuality. Insofar as intercultural methods for evaluating factual and logical statements exist, people from other cultures should at least be able to understand these inconsistencies or mistaken factual beliefs and use them as basis for making some judgments having intercultural *moral* authority.

First, according to these studies the main reason given for performing female circumcision/genital mutilation is that it is regarded as a religious requirement. Most of the people practicing this ritual are Muslims, but it is not a practice required by the Koran (El Dareer 1982; Ntiri 1993). El Dareer writes: "Circumcision of women is not explicitly enjoined in the Koran, but there are two implicit sayings of the Prophet Mohammed: 'Circumcision is an ordinance in men and an embellishment in women' and, reportedly Mohammed said to Om Attiya, a woman who circumcised girls in El Medina, 'Do not go deep. It is more illuminating to the face and more enjoyable to the husband.' Another version says, 'Reduce but do not destroy. This is enjoyable to the woman and preferable to the man.' But there is nothing in the Koran to suggest that the Prophet commanded that women be circumcised. He advised that it was important to both sexes that very little should be

From Loretta M. Kopelman, "Female Circumcision/Genital Mutilation and Ethical Relativism," *Second Opinion*, vol. 20, no. 2 (October 1994). Copyright © 1994 by The Park Ridge Center for the Study of Health, Faith, and Ethics, 211 East Ontario, Suite 800, Chicago, IL 60611. Reprinted by permission. Notes and references omitted.

taken" (1992:72). Female circumcision/genital mutilation, moreover, is not practiced in the spiritual center of Islam, Saudi Arabia (Calder et al. 1993). Another reason for questioning this as a Muslim practice is that clitoridectomy and infibulation predate Islam, going back to the time of the pharaohs (Abdalla 1982; El Dareer 1992).

Second, many argue that the practice helps to preserve group identity. When Christian colonialists in Kenya introduced laws opposing the practice of female circumcision in the 1930s, African leader Kenyatta expressed a view still popular today: "This operation is still regarded as the very essence of an institution which has enormous educational, social, moral and religious implications, quite apart from the operation itself. For the present, it is impossible for a member of the [Kikuyu] tribe to imagine an initiation without clitoridectomy . . . the abolition of IRUA [the ritual operation] will destroy the tribal symbol which identifies the age group and prevent the Kikuyu from perpetuating that spirit of collectivism and national solidarity which they have been able to maintain from time immemorial" (Scheper-Hughes 1991:27). In addition, the practice is of social and economic importance to older women who are paid for performing the rituals (El Dareer 1982; Koso-Thomas 1987; Abdalla 1982; Ginsberg 1991).

Drs. Koso-Thomas, El Dareer, and Abdalla agree that people in these countries support female circumcision as a good practice, but only because they do not understand that it is a leading cause of sickness or even death for girls, mothers, and infants, and a major cause of infertility, infection, and maternal-fetal and marital complications. They conclude that these facts are not confronted because these societies do not speak openly of such matters. Abdalla writes, "There is no longer any reason, given the present state of progress in science, to tolerate confusion and ignorance about reproduction and women's sexuality" (1982:2). Female circumcision/genital mutilation is intended to honor women as male circumcision honors men, and members of cultures where the surgery is practiced are shocked by the analogy of clitoridectomy to removal of the penis (El Dareer 1982).

Third, the belief that the practice advances health and hygiene is incompatible with stable data from surveys done in these cultures, where female circumcision/genital mutilation has been linked to mortality or morbidity such as shock, infertility, infections, incontinence, maternal-fetal complications, and protracted labor. The tiny hole generally left for blood and urine to pass is a constant source of infection (El Dareer 1982; Koso-Thomas 1987; Abdalla 1982; Calder et al. 1993; Ntiri 1993). Koso-Thomas writes, "As for cleanliness, the presence of these scars prevents urine and menstrual flow escaping by the normal channels. This may lead to acute retention of urine and menstrual flow, and to a condition known as *hematocolpos,* which is highly detrimental to the health of the girl or woman concerned and causes odors more offensive than any that can occur through the natural secretions" (Koso-Thomas 1987:10). Investigators completing a recent study wrote: "The risk of medical complications after female circumcision is very high as revealed by the present study [of 290 Somali women, conducted in the capital of Mogadishu]. Complications which cause the death of the young girls must be a common occurrence especially in the rural areas. . . . Dribbling urine incontinence, painful menstruations, haematocolpos and painful intercourse are facts that Somali women have to live with—facts that strongly motivate attempts to change the practice of female circumcision" (Dirie and Lindmark 1992:482).

Fourth, investigators found that circumcision is thought necessary in these cultures to preserve virginity and family honor and to prevent immorality. Type 3 circumcision [in which the clitoris and most or all of the labia minora are removed] is used to keep women from having sexual intercourse before marriage and conceiving illegitimate children. In addition, many believe that Types 2 [in which the clitoris, the labia minora, and parts of the labia majora are removed] and 3 circumcision must be done because uncircumcised women have excessive and uncontrollable sexual drives. El Dareer, however, believes that this view is not consistently held—that women in the Sudan are respected and that Sudanese men would be shocked to apply this sometimes-held cultural view to members of their own families. This reason also seems incompatible with the general view, which investigators found was held by both men and women in these cultures, that sex cannot be pleasant for women (El Dareer 1982; Koso-Thomas 1987; Abdalla 1982). In addition, female circumcision/genital mutilation offers no foolproof way to promote chastity and can even lead to promiscuity because it does not diminish desire or libido even where it makes orgasms impossible (El Dareer 1982). Some women continually seek experiences with new sexual partners because they are left unsatisfied in their sexual encounters (Koso-Thomas 1987). Moreover, some pretend to be virgins by getting stitched up tightly again (El Dareer 1982).

Fifth, interviewers found that people practicing female circumcision/ genital mutilation believe that it furthers marriage goals, including greater sexual pleasure for men. To survive economically, women in these cultures must marry, and they will not be acceptable marriage partners unless they have undergone this ritual surgery (Abdalla 1982; Ntiri 1993). It is a curse, for example, to say that someone is the child of an uncircumcised woman (Koso-Thomas 1987). The widely held belief that infibulation enhances women's beauty and men's sexual pleasure makes it difficult for women who wish to marry to resist this practice (Koso-Thomas 1987; El Dareer 1992). Some men from these cultures, however, report that they enjoy sex more with uncircumcised women (Koso-Thomas 1987). Furthermore, female circumcision/ genital mutilation is inconsistent with the established goals of some of these cultures because it is a leading cause of disability and contributes to the high mortality rate among mothers, fetuses, and children. Far from promoting the goals of marriage, it causes difficulty in consummating marriage, infertility, prolonged and obstructed labor, and morbidity and mortality.

Criticisms of Ethical Relativism

Examination of the debate concerning female circumcision suggests several conclusions about the extent to which people from outside a culture can understand or contribute to moral debates within it in a way that has moral force. First, the fact that a culture's moral and religious views are often intertwined with beliefs that are open to rational and empirical evaluation can be a basis of cross-cultural examination and intercultural moral criticism (Bambrough 1979). Defenders of female circumcision/genital mutilation do not claim that this practice is a moral or religious requirement and end the discussion; they are willing to give and defend reasons for their views. For example, advocates of female circumcision/genital mutilation claim that it benefits women's health and well-being. Such claims are open to cross-cultural examination because information is available to determine whether the practice promotes health or cause morbidity or mortality. Beliefs that the practice enhances fertility and promotes health, that women cannot have orgasms, and that allowing the baby's head to touch the clitoris during delivery causes death to the baby are incompatible with stable medical data (Koso-Thomas 1987). Thus an opening is allowed for genuine cross-cultural discussion or criticism of the practice.

Some claims about female circumcision/genital mutilation, however, are not as easily open to cross-cultural understanding. For example, cultures practicing the Type 3 surgery, infibulation, believe that it makes women more beautiful. For those who are not from these cultures, this belief is difficult to understand, especially when surveys show that many women in these cultures, when interviewed, attributed to infibulation their keloid scars, urine retention, pelvic infections, puerperal sepsis, and obstetrical problems (Ntiri 1993; Abdalla 1982). Koso-Thomas writes: "None of the reasons put forward in favor of circumcision have any real scientific or logical basis. It is surprising that aesthetics and the maintenance of cleanliness are advanced as grounds for female circumcision. The scars could hardly be thought of as contributing to beauty. The hardened scar and stump usually seen where the clitoris should be, or in the case of the infibulated vulva, taut skin with an ugly long scar down the middle, present a horrifying picture" (Koso-Thomas 1987:10). Thus not everyone in these cultures believes that these rituals enhance beauty; some find such claims difficult to understand.

Second, the debate over female circumcision/genital mutilation illustrates another difficulty for defenders of this version of ethical relativism concerning the problem of differentiating cultures. People who brought the practice of female circumcision/genital mutilation with them when they moved to another nation still claim to be a distinct cultural group. Some who moved to Britain, for example, resent the interference in their culture represented by laws that condemn the practice as child abuse (Thompson 1989). If ethical relativists are to appeal to cultural approval in making the final determination of what is good or bad, right or wrong, they must tell us how to distinguish one culture from another.

How exactly do we count or separate cultures? A society is not a nation-state, because some social groups have distinctive identities within nations. If we do not define societies as nations, however, how do we distinguish among cultural groups, for example, well enough to say that an action is child abuse in one culture but not in another? Subcultures in nations typically overlap and have many variations. Even if we could count cultural groups well enough to say exactly how to distinguish one culture from another, how and when would this be relevant? How big or old or vital must a culture, subculture, group, or cult be in order to be recognized as a society whose moral distinctions are self-contained and self-justifying?

A related problem is that there can be passionate disagreement, ambivalence, or rapid changes within a culture or group over what is approved or disapproved. According to ethical relativism, where there is significant disagreement within a culture there is no way to determine what is right or wrong. But what disagreement is significant? As we saw, some people in these cultures, often those with higher education, strongly disapprove of female circumcision/genital mutilation and work to stop it (El Dareer 1982; Koso-Thomas 1987; Ntiri 1993; Dirie and Lindmark 1992; Abdalla 1982). Are they in the same culture as their friends and relatives who approve of these rituals? It seems more accurate to say that people may belong to various groups that overlap and have many variations. This description, however, makes it difficult for ethical relativism to be regarded as a helpful theory for determining what is right or wrong. To say that something is right when it has cultural approval is useless if we cannot identify the relevant culture. Moreover, even where people agree about the rightness of certain practices, such as these rituals, they can sometimes be inconsistent. For example, in reviewing reasons given within cultures where female circumcision/genital mutilation is practiced, we saw that there was some inconsistency concerning whether women needed this surgery to control their sexual appetites, to make them more beautiful, or to prevent morbidity or mortality. Ethical relativists thus have extraordinary problems offering a useful account of what counts as a culture and establishes cultural approval or disapproval.

Third, despite some clear disagreement such as that over the rightness of female circumcision/genital mutilation, people from different parts of the world share common goals like the desirability of promoting people's health, happiness, opportunities, and cooperation, and the wisdom of stopping war, pollution, oppression, torture, and exploitation. These common goals make us a world community, and using shared methods of reasoning and evaluation, we can discuss how well they are understood or how well they are implemented in different parts of our world community. We can use shared goals to assess whether female circumcision/genital mutilation is more like respect or oppression, more like enhancement or diminishment of opportunities, or more like pleasure or torture. While there are, of course, genuine differences between citizens of the world, it is difficult to comprehend how they could be identified unless we could pick them out against a background of our similarities. Highlighting our differences, however useful for some purposes, should not eclipse the truth that we share many goals and values and are similar enough that we can assess each other's views as rational beings in a way that has moral force. Another way to express this is to say that we should recognize universal human rights or be respectful of each other as persons capable of reasoned discourse.

Fourth, this version of ethical relativism, if consistently held, leads to the abhorrent conclusion that we cannot make intercultural judgments with moral force about societies that start wars, practice torture, or exploit and oppress other groups; as long as these activities are approved in the society that does them, they are allegedly right. Yet the world community believed that it was making a cross-cultural judgment with moral force when it criticized the Communist Chinese government for crushing a pro-democracy student protest rally, the South Africans for upholding apartheid, the Soviets for using psychiatry to suppress dissent, and the Bosnian Serbs for carrying out the siege of Sarajevo. And the judgment was expressed without anyone's ascertaining whether the respective actions had widespread approval in those countries. In each case, representatives from the criticized society usually said something like, "You don't understand why this is morally justified in our culture even if it would not be in your society." If ethical relativism were convincing, these responses ought to be as well.

Relativists who want to defend sound social cross-cultural and moral judgments about the value of freedom and human rights in other cultures seem to have two choices. On the one hand, if they agree that some cross-cultural norms have moral authority, they should also agree that some intercultural judgments about female circumcision/genital mutilation may have moral authority. Some relativists take this route (see, for example, Sherwin 1992), thereby abandoning the version of ethical relativism being criticized herein. On the other hand, if they defend this version of ethical relativism yet make cross-cultural moral judgments about the importance of values like tolerance, group benefit, and the survival of cultures, they will have to admit to an inconsistency in their arguments. For example, anthropologist Scheper-Hughes (1991) advocates tolerance of other cultural value systems; she fails to see that she is saying that tolerance between cultures is *right* and that this is a cross-cultural moral judgment using a moral norm (tolerance). Similarly, relativists who say it is wrong to eliminate rituals that give meaning to other cultures are also inconsistent in making a judgment that presumes to have genuine cross-cultural moral authority. Even the sayings sometimes used by defenders of ethical relativism—such as "When in Rome do as the Romans" (Scheper-Hughes 1991)—mean it is *morally permissible* to adopt all the cultural norms in operation wherever one finds oneself. Thus it is not consistent for defenders of this version of ethical relativism to make intercultural moral judgments about tolerance, group benefit, intersocietal respect, or cultural diversity.

The burden of proof, then, is upon defenders of this version of ethical relativism to show why we cannot do something we think we sometimes do very well, namely, engage in intercultural moral discussion, cooperation, or criticism and give support to people whose welfare or rights are in jeopardy in other cultures. In addition, defenders of ethical relativism need to explain how we can justify the actions of international professional societies that take moral stands in adopting policy. For example, international groups may take moral stands that advocate fighting pandemics, stopping wars, halting oppression, promoting health education, or eliminating poverty, and they seem to have moral authority in some cases. Some might respond that our professional groups are themselves cultures of a sort. But this response raises the . . . problem of how to individuate a culture or society. . . .

Comment

We have sufficient reason, therefore, to conclude that these rituals of female circumcision/genital mutilation are wrong. For me to say they are wrong does not mean that they are disapproved by most people in my culture but wrong for reasons similar to those given by activists within these cultures who are working to stop these practices. They are wrong because the usual forms of the surgery deny women orgasms and because they cause medical complications and even death. It is one thing to say that these practices are wrong and that activists should be supported in their efforts to stop them; it is another matter to determine how to do this effectively. All agree that education may be the most important means to stop these practices. Some activists in these cultures want an immediate ban (Abdalla 1982). Other activists in these cultures encourage Type 1 circumcision (pricking or removing the clitoral hood) in order to "wean" people away from Types 2 and 3 by substitution. Type 1 has the least association with morbidity or mortality and, if there are no complications, does not preclude sexual orgasms in later life. The chance of success through this tactic is more promising and realistic, they hold, than what an outright ban would achieve; and people could continue many of their traditions and rituals of welcome without causing so much harm (El Dareer 1982). Other activists in these countries, such as Raquiya Abdalla, object to equating Type 1 circumcision in the female with male circumcision: "To me and to many others, the aim and results of any form of circumcision of women are quite different from those applying to the circumcision of men" (1982:8). Because of the hazards of even Type 1 circumcision, especially for infants, I agree with the World Health Organization and the American Medical Association that it would be best to stop all forms of ritual genital surgery on women. Bans have proven ineffective: this still-popular practice has been illegal in most countries for many years (Rushwan 1990; Ntiri 1993; El Dareer 1982). Other proposals by activists focus on education, fines, and carefully crafted legislation (El Dareer 1982; Abdalla 1982; Ozumba 1992; Dirie and Lindmark 1992; WHO 1992).

The critique of the reasons given to support female circumcision/genital mutilation in cultures where it is practiced shows us how to enter discussions, disputes, or assessments in ways that can have moral authority. We share common needs, goals, and methods of reasoning and evaluation. Together they enable us to evaluate many claims across cultures and sometimes to regard ourselves as part of a world community with interests in promoting people's health, happiness, empathy, and opportunities as well as desires to stop war, torture, pandemics, pollution, oppression, and injustice. Thus, ethical relativism—the view that to say something is right means it has cultural approval and to say it is wrong means it has cultural disapproval—is implausible as a useful theory, definition, or account of the meaning of moral judgments. The burden of proof therefore falls upon upholders of this version of ethical relativism to show why criticisms of other cultures always lack moral authority. Although many values are culturally determined and we should not impose moral judgments across cultures hastily, we sometimes know enough to condemn practices approved in other cultures. For example, we can understand enough of the debate about female circumcision/genital mutilation to draw some conclusions: it is wrong, oppressive, and not a voluntary practice in the sense that the people doing it comprehend information relevant to their decision. Moreover, it is a ritual, however well-meant, that violates justifiable and universal human rights or values supported in the human community, and we should promote international moral support for advocates working to stop the practice wherever it is carried out.

NO

P. Masila Mutisya

A Symbolic Form of Female Circumcision Should Be Allowed for Those Who Want It

In recent years, the issue of female circumcision has provoked heated discussion here in the United States and far from its cultural origins in Africa. As controversial as it is, the issue of female circumcision raises a very important point that needs attention across the board when we are dealing with cultural behaviors, traditions, and practices that are brought by immigrants into a foreign culture. Whether we are dealing with a sexual practice like female circumcision, parentally arranged marriages, child marriages, or a non-sexual custom, we must deal clearly with the implications of cross-cultural, intercultural and multicultural education. This need for cross-cultural sensitivity and understanding is fairly obvious from the blanket condemnations of all forms of female circumcision as a brutalization of women, and the parallel silence about its cultural meaning as an important rite of passage for women. There is certainly a lot of ignorance about African cultures among Americans, both in the general population with its vocal feminist advocacy groups as well as among our legislators and health care professionals. There is a real need for better understanding of these rich cultural traditions.

The issue here is not one of cultural relativism, or the lack of it. What I am concerned about is that it is all too easy to misinterpret the symbolism and meaning of a traditional cultural rite. Unless we understand the various forms of female circumcision and its cultural importance as part of a girl's rite of passage to womanhood we run the serious risk of doing more harm than good. Lack of understanding of the values of one culture leads to the imposition of the views and interpretations of the cultural majority on new minorities within a nation. This has often been the case in the United States with the miseducation and misinterpretation of many aspects of African cultures, as well as other cultures in this nation. This in turn leads to conflicts in social and psychological awareness that affect the identities of different people in our multicultural society. People of African descent seem to be more affected by this than others.

Loretta Kopelman's call for the abolition of all forms of female circumcision is a clear example of this cultural imperialism. This misunderstanding is also evident in ongoing discussions of female circumcision on the internet and in various journals.

In her discussion of female circumcision, Kopelman, a professor of medical humanities, attacks the cultural relativism theory. She argues that certain moral absolutes apply across the board to all cultures and that these principles clearly dictate that all forms of female circumcision should be banned regardless of its particular form and its symbolic role as a rite of passage in some African cultures. She maintains that the reasons given to explain why these rituals exist have no validity or value. For her, female circumcision falls in the same category as murder of the innocent and therefore should be totally banned.

I speak as an educator who understands the symbolism of the African rites of passage very well because I am part of one African culture in which this educational rite of passage is practiced. I find no evidence in Kopelman's arguments to indicate that she has any understanding of or appreciation for objective cross-cultural, intercultural, and multicultural interpretations. Her arguments are a classic example of how most westerners, rooted in the cultures of Europe and North America, so easily assume the role of dictating and imposing their morality on non-westerners without offering any viable alternative or accommodation. I think this is a way of saying that the people who have practiced these and other rituals for thousands of years before and after coming in contact with westerners, must abolish their culture and be assimilated into the dominant western Euro-American value and moral system, even though—and this is one of my major arguments—the western Euro-American culture which she seeks to impose on all others has very few if any educational culturally-based rites of passage for their youth. Barring marriage and death rituals, it is practically devoid of all rites of passage.

Most of the traditional education of African boys and girls for adulthood is informal. However, initiation rites, such as female circumcision, can be considered formal because they occur in a public community setting with specific symbolic activities and ceremonies, which differ according to the individual society. In those cultures where female circumcision is practiced, this community-based ritual is a formal recognition that the girl has successfully completed her preparation for womanhood and is ready for marriage. (The examples I cite below are mostly from the Kamba and Gikuyu people and Bantu ethnic groups.)

An African child's education for adulthood is matched with its cognitive development and readiness, and may begin anywhere between ages 4 and 12. Young girls are taught the skills of a woman, learning to cook, manage a home and handle other chores related to their domestic responsibilities. They are also taught the social importance of these responsibilities in terms of women's role as the pillars of society. They learn respect for their elders and their lineage, how to communicate without being offensive, an appreciation of their tribal or clan laws and their ethnic identity. An African child's education for adult responsibilities includes learning about their sexuality and the taboos of their culture related to sexual relationships. Such taboos include sexual abstinence until marriage and ways of dealing with temptations. Girls learn who they should and should not marry, how to make love to a man while enjoying themselves, how to avoid pregnancy because there are terrible consequences if one becomes pregnant before marriage, and also how to avoid divorce for irresponsible reasons. In our cultures, grandparents and aunts are usually responsible for educating girls for womanhood. Boys are given similar gender appropriate education in their youthful years.

Depending on the particular tribal culture, completion of this educational process is certified by a formal ritual such as female circumcision. Both the educational process and the formal ritual are essential because together they prepare the boy or girl for marriage. Without this education and a declaration of adulthood provided by a formal ritual capping the education, one is not eligible for marriage and is still considered a child.

I strongly disagree with Kopelman's position that *all* forms of female circumcision should be banned. I do agree, however, with her call for a ban on any mutilation and/or infibulation that involves cutting or severing of any part of a female genitalia for whatever reasons given, when this is known to result in any health or fertility complication or disorder whether minor or major.

My proposed solution stems from an understanding of the symbolic function female circumcision plays in the passage of an African girl into womanhood, and the reinforcement this ritual cutting plays in affirming the responsibilities of the African male. Kopelman's argument is based on a total distortion of the vital function female circumcision plays in the education girls from some African traditions need in their transition to womanhood. The reasons Kopelman cites are widely accepted by non-Africans (and some Africans) who do not truly understand or appreciate the depths of African rites of passage. I have provided details on this distortion elsewhere, in an article published in the *Journal of Black Studies* on "Demythologization and Demystification of African Initiation Rites: A Positive and Meaningful Education Aspect Heading for Extinction." In that article I pointed out the stereotypes critics of the African rites of passage use in misinterpreting this practice. Most of the stereotyped arguments do not acknowledge the considerable education that precedes the circumcision ceremony. This education provides an essential base of knowledge for the young woman to make the transition from childhood to adulthood. This education incorporates sex education, discipline, moral foundation, and gender awareness, a rare aspect in the socialization of today's youth in the United States of America.

My argument is that the education that precedes female circumcision enhances the psychological and social aspects that help shape the identity of African womanhood. This will be lost if the ritual is discontinued. These rites of passage provide a foundation of one's entire life which involves the awareness of the rules of the society and philosophy that guides such rules. This foundation provides young women—and men—with the essence of who they are and the framework of what they aspire to be. It provides the young person with confidence, efficacy and self-respect, which enhances the capacity to respect and value others as human beings. After this lesson, it is hard for the young person to take someone else's life or his/her own, a common occurrence in western societies. It is also establishes ownership of property, beginning with the gifts the initiates receive. This leads to developing responsible management skills needed to survive throughout a woman's life. The initiation and the knowledge achieved before and after circumcision give a young woman (or man) a sense of belonging or permanence. Consequently, one is very unlikely to find a young initiate feeling alienated from her or his society as we see in today's societies where children and teens find their identity in joining gangs or cults. Even in Africa today teenage pregnancies and youth violence, which were unheard of in precolonial times, are on the rise. Unfortunately these pregnancies are mostly caused by older men with teenage girls. Before the colonial powers began their campaign against African rites of passage, teen pregnancies were rare because both the teenagers and the older men knew that it was taboo to have sex before marriage and to have children one is not going to be responsible for.

Stereotypical Reasons Given by Kopelman and Others

Kopelman begins her argument for banning all female circumcision by citing several studies conducted by people who come from places where female infibulation and genital mutilation are widely practiced. Using these studies, she lists five reasons she attributes to those seeking to justify this practice: (1) This ritual satisfies a religious requirement, (2) It preserves group identity, (3) It helps maintain cleanliness, (4) It preserves virginity and family honor and prevents immorality, and (5) It furthers marriage goals, including greater sexual pleasure. Invalid as these reasons may be in supporting the morality and acceptability of female circumcision, the problem is that they are common "straw men" arguments set up by opponents of all female circumcision because they are easily refuted. In focusing on these stereotyped and culturally biased reasons, Kopelman and other critics totally ignore and fail to deal with the main purpose of why the circumcision ritual is performed by most Africans.

Of course, anyone who is presented with these five superficial arguments and is not informed about the true core meaning of female circumcision would be easily convinced that the ritual is barbarous and should be stopped immediately. Kopelman fails to point out why this ritual has prevailed for such a long time. Instead, she focuses on the most brutal and inhumane aspects (infibulation and mutilation), which are practiced by just a few African groups. She refers to these groups as Islamic-influenced peoples, even though she admits that among the few people who practice the extreme version, their practice predates the Islamic era. Nor does she explain which particular group of people or pharonic era first practiced these extremes. This careless reference leads people to forget that there are many other forms of the ritual which have the same symbolic meaning but do not involve the extremes of infibulation or clitoridectomy. These practices are performed safely. Some do not even involve circumcision but scarification for the purpose of shedding a little blood, a symbol of courage that is a universal component of male adolescent rites of passage. It is easy for someone like Kopelman not too see the importance of this symbolism, especially when she does not have any similar positive educational experience with which to compare it. Her argument therefore paints with a broad brush on the diversity within the African continent, and her position takes away the very essence of being of most Africans. Also, like other insensitive commentators on African cultures, she fails to point out how the influence of chastity and preservation of virginity for "man's pleasure" has been introduced in both cultural and religious perspectives from outside black Africa. European missionaries and colonialists, preceded by Arabs, followed the same pattern she adopts. Such attitudes have resulted in many Africans abandoning their traditional ways of life. This has created the many identity crises that Africans experience today.

As Africans have adopted attitudes alien to their culture when they interact with the non-Africans who reject and penalize their practice of traditional rites of passage, identity crises have gripped African societies. Examples of such crises are the increase of violence, teen pregnancies, and genocide, which were rare when the rites of passage were in effect. These crises have culminated in the destruction of the base foundation that guides Africans in conceptualizing who they are as human beings. This destruction of traditional cultures and their rites of passage has also resulted in Africans being viewed as objects of exploitation marginal to European culture, and becoming subjects to be acted upon rather than actors of their own way of life, for example, defining who they are as opposed to being defined by others. Kopelman adds wounds to the deep destruction of African cultures that has been imposed on them through miseducation. Like the colonialists before her, she is driven by hegemony in her value system and judgments of other cultures.

A Culturally Sensitive Alternative

In calling for the total abolition of all forms of female circumcision, Kopelman fails to offer any alternative that might be culturally accepted by both African immigrants and those adhering to the dominant Euro-American values of the United States. Instead of suggesting a substitute ritual that would fulfill the main purpose of female circumcision, Kopelman describes all forms of this varied cultural practice, even the most simple and symbolic, as a brutal ritual. She obviously does not think the people who practice this ritual are capable of making adjustments to end the atrocities and sometimes deadly consequences that frequently accompany this rite when practiced in lands where the majority of people have little or no knowledge of sterile techniques or access to modern medical care. She ignores the possibility that an alternative ritual might be accepted by peoples who have practiced female circumcision for centuries.

Let me cite an example of what I mean by a mutually acceptable form of female circumcision that would respect the ancient traditions of some African immigrants and at the same time avoid all the negative consequences of genital mutilation and infibulation. This simple but elegant alternative emerged from discussions between the staff at one American hospital and a group of Somali and other African refugees who have recently settled in Seattle, Washington, clinging to their traditions and insisting that their daughters undergo the ritual of genital cutting.

The staff at Seattle's Harborview Medical Center faced this problem when refugee mothers were asked before delivery if they wanted their baby circumcised if it was a boy. Some mothers responded, "Yes, and also if it is a girl." The hospital, which has a long history of sensitivity to diverse cultures and customs, convened a committee of doctors to discuss what to do about the requests. The hospital staff proposed a compromise, a simple, symbolic cut in the clitoral hood to draw a couple of drops of blood, which could be used in the ritual to bond the girl with the earth, her family and clan. Despite the sensationalized publicity given to the more brutal forms of genital mutilation and infibulation, this symbolic nicking of the clitoral hood to shed a few drops of blood is in fact what most Africans outside Somalia, the Sudan, and Ethiopia do in their female circumcisions.

However, when this suggested alternative became public knowledge, it threw the liberal city of Seattle into turmoil.

Mazurka Ramsey, an Ethiopian immigrant whose San Jose–based group, Forward USA, seeks to eliminate the ritual completely, asked: "How dare it even cross their mind? What the Somali, what the immigrants like me need is an education, not sensitivity to culture." Unlike Ramsey, who is eager to cast off her cultural heritage and adopt American values, other refugee parents continue to press to have their daughters circumcised, even though the Seattle Somali community has essentially agreed that the practice should be ended.

"You cannot take away the rights of families and women," Hersi Mohamed, a Somali elder, said. "As leaders and elders of the community we cannot force a mother to accept the general idea of the community. She can say, 'I want my girl to have letting of blood.'"

Though this is an issue physicians and hospitals across the country are facing with increasing regularity, Harborview is the only hospital so far to discuss the problem openly as a public health issue, rather than treating it simply as an outdated barbaric rite that should be wiped out and totally banned.

A new federal law, in effect since April 1997, sets a prison sentence of up to 5 years for anyone who "circumcises, excises, or infibulates" the genitals of girls under age 18. With some 150,000 females of African origin in the United States having already been cut or facing the possibility of being cut, the compromise suggested by Harborview Hospital makes good sense as an attempt to save girls from the most drastic forms of this ritual.

As the *Chicago Tribune* reported:

> "It would be a small cut to the prepuce, the hood above the clitoris, with no tissue excised, and this would be conducted under local anesthetic for children old enough to understand the procedure and give consent in combination with informed consent of the parents," said Harborview spokeswoman Tina Mankowski.
>
> "We are trying to provide a relatively safe procedure to a population of young women who traditionally have had some horrendous things done to them," she said, but added, "We are not now doing female circumcisions at Harborview, nor are we considering doing female circumcisions."
>
> Whether the proposal would be prohibited by the new law is one of the legal questions being reviewed by the Washington state attorney general.

The hospital's medical director will make no final decision on the proposal until the legal review is completed and a community-wide discussion is held, Mankowski said.

The Seattle area is home to about 3,500 members of a fast-growing Somali community. Some Somali and other African immigrants here have made it clear how deeply ingrained the practice is in their cultural and religious views.

Somali men and women told *The Seattle Times* their daughters would be shamed, dishonored and unmarriageable if they were not cut, an act they believe shows their purity.

They also said that if they could not get it done in the U.S. they would pay the $1,500 fare to fly their daughters to their homeland, where they face the extreme version of the cutting ritual. Some, but not all, of them said a symbolic cut on their daughters would be enough.

Unfortunately, the compromise collapsed when a group of feminists threatened to file a lawsuit charging the hospital staff with violation of the new federal law.

Instead of being creative and flexible like the staff at Harborview Hospital, Kopelman takes a dogmatic culturally-biased stance and calls on us to get rid of a cultural practice that predates European cultures, a custom that provides a foundation for many Africans' cultural identity. In essence, she suggests that Africans should abandon their way of life and become culture-less or ritualless societies just as American society is. When a culture has no meaningful rites of passage for its youth, the young grow up without a sense of belonging, continuity and permanence, an experience of many youth and adults in both contemporary Africa and present American societies. As a result, psychologists and other mental health professionals are needed to provide a substitute ritual and rite of passage for many youth and adults looking for their identity. This search was unnecessary and rare in traditional African societies because they had meaningful rites of passage. Without a good foundation of identity development based on meaningful traditional rites of passage, many recent young immigrants from Africa try to cope or compensate with facial reconstructions, liposuctions, changing of skin color or bleaching (melanin) destruction, selfhate, bulemia, obesity, suicides and other types of self-abuse. Without rituals to confirm their respect for women, immigrant African males may come to treat women as objects as opposed to equal human beings.

The alternative I propose is a careful interpretation of the meaning of other peoples' cultures and examining them from their own perspective before jumping to judgments. Failure to take this approach only makes the situation worse. I therefore propose an alternative of just nicking the clitoris enough to perform the symbolic rituals. This would be preceded by the most important part, the education of a girl for the responsibilities of womanhood and a full explanation of the importance of the practice. This nicking would of course be done in a sanitized condition by a licensed physician. A careful analysis, as free of cultural bias as possible, should allow the continuation of many rites of passage that are an ancient part of immigrant cultures.

I also suggest that before we make sweeping generalizations about cultural practices, we should try to look into the perspective of the people we are trying to critique. Some practices may be a little difficult to understand, but with a careful, sensitive approach, it may be simpler than one might think. A great way to attempt to understand others is to learn their language as an avenue to a better understanding of the values and philosophical perspective. This is close to "walking in someone else's shoes," the best practice in cross-cultural and inter-cultural awareness.

POSTSCRIPT

Should Female
Circumcision Be Banned?

Sociologists and cultural anthropologists talk about "enculturation" as the process whereby people from one society and culture migrate from their homeland to another place where they have to adjust to a new culture with different values, attitudes, and behaviors.

Enculturation is a two-sided process. The obvious side involves the adjustments that the immigrants must make as they become acquainted with and part of the new society. The immigrants slowly, sometimes painfully, adjust their attitudes, behaviors, and values to accommodate the dominant majority society in which they are one of perhaps many minorities. They also gradually adopt some of the majority values and behaviors, even as they modify their own traditions. Sometimes, to avoid conflict, they may conceal from outsiders some of their more "unusual" attitudes and behaviors—"unusual" meaning unfamiliar to the majority—to avoid being singled out and discriminated against.

The less obvious side of enculturation is the inevitable adjustments that occur among people in the majority culture as they encounter and interact with minority immigrants who are in the process of moving into the mainstream and becoming part of the general culture. The issue of female genital cutting is typical of this process.

In late 1997 a report from Kenya illustrated the advantages of cultural sensitivity and the need to avoid imposing our values on other cultures. This report was published by Maendeleo ya Wanawake, the Kenyan national women's organization, and the Seattle, Washington–based Program for Appropriate Technology in Health, a nonprofit international organization for women's and children's health. They reported that a growing number of rural Kenyan families are turning to a new ritual called *Ntanira na Mugambo,* or "Circumcision Through Words." Developed by several Kenyan and international nongovernmental agencies working together for six years, "Circumcision Through Words" brings young girls together for a week of seclusion during which they learn traditional teachings about their coming roles as women, parents, and adults in the community, as well as more modern messages about personal health, reproductive issues, hygiene, communications skills, self-esteem, and dealing with peer pressure. A community celebration of song, dance, and feasting affirms the girls and their new place in the community.

As more and more immigrants enter the United States and become part of its ethnic and cultural diversity, the challenges of enculturation are likely to become more complex and demanding. Hence the importance of understanding the current debate over female circumcision. Most articles on the subject denounce the practice and call for a complete ban on any form of female circumcision. This side has now been canonized by enactment of the federal ban. As of late 1997 only P. Masila Mutisya has dared to raise the possibility of some kind of accommodation. What do you think of this seemingly one-sided debate?

Suggested Readings

R. Abcaria, "Rite or Wrong: Female Circumcisions Are Still Performed on African Continent," *Fayetteville Observer Times* (June 14, 1993).

A. M. A'Haleem, "Claiming Our Bodies and Our Rights: Exploring Female Circumcision as an Act of Violence," in M. Schuler, ed., *Freedom From Violence: Women's Strategies From Around the World* (Widbooks, 1992).

M. B. Assad, "Female Circumcision in Egypt: Social Implications, Current Research, and Prospects for Change," *Studies in Family Planning* (January 1980).

T. Brune, "Compromise Plan on Circumcision of Girls Gets Little Support," *Chicago Tribune* (October 28, 1996).

E. Dorkenoo, *Cutting the Rose: Female Genital Mutilation—The Practice and Its Prevention* (Minority Rights Group, 1994).

O. Koso-Thomas, *The Circumcision of Women: A Strategy for Eradication* (Zed Books, 1992).

M. Mutisya, "Demythologization and Demystification of African Initiation Rites: A Positive and Meaningful Educational Aspect Heading for Extinction," *Journal of Black Studies* (September 1996).

C. M. Nangoli, *No More Lies About Africa: Here Is the Truth From an African* (African Heritage Publishers, 1986).

Federal Communications Commission (FCC)

The FCC is a U.S. government agency charged with regulating interstate and international communications by radio, television, wire, satellite, and cable.

http://www.fcc.gov

Electronic Frontier Foundation

The Electronic Frontier Foundation works to educate the press, policymakers, and the general public about civil liberties issues related to technology.

http://www.eff.org.

Rape, Abuse, & Incest National Network (RAINN)

RAINN is the nation's largest anti-sexual assault organization. It operates the National Sexual Assault Hotline at 1-800-656-HOPE and carries out programs to prevent sexual assault, help victims, and ensure that rapists are brought to justice.

http://www.rainn.org/

Stem Cell Information

This Web site, operated by the National Institutes of Health, provides basic information on stem cells and links describing the status of research and federal policy.

http://stemcells.nih/gov

The Kinsey Institute for Research

The Kinsey Institute for Research is a private, not-for-profit corporation affiliated with Indiana University. The Kinsey Institute promotes interdisciplinary research and scholarship in the fields of human sexuality, gender, and reproduction.

http://www.indiana.edu/~kinsey/

Alternatives to Marriage Project

The Alternatives to Marriage Project advocates for equality and fairness for unmarried people, including people who choose not to marry, cannot marry, or live together before marriage.

http://www.unmarried.org

National Marriage Project

The mission of the National Marriage Project is to provide research and analysis on the state of marriage in America and to educate the public on the social, economic, and cultural conditions affecting marital success and child well-being.

http://marriage.rutgers.edu

PART 2

Social Issues

*C*ompeting *philosophical forces drive concerns about human sexuality on a societal level. Some are primarily focused on the well-being of individuals (or groups of individuals) and their right to individual expression versus their protection from harm; others are mainly concerned with either maintaining or questioning established social norms; still others are engaged by the question of whether or not tax dollars should be used to fund programs and research not endorsed by all. This section examines eight such questions that affect our social understanding of sexuality.*

- Should Sexual Content on the Internet Be Restricted?

- Should the FCC Restrict Broadcast "Indecency"?

- Is Pornography Harmful to Women?

- Is Pedophilia Always Harmful?

- Should Federal Funding of Stem Cell Research Be Restricted?

- Should Sexuality Research Receive Public Funding?

- Do Schools Perpetuate a Gender Bias?

- Should Society Support Cohabitation Before Marriage?

ISSUE 10

Should Sexual Content on the Internet Be Restricted?

YES: Stephen G. Breyer, from the dissenting opinion in *Ashcroft v. American Civil Liberties Union* (June 29, 2004)

NO: Anthony M. Kennedy, from the Court's opinion in *Ashcroft v. American Civil Liberties Union* (June 29, 2004)

ISSUE SUMMARY

YES: In a dissenting opinion, United States Supreme Court Justice Stephen G. Breyer argues that the Child Online Protection Act does not impose an unreasonable burden on free speech, and should have been upheld by the high court.

NO: Explaining the Supreme Court's decision to strike down the Child Online Protection Act, Justice Anthony M. Kennedy says that filtering software is a better and less restrictive alternative for protecting children from sexual content on the Internet.

Sexual content is available *everywhere* on the Internet. A search for the word "sex" on the popular search engine google.com yields 181 million results. Many of these links will direct Internet travelers to erotic or pornographic sites, but many of the links will also lead to useful information sites. Among the first sites listed in a Google search will be sxetc.org, a reliable sexuality information Web site by teens for teens. Another site, safersex.org, will give viewers helpful hints about protection from sexually transmitted infections. Other non-pornographic sites returned in such a search include links to the Kinsey Institute and the Sexuality Information and Education Council of the United States (SIECUS), not to mention fan sites for HBO's popular *Sex and the City* and one for the punk rock band, the Sex Pistols! (One can even find a link for this book in such a search!)

Despite the many useful and "legitimate" Web sites that are returned when searching for "sex" online, there are also many that concern people. Erotic, obscene, or pornographic material is a click away for anyone who looks for it. Sometimes sexual material finds Web surfers, even when they aren't looking. Instant messages may pop up on one's screen offering unsolicited links to view erotic pictures. Unwelcome e-mail may offer discounts on Viagra or penis and breast enhancements. Most adults will navigate the Internet through unwanted material without worrying too much about it, but passions heat up when it comes to sexual material that arrives on the computer screens of children.

The Child Online Protection Act (COPA) was drafted by Congress to address the high volume of sexual content to which children may be routinely exposed when connected to the Internet. Other media have governmentally imposed restrictions on sexual content. Television and radio are limited in the sexual content it can depict or discuss. Newspapers and magazines also limit sexual content. When sexual content is their trade (such as *Playboy* or other erotic magazines), age and access restrictions apply.

COPA was conceptualized to address unregulated sexual content online deemed "harmful to minors" by requiring Web sites with such material to have their patrons give their credit card information for entry (or to otherwise employ technology to prevent minors from accessing the Web site). COPA would impose penalties of $50,000 and six months in prison for those who would knowingly post material that is "harmful to minors" without such mechanisms to prevent minors from entering.

Free speech advocates challenged COPA in court. The American Civil Liberties Union (ACLU) argued that sexual content could already be regulated by concerned parents using filtering software to prevent their children from viewing sexual material online. Such technology, the ACLU argued, would protect minors from material their parents did not want them to see, while not imposing any new burdens on providers or legitimate consumers of erotic materials. The challenge eventually made its way to the United States Supreme Court, in the form of a "writ of certiorari" (or a request for the Supreme Court to review a lower court's decision). After reviewing the case, the Supreme Court upheld the decisions of lower courts, effectively striking down COPA.

In the following essays, Supreme Court Justices Stephen G. Breyer and Anthony M. Kennedy explain their differing perspectives on this decision. Justice Breyer argues that the high court should have upheld COPA, since it did not impose unreasonable expectations on Web site providers. In speaking for the court majority, Justice Kennedy argues that Internet filtering software is less restrictive than COPA, and likely more effective in restricting children's access to material that may cause harm.

Stephen G. Breyer

 **YES**

John D. Ashcroft, Attorney General, Petitioner *v.* American Civil Liberties Union et al.

Justice Breyer, with whom The Chief Justice and Justice O'Connor join, dissenting.

The Child Online Protection Act (Act), seeks to protect children from exposure to commercial pornography placed on the Internet. It does so by requiring commercial providers to place pornographic material behind Internet "screens" readily accessible to adults who produce age verification. The Court recognizes that we should "'proceed . . . with care before invalidating the Act,'" while pointing out that the "imperative of according respect to the Congress . . . does not permit us to depart from well-established First Amendment principles." I agree with these generalities. Like the Court, I would subject the Act to "the most exacting scrutiny," requiring the Government to show that any restriction of nonobscene expression is "narrowly drawn" to further a "compelling interest" and that the restriction amounts to the "least restrictive means" available to further that interest.

Nonetheless, my examination of (1) the burdens the Act imposes on protected expression, (2) the Act's ability to further a compelling interest, and (3) the proposed "less restrictive alternatives" convinces me that the Court is wrong. I cannot accept its conclusion that Congress could have accomplished its statutory objective—protecting children from commercial pornography on the Internet—in other, less restrictive ways.

I

Although the Court rests its conclusion upon the existence of less restrictive alternatives, I must first examine the burdens that the Act imposes upon protected speech. That is because the term "less restrictive alternative" is a comparative term. An "alternative" is "less restrictive" only if it will work less First Amendment harm than the statute itself, while at the same time similarly furthering the "compelling" interest that prompted Congress to enact the statute. Unlike the majority, I do not see how it is possible to make this comparative

Ashcroft v. American Civil Liberties Union, United States Supreme Court, No. 03-218 (June 29, 2004).

determination without examining both the extent to which the Act regulates protected expression and the nature of the burdens it imposes on that expression. That examination suggests that the Act, properly interpreted, imposes a burden on protected speech that is no more than modest.

A

The Act's definitions limit the material it regulates to material that does not enjoy First Amendment protection, namely legally obscene material, and very little more. A comparison of this Court's definition of unprotected, "legally obscene," material with the Act's definitions makes this clear.

Material is legally obscene if

> "(a) . . . 'the average person, applying contemporary community standards' would find that the work, taken as a whole, appeals to the prurient interest . . . ; (b) . . . the work depicts or describes, in a patently offensive way, sexual conduct specifically defined by the applicable state law; and (c) . . . the work, taken as a whole, lacks serious literary, artistic, political, or scientific value."

The present statute defines the material that it regulates as material that meets all of the following criteria:

> "(A) the average person, applying contemporary community standards, would find, taking the material as a whole *and with respect to minors,* [that the material] is designed to appeal to, or is designed to pander to, the prurient interest;
>
> "(B) [the material] depicts, describes, or represents, in a manner patently offensive *with respect to minors,* an actual or simulated sexual act or sexual contact, an actual or simulated normal or perverted sexual act, or a lewd exhibition of the genitals or post-pubescent female breast; and
>
> "(C) [the material] taken as a whole, lacks serious literary, artistic, political, or scientific value *for minors.*"

Both definitions define the relevant material through use of the critical terms "prurient interest" and "lacks serious literary, artistic, political, or scientific value." Insofar as material appeals to, or panders to, "the prurient interest," it simply seeks a sexual response. Insofar as "patently offensive" material with "no serious value" simply seeks that response, it does not seek to educate, it does not seek to elucidate views about sex, it is not artistic, and it is not literary. Compare, *e.g., Erznoznik* v. *Jacksonville* (invalidating an ordinance regulating nudity in films, where the ban was not confined to "sexually explicit nudity" or otherwise limited), with *Ginzburg* v. *United States* (finding unprotected material that was "created, represented, and sold solely as a claimed instrument of the sexual stimulation it would bring"). That is why this Court, in *Miller* [v. *California*], held that the First Amendment did not protect material that fit its definition.

The only significant difference between the present statute and *Miller's* definition consists of the addition of the words "with respect to minors," and "for minors." But the addition of these words to a definition that would otherwise cover only obscenity expands the statute's scope only slightly. That is because the material in question (while potentially harmful to young children) must, first, appeal to the "prurient interest" of, *i.e.,* seek a sexual response from, some group of adolescents or postadolescents (since young children normally do not so respond). And material that appeals to the "prurient interest[s]" of some group of adolescents or postadolescents will almost inevitably appeal to the "prurient interest[s]" of some group of adults as well.

The "lack of serious value" requirement narrows the statute yet further— despite the presence of the qualification "for minors." That is because one cannot easily imagine material that has serious literary, artistic, political, or scientific value for a significant group of adults, but lacks such value for any significant group of minors. Thus, the statute, read literally, insofar as it extends beyond the legally obscene, could reach only borderline cases. And to take the words of the statute literally is consistent with Congress' avowed objective in enacting this law; namely, putting material produced by professional pornographers behind screens that will verify the age of the viewer.

These limitations on the statute's scope answer many of the concerns raised by those who attack its constitutionality. Respondents fear prosecution for the Internet posting of material that does not fall within the statute's ambit as limited by the "prurient interest" and "no serious value" requirements; for example: an essay about a young man's experience with masturbation and sexual shame; "a serious discussion about birth control practices, homosexuality, . . . or the consequences of prison rape"; an account by a 15-year-old, written for therapeutic purposes, of being raped when she was 13; a guide to self-examination for testicular cancer; a graphic illustration of how to use a condom; or any of the other postings of modern literary or artistic works or discussions of sexual identity, homosexuality, sexually transmitted diseases, sex education, or safe sex, let alone Aldous Huxley's Brave New World, J. D. Salinger's Catcher in the Rye, or, as the complaint would have it, "Ken Starr's report on the Clinton-Lewinsky scandal."

These materials are *not* both (1) "designed to appeal to, or . . . pander to, the prurient interest" of significant groups of minors *and* (2) lacking in "serious literary, artistic, political, or scientific value" for significant groups of minors. Thus, they fall outside the statute's definition of the material that it restricts, a fact the Government acknowledged at oral argument.

I have found nothing elsewhere in the statute's language that broadens its scope. Other qualifying phrases, such as "taking the material as a whole" and "for commercial purposes" limit the statute's scope still more, requiring, for example, that individual images be considered in context. In sum, the Act's definitions limit the statute's scope to commercial pornography. It affects unprotected obscene material. Given the inevitable uncertainty about how to characterize close-to-obscene material, it could apply to (or chill the production of) a limited class of borderline material that courts might ultimately find is protected. But the examples I have just given fall outside that class.

B

The Act does not censor the material it covers. Rather, it requires providers of the "harmful to minors" material to restrict minors' access to it by verifying age. They can do so by inserting screens that verify age using a credit card, adult personal identification number, or other similar technology. In this way, the Act requires creation of an internet screen that minors, but not adults, will find difficult to bypass.

I recognize that the screening requirement imposes some burden on adults who seek access to the regulated material, as well as on its providers. The cost is, in part, monetary. The parties agreed that a Web site could store card numbers or passwords at between 15 and 20 cents per number. And verification services provide free verification to Web site operators, while charging users less than $20 per year. According to the trade association for the commercial pornographers who are the statute's target, use of such verification procedures is "standard practice" in their online operations.

In addition to the monetary cost, and despite strict requirements that identifying information be kept confidential, the identification requirements inherent in age-screening may lead some users to fear embarrassment. Both monetary costs and potential embarrassment can deter potential viewers and, in that sense, the statute's requirements may restrict access to a site. But this Court has held that in the context of congressional efforts to protect children, restrictions of this kind do not automatically violate the Constitution. And the Court has approved their use. See, *United States* v. *American Library Assn., Inc.* ("[T]he Constitution does not guarantee the right to acquire information at a public library without any risk of embarrassment"). (O'Connor, J., concurring in judgment in part and dissenting in part) (calling the age-verification requirement similar to "a bouncer [who] checks a person's driver's license before admitting him to a nightclub").

In sum, the Act at most imposes a modest additional burden on adult access to legally obscene material, perhaps imposing a similar burden on access to some protected borderline obscene material as well.

II

I turn next to the question of "compelling interest," that of protecting minors from exposure to commercial pornography. No one denies that such an interest is "compelling." Rather, the question here is whether the Act, given its restrictions on adult access, significantly advances that interest. In other words, is the game worth the candle?

The majority argues that it is not, because of the existence of "blocking and filtering software." The majority refers to the presence of that software as a "less restrictive alternative." But that is a misnomer—a misnomer that may lead the reader to believe that all we need do is look to see if the blocking and filtering software is less restrictive; and to believe that, because in one sense it is (one can turn off the software), that is the end of the constitutional matter.

But such reasoning has no place here. Conceptually speaking, the presence of filtering software is not an *alternative* legislative approach to the problem of protecting children from exposure to commercial pornography. Rather, it is part of the status quo, *i.e.*, the backdrop against which Congress enacted the present statute. It is always true, by definition, that the status quo is less restrictive than a new regulatory law. It is always less restrictive to do *nothing* than to do *something*. But "doing nothing" does not address the problem Congress sought to address–namely that, despite the availability of filtering software, children were still being exposed to harmful material on the Internet.

Thus, the relevant constitutional question is not the question the Court asks: Would it be less restrictive to do nothing? Of course it would be. Rather, the relevant question posits a comparison of (a) a status quo that includes filtering software with (b) a change in that status quo that adds to it an age-verification screen requirement. Given the existence of filtering software, does the problem Congress identified remain significant? Does the Act help to address it? These are questions about the relation of the Act to the compelling interest. Does the Act, compared to the status quo, significantly advance the ball? (An affirmative answer to these questions will not justify "[a]ny restriction on speech," as the Court claims, for a final answer in respect to constitutionality must take account of burdens and alternatives as well.)

The answers to these intermediate questions are clear: Filtering software, as presently available, does not solve the "child protection" problem. It suffers from four serious inadequacies that prompted Congress to pass legislation instead of relying on its voluntary use. First, its filtering is faulty, allowing some pornographic material to pass through without hindrance. Just last year, in *American Library Assn.*, Justice Stevens described "fundamental defects in the filtering software that is now available or that will be available in the foreseeable future." He pointed to the problem of underblocking: "Because the software relies on key words or phrases to block undesirable sites, it does not have the capacity to exclude a precisely defined category of images." That is to say, in the absence of words, the software alone cannot distinguish between the most obscene pictorial image and the Venus de Milo. No Member of this Court disagreed.

Second, filtering software costs money. Not every family has the $40 or so necessary to install it. By way of contrast, age screening costs less.

Third, filtering software depends upon parents willing to decide where their children will surf the Web and able to enforce that decision. As to millions of American families, that is not a reasonable possibility. More than 28 million school age children have both parents or their sole parent in the work force, at least 5 million children are left alone at home without supervision each week, and many of those children will spend afternoons and evenings with friends who may well have access to computers and more lenient parents.

Fourth, software blocking lacks precision, with the result that those who wish to use it to screen out pornography find that it blocks a great deal of material that is valuable. As Justice Stevens pointed out, "the software's reliance on words to identify undesirable sites necessarily results in the blocking of thousands of pages that contain content that is completely innocuous for both adults and minors, and that no rational person could conclude matches the filtering companies' category definitions, such as pornography or sex." Indeed, the American Civil Liberties Union (ACLU), one of the respondents here, told Congress that filtering software "block[s] out valuable and protected information, such as information about the Quaker religion, and web sites including those of the American Association of University Women, the AIDS Quilt, the Town Hall Political Site (run by the Family Resource Center, Christian Coalition and other conservative groups)." The software "is simply incapable of discerning between constitutionally protected and unprotected speech." It "inappropriately blocks valuable, protected speech, and does not effectively block the sites [it is] intended to block."

Nothing in the District Court record suggests the contrary. No respondent has offered to produce evidence at trial to the contrary. No party has suggested, for example, that technology allowing filters to interpret and discern among images has suddenly become, or is about to become, widely available. Indeed, the Court concedes that "[f]iltering software, of course, is not a perfect solution to the problem."

In sum, a "filtering software status quo" means filtering that underblocks, imposes a cost upon each family that uses it, fails to screen outside the home, and lacks precision. Thus, Congress could reasonably conclude that a system that relies entirely upon the use of such software is not an effective system. And a law that adds to that system an age-verification screen requirement significantly increases the system's efficacy. That is to say, at a modest additional cost to those adults who wish to obtain access to a screened program, that law will bring about better, more precise blocking, both inside and outside the home.

The Court's response—that 40% of all pornographic material may be of foreign origin—is beside the point. Even assuming (I believe unrealistically) that *all* foreign originators will refuse to use screening, the Act would make a difference in respect to 60% of the Internet's commercial pornography. I cannot call that difference insignificant.

The upshot is that Congress could reasonably conclude that, despite the current availability of filtering software, a child protection problem exists. It also could conclude that a precisely targeted regulatory statute, adding an age-verification requirement for a narrow range of material, would more effectively shield children from commercial pornography.

Is this justification sufficient? The lower courts thought not. But that is because those courts interpreted the Act as imposing far more than a modest burden. They assumed an interpretation of the statute in which it reached far beyond legally obscene and borderline-obscene material, affecting material that, given the interpretation set forth above, would fall well outside the Act's scope. But we must interpret the Act to save it, not to destroy it. So interpreted, the Act imposes a far lesser burden on access to protected material. Given the modest nature of that burden and the likelihood that the Act will significantly further Congress' compelling objective, the Act may well satisfy the First Amendment's stringent tests. Indeed, it does satisfy the First Amendment unless, of course, there is a genuine alternative, "less restrictive" way similarly to further that objective.

III

I turn, then, to the actual "less restrictive alternatives" that the Court proposes. The Court proposes two real alternatives, *i.e.,* two potentially less restrictive ways in which Congress might alter the status quo in order to achieve its "compelling" objective.

First, the Government might "act to encourage" the use of blocking and filtering software. The problem is that any argument that rests upon this alternative proves too much. If one imagines enough government resources devoted to the problem and perhaps additional scientific advances, then, of course, the use of software might become as effective and less restrictive. Obviously, the Government could give all parents, schools, and Internet cafes free computers with filtering programs already installed, hire federal employees to train parents and teachers on their use, and devote millions of dollars to the development of better software. The result might be an alternative that is extremely effective.

But the Constitution does not, because it cannot, require the Government to disprove the existence of magic solutions, *i.e.,* solutions that, put in general terms, will solve any problem less restrictively but with equal effectiveness.

Otherwise, "the undoubted ability of lawyers and judges," who are not constrained by the budgetary worries and other practical parameters within which Congress must operate, "to imagine *some* kind of slightly less drastic or restrictive an approach would make it impossible to write laws that deal with the harm that called the statute into being." As Justice Blackmun recognized, a "judge would be unimaginative indeed if he could not come up with something a little less 'drastic' or a little less 'restrictive' in almost any situation, and thereby enable himself to vote to strike legislation down." Perhaps that is why no party has argued seriously that additional expenditure of government funds to encourage the use of screening is a "less restrictive alternative."

Second, the majority suggests decriminalizing the statute, noting the "chilling effect" of criminalizing a category of speech. To remove a major sanction, however, would make the statute less effective, virtually by definition.

IV

My conclusion is that the Act, as properly interpreted, risks imposition of minor burdens on some protected material—burdens that adults wishing to view the material may overcome at modest cost. At the same time, it significantly helps to achieve a compelling congressional goal, protecting children from exposure to commercial pornography. There is no serious, practically available "less restrictive" way similarly to further this compelling interest. Hence the Act is constitutional.

V

The Court's holding raises two more general questions. First, what has happened to the "constructive discourse between our courts and our legislatures" that "is an integral and admirable part of the constitutional design"? After eight years of legislative effort, two statutes, and three Supreme Court cases the Court sends this case back to the District Court for further proceedings. What proceedings? I have found no offer by either party to present more relevant evidence. What remains to be litigated? I know the Court says that the parties may "introduce further evidence" as to the "relative restrictiveness and effectiveness of alternatives to the statute." But I do not understand what that new evidence might consist of.

Moreover, Congress passed the current statute "[i]n response to the Court's decision in *Reno [v. American Civil Liberties Union]*" striking down an earlier statutory effort to deal with the same problem. Congress read *Reno* with care. It dedicated itself to the task of drafting a statute that would meet each and every criticism of the predecessor statute that this Court set forth in *Reno*. It incorporated language from the Court's precedents, particularly the *Miller* standard, virtually verbatim. And it created what it believed was a statute that would protect children from exposure to obscene professional pornography without obstructing adult access to material that the First Amendment protects. What else was Congress supposed to do?

I recognize that some Members of the Court, now or in the past, have taken the view that the First Amendment simply does not permit Congress to legislate in this area. ("[T]he Federal Government is without any power whatever under the Constitution to put any type of burden on speech and expression of ideas of any kind"). Others believe that the Amendment does not permit Congress to legislate in certain ways, *e.g.*, through the imposition of criminal penalties for obscenity. There are strong constitutional arguments favoring these views. But the Court itself does not adopt those views. Instead, it finds that the Government has not proved the nonexistence of "less restrictive alternatives." That finding, if appropriate here, is universally appropriate. And if universally appropriate, it denies to Congress, in practice, the legislative leeway that the Court's language seem to promise. If this statute does not pass the Court's "less restrictive alternative" test, what does? If nothing does, then the Court should say so clearly.

As I have explained, I believe the First Amendment permits an alternative holding. We could construe the statute narrowly—as I have tried to do—removing nearly all protected material from its scope. By doing so, we could reconcile its language with the First Amendment's demands. We would "save" the statute, "not . . . destroy it." And in the process, we would permit Congress to achieve its basic child-protecting objectives.

Second, will the majority's holding in practice mean greater or lesser protection for expression? I do not find the answer to this question obvious. The Court's decision removes an important weapon from the prosecutorial arsenal. That weapon would have given the Government a choice—a choice other than "ban totally or do nothing at all." The Act tells the Government that, instead of prosecuting bans on obscenity to the maximum extent possible (as respondents have urged as yet another "alternative"), it can insist that those who make available material that is obscene or close to obscene keep that material under wraps, making it readily available to adults who wish to see it, while restricting access to children. By providing this third option—a "middle way"—the Act avoids the need for potentially speech-suppressing prosecutions.

That matters in a world where the obscene and the nonobscene do not come tied neatly into separate, easily distinguishable, packages. In that real world, this middle way might well have furthered First Amendment interests by tempering the prosecutorial instinct in borderline cases. At least, Congress might have so believed. And this likelihood, from a First Amendment perspective, might ultimately have proved more protective of the rights of viewers to retain access to expression than the all-or-nothing choice available to prosecutors in the wake of the majority's opinion.

For these reasons, I dissent.

NO ⬅

John D. Ashcroft, Attorney General, Petitioner *v.* American Civil Liberties Union et al.

Justice Kennedy delivered the opinion of the Court.

This case presents a challenge to a statute enacted by Congress to protect minors from exposure to sexually explicit materials on the Internet, the Child Online Protection Act (COPA). We must decide whether the Court of Appeals was correct to affirm a ruling by the District Court that enforcement of COPA should be enjoined because the statute likely violates the First Amendment.

In enacting COPA, Congress gave consideration to our earlier decisions on this subject, in particular the decision in *Reno* v. *American Civil Liberties Union* (1997). For that reason, "the Judiciary must proceed with caution and . . . with care before invalidating the Act." The imperative of according respect to the Congress, however, does not permit us to depart from well-established First Amendment principles. Instead, we must hold the Government to its constitutional burden of proof.

Content-based prohibitions, enforced by severe criminal penalties, have the constant potential to be a repressive force in the lives and thoughts of a free people. To guard against that threat the Constitution demands that content-based restrictions on speech be presumed invalid, and that the Government bear the burden of showing their constitutionality. This is true even when Congress twice has attempted to find a constitutional means to restrict, and punish, the speech in question.

This case comes to the Court on certiorari review of an appeal from the decision of the District Court granting a preliminary injunction. The Court of Appeals reviewed the decision of the District Court for abuse of discretion. Under that standard, the Court of Appeals was correct to conclude that the District Court did not abuse its discretion in granting the preliminary injunction. The Government has failed, at this point, to rebut the plaintiffs' contention that there are plausible less restrictive alternatives to the statute. Substantial practical considerations, furthermore, argue in favor of upholding the injunction and allowing the case to proceed to trial. For those reasons, we affirm the

Ashcroft v. American Civil Liberties Union, United States Supreme Court, No. 03-218 (June 29, 2004).

decision of the Court of Appeals upholding the preliminary injunction, and we remand the case so that it may be returned to the District Court for trial on the issues presented.

I

A

COPA is the second attempt by Congress to make the Internet safe for minors by criminalizing certain Internet speech. The first attempt was the Communications Decency Act of 1996. The Court held the CDA unconstitutional because it was not narrowly tailored to serve a compelling governmental interest and because less restrictive alternatives were available.

In response to the Court's decision in *Reno*, Congress passed COPA. COPA imposes criminal penalties of a $50,000 fine and six months in prison for the knowing posting, for "commercial purposes," of World Wide Web content that is "harmful to minors." Material that is "harmful to minors" is defined as:

"any communication, picture, image, graphic image file, article, recording, writing, or other matter of any kind that is obscene or that—

"(A) the average person, applying contemporary community standards, would find, taking the material as a whole and with respect to minors, is designed to appeal to, or is designed to pander to, the prurient interest;

"(B) depicts, describes, or represents, in a manner patently offensive with respect to minors, an actual or simulated sexual act or sexual contact, an actual or simulated normal or perverted sexual act, or a lewd exhibition of the genitals or post-pubescent female breast; and

"(C) taken as a whole, lacks serious literary, artistic, political, or scientific value for minors."

"Minors" are defined as "any person under 17 years of age." A person acts for "commercial purposes only if such person is engaged in the business of making such communications." "Engaged in the business," in turn, "means that the person who makes a communication, or offers to make a communication, by means of the World Wide Web, that includes any material that is harmful to minors, devotes time, attention, or labor to such activities, as a regular course of such person's trade or business, with the objective of earning a profit as a result of such activities (although it is not necessary that the person make a profit or that the making or offering to make such communications be the person's sole or principal business or source of income)."

While the statute labels all speech that falls within these definitions as criminal speech, it also provides an affirmative defense to those who employ specified means to prevent minors from gaining access to the prohibited materials on their Web site. A person may escape conviction under the statute by demonstrating

NO / Anthony M. Kennedy

that he "has restricted access by minors to material that is harmful to minors—

> "(A) by requiring use of a credit card, debit account, adult access code, or adult personal identification number;
>
> "(B) by accepting a digital certificate that verifies age, or
>
> "(C) by any other reasonable measures that are feasible under available technology."

Since the passage of COPA, Congress has enacted additional laws regulating the Internet in an attempt to protect minors. For example, it has enacted a prohibition on misleading Internet domain names in order to prevent Web site owners from disguising pornographic Web sites in a way likely to cause uninterested persons to visit them (giving, as an example, the Web site "whitehouse.com"). It has also passed a statute creating a "Dot Kids" second-level Internet domain, the content of which is restricted to that which is fit for minors under the age of 13.

B

Respondents, Internet content providers and others concerned with protecting the freedom of speech, filed suit in the United States District Court for the Eastern District of Pennsylvania. They sought a preliminary injunction against enforcement of the statute. After considering testimony from witnesses presented by both respondents and the Government, the District Court issued an order granting the preliminary injunction. The court first noted that the statute would place a burden on some protected speech. The court then concluded that respondents were likely to prevail on their argument that there were less restrictive alternatives to the statute: "On the record to date, it is not apparent . . . that [petitioner] can meet its burden to prove that COPA is the least restrictive means available to achieve the goal of restricting the access of minors" to harmful material. In particular, it noted that "[t]he record before the Court reveals that blocking or filtering technology may be at least as successful as COPA would be in restricting minors' access to harmful material online without imposing the burden on constitutionally protected speech that COPA imposes on adult users or Web site operators."

The Government appealed the District Court's decision to the United States Court of Appeals for the Third Circuit. The Court of Appeals affirmed the preliminary injunction, but on a different ground. The court concluded that the "community standards" language in COPA by itself rendered the statute unconstitutionally overbroad. We granted certiorari and reversed, holding that the community-standards language did not, standing alone, make the statute unconstitutionally overbroad. We emphasized, however, that our decision was limited to that narrow issue. We remanded the case to the Court of Appeals to reconsider whether the District Court had been correct to grant the preliminary injunction. On remand, the Court of Appeals again affirmed the District Court. The Court of Appeals concluded that the statute was not narrowly tailored to serve a compelling Government interest, was overbroad, and was not the least restrictive means available for the Government to serve the interest of preventing minors from using the Internet to gain access to materials that are harmful to them. The Government once again sought review from this Court, and we again granted certiorari.

II

A

"This Court, like other appellate courts, has always applied the abuse of discretion standard on the review of a preliminary injunction." *Walters* v. *National Assn. of Radiation Survivors.* "The grant of appellate jurisdiction does not give the Court license to depart from established standards of appellate review." If the underlying constitutional question is close, therefore, we should uphold the injunction and remand for trial on the merits. Applying this mode of inquiry, we agree with the Court of Appeals that the District Court did not abuse its discretion in entering the preliminary injunction. Our reasoning in support of this conclusion, however, is based on a narrower, more specific grounds than the rationale the Court of Appeals adopted. The Court of Appeals, in its opinion affirming the decision of the District Court, construed a number of terms in the statute, and held that COPA, so construed, was unconstitutional. None of those constructions of statutory terminology, however, were relied on by or necessary to the conclusions of the District Court. Instead, the District Court concluded only that the statute was likely to burden some speech that is protected for adults, which petitioner does not dispute. As to the definitional disputes, the District Court concluded only that respondents' interpretation was "not unreasonable," and relied on their interpretation only to conclude that respondents had standing to challenge the statute, which, again, petitioner does not dispute. Because we affirm the District Court's decision to grant the preliminary injunction for the reasons relied on by the District Court, we decline to consider the correctness of the other arguments relied on by the Court of Appeals.

The District Court, in deciding to grant the preliminary injunction, concentrated primarily on the argument that there are plausible, less restrictive alternatives to COPA. A statute that "effectively suppresses a large amount of speech that adults have a constitutional right to receive and to address to one another ... is unacceptable if less restrictive alternatives would be at least as effective in achieving the legitimate purpose that the statute was enacted to serve." When plaintiffs challenge a content-based speech restriction, the burden is on the Government to prove that the proposed alternatives will not be as effective as the challenged statute.

In considering this question, a court assumes that certain protected speech may be regulated, and then asks what is the least restrictive alternative that can be used to achieve that goal. The purpose of the test is not to consider whether the challenged restriction has some effect in achieving Congress' goal, regardless of the restriction it imposes. The purpose of the test is to ensure that speech is restricted no further than necessary to achieve the goal, for it is important to assure that legitimate speech is not chilled or punished. For that reason, the test does not begin with the status quo of existing regulations, then ask whether the challenged restriction has some additional ability to achieve Congress' legitimate interest. Any restriction on speech could be justified under that analysis. Instead, the court should ask whether the challenged regulation is the least restrictive means among available, effective alternatives.

In deciding whether to grant a preliminary injunction stage, a district court must consider whether the plaintiffs have demonstrated that they are likely to prevail on the merits. (The court also considers whether the plaintiff has shown irreparable injury but the parties in this case do not contest the correctness of the District Court's conclusion that a likelihood of irreparable injury had been established.) As the Government bears the burden of proof on the ultimate question of COPA's constitutionality, respondents must be deemed likely to prevail unless the Government has shown that respondents' proposed less restrictive alternatives are less effective than COPA. Applying that analysis, the District Court concluded that respondents were likely to prevail. That conclusion was not an abuse of discretion, because on this record there are a number of plausible, less restrictive alternatives to the statute.

The primary alternative considered by the District Court was blocking and filtering software. Blocking and filtering software is an alternative that is less restrictive than COPA, and, in addition, likely more effective as a means of restricting children's access to materials harmful to them. The District Court, in granting the preliminary injunction, did so primarily because the plaintiffs had proposed that filters are a less restrictive alternative to COPA and the Government had not shown it would be likely to disprove the plaintiffs' contention at trial.

Filters are less restrictive than COPA. They impose selective restrictions on speech at the receiving end, not universal restrictions at the source. Under a filtering regime, adults without children may gain access to speech they have a right to see without having to identify themselves or provide their credit card information. Even adults with children may obtain access to the same speech on the same terms simply by turning off the filter on their home computers. Above all, promoting the use of filters does not condemn as criminal any category of speech, and so the potential chilling effect is eliminated, or at least much diminished. All of these things are true, moreover, regardless of how broadly or narrowly the definitions in COPA are construed.

Filters also may well be more effective than COPA. First, a filter can prevent minors from seeing all pornography, not just pornography posted to the Web from America. The District Court noted in its factfindings that one witness estimated that 40% of harmful-to-minors content comes from overseas. COPA does not prevent minors from having access to those foreign harmful materials. That alone makes it possible that filtering software might be more effective in serving Congress' goals. Effectiveness is likely to diminish even further if COPA is upheld, because the providers of the materials that would be covered by the statute simply can move their operations overseas. It is not an answer to say that COPA reaches some amount of materials that are harmful to minors; the question is whether it would reach more of them than less restrictive alternatives. In addition, the District Court found that verification systems may be subject to evasion and circumvention, for example by minors who have their own credit cards. Finally, filters also may be more effective because they can be applied to all forms of Internet communication, including e-mail, not just communications available via the World Wide Web.

That filtering software may well be more effective than COPA is confirmed by the findings of the Commission on Child Online Protection, a blue-ribbon commission created by Congress in COPA itself. Congress directed the Commission to evaluate the relative merits of different means of restricting minors' ability to gain access to harmful materials on the Internet. It unambiguously found that filters are more effective than age-verification requirements (assigning a score for "Effectiveness" of 7.4 for server-based filters and 6.5 for client-based filters, as compared to 5.9 for independent adult-id verification, and 5.5 for credit card verification). Thus, not only has the Government failed to carry its burden of showing the District Court that the proposed alternative is less effective, but also a Government Commission appointed to consider the question has concluded just the opposite. That finding supports our conclusion that the District Court did not abuse its discretion in enjoining the statute.

Filtering software, of course, is not a perfect solution to the problem of children gaining access to harmful-to-minors materials. It may block some materials that are not harmful to minors and fail to catch some that are. Whatever the deficiencies of filters, however, the Government failed to introduce specific evidence proving that existing technologies are less effective than the restrictions in COPA. The District Court made a specific factfinding that "[n]o evidence was presented to the Court as to the percentage of time that blocking and filtering technology is over- or underinclusive." In the absence of a showing as to the relative effectiveness of COPA and the alternatives proposed by respondents, it was not an abuse of discretion for the District Court to grant the preliminary injunction. The Government's burden is not merely to show that a proposed less restrictive alternative has some flaws; its burden is to show that it is less effective. It is not enough for the Government to show that COPA has some effect. Nor do respondents bear a burden to introduce, or offer to introduce, evidence that their proposed alternatives are more effective. The Government has the burden to show they are less so. The Government having failed to carry its burden, it was not an abuse of discretion for the District Court to grant the preliminary injunction.

One argument to the contrary is worth mentioning—the argument that filtering software is not an available alternative because Congress may not require it to be used. That argument carries little weight, because Congress undoubtedly may act to encourage the use of filters. We have held that Congress can give strong incentives to schools and libraries to use them. It could also take steps to promote their development by industry, and their use by parents. It is incorrect, for that reason, to say that filters are part of the current regulatory status quo. The need for parental cooperation does not automatically disqualify a proposed less restrictive alternative. ("A court should not assume a plausible, less restrictive alternative would be ineffective; and a court should not presume parents, given full information, will fail to act"). In enacting

COPA, Congress said its goal was to prevent the "widespread availability of the Internet" from providing "opportunities for minors to access materials through the World Wide Web in a manner that can frustrate parental supervision or control." COPA presumes that parents lack the ability, not the will, to monitor what their children see. By enacting programs to promote use of filtering software, Congress could give parents that ability without subjecting protected speech to severe penalties.

The closest precedent on the general point is our decision in *Playboy Entertainment Group*. *Playboy Entertainment Group*, like this case, involved a content-based restriction designed to protect minors from viewing harmful materials. The choice was between a blanket speech restriction and a more specific technological solution that was available to parents who chose to implement it. Absent a showing that the proposed less restrictive alternative would not be as effective, we concluded, the more restrictive option preferred by Congress could not survive strict scrutiny. In the instant case, too, the Government has failed to show, at this point, that the proposed less restrictive alternative will be less effective. The reasoning of *Playboy Entertainment Group*, and the holdings and force of our precedents require us to affirm the preliminary injunction. To do otherwise would be to do less than the First Amendment commands. "The starch in our constitutional standards cannot be sacrificed to accommodate the enforcement choices of the Government."

B

There are also important practical reasons to let the injunction stand pending a full trial on the merits. First, the potential harms from reversing the injunction outweigh those of leaving it in place by mistake. Where a prosecution is a likely possibility, yet only an affirmative defense is available, speakers may self-censor rather than risk the perils of trial. There is a potential for extraordinary harm and a serious chill upon protected speech. The harm done from letting the injunction stand pending a trial on the merits, in contrast, will not be extensive. No prosecutions have yet been undertaken under the law, so none will be disrupted if the injunction stands. Further, if the injunction is upheld, the Government in the interim can enforce obscenity laws already on the books.

Second, there are substantial factual disputes remaining in the case. As mentioned above, there is a serious gap in the evidence as to the effectiveness of filtering software. For us to assume, without proof, that filters are less effective than COPA would usurp the District Court's factfinding role. By allowing the preliminary injunction to stand and remanding for trial, we require the Government to shoulder its full constitutional burden of proof respecting the less restrictive alternative argument, rather than excuse it from doing so.

Third, and on a related point, the factual record does not reflect current technological reality—a serious flaw in any case involving the Internet. The technology of the Internet evolves at a rapid pace. Yet the factfindings of the District Court were entered in February 1999, over five years ago. Since then, certain facts about the Internet are known to have changed. Compare (36.7 million Internet hosts as of July 1998) with Internet Systems Consortium,

Internet Domain Survey, Jan. 2004, `http://www.isc.org/index.pl?/ops/ds` (as visited June 22, 2004, and available in the Clerk of Court's case file) (233.1 million hosts as of Jan. 2004). It is reasonable to assume that other technological developments important to the First Amendment analysis have also occurred during that time. More and better filtering alternatives may exist than when the District Court entered its findings. Indeed, we know that after the District Court entered its factfindings, a congressionally appointed commission issued a report that found that filters are more effective than verification screens.

Delay between the time that a district court makes factfindings and the time that a case reaches this Court is inevitable, with the necessary consequence that there will be some discrepancy between the facts as found and the facts at the time the appellate court takes up the question. We do not mean, therefore, to set up an insuperable obstacle to fair review. Here, however, the usual gap has doubled because the case has been through the Court of Appeals twice. The additional two years might make a difference. By affirming the preliminary injunction and remanding for trial, we allow the parties to update and supplement the factual record to reflect current technological realities.

Remand will also permit the District Court to take account of a changed legal landscape. Since the District Court made its factfindings, Congress has passed at least two further statutes that might qualify as less restrictive alternatives to COPA—a prohibition on misleading domain names, and a statute creating a minors-safe "Dot Kids" domain. Remanding for trial will allow the District Court to take into account those additional potential alternatives.

On a final point, it is important to note that this opinion does not hold that Congress is incapable of enacting any regulation of the Internet designed to prevent minors from gaining access to harmful materials. The parties, because of the conclusion of the Court of Appeals that the statute's definitions rendered it unconstitutional, did not devote their attention to the question whether further evidence might be introduced on the relative restrictiveness and effectiveness of alternatives to the statute. On remand, however, the parties will be able to introduce further evidence on this point. This opinion does not foreclose the District Court from concluding, upon a proper showing by the Government that meets the Government's constitutional burden as defined in this opinion, that COPA is the least restrictive alternative available to accomplish Congress' goal.

⋅⟨◉⟩⋅

On this record, the Government has not shown that the less restrictive alternatives proposed by respondents should be disregarded. Those alternatives, indeed, may be more effective than the provisions of COPA. The District Court did not abuse its discretion when it entered the preliminary injunction. The judgment of the Court of Appeals is affirmed, and the case is remanded for proceedings consistent with this opinion.

It is so ordered.

POSTSCRIPT

Should Sexual Content on the Internet Be Restricted?

The Supreme Court's rejection of COPA may not be the final word on the subject. As Justice Kennedy noted, the high court does not outright reject Congress's ability to legislate to limit minors' access to sexual material; it only rejects their attempt in this case as too restrictive.

Although Justice Kennedy championed the benefits of Internet filtering software, they also have limits. Such software is of varying quality, and while it might block out the pornography that is of concern, some programs are over-ambitious, also restricting access to some very helpful sexual information, like Planned Parenthood's teenwire.com, Web sites that provide information for gay and lesbian young people (like youthresource.com), or even the federal government's own iwannaknow.org.

If the burden of restricting material that is "harmful to minors" is placed on individuals, should they also bear the expense of filtering software? New televisions are required to have a "v-chip" installed—a device that when activated restricts sexual or violent content. Should new computers similarly be required to have filtering software bundled with other software? And what settings should apply? Or should that be left up to the individuals who use—or do not use—the software? What about public facilities like libraries, universities, and hotel lobbies?

Further, what do you think of COPA's definition of what is "harmful to minors"? It specifically describes sexual content but does not address violence. If the purpose of legislation is truly to protect minors from harm, should it also restrict access to violent imagery? And if so, what would the implications of such legislation be? Would news information Web sites like cnn.com and msnbc.com need to obtain one's credit card data before permitting access to stories and images about war or a murder investigation? What material, if any, would you want to see restricted, either through a credit card entry system or through filtering software?

Finally, the inexact nature of cyberspace also raises the question of jurisdiction. Where exactly *is* a person when they are downloading or uploading something on the Web? Do the laws of the physical place apply? Take, for example, a person who creates a Web site from his or her home in one city, and then uploads (adds) material to that Web site from another city—or from another country. Whose laws apply? If legislation like COPA were upheld, would providers of sexual material seek to establish foreign universal resource locators (URLs) where such laws do not apply, in order to maintain their Web sites without restrictions?

Suggested Readings

W. Adamson, "Sex in the City: What Happened at the Minneapolis Public Library," *Off Our Backs* (May–June 2004).

Associated Press, "Justices Block Internet Porn Law," msnbc.com (June 29, 2004).

A. Beeson, "Online Porn Law—COPA Opponent," *Washington Post* (June 30, 2004).

P. Brick and B. Taverner, "Savvy Websites: In Search of Accurate Sexuality Information on the 'Net," *Positive Images: Teaching Abstinence, Contraception, and Sexual Health* (Planned Parenthood of Greater Northern, New Jersey, 2001).

M. Heins, "The Right Result; The Wrong Reason," *The Free Expression Policy Project* (July 1, 2004).

K. Lehmann, "Avoiding Pornography Landmines While Traveling the Information Superhighway: Adult Content, You Must be at Least 18 Years of Age to Enter," *Multimedia Schools* (May–June 2002).

B. Mears, "Supreme Court Affirms Use of Computer Filters in Public Libraries," http://www.cnn.com/2003/LAW/06/24/scotus.internetporn.library/index.html (January 13, 2004).

J. Schwartz, "Antipornography Law Keeps Crashing Into First Amendment," *New York Times* (June 30, 2004).

ISSUE 11

Should the FCC Restrict Broadcast "Indecency"?

YES: Federal Communications Commission, from *FCC Consumer Facts: Obscene, Profane, and Indecent Broadcasts,* http://www.fcc.gov/eb/Orders/2001/fcc01090.doc (2001)

NO: Judith Levine, from "Is 'Indecency' Harmful to Minors?" An Adaptation of an Article from *Extra! Fairness in Accuracy and Reporting (FAIR)* (October 2004)

ISSUE SUMMARY

YES: The Federal Communications Commission (FCC), a U.S. government agency charged with regulating the content of the broadcast airways, including television and radio, outlines what it defines as "indecent" broadcast material and describes its enforcement policy.

NO: Author Judith Levine traces the history of censorship in the United States, and argues that much of what the FCC has determined is "indecent" sexual speech is not, in fact, harmful to children.

In January 2004, about 100 million viewers tuned in to CBS to watch the New England Patriots defeat the Carolina Panthers in Superbowl XXXVIII. But talk at water coolers, breakfast tables, and classrooms around the country the next day had little to do with the heroics of quarterback Tom Brady, nor about Adam Vinatieri's 41-yard field goal with four seconds left. Instead, the nation was talking about performer Janet Jackson's breast. During the half-time performance, Jackson's breast was exposed by co-star Justin Timberlake, revealing a nearly bare breast, with her nipple covered by a star-shaped pastie. The incident caused a national uproar. Nielson ratings estimated that about one in five children between the ages of 2 and 11 witnessed the event. (And those who did not see it live had ample time so see the incident ad infinitum in the news media coverage that followed.) It remained a feature news story for days and then weeks, as commentators and news analysts examined who was responsible, and how severely they should be punished.

CBS and Jackson apologized, Timberlake called it an unfortunate "wardrobe malfunction," and much of America wondered what effect the incident would have on children.

Meanwhile, the Federal Communications Commission (FCC) was not amused. The governmental agency charged with enforcing "indecency" violations reported having received more than a half million complaints. The FCC began holding hearings about increasing the monetary fines and proceeded to scrutinize the alleged violations of other performers and media outlets. When the FCC fined Clear Channel Communications $495,000 for sexual content aired in six Howard Stern shows, Clear Channel dropped Stern from all its radio outlets. The fine was significant as it marked a departure from the FCC's standard practice of fining. In this case, each "indecent" utterance was fined individually; previously, the FCC would fine an entire program the maximum $27,500, regardless of the number of violations on each show.

What is "indecent"? The FCC defines it as "language or material that, in context, depicts or describes, in terms patently offensive as measured by contemporary community broadcast standards for the broadcast medium, sexual or excretory organs or activities." Such material is protected as free speech by the First Amendment. However, the FCC is empowered to restrict the times of day that such material can be aired, under the premise that children need to be protected from indecency. Indecent material may not be aired between 6 a.m. and 10 p.m. Likewise, "profanity" may not be aired during these times. "Profane" material includes "personally reviling epithets naturally tending to provoke violent resentment or denoting language so grossly offensive to members of the public who actually hear it as to amount to a nuisance."

Still, the definitions of "indecency" and "profanity" are quite subjective and may require further clarification. The same is true for material that is "obscene," which may not be aired at all. In the following essays, the FCC elaborates on its definitions of indecency, profanity, and obscenity, giving case examples to illustrate its enforcement policy more clearly. In response, Judith Levine argues that the very premise of restricting indecent material is flawed, as there is no evidence that sexual speech harms children.

YES

Enforcement Policies Regarding Broadcast Indecency

I. Introduction

The Commission issues this Policy Statement to provide guidance to the broadcast industry regarding our case law and our enforcement policies with respect to broadcast indecency. This document is divided into five parts. Section I gives an overview of this document. Section II provides the statutory basis for indecency regulation and discusses the judicial history of such regulation. Section III describes the analytical approach the Commission uses in making indecency determinations. This section also presents a comparison of selected rulings intended to illustrate the various factors that have proved significant in resolving indecency complaints. The cited material refers only to broadcast indecency actions and does not include any discussion of case law concerning indecency enforcement actions in other services regulated by this agency such as cable, telephone, or amateur radio. Section IV describes the Commission's broadcast indecency enforcement process. Section V is the conclusion.

II. Statutory Basis/Judicial History

It is a violation of federal law to broadcast obscene or indecent programming. Specifically, Title 18 of the United States Code, Section 1464 (18 U.S.C. § 1464), prohibits the utterance of "any obscene, indecent, or profane language by means of radio communication." Congress has given the Federal Communications Commission the responsibility for administratively enforcing 18 U.S.C. § 1464. In doing so, the Commission may revoke a station license, impose a monetary forfeiture, or issue a warning for the broadcast of indecent material.

The FCC's enforcement policy has been shaped by a number of judicial and legislative decisions. In particular, because the Supreme Court has determined that obscene speech is not entitled to First Amendment protection, obscene speech cannot be broadcast at any time. In contrast, indecent speech is protected by the First Amendment, and thus, the government must both identify a compelling interest for any regulation it may impose on indecent

From the *FCC Consumer Facts: Obscene, Profane, and Indecent Broadcasts*, 2001. Federal Communications Commission. Notes omitted.

speech and choose the least restrictive means to further that interest. Even under this restrictive standard, the courts have consistently upheld the Commission's authority to regulate indecent speech, albeit with certain limitations.

FCC v. Pacifica Foundation provides the judicial foundation for FCC indecency enforcement. In that case, the Supreme Court held that the government could constitutionally regulate indecent broadcasts. In addition, the Court quoted the Commission's definition of indecency with apparent approval. The definition, "language or material that, in context, depicts or describes, in terms patently offensive as measured by contemporary community standards for the broadcast medium, sexual or excretory activities or organs," has remained substantially unchanged since the time of the *Pacifica* decision. Moreover, the definition has been specifically upheld against constitutional challenges in the *Action for Children's Television (ACT)* cases in the D.C. Circuit Court of Appeals. Further, in *Reno v. ACLU*, the U.S. Supreme Court struck down an indecency standard for the Internet but did not question the constitutionality of our broadcast indecency standard. Rather, the Court recognized the "special justifications for regulation of the broadcast media that are not applicable to other speakers."

Although the D.C. Circuit approved the FCC's definition of indecency in the *ACT* cases, it also established several restrictive parameters on FCC enforcement. The court's decisions made clear that the FCC had to identify the compelling government interests that warranted regulation and also explain how the regulations were narrowly tailored to further those interests. In *ACT I*, the court rejected as inadequately supported the Commission's determination that it could reach and regulate indecent material aired as late as 11:00 p.m., and remanded the cases involved to the Commission for proceedings to ascertain the proper scope of the "safe harbor" period, that is, the time during which indecent speech may be legally broadcast. Before the Commission could comply with the court's remand order, however, Congress intervened and instructed the Commission to adopt rules that enforced the provisions on a "24 hour per day basis." The rule adopted to implement this legislative mandate was stayed and was ultimately vacated by the court in *ACT II* as unconstitutional. In 1992, responding to the decision in *ACT II*, Congress directed the Commission to adopt a new "safe harbor"—generally 12 midnight to 6:00 a.m., but 10:00 p.m. to 6:00 a.m. for certain noncommercial stations. The Commission implemented this statutory scheme in January 1993. Before this rule could become effective, however, the court stayed it pending judicial review. In 1995, the D.C. Circuit, *en banc*, held in *ACT III* that there was not a sufficient justification in the record to support a preferential "safe harbor" period for noncommercial stations and that the more restrictive midnight to 6:00 a.m. "safe harbor" for commercial stations was therefore unconstitutional. The court concluded, however, that the less restrictive 10:00 p.m. to 6:00 a.m. "safe harbor" had been justified as a properly tailored means of vindicating the government's compelling interest in the welfare of children and remanded the case to the Commission "with instructions to limit its ban on the broadcasting of indecent programs to the period from 6:00 a.m. to 10:00 p.m."

The Commission implemented the court's instructions by appropriately conforming. These changes became effective on August 28, 1995.

Thus, outside the 10:00 p.m. to 6:00 a.m. safe harbor, the courts have approved regulation of broadcast indecency to further the compelling government interests in supporting parental supervision of children and more generally its concern for children's well being. The principles of enforcement articulated below are intended to further these interests.

III. Indecency Determinations

A. Analytical Approach

Indecency findings involve at least two fundamental determinations. First, the material alleged to be indecent must fall within the subject matter scope of our indecency definition—that is, the material must describe or depict sexual or excretory organs or activities.

Second, the broadcast must be *patently offensive* as measured by contemporary community standards for the broadcast medium. In applying the "community standards for the broadcast medium" criterion, the Commission has stated:

The determination as to whether certain programming is patently offensive is not a local one and does not encompass any particular geographic area. Rather, the standard is that of an average broadcast viewer or listener and not the sensibilities of any individual complainant.

In determining whether material is patently offensive, the *full context* in which the material appeared is critically important. It is not sufficient, for example, to know that explicit sexual terms or descriptions were used, just as it is not sufficient to know only that no such terms or descriptions were used. Explicit language in the context of a *bona fide* newscast might not be patently offensive, while sexual innuendo that persists and is sufficiently clear to make the sexual meaning inescapable might be. Moreover, contextual determinations are necessarily highly fact-specific, making it difficult to catalog comprehensively all of the possible contextual factors that might exacerbate or mitigate the patent offensiveness of particular material. An analysis of Commission case law reveals that various factors have been consistently considered relevant in indecency determinations. By comparing cases with analogous analytical structures, but different outcomes, we hope to highlight how these factors are applied in varying circumstances and the impact of these variables on a finding of patent offensiveness.

B. Case Comparisons

The principal factors that have proved significant in our decisions to date are: (1) the *explicitness or graphic nature* of the description or depiction of sexual or excretory organs or activities; (2) whether the material *dwells on or repeats at length* descriptions of sexual or excretory organs or activities; (3) *whether the material appears to pander or is used to titillate*, or *whether the material appears to have been presented for its shock value.* In assessing all of the factors, and particularly the third factor, the overall context of the broadcast in which the disputed material appeared is critical. Each indecency case presents its own particular mix of these, and possibly other, factors, which must be balanced to ultimately determine whether the material is patently offensive and therefore indecent. No single factor generally provides the basis for an indecency finding. To illustrate the noted factors, however, and to provide a sense of the weight these considerations have carried in specific factual contexts, a comparison of cases has been organized to provide examples of decisions in which each of these factors has played a particularly significant role, whether exacerbating or mitigating, in the indecency determination made.

It should be noted that the brief descriptions and excerpts from broadcasts that are reproduced in this document are intended only as a research tool and should not be taken as a meaningful selection of words and phrases to be evaluated for indecency purposes without the fuller context that the tapes or transcripts provide. The excerpts from broadcasts used in this section have often been shortened or compressed. In order to make the excerpts more readable, however, we have frequently omitted any indication of these ellipses from the text. Moreover, in cases where material was included in a complaint but not specifically cited in the decision based on the complaint, we caution against relying on the omission as if it were of decisional significance. For example, if portions of a voluminous transcript are the object of an enforcement action, those portions not included are not necessarily deemed not indecent. The omissions may be the result of an editing process that attempted to highlight the most significant material within its context. No inference should be drawn regarding the material deleted.

1. Explicitness/Graphic Description Versus Indirectness/Implication

The more explicit or graphic the description or depiction, the greater the likelihood that the material will be considered patently offensive. Merely because the material consists of double entendre or innuendo, however, does not preclude an indecency finding if the sexual or excretory import is unmistakable.

Following are examples of decisions where the explicit/graphic nature of the description of sexual or excretory organs or activities played a central role in the determination that the broadcast was indecent.

WYSP(FM), Philadelphia, PA: "Howard Stern Show"

> *God, my testicles are like down to the floor . . . you could really have a party with these . . . Use them like Bocci balls.*
>
> *(As part of a discussion of lesbians) I mean to go around porking other girls with vibrating rubber products . . .*
>
> *Have you ever had sex with an animal? Well, don't knock it. I was sodomized by Lambchop.*

Indecent Warning Issued. Excerpted material (only some of which is cited above) consisted of "vulgar and lewd references to the male genitals and to masturbation and sodomy broadcast in the context of . . . 'explicit references to masturbation, ejaculation, breast size, penis size, sexual intercourse, nudity, urination, oral-genital contact, erections, sodomy, bestiality, menstruation and testicles.'"'. . .

KROQ(FM), Los Angeles, CA: "You Suck" Song

> *I know you're really proud cause you think you're well hung but I think its time you learn how to use your tongue. You say you want things to be even and you want things to be fair but you're afraid to get your teeth caught in my pubic hair. If you're lying there expecting me to suck your dick, you're going to have to give me more than just a token lick. . . . Go down baby, you suck, lick it hard and move your tongue around. If you're worried about babies, you can lower your risk, by giving me that special cunnilingus kiss. . . . you can jiggle your tongue on my clit. Don't worry about making me have an orgasm. . . . You asshole, you shit. I know it's a real drag, to suck my cunt when I'm on the rag. . . . You tell me it's gross to suck my yeast infection. How do you think I feel when I gag on your erection.*

Indecent—NAL Issued. (graphically and explicitly describes sexual and excretory organs or activities).
. . . Less explicit material and material that relies principally on innuendo to convey a sexual or excretory meaning have also been cited by the Commission as actionably indecent where the sexual or excretory meaning was unmistakable. . . .

KGB-FM, San Diego, CA: "Candy Wrapper" Song

> *I whipped out my Whopper and whispered, Hey, Sweettart, how'd you like to Crunch on my Big Hunk for a Million Dollar Bar? Well, she immediately went down on my Tootsie Roll and you know, it was like pure Almond Joy. I couldn't help but grab her delicious Mounds, . . . this little Twix had the Red Hots. . . . as my Butterfinger went up her tight little Kit Kat, and she started to scream Oh, Henry! Oh, Henry! Soon she was fondling my Peter Paul, and Zagnuts and I knew it wouldn't be long before I blew my Milk Duds clear to Mars and gave her a taste of the old Milky Way. . . . I said, Look . . . why don't you just take my Whatchamacallit and slip it up your Bit-O-Honey. Oh, what a piece of Juicy Fruit she was too. She screamed Oh, Crackerjack. You're better than the Three Musketeers! as I rammed my Ding Dong up her Rocky Road and into her Peanut Butter Cup. Well, I was giving it to her Good'n Plenty, and all of a sudden, my Starburst. . . . she started to grow a bit Chunky and . . . Sure enough, nine months later, out popped a Baby Ruth.*

Indecent—NAL Issued. ("While the passages arguably consist of double entendre and indirect references, the language used in each passage was understandable and clearly capable of a specific sexual meaning and, because of the context, the sexual import was inescapable."); ("notwithstanding the use of candy bar names to symbolize sexual activities, the titillating and pandering nature of the song makes any thought of candy bars peripheral at best"). . . .

KMEL(FM), San Francisco, CA: "Rick Chase Show"; "Blow Me" Song

> *Blow me, you hardly even know me, just set yourself below me and blow me,*
> *tonight. Hey, a handy would certainly be dandy, but it's not enough to slow*
> *(unintelligible) me, hey, you gotta blow me all night. Hey, when you pat your*
> *lips that way, I want you night and day, when you squeeze my balls so tight.*
> *I want to blow my love, hey, with all my might.*

Indecent—NAL Issued. Commission found that the language dwelled on descriptions of sexual organs and activities, "was understandable and clearly capable of a specific sexual meaning and, because of the context, the sexual import was inescapable."

Compare the following case in which the material aired was deemed not to be actionably indecent.

WFBQ(FM)/WNDE(AM), Indianapolis, IN: "Elvis" and "Power, Power, Power"

> *As you know, you gotta stop the King, but you can't kill him . . . So you talk to*
> *Dick Nixon, man you get him on the phone and Dick suggests maybe getting*
> *like a mega-Dick to help out, but you know, you remember the time the King ate*
> *mega-Dick under the table at a 095 picnic . . . you think about getting mega-*
> *Hodgie, but that's no good because you know, the King was a karate dude . . .*
>
> *Power! Power! Power! Thrust! Thrust! Thrust! First it was Big Foot, the*
> *monster car crunching 4x4 pickup truck. Well, move over, Big Foot! Here comes*
> *the most massive power-packed monster ever! It's Big Peter! (Laughter) Big Peter*
> *with 40,000 Peterbilt horsepower under the hood. It's massive! Big Peter! For-*
> *merly the Big Dick's Dog Wiener Mobile. Big Peter features a 75-foot jacked up*
> *monster body. See Big Peter crush and enter a Volvo. (Laughter) . . . strapped*
> *himself in the cockpit and put Big Peter through its paces. So look out Big Foot!*
> *Big Peter is coming! Oh my God! It's coming! Big Peter! (Laughter)*

Not Indecent. The licensee provided a fuller transcript of the cited "Elvis" excerpt and explained the context in which it was aired, arguing that no sexual meaning was intended and that no such meaning would be reasonably understood from the material taken as a whole. The licensee also explained the regional humor of the Power, Power, Power excerpt and the context in which it was broadcast. The Mass Media Bureau held that the material was not indecent because the "surrounding contexts do not appear to provide a background against which a sexual import is inescapable."

In assessing explicitness, the Commission also looks to the audibility of the material as aired. If the material is difficult or impossible to understand, it may not be actionably indecent. However, difficulty in understanding part of the material or an attempt to obscure objectionable material will not preclude a finding of indecency where at least some of the material is recognizable or understandable.

KGB-FM, San Diego, CA: "Sit on My Face" Song

> *Sit on my face and tell me that you love me. I'll sit on your face and tell you I*
> *love you, too. I love to hear you moralize when I'm between your thighs. You*

blow me away. Sit on my face and let me embrace you. I'll sit on your face and then I'll love you (?) truly. Life can be fine, if we both sixty-nine. If we sit on faces (?) the ultimate place to play (?). We'll be blown away.

Indecent—NAL Issued. The song was found to be actionably indecent despite English accent and "ambient noise" because the lyrics were sufficiently understandable.

WWKX(FM), Woonsocket, RI: "Real Deal Mike Neil Show"

Douche bag, hey what's up, fu(Bleep)ck head? . . . You his fuck (Bleep) ho or what? You his fuck (Bleep) bitch man, where you suck his dick every night? . . . Suck some di(Bleep)ck make some money for Howard and pay your pimp okay?

Indecent—NAL Issued. Material was found to be actionably indecent despite attempt to obscure objectionable language because "editing was ineffective and merely resulted in a "bleep" in the middle of clearly recognizable words (or in some cases a "bleep" after the word)." The Mass Media Bureau held that "[b]ecause the words were recognizable, notwithstanding the editing," they were indecent within the context used in this broadcast.

2. Dwelling/Repetition versus Fleeting Reference

Repetition of and persistent focus on sexual or excretory material have been cited consistently as factors that exacerbate the potential offensiveness of broadcasts. In contrast, where sexual or excretory references have been made once or have been passing or fleeting in nature, this characteristic has tended to weigh against a finding of indecency.

WXTB(FM), Clearwater, FL: "Bubba, The Love Sponge"

Could you take the phone and rub it on you Chia Pet? Oh, let me make sure nobody is around. Okay, hang on a second (Rubbing noise). Okay I did it. . . . Now that really your little beaver? That was mine. Your what? That was my little beaver? Oh I love when a girl says beaver. Will you say it again for me honey please? It was my little beaver. . . . Will you say, Bubba come get my beaver? Bubba, would come get my little beaver? . . . tell me that doesn't do something for you. That is pretty sexy. . . . bring the beaver. It will be with me. We got beaver chow. I can't wait, will you say it for me one more time? Say what? My little beaver or Bubba come get my little beaver? Okay, Bubba come get my beaver. Will you say, Bubba come hit my beaver? Will you say it? Bubba, come hit my beaver. That is pretty sexy, absolutely. Oh, my God, beaver.

Indecent—NAL Issued.

WXTB(FM), Clearwater, FL: "Bubba, The Love Sponge"

Well, it was nice big fart. I'm feeling very gaseous at this point but there, so far has been no enema reaction, as far as. There's been no, there's been no expelling? No expelling. But I feel mucus rising. . . . Can't go like. (Grunting sound) Pushing, all I keep doing is putting out little baby farts. . . . on the toilet ready to go. . . . Push it, strain it. It looks normal. Just average, average. Little rabbit one. Little rabbit pellets. I imagine maybe, we'll break loose. Push hard Cowhead. I'm pushing, I got veins popping out of my forehead. Go ahead, those moles might pop right off. You can tell he's pushing. I'm out of breath. One more, last one. One big push.

Indecent—NAL Issued. The cited material dwells on excretory activities and the Commission found it to be patently offensive.

Compare the following cases where material was found not indecent because it was fleeting and isolated.

WYBB(FM), Folly Beach, SC: "The Morning Show"

The hell I did, I drove mother-fucker, oh. Oh.

Not Indecent. The "broadcast contained only a fleeting and isolated utterance which, within the context of live and spontaneous programming, does not warrant a Commission sanction."

KPRL(AM)/KDDB(FM), Paso Robles, CA: News Announcer Comment

Oops, fucked that one up.

Not Indecent. The "news announcer's use of single expletive" does not "warrant further Commission consideration in light of the isolated and accidental nature of the broadcast."

In contrast, even relatively fleeting references may be found indecent where other factors contribute to a finding of patent offensiveness. Examples of such factors illustrated by the following cases include broadcasting references to sexual activities with children and airing material that, although fleeting, is graphic or explicit.

3. . . . Presented in a Pandering or Titillating Manner or for Shock Value
The apparent purpose for which material is presented can substantially affect whether it is deemed to be patently offensive as aired. In adverse indecency findings, the Commission has often cited the pandering or titillating character of the material broadcast as an exacerbating factor. Presentation for the shock value of the language used has also been cited. As Justice Powell stated in his opinion in the Supreme Court's decision affirming the Commission's determination that the broadcast of a comedy routine was indecent, "[T]he language employed is, to most people, vulgar and offensive. It was chosen specifically for this quality, and it was repeated over and over as a sort of verbal shock treatment." On the other hand, the manner and purpose of a presentation may well preclude an indecency determination even though other factors, such as explicitness, might weigh in favor of an indecency finding. In the following cases, the decisions looked to the manner of presentation as a factor supporting a finding of indecency.

KLOL(FM), Houston, TX: "Stevens & Pruett Show"

Sex survey lines are open. Today's question, it's a strange question and we hope we have a lot of strange answers. What makes your hiney parts tingle? When my husband gets down there and goes (lips noise). . . . I love oral sex. . . . Well, my boyfriend tried to put Hershey kisses inside of me and tried to lick it out and it took forever for him to do it.

Indecent—NAL Issued. Explicit description in a program that focused on sexual activities in a lewd, vulgar, pandering and titillating manner.

WEBN(FM), Cincinnati, OH: "Bubba, The Love Sponge"

All I can say is, if you were listening to the program last night you heard Amy and Stacy . . . come in here, little lesbians that they are. Little University of Cincinnati ho's and basically that we could come over and watch them. We got over to the house. . . . They start making out a little bit. They go to bed. They get, they start, they're starting like a mutual 69 on the bed. Guido all of a sudden whips it out. . . . Rather than take care of each other . . . Guido is like knee deep with the butch bitch and all of a sudden here is the fem bitch looking at me. Hot. I get crazy. I hook up a little bit. Then Guido says, hey, I done got mine, how about we switching? So I went into the private bedroom with the butch bitch and then got another one.

Indecent—NAL Issued. . . . In determining whether broadcasts are presented in a pandering or titillating manner, the context of the broadcast is particularly critical. Thus, even where language is explicit, the matter is graphic, or where there is intense repetition of vulgar terms, the presentation may not be pandering or titillating, and the broadcast may not be found actionably indecent.

. . . WABC-TV, New York, NY: "Oprah Winfrey Show" (How to Make Romantic Relations with Your Mate Better)

Okay, for all you viewers out there with children watching, we're doing a show today on how to make romantic relations with your mate better. Otherwise known as s-e-x. . . . I'm very aware there are a number of children who are watching and so, we're going to do our best to keep this show rated "G" but just in case, you may want to send your kids to a different room. And we'll pause for a moment while you do that. . . . According to experts and recent sex surveys the biggest complaints married women have about sex are . . . their lovemaking is boring . . . American wives all across the country have confessed to using erotic aids to spice up their sex life and . . . thousands of women say they fantasize while having sex with their husbands. . . . And most women say they are faking it in the bedroom.

[Quiz:] I like the way my partner looks in clothing. . . . I like the way my partner looks naked. . . . I like the way my partner's skin feels. . . . I like the way my partner tastes. . . .

[Psychologist and panelists:] Do you know that you can experience orgasm, have you experienced that by yourself? No, I have not . . . Okay, one of the things that, well, you all know what I'm talking about. . . . You need to at least know how to make your body get satisfied by yourself. Because if

you don't know how to do it, how is he going to figure it out? He doesn't have your body parts, he doesn't know.

Not Indecent.   Subject matter alone does not render material indecent. Thus, while material may be offensive to some people, in context, it might not be actionably indecent.

. . . WSMC-FM, Collegedale, TN: "All Things Considered" [National Public Radio]

Mike Schuster has a report and a warning. The following story contains some very rough language. [Excerpt from wiretap of telephone conversation in which organized crime figure John Gotti uses "fuck" or "fucking" 10 times in 7 sentences (110 words).]

Not Indecent.   Explicit language was integral part of a bona fide news story concerning organized crime; the material aired was part of a wiretap recording used as evidence in Gotti's widely reported trial. The Commission explained that it did "not find the use of such [coarse] words in a legitimate news report to have been gratuitous, pandering, titillating or otherwise "patently offensive" as that term is used in our indecency definition."
   . . . Compare the following cases where licensees unsuccessfully claimed that, because of the context of the broadcasts (*i.e.*, alleged news stories), the broadcasts were not pandering.

KSD-FM, St. Louis, MO: "The Breakfast Club"

I've got this Jessica Hahn interview here in Playboy. I just want to read one little segment . . . the good part.
   "[Jim Bakker] has managed to completely undress me and he's sitting on my chest. He's really pushing himself, I mean the guy was forcing himself. He put his penis in my mouth . . . I'm crying, tears are coming, and he is letting go. The guy came in my mouth. My neck hurts, my throat hurts, my head feels like it's going to explode, but he's frustrated and determined, determined enough that within minutes he's inside me and he's on top and he's holding my arms. He's just into this, he's inside me now. Saying, when you help the shepherd, you're helping the sheep."
   (followed by air personality making sheep sounds) This was rape. Yeah, don't you ever come around here Jim Bakker or we're going to cut that thing off.

Indecent—NAL Issued.   The broadcast contained excerpts from a *Playboy* magazine account of the alleged rape of Jessica Hahn by the Rev. Jim Bakker. The licensee explained the broadcast was newsworthy "banter by two on-air personalities reflecting public concern, criticism, and curiosity about a public figure whose reputedly notorious behavior was a widespread media issue at the time." Responding to the licensee's argument, the Mass Media Bureau stated that "although the program . . . arguably concerned an incident that was at the time 'in the news,' the particular material broadcast was not only exceptionally explicit and vulgar, it was . . . presented in a pandering manner. In short, the rendition of the details of the alleged rape was, in context, patently offensive."

. . . KSJO(FM), San Jose, California: Lamont & Tonelli Show

> ". . . she should go up and down the shaft about five times, licking and sucking and on the fifth swirl her tongue around the head before going back down. . . ."
> "Show us how its done" (evidently the guest had some sort of a prop).
> "Well, if this was a real penis, it would have a ****ridge, I would like (sic) around the ridge like this. . . ."
> [laughter, comments such as 'oh yeah, baby'].

Indecent—NAL Issued. The licensee claimed that the program was a clinical discussion of oral sex. The Enforcement Bureau rejected this argument on the grounds that the disc jockeys' comments on her material showed that the material was offered in a pandering and titillating manner. "The disc jockeys' invitation to have Dr. Terry use a prop on a radio program, and their laughter and statements (such as "oh yeah, baby") while she conducted that demonstration shown that the material was intended to be pandering and titillating as opposed to a clinical discussion of sex."

The absence of a pandering or titillating nature, however, will not necessarily prevent an indecency determination, as illustrated by the following case.

WIOD(AM), Miami, FL: "Penis Envy" Song

> If I had a penis, . . . I'd stretch it and stroke it and shove it at smarties . . . I'd stuff it in turkeys on Thanksgiving day. . . . If I had a penis, I'd run to my mother, Comb out the hair and compare it to brother. I'd lance her, I'd knight her, my hands would indulge. Pants would seem tighter and buckle and bulge. (Refrain) A penis to plunder, a penis to push, 'Cause one in the hand is worth one in the bush. A penis to love me, a penis to share, To pick up and play with when nobody's there. . . . If I had a penis, . . . I'd force it on females, I'd pee like a fountain. If I had a penis, I'd still be a girl, but I'd make much more money and conquer the world.

Indecent—NAL Issued. The Mass Media Bureau found the material to be patently offensive. In response to the licensee's assertion that this song was not pandering or titillating and therefore should not be considered indecent, the Bureau stated: "We believe . . . that it is not necessary to find that the material is pandering or titillating in order to find that its references to sexual activities and organs are patently offensive. (Citations omitted.) Moreover, humor is no more an absolute defense to indecency . . . than is music or any other one component of communication."

IV. Enforcement Process

The Commission does not independently monitor broadcasts for indecent material. Its enforcement actions are based on documented complaints of indecent broadcasting received from the public. Given the sensitive nature of these cases and the critical role of context in an indecency determination, it is important that the Commission be afforded as full a record as possible to evaluate allegations of indecent programming. In order for a complaint to be considered, our practice is that it must generally include: (1) a full or partial tape or transcript or significant excerpts of the program; (2) the date and time of the broadcast; and (3) the call sign of the station involved. Any tapes or other documentation of the programming supplied by the complainant, of necessity, become part of the Commission's records and cannot be returned. Documented complaints should be directed to the FCC, Investigations and Hearings Division, Enforcement Bureau, 445 Twelfth Street, S.W., Washington, D.C. 20554.

If a complaint does not contain the supporting material described above, or if it indicates that a broadcast occurred during "safe harbor" hours or the material cited does not fall within the subject matter scope of our indecency definition, it is usually dismissed by a letter to the complainant advising of the deficiency. In many of these cases, the station may not be aware that a complaint has been filed.

If, however, the staff determines that a documented complaint meets the subject matter requirements of the indecency definition and the material complained of was aired outside "safe harbor" hours, then the broadcast at issue is evaluated for patent offensiveness. Where the staff determines that the broadcast is not patently offensive, the complaint will be denied. If, however, the staff determines that further enforcement action might be warranted, the Enforcement Bureau, in conjunction with other Commission offices, examines the material and decides upon an appropriate disposition, which might include any of the following: (1) denial of the complaint by staff letter based upon a finding that the material, in context, is not patently offensive and therefore not indecent; (2) issuance of a Letter of Inquiry (LOI) to the licensee seeking further information concerning or an explanation of the circumstances surrounding the broadcast; (3) issuance of a Notice of Apparent Liability (NAL) for monetary forfeiture; and (4) formal referral of the case to the full Commission for its consideration and action. Generally, the last of these alternatives is taken in cases where issues beyond straightforward indecency violations may be involved or where the potential sanction for the indecent programming exceeds the Bureau's delegated forfeiture authority of $25,000.

Where an LOI is issued, the licensee's comments are generally sought concerning the allegedly indecent broadcast to assist in determining whether the material is actionable and whether a sanction is warranted. If it is determined that no further action is warranted, the licensee and the complainant will be so advised. Where a *preliminary* determination is made that the material was aired and was indecent, an NAL is issued. If the Commission previously determined that the broadcast of the same material was indecent, the subsequent broadcast constitutes egregious misconduct and a higher forfeiture amount is warranted.

The licensee is afforded an opportunity to respond to the NAL, a step which is required by statute. Once the Commission or its staff has considered any response by the licensee, it may order payment of a monetary penalty by issuing a Forfeiture Order. Alternatively, if the preliminary finding of violation in the NAL is successfully rebutted by the licensee, the NAL may be rescinded. If a Forfeiture Order is issued, the monetary penalty assessed may either be the same as specified in the NAL or it may be a lesser amount if the licensee has demonstrated that mitigating factors warrant a reduction in forfeiture.

A Forfeiture Order may be appealed by the licensee through the administrative process under several different provisions of the Commission's rules. The licensee also has the legal right to refuse to pay the fine. In such a case, the Commission may refer the matter to the U.S. Department of Justice, which can initiate a trial *de novo* in a U.S. District Court. The trial court may start anew to evaluate the allegations of indecency.

V. Conclusion

The Commission issues this Policy Statement to provide guidance to broadcast licensees regarding compliance with the Commission's indecency regulations. By summarizing the regulations and explaining the Commission's analytical approach to reviewing allegedly indecent material, the Commission provides a framework by which broadcast licensees can assess the legality of airing potentially indecent material. Numerous examples are provided in this document in an effort to assist broadcast licensees. However, this document is not intended to be an all-inclusive summary of every indecency finding issued by the Commission and it should not be relied upon as such. There are many additional cases that could have been cited. Further, as discussed above, the excerpts from broadcasts quoted in this document are intended only as a research tool. A complete understanding of the material, and the Commission's analysis thereof, requires review of the tapes or transcripts and the Commission's rulings thereon.

OBSCENE, PROFANE, AND INDECENT BROADCASTS: FCC CONSUMER FACTS

It's Against the Law

It is a violation of federal law to broadcast **obscene** programming at any time. It is also a violation of federal law to broadcast **indecent** or **profane** programming during certain hours. Congress has given the Federal Communications Commission (FCC) the responsibility for administratively enforcing the law that governs these types of broadcasts. The Commission may revoke a station license, impose a monetary forfeiture, or issue a warning, for the broadcast of obscene or indecent material.

Obscene Broadcasts Are Prohibited at All Times

Obscene speech is not protected by the First Amendment and cannot be broadcast at any time. To be obscene, material must meet a three-prong test:

- An average person, applying contemporary community standards, must find that the material, as a whole, appeals to the prurient interest;

- The material must depict or describe, in a patently offensive way, sexual conduct specifically defined by applicable law; and
- The material, taken as a whole, must lack serious literary, artistic, political, or scientific value.

Indecent Broadcast Restrictions

The FCC has defined broadcast indecency as "language or material that, in context, depicts or describes, in terms patently offensive as measured by contemporary community broadcast standards for the broadcast medium, sexual or excretory organs or activities." Indecent programming contains patently offensive sexual or excretory references that do not rise to the level of obscenity. As such, the courts have held that indecent material is protected by the First Amendment and cannot be banned entirely. It may, however, be restricted in order to avoid broadcast during times of the day when there a reasonable risk that children may be in the audience.

Consistent with a federal statute and federal court decisions interpreting the indecency statute, the Commission adopted a rule pursuant to which broadcasts—both on television and radio—that fit within the indecency definition and that are aired between 6:00 a.m. and 10:00 p.m. are subject to indecency enforcement action.

Profane Broadcast Restrictions

The FCC has defined profanity as including language that "denot[es] certain of those personally reviling epithets naturally tending to provoke violent resentment or denoting language so grossly offensive to members of the public who actually hear it as to amount to a nuisance."

Like indecency, profane speech is prohibited on broadcast radio and television between the hours of 6 a.m. to 10 p.m.

Enforcement Procedures and Filing Complaints

Enforcement actions in this area are based on documented complaints received from the public about indecent, profane, or obscene broadcasting. The FCC's staff reviews each complaint to determine whether it has sufficient information to suggest that there has been a violation of the obscenity, profanity, or indecency laws. If it appears that a violation may have occurred, the staff will start an investigation by sending a letter of inquiry to the broadcast station. Otherwise, the complaint will be dismissed or denied.

Context

In making indecency and profanity determinations, context is key! The FCC staff must analyze what was actually said during the broadcast, the meaning of what was said, and the context in which it was stated. Accordingly, the FCC asks complainants to provide the following information:

- *Information regarding the details of what was actually said (or depicted) during the allegedly indecent, profane or obscene broadcast.* There is flexibility on how a complainant may provide this information. complainant may submit a significant excerpt of the program describing what was actually said (or depicted) or a full or partial recording (e.g., tape) or transcript of the material.

In whatever form the complainant decides provide the information, it must be sufficiently detailed so the FCC can determine the words and language actually used during the broadcast and the context of those words or language. Subject matter alone is not a determining factor of whether material is obscene, profane, or indecent. For example, stating only that the broadcast station "discussed sex" or had a "disgusting discussion of sex" during a program is not sufficient. Moreover, the FCC must know the context when analyzing whether specific, isolated words are indecent or profane. The FCC does not require complainants to provide recordings or transcripts in support of their complaints. Consequently, failure to provide a recording or transcript of a broadcast, in and of itself, will not lead to automatic dismissal or denial of a complaint.

- *The date and time of the broadcast.* Under federal law, if the FCC assesses a monetary forfeiture against a broadcast station for violation of a rule, it must specify the date the violation occurred. Accordingly, it is important that complainants provide the date the material in question was broadcast. A broadcaster's right to air indecent or profane speech is protected between the hours of 10 p.m. and 6 a.m. Consequently, the FCC must know the time of day that the material was broadcast.
- *The call sign of the station involved.*

Of necessity, any documentation you provide the FCC about your complaint becomes part of the FCC's records and may not be returned. Complaints containing this information should directed to:

Federal Communications Commission

Enforcement Bureau

Investigations and Hearings Division

445 12th St., SW, Room 3-B443

Washington, DC 20554

You may also file a complaint electronically using the FCC Form 475 (complaint form) at **http://www.fcc.gov/cgb/complaints.html** or by e-mail at **www.fccinfo@fcc.gov**.

Judith Levine

Is "Indecency" Harmful to Minors?

"For more than 75 years . . . Congress has entrusted the FCC with protecting children from broadcast indecency," the Federal Communications Commission's chief enforcer David H. Solomon declared in April, 2004. "There's no question that the FCC is taking indecency enforcement very seriously these days."

No question indeed. Solomon was referring to the commission's new regulatory enthusiasm—some would call it a crusade—spearheaded by Chairman Michael Powell, seconded by President Bush, and toughened by two GOP bills to raise fines from the current maximum of $27,500 to as high as a half-million dollars; the laws would also revoke licenses after "three strikes." Solomon crowed about enlivening the definition of indecency—"language or material that, in context, depicts or describes, in terms patently offensive as measured by contemporary community standards for the broadcast medium, sexual or excretory organs or activities"—with a broader subset of "profanity." In addition to blasphemy (an already questionable concept in a secular nation), the commission would prohibit as profane any "personally reviling epithets naturally tending to provoke violent resentment" or language "so grossly offensive. . . . as to amount to a nuisance." The "F-word," as the commission delicately refers to it, would hereafter be considered such a violently resentment-provoking nuisance.

And, oh yes, the FCC "remain[ed] strongly committed" to the First Amendment.

Powell had been itching to act. In January, 2003, his enforcers ruled that the Bono's exclamation on NBC's Golden Globe awards—"Fucking brilliant!"—was not profane. All year on Clear Channel radio, Bubba the Love Sponge nattered on about "waxing [his] carrot," Howard Stern discussed cum with porn stars.

But the last straw was half-time, Superbowl 2004. During a song-and-dance duet, a scripted bodice-rip by Justin Timberlake resulted in the momentary baring of Janet Jackson's right breast, bedecked with a sunburst-shaped "nipple shield." Organized conservatives predicted the end of civilization and helped mobilize a half-million complaints to CBS. Powell told the press of his cozy family "celebration" being ambushed by this "classless, crass, and deplorable stunt," and vowed to investigate. Rejecting Timberlake's claim of a "wardrobe malfunction," the FCC in July found the performance indecent—to the tune of $550,000 in fines against Viacom Inc., parent company to the 20 CBS affiliates that aired the show.

While civil libertarians protested the supersized penalties and the ever-vaguer regulations, media companies sped to adopt failsafe policies. Scripts from *NYPD Blue* to *Masterpiece Theatre* were scrubbed, on-air personalities were muzzled and non-compliers canned. Clear Channel dumped Stern, and at Santa Monica-based KCRW-FM, Sandra Tsing Loh lost her $150-a-week job when the "F-word" slipped by un-bleeped during a commentary on knitting (the station later offered the position back, but Loh declined). The FCC praised such "voluntary action." Many producers called it scared s—less self-censorship.

The concept of indecency is inextricably linked to protecting children, which is why most sexual speech is prohibited on radio and commercial television between 6 a.m. and 10 p.m., when minors might be in the audience. According to veteran civil liberties attorney Marjorie Heins, laws are routinely passed and upheld in court based on the notion that witnessing sexual words and images is harmful to minors. Even among those who challenge the laws' free-speech infringements, few question this truism.

But there is no evidence that sexual speech harms children.

The idea that young (or female or feeble) minds are vulnerable to media-induced bad thoughts, which might lead to bad acts, might be called the founding principle of obscenity law. In 1868, an English anti-clerical pamphlet called "The Confessional Unmasked" was deemed punishably obscene because its text might "suggest to the minds of the young of either sex, and even to persons of more advanced years, thoughts of a most impure and libidinous character."

The worry that mobilizes the law, while neither pan-historic nor universal, is nonetheless old and enduring. In 1700, an English anti-masturbation treatise called *Onania, or the Heinous Sin of Self-Pollution, And All its Frightful Consequences, in Both Sexes consider'd, &c* became a best-seller with such warnings as "*Dogs* in the Streets and *Bulls* in the Fields may do mischief to Debauch's Fancy's, and it is possible that either Sex may be put in mind of Lascivious Thoughts, by their own *Poultry.*"

In the late 19th century, while Anthony Comstock scoured daily newspapers for censorable "traps for the young," the New York Society for the Prevention of Cruelty to Children "kept a watchful eye upon the so-called Museums of the City," whose advertisements were "like magnets to curious children." According to one of the society's reports, a play featuring "depravity, stabbing, shooting, and blood-shedding" so traumatized a 10-year-old girl that she was found "wander[ing] aimlessly along Eighth Avenue as if incapable of ridding herself of the dread impressions that had filled her young mind."

By 1914, essayist Agnes Repellier was inveighing against a film and publishing industry "coining money" creating a generation hypersophisticated in sin. "[Children's] sources of knowledge are manifold, and astoundingly explicit," she wrote in *The Atlantic*. Perhaps the first to propose a movie-rating system, Repellier asked "the authorities" to bar children "from all shows dealing with prostitution." And in 1934, Dr. Ira S. Wile indicted "lurid movies, automobiles, speed, jazz, [and] literature tinged with pornography," among the causes of "The Sexual Problems of Adolescence."

After jazz came comic books, then rock 'n' roll, hip-hop, videogames, Internet porn—it's a miracle anyone has survived childhood with sufficient morality to protect the next generation from corruption.

In spite of all this hand-wringing, though, evidence of the harm of exposure to sexually explicit images or words in childhood is inconclusive, even nonexistent. The 1970 U.S. Commission on Obscenity and Pornography, the "Lockhart Commission," failed to find harm to children in viewing erotica, and even suggested such exposure could "facilitate much needed communication between parent and child over sexual matters."

In a survey of 3,200 elementary school kids in the 1970s (before MTV!), "the most productive responses were elicited with the instructions, 'Why children shouldn't be allowed to see R and X rated movies'; or 'What is in R and X rated movies that children are too young to know about?' Here, the children proceeded with aplomb to tell all that they knew but were not supposed to know," wrote the study's authors. The conclusion: Children are sexual, they know about sex, and this does not harm them. Their "innocence" is an adult fantasy.

Assembled to overturn the 1970 findings, the Reagan Administration's 1985 Commission on Pornography (the "Meese Commission") could not establish factual links between sexual explicit materials and antisocial behavior either. The lion's share of the testimony it heard concerned adult consumers, yet the commission pitched its pro-restriction recommendations to popular fears about children: "For children to be taught by these materials that sex is public, that sex is commercial, and that sex can be divorced from any degree of affection, love, commitment, or marriage," the report read, "is for us the wrong message at the wrong time."

Indeed, some research suggests that *less* exposure to sexual materials may be worse for children than more. Interviews of sex criminals including child molesters reveal that the children who eventually became rapists were usually less exposed to pornography than other kids. In general, according to Johns Hopkins University sexologist John Money, "the majority of patients with paraphilias"—deviant sexual fantasies and behaviors—"described a strict anti-sexual upbringing in which sex was either never mentioned or was actively repressed or defiled." On a less criminal note, students who attend sex ed classes in which a wide range of sexual topics are discuss do far better than those in abstinence-only classes in protecting themselves against pregnancy and disease and negotiating their sexual relationships.

So what about these fresh corrupting "indecencies"? Anecdotal evidence suggests the breast, the F-word, or anything Bubba says are not news to any child who isn't Amish. Eighth-graders interviewed after the Superbowl evinced only mild concern—for their younger siblings. "I thought the end was a little bit inappropriate," commented one girl, "being that kids of all ages were watching it."

And Bono's outburst? In a successful appeal of NBC's exoneration, Parents Television Coalition argued that the singer could "enlarge a child's vocabulary. . . in a manner that many, if not most, parents would find highly detrimental and objectionable."

To test this thesis, I googled "swearing and children." A hundred-fifty-five thousand hits proved PTC right on one claim: parents object to their kids' swearing. On the other, though, the evidence is shaky. Kent State psychologist Timothy Jay, an expert on cursing, told NPR that as soon as kids can speak, they start to cuss—because everyone around them does. Nevertheless, every online "expert" predicts parental surprise: "What a shock [when] a foul word escapes your little angel's lips!"

As with much objection to victimless crimes, a circular logic emerges. Kids curse, often in "inappropriate" settings like Grandma's house or kindergarten, to gain attention, to shock. This works (see above) because, well, cursing is inappropriate. Cursing is inappropriate because it is shocking and shocking because it is inappropriate.

Older kids curse to be like other kids, say the experts. Which came first, the kids cursing or the other kids cursing, is never clear. As for harms to children, the worst one mentioned is that cursing elicits punishment. Cursing is bad because it is shocking and shocking because bad; bad because inappropriate and inappropriate because bad; punishable because harmful and harmful because punished.

But cursing can be reined in with gentle discipline (aka punishment). Since it is a minor offense, mouth-washing with soap is not recommended. Adult cursing, on the other hand, is "highly detrimental" to children; thus, fines up to $500,000 are recommended.

When discussing sexual speech, child-development experts often invoke "age-appropriateness," a determination of high sensitivity, with miscalculations carrying grave consequences (Penelope Leach: "Although secrecy makes for dangerous ignorance, too much openness can turn on what is meant to stay turned off until later"). This leads to movie and TV ratings indicating that this film is okay for 13-year-olds but not 12-year-olds, that one for 17-year-olds but only when accompanied by an adult (who could be 18).

Given the gradual and idiosyncratic nature of children's maturation, the timing mechanism of a sexual education probably resembles a sundial more than the IBM Olympic stopwatch. Parents needn't worry so much. But efforts to delineate the boundary between child and adolescent, adolescent and adult, express an anxiety far greater than whether a breast that is appropriate at 10:30 p.m. is inappropriate at 9:30.

What scares us is that these boundaries, if they ever existed, are disappearing.

Philippe Ariès, founder of childhood history, famously proposed that before the 18th Century, there was no such thing as childhood. At seven, a 17th Century person might become a maid or shoemaker's apprentice; by 14 he could be a soldier, a king, or a parent; by 40, he'd likely be dead. The 18th Century Romantics gave us the Innocent Child, uncorrupted by adult knowledge; the following century, the Victorians figured childhood innocence sexual in nature, even as the dangers and pleasures of the Industrial Revolution gave the lie to this wishful invention.

We have not left off trying to fortify the official wall between childhood and adulthood. Twentieth-century innovations from Freudian psychology to child labor laws laid heavy bricks in it. But in our century, globalized economies and proliferating communications technologies are kicking that wall down. Worldwide, children work in sweatshops, invest in stocks, commit crimes, join armies. Even "sheltered" children watch the same videos, listen to the same music, and surf the same Web sites as adults. They know about sex and they engage in sex.

While we locate them in a separate political category, a medical specialty, a market niche—and an FCC-patrolled time slot. But children in the 21st Century may be more like adults than they have been since the 17th Century.

It is unlikely the air will get less dense with information, or with sex—and no law, no Internet filter or vigilant parent can keep tabs on every pixel that passes before a child's eyes. All adults can do is help kids understand and negotiate the sexual world.

But the campaign against indecency is bigger than children. Parents Television Council and their allies in and outside government would like to Bowdlerize the public sphere entirely. So far, the courts have limited attempts, such as numerous online decency statutes, that would reduce all communications to a level appropriate to the Teletubbies.

Still, it is wrong to see censorship as bad for adults and good for children. Everyone can benefit from abundant accurate, realistic sexual information and diverse narratives and images of bodies and sex. In sex as in politics, only more speech can challenge bad speech. We won't all agree on what is bad, but it is time to wrest those definitions from the hands of radical moralists.

POSTSCRIPT

Should the FCC Restrict Broadcast "Indecency"?

All broadcast outlets are responsible for knowing the FCC's policies regarding obscenity, indecency, and profanity. Ironically, station managers who carefully read the FCC's own publication, with all its vivid case studies, could reasonably determine the document itself to be obscene, indecent, and profane. Indeed, portions of the FCC's Enforcement Policies were too obscene to include in this text, as they cited crude jokes about pedophilia, for example. One must wonder how professionals in radio and television respond when such an obscene document arrives in the mail from the FCC. On the other hand, explicit guidance is necessary for station managers to fully understand what may and may not be aired.

The examples cited in the FCC's Enforcement Policies may not always seem congruous. Further, some argue that the FCC has not been even-handed in its enforcement. Howard Stern, a frequent target of the FCC, routinely directs listeners to lodge complaints against other shows, like the *Oprah Winfrey Show,* when it features graphic discussions of sex, or *60 Minutes* when a singer missed a lyric and said, "Shit!"

On Veterans Day in November 2004, ABC aired the movie *Saving Private Ryan* in prime time, uncut with all its expletives and graphic violent war imagery. Sixty-six ABC affiliates refused to air the film, uncertain about whether the FCC would levy substantial fines for every single expletive uttered throughout the film, or if it would regard the film's airing as a patriotic way to honor veterans of World War II. To date, the FCC has taken no action against ABC or the affiliates who aired it, despite clear violations of the FCC policy on indecency.

If the FCC were to take action on the airing of *Saving Private Ryan,* it could only fine ABC based on its airing of expletives. No portion of the FCC policy restricts airing violent imagery. Thus, scenes in which soldiers are maimed are deemed acceptable for viewing, but any utterance of "fuck" would be categorically harmful to children.

What is harmful to children? Is sexual speech and sexual imagery inherently harmful as the FCC policy suggests? Do you agree with Levine when she rejects the idea that sexual material is harmful to children? What do you make of the various cases cited by the FCC? Would you decide differently for any of those cases? Which ones? What other content, if any, do you believe should be restricted as "indecent," or as harmful to children? What penalties would you impose for stations that violate these restrictions?

Suggested Readings

J. Levine, *Harmful to Minors: The Perils of Protecting Children from Sex* (University of Minnesota Press, 2002).

Parents' Television Council, "Basic Cable Awash in Raunch," `http://www.parentstv.org/PTC/publications/reports/2004cablestudy/main.asp` (November 2004).

Parent's Television Council, "Dereliction of Duty: How the Federal Communications Commission has Failed the Public," `http://www.parentstv.org/PTC/publications/reports/fccwhitepaper/main.asp` (February 3, 2004).

R. Pugh, "Decency Advocate: ABC's Ryan Broadcast Flouted FCC Rules— What Now?," `http://headlines.agapepress.org/archive/11/afa/172004b.asp` (November 17, 2004).

F. Rich, "The Great Indecency Hoax," *New York Times* (November 28, 2004).

T. Shales, "Michael Powell Exposed! The FCC Chairman Has No Clothes," *Washington Post* (November 21, 2004).

United States Government Printing Office, *Can You Say That on TV?: An Examination of the FCC's Enforcement with Respect to Broadcast Indecency: Hearing Before the Subcommittee on Teleco* (2004).

ISSUE 12

Is Pornography Harmful to Women?

YES: Elizabeth Cramer et al., from "Violent Pornography and Abuse of Women: Theory to Practice," *Violence and Victims* (vol. 13, no. 4, 1998)

NO: Nadine Strossen, from "The Perils of Pornophobia," *The Humanist* (May/June 1995)

ISSUE SUMMARY

YES: Researchers Elizabeth Cramer et al. state that their study of abused women shows that the use of pornography by males is directly linked with the physical and sexual abuse of women.

NO: Professor of law Nadine Strossen argues that misguided assaults on pornography have resulted in the naive belief that pornography is a major weapon that men use to degrade and dominate women.

Although the First Amendment to the U.S. Constitution protects freedom of speech, Americans have always had restraints on what they can say and write in public. Over 70 years ago, Chief Justice Oliver Wendell Holmes ruled that the First Amendment does not give someone the right to shout "Fire!" in a crowded theater because of the harm such an act could cause. This court ruling supports the efforts of some anti-pornography feminists, who contend that the violence and degrading portrayals of women found in pornography can lead to the abuse of women in real life. Feminists Andrea Dworkin and Catharine MacKinnon call for banning not only "traditional" pornography but also publications, acts, and verbalizations that can be construed as offensive and demeaning to women. Dworkin and MacKinnon define pornography as the major weapon in a cultural war between females and males that permeates every aspect of American lives and society.

At the root of the debate is how we define pornography. Feminist Pat Califia points out that some feminists, as well as the organization Women Against Violence in Pornography and the Media (WAVPM), have adopted a very broad definition. Califia states that according to their definition, "Pornography can include a picture of a woman whose body is smeared with honey, a woman stabbing a man in the back, or a woman dressed in leather towering over two men, as well as films showing various sex acts. This vague definition allowed them to support their contention that pornography objectifies and demeans women, since any image that is objectifying and demeaning is called pornographic." This definition also allows some to maintain that they are fighting against sexist stereotypes of women and not trying to censor sexually explicit material. In their view, misogyny (the hatred of women) is more prevalent and pernicious in pornography than in any other type of media.

Some counter that the focus and efforts of those who oppose pornography are an example of elitist white females worrying about themselves and their "sensitivities" while they ignore the very real physical violence that inner-city residents, women and men alike, face daily. Instead of trying to work out an agreement on what is pornographic, some maintain that the focus should be on gaining greater political and economic equality for women.

As you read the selections, try to develop a classification of different types of pornography. How should the new feminist-produced soft-core pornography, some of which appears in magazines like *Cosmopolitan,* that portrays women as persons who enjoy sexual pleasure as much as men do be viewed? How should pornography produced by gays and lesbians for gay and lesbian readers be viewed? What about erotic romantic novels? Decide which types you might want to make illegal, if any. Do you believe society would benefit from restricting or banning some types of sexually explicit material? For instance, should soft-core pornography, which involves nudity and genital depictions, be treated the same as hard-core pornography, which involves graphic presentation of sexual play, intercourse, and oral sex? What about pornography that includes anal sex, light and/or heavy bondage, bestiality, or other fetishistic behavior? What about topless dancers at bars, strippers on stage or at parties, or live sex acts on stage? How should suggestive advertisements, telephone sex, or "cybersex" on the Internet be viewed?

You may also want to think about what role pornography plays in American-society. Why does so much pornography depict violent sex, and the degradation and victimization of women? Is pornography a symptom of a psychologically unhealthy society, or a healthy safety valve in a society that is basically uncomfortable with sexuality? If we were more accepting and had a positive view of sex that allowed it a natural place in our daily lives, would hard-core pornography continue to sell as well as it does today?

In the following selections, Elizabeth Cramer et al. present the results of a study to demonstrate the correlation between the abuse of women and the use of pornography by the abuser. Nadine Strossen argues that the condemnation of pornography can be carried too far and that universal censorship is not the solution to end violence against women.

YES ⬅

Elizabeth Cramer et al.

Violent Pornography and Abuse of Women: Theory to Practice

T he charge has been made that pornography is the theory and rape is the practice (Kramarae & Treechler, 1985). The final report of the Attorney General's Commission on Pornography (1986), also known as the Meese Commission, stated that there was indeed a connection between persons' use of violent pornography and their use of violence in intimate relationships. The Meese Commission defined pornography as "material predominantly sexually specific and intended for the purpose of sexual arousal" (p. 228–29). They further divided pornography into two subcategories: (1) erotica, which features nudity and explicit consensual sex, and (2) pornography, which contains both non-violent materials depicting domination and humiliation, and sexually explicit material containing violence. Only the latter category was used to define pornography in the present study. Degrading and violent sexual materials have been identified as potentially the most damaging of all types of erotica to the formation of egalitarian, mutually satisfying relationships (Linz, Donerstein, & Penrod, 1988).

Theory to Practice

Does the theory of pornography (that using pornographic materials actually teaches the user that women are there for the gratification of men, and that women enjoy the sexual "liberation" that violence brings) become the practice of pornography? Social learning theory states that we learn about how to act in social situations by observing society around us (Bandura, 1977). Cowan, Lee, Levy, and Smyer (1988) did a content analysis of 45 adult only, x-rated films randomly selected from a list of 121 adult movie titles readily available from a family videocassette store. They found that 60% of the video time was devoted to explicit portrayals of sexual acts. Of these depictions, 78% were coded as dominant and 82% as exploitive, with men doing almost 80% of the dominating/exploiting. Where women were shown as dominating/exploiting, their targets were most frequently other women. A woman's rape was shown in over half of the films, and 90% of the rapists were men. Physically aggressive acts appeared in 73% of the movies. Status inequities were shown with the

From Elizabeth Cramer, Judith McFarlane, Barbara Parker, Karen Soeken, Concepcion Silva, and Sally Reel, "Violent Pornography and Abuse of Women: Theory to Practice," *Violence and Victims*, vol. 13, no. 4 (1998). Copyright © 1998 by Springer Publishing Company, Inc. Reprinted by permission of Springer Publishing Company, Inc., New York 10012. References omitted.

men portrayed as professionals, and the women as secretaries, homemakers, students. . . . The authors state that "the message that men receive from these videos . . . is a distorted characterization of both male and female sexuality that is particularly degrading to women" (p. 309). . . .

There is also a racist component in portrayals of pornographic sex. In an examination of the covers of 60 pornographic magazines and a content analysis of 7 pornographic books, Mayall and Russell (1993) found that African American women were "portrayed in a variety of derogatory and stereotypic ways—as animalistic, incapable of self-control, sexually depraved, impulsive, unclean. . . ." Jewish women were also identified as a separate class, with these women being spoken of as "Jewish whores," "Yiddish swine," etc., and portrayed as submitting to, and enjoying, sexual degradation by Aryan "masters" (p. 176). . . .

Since more than 25% of all women will suffer from a sexual attack during their lifetime (Remer & Witten, 1988) and women's enjoyment of rape is a common theme in pornography (Cowan et al., 1988; Russell et al., 1993), the question of whether viewers of pornography have callous views of rape and/or are more likely to deny men's responsibility in cases of rape has been raised. Malamuth (1981) in a study of 271 male and female students found that exposure to sexually violent films increased men's acceptance of both rape myths ("women say no when they mean yes," "most women who have been raped were asking for it," "many women secretly want to be raped") and interpersonal violence against women. (Interestingly, women in the study were less accepting of rape myths and interpersonal violence after viewing sexually violent films.) Findings similar to these have been supported by Demare, Briere and Lips (1988), Garcia (1986), Linz, Donnerstein, and Penrod (1988), Malamuth and Check (1985). Linz, Donnerstein and Penrod (1984) found that exposure to one film juxtaposing sexual situations and violence per day for 5 days lowered the subjects' anxiety and depressive reactions to the violence in these films over the course of viewing. Subjects who rated the material as progressively less offensive or violent over the course of the series were also more likely to view the victim as responsible for her assault, judged her as offering less resistance to her abuser, and found her less sympathetic, less attractive and less worthy as an individual at the end of the series.

All of the studies mentioned above have taken place in a laboratory setting, and the criticism can be leveled at them that a laboratory is very different from real life. Does pornography relate to the abuse of women outside of the laboratory setting? The authors' previous study found a correlation between battering of women and pornography use by the abuser in a more naturalistic setting (Cramer & McFarlane, 1994). In this study, 87 women pressing charges of physical abuse against an intimate partner were asked if this partner used violent pornography. Forty percent of the women reported pornography use by the abuser. Of these, 35 women (53%) stated that they had been asked or forced to enact scenes they had been shown. Thirty-six (40%) of the subjects had been raped and of these, 74% stated that their partner had used pornography. Twenty-six percent of the women had been reminded of pornography during the abuse incidents. Sommers and Check (1987) also found that battered women experienced significantly more sexual aggression from their partners than the nonbattered control group and that 39% of these women (vs. 3% of the controls) answered yes to the question of whether their partner had ever tried to get them to act out pornographic scenes they had viewed. Russell and colleagues (1985) stated that 14% of a random selection of 930 women from the San Francisco area reported that they had been asked to pose for pornographic pictures, and 10% had been upset by a partner trying to enact scenes from the pornography that had been seen. In a study with current and former prostitutes in the San Francisco Bay area Silbert and Pines (1993) found that 24% of 193 women who had been raped mentioned allusions to pornographic material on the part of the rapist during the assault. This figure is even more significant when it is understood that these comments were spontaneously offered by correspondents during the course of interviews soliciting information about their sexual assault experiences, with no reference to the issues of pornography being made by the interviewer. . . .

Procedures

A prospective cohort design was followed. Approximately equal numbers of African American, non-Hispanic Anglo-American, and Hispanic women, who reported abuse in the year prior to or during pregnancy, were assessed for severity of abuse and their partners' use of pornography, and then assigned to an intervention or control group and followed until the baby was 12 months of age. . . .

Sample   This report is from 198 abused women of whom 35.4% ($n = 70$) are African American, 32.8% ($n = 65$) Hispanic (primarily Mexican and Mexican-American), and 31.8% ($n = 63$) are White American women. (Hispanic was defined as non-Anglo and non-African American and of Spanish speaking decent.)

The women were between the ages of 14 and 42, with a mean age of 23.2 years (standard deviation = 5.6); 29.6% were teenagers (i.e., 19 years or less). All women had incomes below the poverty level as defined using each state's criteria for Women, Infants, and Children (WIC) program eligibility.

Instruments

Abuse Screen

The Abuse Screen consists of five questions to determine abuse status and perpetrator within a defined period of time. (See Box). . . .

Index of Spouse Abuse (ISA)

The ISA is a 30-item, self-report scale designed to measure the severity or magnitude of physical (ISA-P) and nonphysical (ISA-NP) abuse inflicted on a woman by her male partner (Hudson & McIntosh, 1981). . . .

Danger Assessment Scale (DAS)

The DAS, consisting of 14 items with yes/no response format, is designed to assist abused women in determining their potential danger of homicide (Campbell, 1986). All items refer to risk factors that have been associated with homicides in situations involving battering. . . .

(CIRCLE <u>YES</u> OR <u>NO</u> FOR EACH QUESTION)

1. Have you **EVER** been emotionally or physically abused by your **partner or someone** important **to you?**   YES   NO
2. **IN THE YEAR BEFORE YOU WERE PREGNANT,** were you pushed, shoved, slapped, hit, kicked or otherwise physically hurt by someone?   YES   NO
   If YES, by whom?_____
3. **WHILE YOU WERE PREGNANT** were you pushed, shoved, slapped, hit, kicked or otherwise physically hurt by someone?   YES   NO
   If YES, by whom?_____
4. **IN THE YEAR BEFORE YOU WERE PREGNANT,** did anyone force you to have sexual activities?   YES   NO
   If YES, who?_____
5. **WHILE YOU WERE PREGNANT** did anyone force you to have sexual activities?   YES   NO
   If YES, who?_____
6. Are you afraid of your partner or anyone you listed above?   YES   NO

Severity of Violence Against Women Scales (SVAWS)

The SVAWS is a 46-item questionnaire designed to measure two major dimensions: behaviors which threaten physical violence and actual physical violence (Marshall, 1992). Included are nine factors or subscales that have been demonstrated valid through factor analytic techniques: Symbolic Violence and Mild, Moderate, and Serious Threats (Threats of Violence Dimension), and Mild, Minor, Moderate, Serious, and Sexual Violence (Actual Violence Dimension). . . .

Relationship Inventory

The authors designed the Relationship Inventory to assess the status of the relationship including information about the abusers' use of pornography. The following introductory comment was read by the investigators to each woman. "The next questions are about pornography and abuse. We define pornography as sexually violent scenes where a woman is being hurt. For example, the woman is held or tied down." Four questions with a yes/no response option were asked: Does the man who abuses you EVER use pornographic magazines films, or videos? Does the man who abuses you EVER show you or make you look at pornographic scenes in magazines, films or videos? Does the man who abuses you EVER ask you or force you to act out the pornographic scenes he has looked at? Does the man who abuses you EVER ask you or force you to pose for pornographic pictures? . . .

Discussion and Conclusions

The findings of this ethnically stratified cohort study of 198 abused women indicate that 40.9% of the women report use of pornographic material by the abuser with the proportion of pornographic use significantly higher for Whites compared to Blacks and Hispanics. Ethnic differences exist for all four pornographic questions, with a greater proportion of White women responding "yes" to all the pornographic questions. If one accepts social learning theory, this would tend to confirm findings of the 1970 Commission on Pornography and Obscenity which stated that White males use more pornography than other ethnic or racial groups, since most of the relationships in this study did not cross racial lines. These ethnic differences also agree with the authors' earlier study of abuse during pregnancy that found both frequency and severity of physical abuse significantly higher for White women compared to African American and Hispanic women (McFarlane, Parker, Soeken, & Bullock, 1992).

In this study, when three groups were formed according to the abuser's use of pornography and associated involvement of the woman in pornographic activities, violence scores were highest for women reporting the abuser asked or forced them to look at, act out or pose for pornographic scenes, pictures. Severity of violence was not related simply to whether the abuser used pornography.

. . . Stated differently, one out of four abusive men forced their partner to participate with them in their use of pornography. Using other measures of violence, this subsample of abusers was consistently the most violent.

Although some would argue that since forcing a woman to participate in a sexual act is violence, the relationship between these variables is tautological. However, the entire sample was of women currently in a relationship with a violent man and only one fourth of the women reported being forced to participate in pornographic activities. Additional research is needed to further describe the differences between these groups of abusive men.

In considering these findings, several points need to be emphasized. First, in collecting the data, we were careful to define pornography by saying "We are talking about when women are held down or hurt," thus making sure that the women were not reporting on simple nudity. Second, the entire sample was women who had been physically or sexually assaulted by their male partner in the previous 12 months. To summarize, in this sample of 198 women, 2 out of 5 reported that their husband or male partner had used pornographic materials that depicted women in sexually violent scenes. The rate was highest for White women, followed by Hispanic women, with Black women reporting the lowest rate. Of those who did report any use of pornography, approximately 55% of the men forced the women to participate. . . .

Implications exist for both women and men. Requested or forced involvement of women in pornographic activities may indicate the likelihood for increased violence and associated trauma for women. This information can be offered to abused women as part of comprehensive counseling, advocacy, and education. Women provided with information on behaviors associated with increased violence can make informed decisions that protect not only their own safety, but that of their children. Equally important is to provide men with information regarding the degree to which pornography may influence their behavior toward women. Of particular concern is the degree to which pornography is used by men for sexual information. Certainly, to present sexual information to both males and females with an egalitarian relationship of mutual respect will contribute to decreasing violence toward women.

NO ↩

Nadine Strossen

The Perils of Pornophobia

In 1992, in response to a complaint, officials at Pennsylvania State University unceremoniously removed Francisco de Goya's masterpiece, *The Nude Maja,* from a classroom wall. The complaint had not been lodged by Jesse Helms or some irate member of the Christian Coalition. Instead, the complainant was a feminist English professor who protested that the eighteenth-century painting of a recumbent nude woman made her and her female students "uncomfortable."

This was not an isolated incident. At the University of Arizona at Tucson, feminist students physically attacked a graduate student's exhibit of photographic self-portraits. Why? The artist had photographed *herself* in her *underwear.* And at the University of Michigan Law School, feminist students who had organized a conference on "Prostitution: From Academia to Activism" removed a feminist-curated art exhibition held in conjunction with the conference. Their reason? Conference speakers had complained that a composite videotape containing interviews of working prostitutes was "pornographic" and therefore unacceptable.

What is wrong with this picture? Where have they come from—these feminists who behave like religious conservatives, who censor works of art because they deal with sexual themes? Have not feminists long known that censorship is a dangerous weapon which, if permitted, would inevitably be turned against them? Certainly that was the irrefutable lesson of the early women's rights movement, when Margaret Sanger, Mary Ware Dennett, and other activists were arrested, charged with "obscenity," and prosecuted for distributing educational pamphlets about sex and birth control. Theirs was a struggle for freedom of sexual expression and full gender equality, which they understood to be mutually reinforcing.

Theirs was also a lesson well understood by the second wave of feminism in the 1970s, when writers such as Germaine Greer, Betty Friedan, and Betty Dodson boldly asserted that women had the right to be free from discrimination not only in the workplace and in the classroom but in the bedroom as well. Freedom from limiting, conventional stereotypes concerning female sexuality was an essential aspect of what we then called "women's liberation." Women should not be seen as victims in their sexual relations with men but as equally assertive partners, just as capable of experiencing sexual pleasure.

But it is a lesson that, alas, many feminists have now forgotten. Today, an increasingly influential feminist pro-censorship movement threatens to impair

From Nadine Strossen, "The Perils of Pornophobia," *The Humanist,* vol. 55, no. 3 (May/June 1995), pp. 7–9. Copyright © 1995 by Nadine Strossen. Reprinted by permission of the author.

the very women's rights movement it professes to serve. Led by law professor Catharine MacKinnon and writer Andrea Dworkin, this faction of the feminist movement maintains that sexually oriented *expression*—not sex-segregated labor markets, sexist concepts of marriage and family, or pent-up rage—is the preeminent cause of discrimination and violence against women. Their solution is seemingly simple: suppress all "pornography."

Censorship, however, is never a simple matter. First, the offense must be described. And how does one define something so infinitely variable, so deeply personal, so uniquely individualized as the image, the word, and the fantasy that cause sexual arousal? For decades, the U.S. Supreme Court has engaged in a Sisyphean struggle to craft a definition of *obscenity* that the lower courts can apply with some fairness and consistency. Their dilemma was best summed up in former Justice Potter Stewart's now famous statement: "I shall not today attempt further to define [obscenity]: and perhaps I could never succeed in intelligibly doing so. But I know it when I see it."

The censorious feminists are not so modest as Justice Stewart. They have fashioned an elaborate definition of *pornography* that encompasses vastly more material than does the currently recognized law of *obscenity*. As set out in their model law (which has been considered in more than a dozen jurisdictions in the United States and overseas, and which has been substantially adopted in Canada), pornography is "the sexually explicit subordination of women through pictures and/or words." The model law lists eight different criteria that attempt to illustrate their concept of "subordination," such as depictions in which "women are presented in postures or positions of sexual submission, servility, or display" or "women are presented in scenarios of degradation, humiliation, injury, torture . . . in a context that makes these conditions sexual." This linguistic driftnet can ensnare anything from religious imagery and documentary footage about the mass rapes in the Balkans to self-help books about women's health. Indeed, the Boston Women's Health Book Collective, publisher of the now-classic book on women's health and sexuality, *Our Bodies, Ourselves,* actively campaigned against the MacKinnon-Dworkin model law when it was proposed in Cambridge, Massachusetts, in 1985, recognizing that the book's explicit text and pictures could be targeted as pornographic under the law.

Although the "MacDworkinite" approach to pornography has an intuitive appeal to many feminists, it is *itself* based on subordinating and demeaning stereotypes about women. Central to the pornophobic feminists—and to many traditional conservatives and right-wing fundamentalists, as well—is the notion that *sex* is inherently degrading to women (although not to men). Not just sexual expression but sex itself—even consensual, nonviolent sex—is an evil from which women, like children, must be protected.

MacKinnon puts it this way: "Compare victims' reports of rape with women's reports of sex. They look a lot alike. . . . The major distinction between intercourse (normal) and rape (abnormal) is that the normal happens so often that one cannot get anyone to see anything wrong with it." And from Dworkin: "Intercourse remains a means or the means of physiologically making a woman inferior." Given society's pervasive sexism, she believes, women cannot freely consent to sexual relations with men; those who do consent are, in Dworkin's words, "collaborators . . . experiencing pleasure in their own inferiority."

These ideas are hardly radical. Rather, they are a reincarnation of disempowering puritanical, Victorian notions that feminists have long tried to consign to the dustbin of history: woman as sexual victim; man as voracious satyr. The MacDworkinite approach to sexual expression is a throwback to the archaic stereotypes that formed the basis for nineteenth-century laws which prohibited "vulgar" or sexually suggestive language from being used in the presence of women and girls.

In those days, women were barred from practicing law and serving as jurors lest they be exposed to such language. Such "protective" laws have historically functioned to bar women from full legal equality. Paternalism always leads to exclusion, discrimination, and the loss of freedom and autonomy. And in its most extreme form, it leads to purdah, in which women are completely shrouded from public view.

꧁꧂

The pro-censorship feminists are not fighting alone. Although they try to distance themselves from such traditional "family-values" conservatives as Jesse Helms, Phyllis Schlafly, and Donald Wildmon, who are less interested in protecting women than in preserving male dominance, a common hatred of sexual expression and fondness for censorship unite the two camps. For example, the Indianapolis City Council adopted the MacKinnon-Dworkin model law in 1984 thanks to the hard work of former council member Beulah Coughenour, a leader of the Indiana Stop ERA movement. (Federal courts later declared the law unconstitutional.) And when Phyllis Schlafly's Eagle Forum and Beverly LaHaye's Concerned Women for America launched their "Enough Is Enough" anti-pornography campaign, they trumpeted the words of Andrea Dworkin in promotional materials.

This mutually reinforcing relationship does a serious disservice to the fight for women's equality. It lends credibility to and strengthens the right wing and its anti-feminist, anti-choice, homophobic agenda. This is particularly damaging in light of the growing influence of the religious right in the Republican Party and the recent Republican sweep of both Congress and many state governments. If anyone doubts that the newly empowered GOP intends to forge ahead with anti-woman agendas, they need only read the party's "Contract with America" which, among other things, reintroduces the recently repealed "gag rule" forbidding government-funded family-planning clinics from even discussing abortion with their patients.

The pro-censorship feminists base their efforts on the largely unexamined assumption that ridding society of pornography would reduce sexism and violence against women. If there were any evidence that this were true, anticensorship feminists—myself included—would be compelled at least to reexamine our opposition to censorship. But there is no such evidence to be found.

A causal connection between exposure to pornography and the commission of sexual violence has never been established. The National Research

Council's Panel on Understanding and Preventing Violence concluded in a 1993 survey of laboratory studies that "demonstrated empirical links between pornography and sex crimes in general are weak or absent." Even according to another research literature survey that former U.S. Surgeon General C. Everett Koop conducted at the behest of the staunchly anti-pornography Meese Commission, only two reliable generalizations could be made about the impact of "degrading" sexual material on its viewers: it caused them to think that a variety of sexual practices was more common than they had previously believed, and to more accurately estimate the prevalence of varied sexual practices.

Correlational studies are similarly unsupportive of the pro-censorship cause. There are no consistent correlations between the availability of pornography in various communities, states and countries and their rates of sexual offenses. If anything, studies suggest an inverse relationship: a greater availability of sexually explicit material seems to correlate not with higher rates of sexual violence but, rather, with higher indices of gender equality. For example, Singapore, with its tight restrictions on pornography, has experienced a much greater increase in rape rates than has Sweden, with its liberalized obscenity laws.

There *is* mounting evidence, however, that MacDworkinite-type laws will be used against the very people they are supposed to protect—namely, women. In 1992, for example, the Canadian Supreme Court incorporated the MacKinnon-Dworkin concept of pornography into Canadian obscenity law. Since that ruling, in *Butler v. The Queen*—which MacKinnon enthusiastically hailed as "a stunning victory for women"—well over half of all feminist bookstores in Canada have had materials confiscated or detained by customs. According to the *Feminist Bookstore News,* a Canadian publication, "The *Butler* decision has been used . . . only to seize lesbian, gay, and feminist material."

Ironically but predictably, one of the victims of Canada's new law is Andrea Dworkin herself. Two of her books, *Pornography: Men Possessing Women* and *Women Hating,* were seized, custom officials said, because they "illegally eroticized pain and bondage." Like the MacKinnon-Dworkin model law, the *Butler* decision makes no exceptions for material that is part of a feminist critique of pornography or other feminist presentation. And this inevitably overbroad sweep is precisely why censorship is antithetical to the fight for women's rights.

The pornophobia that grips MacKinnon, Dworkin, and their followers has had further counterproductive impacts on the fight for women's rights. Censorship factionalism within the feminist movement has led to an enormously wasteful diversion of energy from the real cause of and solutions to the ongoing problems of discrimination and violence against women. Moreover, the "porn-made-me-do-it" defense, whereby convicted rapists cite MacKinnon and Dworkin in seeking to reduce their sentences, actually impedes the aggressive enforcement of criminal laws against sexual violence.

A return to the basic principles of women's liberation would put the feminist movement back on course. We women are entitled to freedom of expression—to read, think, speak, sing, write, paint, dance, photograph, film, and fantasize as we wish. We are also entitled to our dignity, autonomy, and equality. Fortunately, we can—and will—have both.

POSTSCRIPT

Is Pornography Harmful to Women?

The issue of pornography and its potential harms, particularly in reinforcing the subjugation and humiliation of females, is a perplexing one. Efforts to censor speech, writing, and pictorial material (including classical art) have been continuous throughout American history. The success of censorship efforts depends mainly on the dominating views in the particular era in which the efforts are being made, and on whether conservative or liberal views dominate during that period. In the conservative Victorian era, morals crusader Anthony Comstock persuaded Congress to adopt a broadly worded law banning "any book, painting, photograph, or other material design, adapted, or intended to explain human sexual functions, prevent conception, or produce abortion." That 1873 law was in effect for almost a hundred years, until the U.S. Supreme Court declared its last remnants unconstitutional by allowing the sale of contraceptives to married women in 1963 and to single women in 1972.

In 1986, a pornography commission headed by then–Attorney General Edwin Meese maintained that the "totality of evidence" clearly documented the social dangers of pornography and justified severe penalties and efforts to restrict and eliminate it. At the same time, then–Surgeon General C. Everett Koop arrived at conclusions that opposed those of the Meese commission. Koop stated that "Much research is still needed in order to demonstrate that the present knowledge [of laboratory studies] has significant real world implications for predicting [sexual] behavior."

Suggested Readings

K. Davies, "Voluntary Exposure to Pornography and Men's Attitudes Toward Feminism and Rape," *Journal of Sex Research* (1997).

A. Leuchtag, "The Culture of Pornography," *The Humanist* (May/June 1995).

E. Schlosser, "The Business of Pornography," *U.S. News & World Report* (February 10, 1997).

N. Strossen, *Defending Pornography: Free Speech, Sex, and the Fight for Women's Rights* (Scribner, 1995).

B. Thompson, *Soft Core: Moral Crusades Against Pornography in Britain and America* (Cassell, 1995).

ISSUE 13

Is Pedophilia Always Harmful?

YES: Laura Schlessinger, from "Evil Among Us," *Dr. Laura Perspective* (June 1999)

NO: David L. Riegel, from *Understanding Loved Boys and Boylovers* (SafeHaven Foundation Press, 2000)

ISSUE SUMMARY

YES: Radio commentator Laura Schlessinger denounces a study, published by the American Psychological Association (APA), that reexamined the results and conclusions from 59 earlier studies of child sexual abuse (CSA) in more than 35,000 college students. Schlessinger views this study as a "pseudo-scientific" attempt to convince people to accept pedophilia as normal.

NO: Author David L. Riegel summarizes the major findings of the research in question, and criticizes the dismissal of scientific research that challenges common assumptions about CSA and its effects on children.

In 1998, *Psychological Bulletin,* the official publication of the American Psychological Association (APA), contained a research report entitled "A Meta-Analytic Examination of Assumed Properties of Child Sexual Abuse Using College Samples." This report was written by three respected researchers with solid publication records, Bruce Rind (Temple University), Robert Bauserman (Maryland State Health Department), and Philip Tromovitch (University of Pennsylvania). It received some discussion and notice in the academic world, but nothing unusual.

However, a few people alerted Laura Schlessinger, a conservative radio and television commentator. Schlessinger immediately launched a campaign to "rally the troops to fight the enemy at the barricades and save our nation" from being turned into a nation of pedophiles. Joined by The Family Research Council and the National Association for the Research and Therapy of Homosexuality (NARTH), Schlessinger enlisted the aid of a few conservative Washington lawmakers, who prepared a bill condemning the report. On July 12, 1999, Representative Matt Salmon (R-Arizona) called on members of the House of Representatives to condemn what had become known for brevity's sake as "the Rind research or report." The purpose of this study, Salmon maintained, was to make pedophilia normal and acceptable. The representatives unanimously voted to condemn the report. Only a handful of representatives abstained, suspecting that the editors of the *Psychological Bulletin* would not publish a report endorsing and promoting pedophilia, and concerned about the wisdom of condemning a scholarly publication that none of them had seen or read in its full form.

Some believe that the conclusions of the Rind research is good news for some sexual abuse victims. If it is true that many (or even a few) victims do not suffer lifelong consequences from child sexual abuse, and that many victims are not traumatized, permanently damaged, or wounded for life, we might view such findings in a positive insight. But many Americans find this possibility totally unacceptable as it would also require us to rethink the basic assumption that pedophilia is harmful all the time.

While the APA endured harsh public criticism from Congress and media commentators, it also received a letter of support from the Society for the Scientific Study of Sexuality (SSSS), in which the past and present officers urged the APA "to staunchly support the right of sexual scientists to engage in free intellectual inquiry—especially in the area of 'controversial' research," such as the sexuality of children and the long-term consequences of child sexual abuse, incest, and adult-child sex.

In the following selections, Schlessinger maintains that the release of the APA study results is harmful because the findings can be interpreted as validating and "normalizing" pedophilia. David L. Riegel summarizes the major findings of the research and criticizes those who would summarily dismiss research findings.

Laura Schlessinger  **YES**

Evil Among Us

[You may have] heard me on the air lambasting a recent article published in the *Bulletin* of the American Psychological Association, called "A Meta-Analytic Examination of Assumed Properties of Child Sexual Abuse Using College Samples."

In short: The three researchers claim that child sexual abuse does not necessarily cause intense, lasting harm—and go on to suggest that when there is a "willing" sexual encounter between an adult and a child, it be given the "value-neutral" term "adult-child sex!"

I've read and re-read this report until I'm sick to my stomach, and still, putting these words into print leaves me practically speechless—and you know how rare that is.

When I first heard about this, I wanted to disbelieve it. But I've done my research, and I cannot stress strongly enough how deadly serious this is.

This study is the first step on the road toward normalizing pedophilia—just as homosexuality has been mainstreamed, to the point where tolerance is no longer sufficient: We now have to "embrace" it.

I want to recap for you my own journey of discovery in this horrifying story: as I first learned of this study, examined it further, spoke with experts in the field who have excoriated the authors' methodology and their conclusions, and as I received hundreds of outraged, appalled and heartbroken letters from listeners who know all too well the "lasting, pervasive" harm of child sexual abuse—and that it is *never* a "willing," "value-neutral" experience.

The Warning Bell Sounds

It began with a letter.

I was in the middle of my show one day when I received a fax from Don, a father of two, who had just heard Dom Giordano, morning talk show host on my Philadelphia affiliate, WWDB, interview one of the authors of this study. Don wrote:

> "[The author] stated that not all children who engage in sexual contact willingly with an adult show any lasting damage. He further stated that to call this sexual contact 'abuse' is a mistake, because it's consensual . . ." [I believe the researchers had] an agenda that should scare all decent people.

The next time some pervert gets caught with a child, I'm sure this is the first study his scum lawyer will drag out to defend his actions."

I immediately thought, "This is a very intelligent letter, but this can't be happening." I didn't believe it. So we started to track it down.

Next we received a fact sheet from NARTH, an organization I respect: the National Association for Research and Therapy of Homosexuality. The name of NARTH's report was: "The Problem of Pedophilia: Adult-Child Sex Is Not Necessarily Abuse, Say Some Psychologists."

The NARTH article pointed out that one of the authors of the *Bulletin* article had earlier co-authored an article in a special issue of the respected *Journal of Homosexuality* entitled "Male Intergenerational Intimacy." That issue was essentially an advertisement for the "benefits" of pedophilia—asserting that the loving pedophile can offer a child "companionship, security and protection" that neither peers nor parents can provide, and that parents should look on the pedophile "as a partner in the boy's upbringing, someone to be welcomed into their home . . ."!

Here are some excerpts from NARTH's report; I'd like to thank Dr. Joseph Nicolosi, director of NARTH, for giving us permission to quote from it. (I've **boldfaced** some important points.)

"The American Psychological Association did not denounce the positions advanced within the *Journal of Homosexuality*. In fact, just recently, the APA published a new major study written by one of those same *Journal of Homosexuality* writers. The latest article appears in the APA's own prestigious *Psychological Bulletin*. It provides an overview of all of the research studying the harm resulting from childhood sexual abuse.

"**The authors' conclusion? That childhood sexual abuse is, on the average, only slightly associated with psychological harm, and that the harm may not even be due to the sexual experience, but to the negative family factors in the children's backgrounds. When the sexual contact is not coerced, especially when it is experienced by a boy and enjoyed, it may not be harmful at all. . . .**

"**In fact, the authors of the *Psychological Bulletin* article propose another way of understanding pedophilia: That it may be abuse if the child feels bad about the relationship. They are in effect suggesting a repetition of the steps by which homosexuality was normalized.** In its first step toward removing homosexuality from the Diagnostic Manual, the APA said the condition was normal as long as the person didn't feel bad about it. . . .

"According to the latest diagnostic manual (DSM-IV), a person no longer has a psychological disorder simply because he molests children. To be diagnosed as disordered, he must feel anxious about the molestation, or be impaired in his work or social relationships. **Thus, the APA has left room for the psychologically 'normal' pedophile.**"

Now, I have to reiterate a point here that I've tried to make several times on the air. Psychology has become some kind of holy writ to the general public. It's not. *Psychology is not hard science.* Just because a bunch of psychologists make intellectual-sounding pronouncements about the way things are—it ain't necessarily so!

⋅⟨◉⟩⋅

So, let me ask a question of the psychologists and psychiatrists of the world: If pedophilia is not a mental disorder, then what is it? Is it normal?

When homosexuality was dropped from the *DSM*, the agenda became, "Homosexuality is normal." If you said anything to the contrary, that meant you were hateful and bigoted. Deviance became redefined as diversity, and tolerance became defined as acceptance, then celebration. It sounds like we're taking the next step with pedophilia.

To return to the NARTH fact sheet:

> "If psychology indeed recognizes consensual pedophilia as harmless, then civil law and social norms will be under pressure to follow the lead of so-called social science, as indeed they did in the issue of homosexuality. **When psychiatry declared homosexuality normal, our courts and theologians began to rewrite civil law and moral theology based upon what psychiatry said it had discovered through empirical science.**"

Later, Joe Nicolosi sent me a memo that makes some very salient additional points:

1. "The study used a *college-age* sample, which implies that most subjects were likely single. Would the results of this study have been different if they had been conducted with these same subjects ten years later? Would those subjects have been more prone to divorce, alcoholism, and child abuse? Would their spouses agree that they were well-adjusted, sexually and emotionally? We doubt it.
2. "The authors of the study try to make a case for separating 'wrongfulness' (social-moral norms) from 'harmfulness' (psychological damage). We believe that social norms of wrongfulness are not *arbitrary*, but they *evolved* out of the great religious philosophers' time-honored observations of 'harmfulness'—i.e., their finding of psychological damage to the person and society.
3. "The study makes a distinction between *forced* and *consensual* child-adult or adult-teen sex. What minor-age child can make an informed decision to consent to sex?"

The Truth Comes Out

Much as I still didn't want to believe this could be happening, I realized it was time to examine this for myself.

So I got the actual article, published [in July 1998] by the American Psychological Association, in their *Psychological Bulletin*. This is a peer-reviewed publication, which means that some number of clinicians had to read and approve this article for publication. While this may not be a statement of the

APA's official position, I hold them accountable for what I have been told by *numerous* professionals is garbage research.

- First of all, let's look at the title of the report: "A Meta-Analytic Examination . . .": Meta-analysis means you don't do any of your own work; you go into the literature, grab a lot of papers, all done by different people, put them all together, do a lot of math, and publish.
- The researchers chose 59 studies to review. Of these, 38 percent have not been published. They are unpublished master-degree or doctoral dissertations. So 23 of the 59 studies used were not even subject to any kind of peer review—that is, to the technical scrutiny of the psychological community.
- These 59 studies all used self-reporting from college students, who were questioned about the effects of child sexual abuse as they felt them. Think about that term, "self-reporting": That's a brilliant way to do research, right? You have a lot of objectivity there.
- The researchers claim that according to some of these college students' own descriptions, the negative effects of child sexual abuse "were neither pervasive nor typically intense, and that men reacted much less negatively than women." Is this anybody's personal experience? Does this bear any resemblance to anyone you know who was molested as a child?
- According to their findings, two-thirds of sexually abused men and more than one-quarter of sexually abused women "reported neutral or positive reactions." So even in their own study—again keeping in mind the dubious nature of their methods—one-third of the guys and 75 percent of the women were harmed. Aren't statistics a wonderful thing?

•◉•

What really frightens me is the idea that this study will now be used to normalize pedophilia—to change the legal system, and further destroy what I feel has been an ongoing plot against the family.

I'm not alone in this view. I had a discussion with Dr. Gerard van den Aardweg of Holland, who has seen firsthand the inroads made in his country by pedophilia activists.

Dr. van den Aardweg has a Ph.D. in psychology, did his dissertation on homosexuality, has been in private practice for many years, and has written several books and articles on homosexuality, pedophilia, neuroses and family issues.

"Their argument is that scores on some tests do not indicate harm—that if harm is not demonstrated by their way of testing, then harm does not exist," Dr. van den Aardweg says.

"**I think these people are so eager to propagate the normality of adultchild sexual contact that they are blind to the obvious alternative: 'If my test did not show harm, maybe my test did not measure harm.'**"

"These tests are sample questionnaires or short interview questions. At best, they can give a very rude indication of subjectively perceived discomfort. But in very many cases they not even do that. Harm is much more than 'I do or do not feel okay,' or 'I didn't like that experience.' Harm after child sexual abuse is often an increased distress with respect to adults; a distorted and unhealthy view of sexuality; a distorted view of their own or the opposite sex. It can be subsequent sexual abnormalities. It can be marriage and other relational problems later in life; problems functioning as a parent; sometimes later promiscuity; and in many cases, inferiority complexes, because children who have been misused often feel worthless.

"**In short, what these psychologists offer us here is an insult to any really credible scientist of true scientific thinking. It is bogus psychology.**"

A Global Crisis

Now here's a further discussion that Dr. van den Aardweg and I had on the telephone:

Dr. van den Aardweg: I think the sexual reform movements of the Western world have as one of their goals to liberate sexuality in all its forms. And so there is a silent—not so silent here in Holland—cooperation of the sexual reform organizations with the cause of the militant pedophiles. Here it is very clear. For example, our Dutch Association for Sexual Reform has special meetings for pedophiles every week in most Dutch cities.

Dr. Laura: This is scary. In this country, such groups gain power and authority by attacking the opposition as phobic, intolerant of diversity, bigoted and mean.

VDA: You will do a wonderful thing if you make people aware of this, and say to them, "Don't let yourself be intimidated. Don't doubt your own commonsense judgment of these things." Because people are overruled and overwhelmed with all kinds of pseudo-science. They think "Who am I? Perhaps I'm wrong, I'm old-fashioned, I'm a victim of my Western culture." But they have to be supported as to their own convictions.

DL: So the point of liberating the sexual mores in general is, ultimately, to have access to kids.

VDA: Yes.

DL: That's what it's for: getting the kids sexually active and then getting sexually active with the kids. So there are a number of ways for people to take our kids. They can recruit them for the Fatherland's master race, they can take them out of villages and force them to become soldiers, or they can support safe-sex education in schools starting in kindergarten, and have them become active and liberated and available and open to new sexual experiences—like sex with an adult.

VDA: Pedophiles have an obsession. It's not a normal kind of sexual drive, it's a pathological obsession. It is the nucleus of their whole life. Like many disturbed people, their attitude is not that "I have to change," but that "the world has to change." And so, they are the ones to crusade to change the world, and really think that they can eventually get normal fathers and mothers to give their children to pedophiles for educational or enlightenment motivations.

Here in Holland, one of the advocates of pedophilia who just died had received royal distinction some years ago for his work to "liberate" homosexuality, as they say. He was in the Dutch senate as a very esteemed and respected senator.

Be aware: The public does not know what is happening. The pedophile network is worldwide.

Outrage and Anguish

You can imagine the firestorm I set off by devoting an entire hour of my radio show to this topic—as well as follow-ups on several subsequent days.

I hadn't even finished speaking when the faxes began pouring in. Listeners were horrified by what they were hearing. . . . The article—and my outspoken opposition to it—received a great deal of media attention. . . .

⋅◈⋅

And, what a surprise, the American Psychological Association was quick to disassociate itself from the article in its own publication, according to a press release they put out:

> "As a publisher of psychological research, APA publishes thousands of research reports every year.
>
> "But, publication of the findings of a research project within an APA journal is in no way an endorsement of a finding by the Association. . .
>
> "Unfortunately, the findings of this meta-analysis . . . are being misreported by some in the media. The actual findings are that for this segment of the population (college students) being the victim of childhood sexual abuse was found to be less damaging to them than generally believed. However, one overall statement of the results was that students who were the victims of child sexual abuse were, on average, slightly less well-adjusted than students who were not victimized as children . . .
>
> "Those who are reporting that the study says that childhood sexual contact with adults is not harmful to children are misreporting the findings."

Perhaps they hadn't read their own publication: The researchers specifically say that "this poorer adjustment *could not be attributed to CSA [child sexual abuse]* [italics mine—DL] because family environment was consistently confounded with CSA. . . ."

Furthermore, the authors clearly state at the end of their report: *"A willing encounter with positive reactions would be labeled simply* adult-child *sex, a value-neutral term. . . . Moreover, the term* child *should be restricted to nonadolescent children"*—as if a nonadolescent child has the intellectual, psychological or emotional maturity to "willingly" engage in a sexual encounter with an adult!

I'm still flabbergasted by this logic.

NO ↵

David L. Riegel

The Real Evil Among Us

In the spring and summer of 1999, a raging academic and public debate erupted over the July 1998 publication of "A Meta-Analytic Examination of Assumed Properties of Child Sexual Abuse Using College Samples" by Doctors Bruce Rind and Robert Bauserman and graduate student Philip Tromovitch. This fracas, which continues right up to the present, is reminiscent of that which ensued when Doctor Edward Wilson published "Sociobiology" some three decades ago. Dr. Wilson was the first to formalize the idea that social behavior could be explained evolutionarily. Biologists, psychologists, sociologists, and others quickly split into two camps, the battle was joined, accusations and personal attacks flew, and on one occasion a group of disgruntled graduate students snuck up behind Dr. Wilson at a conference, dumped a bucket of water on his head, and shouted "You're all wet!" When careful scientific research shows that time honored and revered "wisdom" is not based in fact, but that a different point of view actually is, there is often a strong and vocal reaction involving misinformation and innuendo in an attempt to discredit the research.

And yet the truths pointed out by Rind *et al.* are nothing new. In 1942 Dr. Karl Menninger, speaking of the effects of sexual experiences of children with older persons in *Love against Hate* (Harcourt, Brace & World, New York), noted: "The assumption is, of course, that children are irreparably ruined by such experiences. . . . I may . . . point out that in the cold light of scientific investigation no such devastating effects usually follow. . ."(p. 284) Over the intervening decades such respected sexologists as Frits Bernard, Larry Constantine, Paul Okami, Theo Sandfort, and many others have investigated these experiences and have generally arrived at the same conclusions as Dr. Menninger.[1] Unfortunately, these findings are still waiting for understanding and acceptance by the general public.

Rind *et al.* and the American Psychological Association (APA), which published the article in one of their journals (*Psychological Bulletin*), have been repeatedly castigated by right wing organizations such as the Family Research Council and the National Association for the Research and Therapy of Homosexuality, as well as by ultraconservative individuals like "Dr. Laura" Schlessinger. There have been indignant news conferences and outraged responses from the child sexual abuse industry; even the United States House of Representative entered the fray by passing a resolution condemning the research, despite the fact that few, if any, of the congresspersons ever read it.

Many of these detractors invoked "morality" in their attacks. But morality is at best a very subjective issue; that which is considered grossly immoral in one society and time can be very acceptable in a different society and/or time. In our own society, masturbation, homosexuality, and premarital cohabitation were all at one time considered immoral, but only a few diehards hold these discredited positions today. The mentoring relationships between pubescent boys and older males in ancient Greece included a sexual component which was accepted in that society. Other societies today have moral expectations that allow for sexual experiences between children and older persons, and there is the possibility that our own society may some day view these matters differently. But, as Rind *et al.* and the APA found out, resistance to enlightenment can be fierce and dogged.

So what actually is this modern day heresy committed by Rind *et al.*, this latest target of witch hunters and book burners? To begin with, the authors took exception to the indiscriminate use of such value-laden terms as "perpetrator," "victim," and "child sexual abuse" (CSA).[2] However, after considering alternatives, they decided to retain these throughout their article simply for convenience, and attend to at least the last of these three terms in their conclusion. Then, simply put, they took 59 previous investigations of "CSA," subjected them to rigorous statistical analyses, and showed that, based on responses from some 35,000 college students, commonly held beliefs in four areas were highly inaccurate: (1) that "CSA" causes harm, (2) that this harm occurs in all cases, (3) that this harm is likely to be intense, and (4) that the effects of "CSA" are equivalent for boys and girls.

These cherished tenets are foundational for the enormously profitable and well entrenched child sexual abuse industry. They are also mainstays for those who are determined to preserve the archaic concept of asexual and innocent children, sexually uninformed robotic chattel property who are to be manipulated, molded, and used however their owners see fit, until they reach an arbitrary age at which they are to be suddenly and magically transformed into intelligent, responsible, and sexually competent adults.

There is no attempt in Rind's research to say that significant psychological damage can never result from non-consensual and coerced sexual relationships between a child and an older person. Rather, the main premises are that the consequences of actual "CSA" are grossly exaggerated, that inadequate consideration has been given to the vast differences in responses of boys versus girls and consensual versus non-consensual experiences, that the clinical terminology is inaccurate and highly biased, and that a revision in attitudes, terminology, perceptions, conclusions, and applications is long since past due.

For most people, large portions of the thirty-two full size double column pages of this research are a nightmare of incomprehensible statistical gibberish. But careful reading and re-reading of the non-statistical portions will give the average reader an understanding of the data, methods, and conclusions.

To wit, here is a summary of the authors' findings, using their own paragraph headings, with respect to four common myths:

- *"CSA" causes harm:*

Most of the 59 sets of data used in the study indicated that people who had experienced "CSA" as children developed more emotional and psychological problems than those who said they had not been exposed to "CSA." But there are several problems here which need to be dealt with, not the least of which is that this correlation is exactly what too many of those 59 investigators expected and wanted to find. Neglect, and such factors as physical, emotional, and mental abuse were either scrambled in with "CSA" or were largely ignored, since there was no perceived need to look any further once the preconceived and desired results had been obtained.

But when these studies were sorted out and properly examined under the microscope of computerized statistical analysis, the assumed relationship between "CSA" and "maladjustment," as emotional and psychological problems are known, diminished almost to the vanishing point. There was some correlation remaining for females, but for males it was so small as to be insignificant. On the other hand, "family environment," which is a catchall for the other forms of abuse described above, had a markedly higher correlation with maladjustment than did "CSA."

The net effect of this aspect of the research was to disprove, in the vast majority of cases, and especially with males, that there is any reason whatsoever to ascribe any significant amount of maladjustment to the occurrence of "CSA."

- *Harm caused by "CSA" occurs in all cases:*

Much of the research done in years past on "CSA" was based on data from clinical populations, i.e., people who sought help for emotional and/or psychological problems. The inevitable result was that the pervasiveness of harm was greatly exaggerated, since only those who perceived themselves as needing treatment were included. Not to mention that clinical psychologists are predisposed to specifically inquire about possible "CSA," and, if there is even a vague hint that it may have occurred, they immediately seize on that "CSA" as the probable cause of any and all maladjustment they can find. There have also been many cases where a "memory" has been elicited simply from the persistent questioning by the psychologist, a memory that was later determined to be based on circumstances that, in fact, never occurred.

Analyses of the data from the non-clinical samples used in the Rind *et al.* study show that this supposed pervasiveness is not the case, since only a small minority of females, and a minuscule number of males, reported that they perceived they had been permanently harmed by their childhood or adolescent sexual encounters. Many of the women reported temporary harm, but many did not. The majority of the men did not even report temporary harm.

- *Harm caused by "CSA" is likely to be intense:*

In the case of a small boy or girl who is forcibly and repeatedly raped by an older man that they had previously loved and trusted, there is good reason to believe that intense psychological harm is likely to result. This is most definitely an extreme and rare example, although, sadly, it does occur. But the data do not support the presupposition that "CSA" causes intense harm except in such rare cases. However, as one author has put it, "children are amazingly resilient," so it cannot be assumed that a severe maladjustment is the inevitable outcome of even this extreme example.

- *The effects of "CSA" are equivalent in boys and girls:*

This position is especially espoused by those who have yet to be convinced that there are very real cognitive, emotional, and behavioral differences between boys and girls. This study continues to demolish any remnants of this concept by demonstrating the completely different attitudes, approaches, and experiences that boys and girls report about sexual activities with significantly older persons. In simple and understandable numbers, the study notes that two thirds of the men who reported "CSA" experiences viewed them at the time as other than negative, and three eighths remembered them as positive. These figures do not take consensuality into account, and it is reasonable to believe that there would be a much larger proportion of positive memories if the non-consensual experiences were eliminated from the computation.

Over two thirds of the women, on the other hand, reported negative feelings, and only one tenth had positive recollections.

Only when unwanted sex is considered separately do the male versus female findings tend toward being equivalent, and even in these cases the association with harm is, on average, small.

⁂

The issue of pejorative, value laden, and inflammatory terminology that Rind *et al.* addressed in their closing paragraphs is also nothing new. In 1990 Okami wrote "Sociopolitical Biases in the Contemporary Scientific Literature on Adult Human Sexual Behavior with Children and Adolescents," which was a chapter in *Pedophilia: Biosocial Dimensions* edited by Feierman and published by Springer-Verlag. Okami notes:

> . . . use of negatively loaded terminology such as "abuse," "assault," . . . "molestation," . . . or "victimization" to refer generically to all adult human sexual behavior with children and adolescents, confounds attempts to understand such interactions and may reflect . . . a serious conflict of interest between scientific inquiry on the one hand and enforcement of social norms or propagation of political ideology on the other (p 99).

As noted earlier, the adverse reactions to this study were swift and vehement. Some were successfully manipulative, as when Representative Matt

Salmon hoodwinked the United States House of Representatives into unanimously approving a hasty resolution denouncing both the research and the researchers. It goes without saying that it would have been political suicide for any member of Congress to vote against condemning what Mr. Salmon trumpeted as "the emancipation proclamation of pedophiles." By approving this absurdity, these congresspersons showed themselves to be politically astute, but totally devoid of any understanding of, or respect for, science, scientists, or scientific principles.

The "Family Research Council" also made a feeble attempt to discredit the research on an imagined procedural blunder reported by an ex-president of the American Psychiatric Association, but wound up with considerable egg on their collective faces when they stated "Of the 59 studies included in the analysis, over 60% of the data are drawn from a single study done 40 years ago." An examination shows, instead of being 60% of the some 35,000 respondents to the 59 studies, that particular study comprised only 4%. Furthermore, because it used somewhat outmoded subjective techniques, and was completed before child abuse researchers began collecting objective data on the effects of "CSA," that study was not used at all in the primary analyses upon which the researchers based their conclusions.

"Dr. Laura" Schlessinger, a talk show host, published a lengthy tirade in her now defunct magazine *Dr. Laura Perspective*, referring to Rind *et al.* as the "Evil Among Us." She began by claiming, but not substantiating, that she has received "hundreds" of letters about the "lasting, pervasive" harm of child sexual abuse. Since her stated positions on these issues effectively solicits such letters, it is not surprising that she receives them. But it is surprising that her claims are in direct opposition to a huge amount of empirical data. She then quoted one of her trusted correspondents as saying that any attorney who would dare represent a "pervert" is "scum," prime examples of the pejorative and inflammatory language that is discussed earlier. Shortly before noting that "because . . . psychologists make intellectual-sounding pronouncements . . . it ain't necessarily so!," she quoted at great length from clinical psychologist Joseph Nicolosi, whose anti-gay agenda is well known. She presented his observations as if they were logical conclusions based on empirical data, when they are actually nothing more than personal and unsupported opinions. One of these is his assertion that no "minor-age child can make an informed decision to consent to sex," which, although it is a position held by some, is the subject of ongoing debate.

After citing more of Nicolosi's misleading and unsupported assertions that were previously refuted in Rind *et al.*, she took aim at the concept of meta-analysis as meaning that "you don't do any of your own work," then contradicted herself by saying that a lot of math—which certainly is "work"—was done! The analyses, discussion, and conclusions in Rind *et al.* also represent a monumental amount of work. Her next targets were masters theses and doctoral dissertations, which she complained are not peer reviewed. Since she holds a doctorate in physiology (but not in the social sciences), she should have been well aware of the fact that such papers are scrutinized by faculty examiners much more thoroughly than most peer reviews. She then took a swipe at "self-reported" behavioral data, failing to take note that the vast majority of human behavioral data are self-reported, whether it be in a personal interview or a questionnaire. Observational data, especially of children, adolescents and adults, are used much less frequently.

She went on to cite a telephone conversation—which she inflated to the status of dealing with a "Global Crisis"—with one Dr. van den Aarweg, yet another member of the psychological discipline she previously dismissed as unscientific. In her part of the conversation, she launched into some very unprofessional and pejorative rhetoric, comparing any attempt at intelligent sex education for children with the Hitler youth groups. In everything she had to say she missed the point that the world view she espouses is only a recent and localized development, and there are many other world views which are or were considered valid by a majority of mankind. Just because a radio talk show host makes intellectual-sounding pronouncements about the way she thinks things ought to be, it doesn't follow that she necessarily is correct.

It is interesting to note that those who have truth and facts on their side are pleased to invite the whole world to investigate both their deliberations and their conclusions. But those who are perpetuating lies and misrepresentations, since they have nothing of substance to say in response, so often resort to innuendo, emotional appeals, irrelevant accusations, and attempts to suppress any discussion of the real issues.

There is no way of accurately determining the inner mindset of the majority of people. Polls tend to get answers on controversial subjects such as childhood sexuality that agree mostly with what people believe they are expected to say, rather than what is actually going on in their minds. And the perceptions perpetuated by the media are mostly derived from the minority of radicals who do the most and loudest screaming. So we can only hope, or perhaps be cautiously optimistic, that beyond the blaring sirens and roaring cannons there is a quiet revolution brewing, a revolution of thinking people who are at long last beginning to realize that for decades they have been spoon fed a diet of misinformation and lies about a very critical factor of human emotional life, that of the sexuality, sexual needs, and the sexual nature of their own precious children.

It took nearly twenty years for Ed Wilson's pioneering work to begin to be accepted and recognized for the insights and wisdom it really contained, but he is now revered as one of the outstanding scientists in sociobiology. How long will it take this time for the dark clouds of the *real* evil among us to be dispelled by the bright sunshine of reason and truth?

Notes

1. See, for example, Bernard, F. (1985). *Paedophilia: A Factual Report.* Rotterdam: Enclave.
2. The term "child sexual abuse" is a pejorative argument in and of itself; however, because so much of the literature is permeated with this term and its acronym, and because Rind *et al.* also reluctantly used it, it is used in this essay for convenience. Such usage does not in any way sanction or endorse the term.

POSTSCRIPT

Is Pedophilia Always Harmful?

In 1986, after examining 300 incest relationships, Warren Farrell, a psychologist teaching at the University of California School of Medicine, concluded that the effects of incest "are perhaps best described as a magnifying glass—magnifying the worst in a poor family environment and the best in a caring and loving family environment." However, in his report titled "The Last Taboo? The Complexities of Incest and Female Sexuality," published in *The Handbook of Sexology, vol. 7* (Elsevier Science, 1991), Farrell noted that "in most family environments it exposes the family fabric to rays of confusion and guilt of such intensity that the magnifying glass burns a hole in all but the strongest."

Whether or not all, most, or only some children who have been involved in adult-child sexual relationships are emotionally and/or psychologically damaged for life, it is clear that adult-child sexual relationships are regarded as socially unacceptable in American culture. There are currently other societies where noncoercive, consensual sexual relations between adults and minors are quite acceptable. In some countries, boys and girls can be given legal consent to sexual relations if they are 12 years old. In the South Pacific, adolescent Melanesian boys and girls are not allowed to have sex with each other before marriage, but the boys are expected to have sex both with an older male and with a boy of their own age. Their first heterosexual experience comes with marriage. In the Cook Islands, Mangaian boys are expected to have sex with many girls but only after an older woman teaches them about the art of sexual pleasuring. But norms regarding sexual readiness that are acceptable in other cultures are widely rejected by U.S. culture. Still, the United States does not have a firm grasp on what it collectively believes about sexual readiness, including sexual contact between adults and minors. The age of consent varies greatly state-to-state, with a low range of 14 (Hawaii) to 18 in several states, including California. As recently as the last century, many states maintained ages of consent of 10 and 12.

Obviously, this is a serious issue that raises important questions. Do you believe adult-child sexual relationships have lifelong damaging effects on the minors involved? Where are the facts, and how should we discover them?

Suggested Readings

J. Duin, "Controversies Cloud APA Convention. Premier Psychological Body's Reports on Child Abuse Still Draw Criticism," *The Washington Times* (August 12, 1999).

G. Goslinga, "Radical Reconsideration of the Concept of Child Sexual Abuse: New Findings by Mauserman, Rind, and Tromovitch", *Koinos* (April 1998).

H. Mirkin, "Sex, Science, and Sin: The Rind Report, Sexual Politics, and American Scholarship," *Sexuality & Culture* (vol. 4, no. 2, 2000).

S. Lamb, "Some Victims Don't Need Pity," *The Boston Globe* (August 1, 1999).

S. Lilienfeld, "When Worlds Collide: Social Science, Politics, and the Rind et al. (1998) Child Sexual Abuse Meta-Analysis," *American Psychologist* (vol. 57, no. 3, 2002).

T. Oellerich, "Rind, Tromovitch, and Bauserman: Politically Incorrect— Scientifically Correct," *Sexuality & Culture* (vol. 4, no. 2, 2000).

K. Parker, "Adult-Child Sex Is Abuse, Plain and Clear," *The Orlando Sentinel* (March 28, 1999).

D. Riegel, *Understanding Loved Boys and Boylovers* (SafeHaven Foundation Press, 2000).

B. Rind and P. Tromovitch, "A Meta-Analytic Review of Findings from National Samples on Psychological Correlates of Child Sexual Abuse," *Journal of Sex Research* (1997).

B. Rind, P. Tromovitch, and R. Bauserman, "A Meta-Analytic Examination of Assumed Properties of Child Sexual Abuse Using College Samples," *Psychological Bulletin* (1998).

B. Rind, P. Tromovitch, and R. Bauserman, "The Validity and Appropriateness of Methods, Analyses, and Conclusions in Rind *et al.* (1998): A Rebuttal of Victimological Critique from Ondersma *et al.* (2001) and Dallam *et al.* (2001)," *Psychological Bulletin* (vol. 127, 2001).

ISSUE 14

Should Federal Funding of Stem Cell Research Be Restricted?

YES: George W. Bush, from Remarks by the President on Stem Cell Research (August 9, 2001)

NO: Douglas F. Munch, from "Why Expanded Stem Cell Research and Less Federal Government Interference Are Needed in the U.S.," An Original Essay Written for This Volume (2002)

ISSUE SUMMARY

YES: President George W. Bush explains his decision to permit limited federal funding of embryonic stem cell research for the purpose of seeking treatments for serious diseases.

NO: Douglas F. Munch, a management consultant to the pharmaceutical and biotechnology industries, criticizes President Bush's decision for not fully reflecting the will of the people and for being too restrictive to have any meaningful impact on medical science and the lives of people affected by serious diseases.

For decades, Americans have debated the subject of abortion, largely with respect to the question, When does life begin? In 2001, this debate took a sharp turn toward arguing the ethics of studying embryonic stem cells for their potential usefulness in treating serious and chronic diseases, like Parkinson's, Alzheimer's, and juvenile diabetes. Embryonic stem cells are derived from human embryos and have the capacity to become any type of human cell. This capacity is a characteristic not shared by fetal tissue or adult stem cells. It is believed that the manipulation and replication of embryonic stem cells can ultimately lead to therapies that could be used to treat diseases that afflict millions.

So, how does this relate to the abortion debate and the question of when life begins? Some opponents of stem cell research believe that a human being is created the moment that sperm and egg meet and cells begin dividing. To these opponents, the scientific use of an embryo's stem cells, which would lead to the embryo's destruction, is no different than killing a human being. Supporters of embryonic stem cell research believe that these embryos, formed a few days after conception and slated for inevitable destruction anyway, are not to be afforded protection at the expense of people with terminal illnesses who could be treated. It is important to note that there are many other subjective opinions about when human life begins, reflecting various individual or religious beliefs.

The surplus of embryos in question is the product of in vitro fertilization, a reproductive process commonly used by infertile couples. In this process, ova (eggs) are fertilized with sperm outside the uterus. The resulting embryo is then implanted inside the uterus. It is a common practice to form several embryos during the in vitro fertilization process, with each serving as "backup" in the event that the preceding implantation fails. Subsequently, most unused embryos are stored indefinitely in a frozen state. Few are intentionally destroyed, and even fewer are donated for medical research.

On August 9, 2001, President George W. Bush informed the nation of his decision to permit limited federal funding of embryonic stem cell research. His decision would permit research on 64 stem cell lines already in existence. Some praised the decision as a fair and reasonable compromise; others feared the limits would prevent any meaningful impact on the lives of millions of people with serious diseases; still others criticized the decision as incongruent with the president's pro-life position. The decision created an atypical rift among "pro-life" individuals and groups. Some, like Pope John Paul II and the National Conference of Catholic Bishops, criticized the decision, while others, like conservative members of Congress (Orrin Hatch, Trent Lott) and the National Right to Life Organization, expressed support for the decision.

A few Hollywood celebrities drew public attention to the subject and lobbied in favor of embryonic stem cell research. Actor Christopher Reeve, who was paralyzed in a horse-riding accident, became a public face of the pro–stem cell research argument. Following Bush's decision, he expressed concern that "[T]his political compromise may seriously hinder progress toward finding treatments and cures for a wide variety of diseases and disorders that affect 100 million Americans." Reeves passed away in October 2004, sparking a resurgence in the stem cell debate less than a month before the November presidential election. Actress Mary Tyler Moore, who has battled juvenile diabetes for 30 years, and actor Michael J. Fox, who has Parkinson's disease, were also vocal supporters of federal research funding. Moore voiced her support for the president's decision, while Fox was skeptical about the limitations. Nancy Reagan, whose husband, former President Ronald Reagan died after battling Alzheimer's disease for many years, has expressed support for stem cell research while staunchly opposing abortion. The former First Lady's public stance illuminates the conflict expressed by many conservatives.

In the following selections, Bush explains his decision to authorize limited federal funding of embryonic stem cell research and describes the ethical arguments he considered in making his decision. Douglas F. Munch comments that Bush's decision does not represent the public interest and falls far too short to enable scientists to develop cures for debilitating and terminal diseases.

YES

George W. Bush

Remarks by the President on Stem Cell Research

THE PRESIDENT: Good evening. I appreciate you giving me a few minutes of your time tonight so I can discuss with you a complex and difficult issue, an issue that is one of the most profound of our time.

The issue of research involving stem cells derived from human embryos is increasingly the subject of a national debate and dinner table discussions. The issue is confronted every day in laboratories as scientists ponder the ethical ramifications of their work. It is agonized over by parents and many couples as they try to have children, or to save children already born.

The issue is debated within the church, with people of different faiths, even many of the same faith coming to different conclusions. Many people are finding that the more they know about stem cell research, the less certain they are about the right ethical and moral conclusions.

My administration must decide whether to allow federal funds, your tax dollars, to be used for scientific research on stem cells derived from human embryos. A large number of these embryos already exist. They are the product of a process called in vitro fertilization, which helps so many couples conceive children. When doctors match sperm and egg to create life outside the womb, they usually produce more embryos than are planted in the mother. Once a couple successfully has children, or if they are unsuccessful, the additional embryos remain frozen in laboratories.

Some will not survive during long storage; others are destroyed. A number have been donated to science and used to create privately funded stem cell lines. And a few have been implanted in an adoptive mother and born, and are today healthy children.

Based on preliminary work that has been privately funded, scientists believe further research using stem cells offers great promise that could help improve the lives of those who suffer from many terrible diseases—from juvenile diabetes to Alzheimer's, from Parkinson's to spinal cord injuries. And while scientists admit they are not yet certain, they believe stem cells derived from embryos have unique potential.

You should also know that stem cells can be derived from sources other than embryos—from adult cells, from umbilical cords that are discarded after

From George W. Bush, Remarks by the President on Stem Cell Research (August 9, 2001).

babies are born, from human placenta. And many scientists feel research on these type of stem cells is also promising. Many patients suffering from a range of diseases are already being helped with treatments developed from adult stem cells.

However, most scientists, at least today, believe that research on embryonic stem cells offer the most promise because these cells have the potential to develop in all of the tissues in the body.

Scientists further believe that rapid progress in this research will come only with federal funds. Federal dollars help attract the best and brightest scientists. They ensure new discoveries are widely shared at the largest number of research facilities and that the research is directed toward the greatest public good.

The United States has a long and proud record of leading the world toward advances in science and medicine that improve human life. And the United States has a long and proud record of upholding the highest standards of ethics as we expand the limits of science and knowledge. Research on embryonic stem cells raises profound ethical questions, because extracting the stem cell destroys the embryo, and thus destroys its potential for life. Like a snowflake, each of these embryos is unique, with the unique genetic potential of an individual human being.

As I thought through this issue, I kept returning to two fundamental questions: First, are these frozen embryos human life, and therefore, something precious to be protected? And second, if they're going to be destroyed anyway, shouldn't they be used for a greater good, for research that has the potential to save and improve other lives?

I've asked those questions and others of scientists, scholars, bioethicists, religious leaders, doctors, researchers, members of Congress, my Cabinet, and my friends. I have read heartfelt letters from many Americans. I have given this issue a great deal of thought, prayer and considerable reflection. And I have found widespread disagreement.

On the first issue, are these embryos human life—well, one researcher told me he believes this five-day-old cluster of cells is not an embryo, not yet an individual, but a pre-embryo. He argued that it has the potential for life, but it is not a life because it cannot develop on its own.

An ethicist dismissed that as a callous attempt at rationalization. Make no mistake, he told me, that cluster of cells is the same way you and I, and all the rest of us, started our lives. One goes with a heavy heart if we use these, he said, because we are dealing with the seeds of the next generation.

And to the other crucial question, if these are going to be destroyed anyway, why not use them for good purpose—I also found different answers. Many argue these embryos are byproducts of a process that helps create life, and we should allow couples to donate them to science so they can be used for good purpose instead of wasting their potential. Others will argue there's no such thing as excess life, and the fact that a living being is going to die does not justify experimenting on it or exploiting it as a natural resource.

At its core, this issue forces us to confront fundamental questions about the beginnings of life and the ends of science. It lies at a difficult moral inter-section, juxtaposing the need to protect life in all its phases with the prospect of saving and improving life in all its stages.

As the discoveries of modern science create tremendous hope, they also lay vast ethical mine fields. As the genius of science extends the horizons of what we can do, we increasingly confront complex questions about what we should do. We have arrived at that brave new world that seemed so distant in 1932, when Aldous Huxley wrote about human beings created in test tubes in what he called a "hatchery."

In recent weeks, we learned that scientists have created human embryos in test tubes solely to experiment on them. This is deeply troubling, and a warning sign that should prompt all of us to think through these issues very carefully.

Embryonic stem cell research is at the leading edge of a series of moral hazards. The initial stem cell researcher was at first reluctant to begin his research, fearing it might be used for human cloning. Scientists have already cloned a sheep. Researchers are telling us the next step could be to clone human beings to create individual designer stem cells, essentially to grow another you, to be available in case you need another heart or lung or liver.

I strongly oppose human cloning, as do most Americans. We recoil at the idea of growing human beings for spare body parts, or creating life for our convenience. And while we must devote enormous energy to conquering disease, it is equally important that we pay attention to the moral concerns raised by the new frontier of human embryo stem cell research. Even the most noble ends do not justify any means.

My position on these issues is shaped by deeply held beliefs. I'm a strong supporter of science and technology, and believe they have the potential for incredible good—to improve lives, to save life, to conquer disease. Research offers hope that millions of our loved ones may be cured of a disease and rid of their suffering. I have friends whose children suffer from juvenile diabetes. Nancy Reagan has written me about President Reagan's struggle with Alzheimer's. My own family has confronted the tragedy of childhood leukemia. And, like all Americans, I have great hope for cures.

I also believe human life is a sacred gift from our Creator. I worry about a culture that devalues life, and believe as your President I have an important obligation to foster and encourage respect for life in America and throughout the world. And while we're all hopeful about the potential of this research, no one can be certain that the science will live up to the hope it has generated.

Eight years ago, scientists believed fetal tissue research offered great hope for cures and treatments—yet, the progress to date has not lived up to its initial expectations. Embryonic stem cell research offers both great promise and great peril. So I have decided we must proceed with great care.

As a result of private research, more than 60 genetically diverse stem cell lines already exist. They were created from embryos that have already been destroyed, and they have the ability to regenerate themselves indefinitely, creating ongoing opportunities for research. I have concluded that we should allow federal funds to be used for research on these existing stem cell lines, where the life and death decision has already been made.

Leading scientists tell me research on these 60 lines has great promise that could lead to breakthrough therapies and cures. This allows us to explore the promise and potential of stem cell research without crossing a fundamental moral line, by providing taxpayer funding that would sanction or encourage further destruction of human embryos that have at least the potential for life.

I also believe that great scientific progress can be made through aggressive federal funding of research on umbilical cord placenta, adult and animal stem cells which do not involve the same moral dilemma. This year, your government will spend $250 million on this important research.

I will also name a President's council to monitor stem cell research, to recommend appropriate guidelines and regulations, and to consider all of the medical and ethical ramifications of biomedical innovation. This council will consist of leading scientists, doctors, ethicists, lawyers, theologians and others, and will be chaired by Dr. Leon Kass, a leading biomedical ethicist from the University of Chicago.

This council will keep us apprised of new developments and give our nation a forum to continue to discuss and evaluate these important issues. As we go forward, I hope we will always be guided by both intellect and heart, by both our capabilities and our conscience.

I have made this decision with great care, and I pray it is the right one.

Thank you for listening. Good night, and God bless America.

NO ↵

Why Expanded Stem Cell Research and Less Federal Government Interference Are Needed in the U.S.

On August 9, 2001, President George W. Bush presented his remarks on stem cell research to the American Public. The President cleverly rode the political fence on his decision to allow stem cell research, but only utilizing those 64 stem cell lines already in existence worldwide. Unfortunately, the President's decision does not go far enough in supporting this important research and that in time, perhaps sooner then he expects, the issue will have to be revisited.

The potential of stem cell research will be realized through the invention of new therapies for currently incurable diseases. Diabetes, heart disease, cancer, Alzheimer's disease, Parkinson's disease, multiple sclerosis and ALS [Lou Gehrig's disease] are some of the diseases expected to benefit from the development of knowledge about stem cells. But that is not all. Stem cell research may open the doors to understanding how genes control cell differentiation. It can also give us much improved insight into new drug development and toxicity to human cells as well as organ transplant rejection.

Why is public funding of this research such a contentious decision? The government sits squarely in the middle of the controversy surrounding the subject. On one side is the vast landscape of government funded research, with medical scientists requesting increased access to embryonic stem cells accompanied by substantially increased funding and support from the National Institutes for Health (NIH) and other government sources. On the other side is an equally vast landscape of public opinion that is divided on highly emotional moral and ethical grounds. This question is further complicated by the President's own conservative theological views and his pronounced political support from the conservative Christian right opposing this research. Since public sentiment drives most political positions in our current age of opinion polls, the arbitrator of public money, largely the political party in power, feels obligated to find its own balance between public funding for public good and defining that good. As a result, while the President's remarks cover the waterfront of stem cell research science and ethics, his decision does not go far enough.

Copyright © 2002 by Douglas F. Munch.

As I view this debate, there are very different points of view coming into play across the nation. There is a definite complex of opposing theological perspectives, coupled with medical/scientific, ethical, and economic points of view.

Theological Perspectives

At the core, the theological debate revolves around the issue of when human life begins. Theologians testifying before the National Bioethics Advisory Commission indicated that religious tradition offers no support to the idea that the fertilized egg goes through some earlier human stage before acquiring the moral status of a person. A commonly expressed conservative position states that human life begins at the moment of conception when the sperm and egg cell are united since the fertilized egg has the potential to become a human being. Other positions vary widely. Some hold that human life begins upon implantation of the egg in the uterus. Historical Catholic teaching and a current Jewish position state that human life begins with quickening (when a pregnant woman can feel fetal movements some time in the fourth month of pregnancy).

Few denominations have taken an official position on the appropriateness of stem cell research. Most church leaders of various denominations appear to be undecided about the matter but some are leaning toward supporting the research. In 1997 the United Church of Christ's General Synod approved serious research on "human pre-embryos through the 14th day of fetal development."

The Episcopal, Evangelical Lutheran, and United Methodist churches have declined to take a position on the matter until . . . their national meetings convene. Other religions are similarly noncommittal. As an example, the Unitarian Universalist Association seems to favor the funding of stem cell work within its pro-science and pro-research tradition, but has reportedly not taken an official position. The Church of Jesus Christ of Latter Day Saints (Mormon Church) similarly is noncommittal on the matter stating that it "merits cautious scrutiny." Reformed Jews, Presbyterian Church USA, and the United Church of Christ seem to be generally favoring the research, although their official positions are not developed and there seem to be many nuances to consider.

Judaism discourages interfering with nature's plan for no good reason, but even Conservative Jews may favor stem cell research. Rabbi Elliott Dorff, Vice Chairman of the Conservative Movement's Committee on Law and Standards, indicated that "the research can serve a common good, combating disease."

There is no Islamic official position in the United States, but Moslem teaching holds that life does not begin until the fertilized egg is attached to the uterine wall, a position which would allow research on embryonic stem cells.

The President's personal and political position appears to be largely influenced by his close relationship with the Christian Conservative Right. Strong opposition to stem cell research has been voiced from both the Roman Catholic Church and the Christian Conservative Right. In a recent visit to the Vatican, the Pope told President Bush that "stem cell research devalues and violates human life." However, these views, and the President's decision, may not be reflected by the general public.

Public Opinion

Recent polls indicate that there is wide support among Americans for stem cell research in contrast to the largely undecided official position of religious authorities. As individuals learn more about the promise of this research and the scientific and ethical implications, the polls show that public opinion favors stem cell research. In an NBC news poll on July 12, 2001, fully 70 percent of Roman Catholics support stem cell research versus 69 percent of the overall U.S. population. Among Catholics, only 22 percent oppose the research versus 23 percent of the overall population. In a June 2001 poll in Utah, the overall population was 62 percent in favor of stem cell research and 27 percent against. Of individuals identifying themselves as "very conservative" 47 percent favored the research while only 35 percent opposed.

The point is that there are many independent views about the humanity of a fertilized egg. Human beings are unable to resolve this fundamental issue on any grounds, scientific or theological, leaving the matter to individual conscience. It is therefore not up to the government to impose an ethical or moral standard about this research. That decision should be up to the individual scientist with funding awarded based on merit for creative scientific thinking that enhances human understanding about these cells, their function and usefulness.

The human race has become cocreators of our world with God. Observation of modern man's impact on our society makes this obvious. Scientists have prevented extinction of animal species, produced transgenic animals used for medical research, genetically modified cell lines for the production of medicine, invented and implemented in-vitro fertilization (IVF), prepared gene replacement therapies to treat disease, and introduced new genes into food products to improve yield and reduce susceptibility to disease. Whether one likes it or not, we humans are already using our gift of free will, intelligence and creativity to alter this world and change the natural course of evolution. The die is cast. It will continue to be our responsibility to use our creative powers and scientific knowledge for ethical and moral purpose from which all people benefit. As cocreators, stem cell research will be no different.

Scientific and Medical Grounds

The President's remarks about the scientific and medical benefit are very favorable toward stem cell research. So favorable that it seems his conclusion to limit the stem cell lines to those existing as of August 9, 2001, is inconsistent with his preamble. But, there are also important issues that the President underplayed in his address.

Human stem cell research is a relatively new medical field. It was only in 1981 that British scientists created the first animal stem cell line from mouse embryos. In 1996 Congress banned the use of federal funding for research where human embryos would be destroyed in the process. Hence, private funding from Geron Corporation enabled scientists at the Wisconsin Alumni Research Foundation (WARF) to develop and patent a method to separate stem cells from the blastocyst in 1998. As of August 9, 2001, there were 64 separate lines of human stem cells available worldwide. Sweden has 24 lines, the U.S. has 20, India has 10, Australia has 6, and Israel has 4. Only these lines are eligible for research funded by the federal government. This by itself is potentially problematic.

Among these 64 lines of stem cells that are approved for funding, many are derived from frozen embryos that are known to be much less robust, reportedly having only 1 chance in 100 of developing to the blastocyst stage (a colony of about 200 undifferentiated stem cells). It is still unknown how many of these lines will be satisfactory for research purposes. Research quality stem cells must have normal chromosomes and genes. They must be able to reproduce without limit and they must be capable of differentiation into all other human cells. While scientists anticipate that these cells will reproduce indefinitely, this is an assumption that may not work out in the future. We cannot know how many of these approved cell lines will develop into useful research material or if they will provide adequate quantities of material to meet research standards and demand.

While stem cells may be obtained from adult tissues (i.e. fat, bone marrow, or brain) and other fetal cell lines (umbilical or placenta), these cells may have started down a differentiation pathway and therefore have more limited research potential. Experts recognize that stem cells from the blastocyst stage of the embryo are ideal because they are completely undifferentiated and have the potential to become any of the approximately 260 cell lines in the human body. Today, medical scientists have only limited knowledge about the theoretical and practical issues necessary to derive therapeutic benefit from the science, although the theoretical potential is great. Additionally, today's stem cells are being grown in a mouse cell culture to trick the stem cells to differentiate, which also limits the research and therapeutic potential due to the potential contamination of the human cells. Much work remains to be done and will be done. If not in the U.S., then the work will be engaged by scientists in other countries where fewer barriers are imposed.

Ethical Issues

The President's remarks appropriately address the possibility of misuse of stem cell research potentially leading to the serious abuse of human reproductive cloning which is properly banned in most countries. However, all technologies have potential for misuse by unscrupulous individuals inclined to manipulate the system for their own ill-gotten gain.

The President appropriately states that the U.S. has a "long and proud record of upholding the highest standards of ethics." We have achieved this record through exercise of individual conscience superimposed over a sound foundation of knowledge, ethics, and through peer pressure from other scientists, not through government imposed legislation. There are already safeguards in the research funding system to protect against such activity—specifically, the long established peer review system awards research grants to worthy (and ethical) projects. Investigational review boards (IRB) protect patients against potentially harmful or immoral clinical research. The system works and the government should not meddle with it or use it as an excuse to install barriers or artificially limit funding for this important work.

In-vitro fertilization (IVF) procedures have produced a large number of unused frozen embryos, as the President correctly pointed out in his remarks. Again, his comments do not adequately address the issues. Unused embryos may remain frozen for many years as they are rarely adopted, donated, or destroyed when they are unwanted. We know that extra embryos are a consequence of IVF.

People choosing to avail themselves of this procedure should be required to undertake the moral and ethical responsibility of determining the disposition of their unused cells as part of their overall decision making and medical informed consent process. I believe that this decision should be required at the time people choose IVF to achieve pregnancy. Otherwise, unused embryos are likely to remain frozen as a burden to society. I would suggest that the options include donation of the embryos for stem cell research purposes. This decision is a personal one, and should be driven by individual conscience. After all, when faced with the tragic death of a child, many parents now take comfort in donating some of the child's tissues to help others as transplants. Should not the same opportunity to benefit others be available to IVF "parents"? If morality is the issue, then where is the morality in abandoning human embryos in a frozen and indeterminate state, leaving them as someone else's problem or to deteriorate in the freezer?

Economic Issues

Several economic factors may also be considered. U.S. Government-funded research has been the most important incubator for new ideas in the world. This support has historically been provided without prior assessment of economic potential. Industries have been started as a result and perhaps hundreds of biotech and health care companies owe their existence to government funded research programs. Inadequate support of stem cell research will unwittingly block the creation of entrepreneurial companies focused on the developing new therapies based on knowledge discovered with federal grant support.

U.S. companies, developing state-of-the-art commercial products for health care, make a substantial contribution to our economy and to maintaining our worldwide superiority in medicine and therapeutics. Supporting basic research at the federal level forms the groundwork for establishing important intellectual property positions for American entrepreneurs and corporations. Placing hurdles in the way of U.S. scientists will move discovery to other nations where there are fewer or no impediments to this research. On August 28th, 2001, the *Washington Post* reported an Indian stem cell scientist to say that the Bush policy "creates a windfall for researchers in such countries as India that do not face such constraints." Another reports that Bush's announcement has opened up a "new pot of gold" for science and business outside the U.S.

By putting political barriers in front of scientists who develop new treatments for disease, we are not only impeding economic and medical progress in the U.S. but also risk losing our leading scientists. Dr. Roger Pedersen, a prominent scientist from the University of California, San Francisco, has announced that he is leaving the U.S. to work in England where research restrictions are not as burdensome. Others will also leave if government restrictions get in the way of science.

Concluding Remarks

Like the President, I have come to express my position on these sensitive matters regarding stem cell research after much thought and personal deliberation. I believe that the views I have presented here support the sanctity of human life. They also allow our American culture to prevail where strong social and ethical values are the underpinnings of the exercise of our gift of free will. Our democratic system enables this to occur. Our federal government should not legislate against its own system by seeking to establish and impose state ethics on our free society.

POSTSCRIPT

Should Federal Funding of Stem Cell Research Be Restricted?

$\mathbf{T}$he question of whether or not embryonic stem cell research should be restricted may come down to fundamental beliefs about the origin of human life. Does life begin at the moment of conception, as many "pro-life" individuals contend? If so, what is to be done with excess embryos already created in the in vitro fertilization process but not destined for implantation? "Pro-choice" individuals may have an easier time with this question, as they reject the belief that a fertilized egg is a human being. The opportunity to improve the lives of people with severe illnesses may be seen as no match to the comparative value of a cluster of cells that is not destined for pregnancy.

In his speech, President George W. Bush raised the issue of human cloning. His statement, "[T]he next step could be to clone human beings to create individual designer stem cells, essentially to grow another you to be available in case you need another heart or lung or liver," requires some clarification. Scientists who have expressed an intention to clone humans are relying on adult stem cells to create a whole cloned human person. Adult cells would be taken from an adult, their DNA injected into a human ovum, and that ovum implanted into a woman's uterus to create a cloned person. Most scientists dismiss this as both unethical and nearly impossible. However, substituting one's DNA for the DNA in embryonic stem cells to create specialized (and perfectly genetically matched cells) is possible.

How do you assess the president's compromise? Did it go far enough or does it fall short of being useful for those afflicted with incurable illnesses? What ethical considerations would guide you in deciding this matter?

Suggested Readings

S. Begley, "Cellular Divide," *Newsweek* (July 9, 2001).

S. Begley, "Did the President Go Far Enough?" *Newsweek* (August 20, 2001).

A. Breznican, "Celebs Supporting Stem Cell Research," *Associated Press* (August 9, 2001).

T. Lindberg, "The Politics of Stem Cell Research: President Bush Got the Headlines He Wanted," *The Washington Times* (August 14, 2001).

"Stem Cell Disappointment," *Arizona Daily Star* (August 12, 2001).

"Stem Cells: Not Far Enough," *The Providence Journal* (August 12, 2001).

The White House, "Fact Sheet: Embryonic Stem Cell Research," available at `http://www.whitehouse.gov` (August 9, 2001).

K. L. Woodward, "A Question of Life or Death: Untangling the Knottiest of Ethical Dilemmas," *Newsweek* (July 9, 2001).

ISSUE 15

Should Sexuality Research Receive Public Funding?

YES: John Bancroft, from "The Medical Community Needs Kinsey's Research Now More Than Ever," *Insight on the News* (March 30, 1998)

NO: Beverly R. Newman, from "Research That Mainstreams Sexual Perversity Does Not Serve the Public Good," *Insight on the News* (March 30, 1998)

ISSUE SUMMARY

YES: John Bancroft, a medical doctor, sexologist, and director of the University of Indiana's Alfred Kinsey Institute for Research in Sex, Gender, and Reproduction, argues that public funding for scientific research on sexuality issues is vital in order to solve some of the major sexual problems that plague the United States.

NO: Beverly R. Newman, a counselor of sexual abuse survivors and a teacher at Ivy Tech College in Indianapolis, Indiana, opposes any public funding of sexuality research by the Kinsey Institute or any other alleged scientific research group because she fears that researchers will follow Alfred Kinsey (1894–1956), whom she calls "a callous, maniacal scientist."

T he United States has an unequaled wealth of sexological research. At the end of the nineteenth century, Celia D. Mosher, a physician and college professor, began to survey her women patients, asking them to describe their sexual and reproductive lives. Thanks to Mosher's scientific curiosity, there is a small but intriguing sample of middle-class, married women's sexual histories that allows some tentative comparisons of women's sexuality at the peak of the Victorian Age and today, one hundred years later. In the early part of the twentieth century, gynecologist Robert Latou Dickinson pioneered the scientific study of human sexuality, marital sex, contraception, women's diseases, and sex problems.

In 1938, Alfred Kinsey, a biology professor at the University of Indiana, was determined to interview 100,000 American men and women about their sex lives. By 1959 his team of colleagues were able to interview 18,000 adults, which was the first scientific picture of the sexual lives of American men and women: when they became sexually active, how often they had sex and what kind of sex, homosexuality and bisexuality; premarital, marital, and extramarital sex; and orgasm. Before Kinsey died in 1956, it seemed that opponents of sex research would be successful in discouraging support for his surveys. In the 1960s, William Masters and Virginia Johnson focused public attention on the scientific study of the physiology and psychology of the human sexual response. For 12 years, Masters and Johnson interviewed and observed individuals experiencing orgasm through masturbation and intercourse. Their research revealed the first detailed scientific information about the stages one goes through from sexual desire to arousal, orgasm, and resolution.

Sexological research in the United States today is considered vital to the management of many social and public health problems. Each year, one million teenage girls become pregnant, a rate twice that of Canada, England, and Sweden, and 10 times that of the Netherlands. This disproportion is similar for teenage abortions. The United States spends $25 billion on social, health, and welfare services for families begun by teenagers. One million Americans are HIV positive and almost one-quarter of a million have died of AIDS. Yet only one in ten American children receives sexuality education that includes information about HIV/AIDS transmission and prevention. One in five adolescent girls in grades eight through eleven is subject to sexual harassment, while three-quarters of girls under age fourteen who have had sexual relations have been raped. These and other public health problems are well documented and increasingly understood in the context of poverty, family trauma, ethnic discrimination, lack of educational opportunities, and inadequate health services. However, there is little recognition among the general public and legislators of the need for sexological research to deal effectively with these problems. Congress has several times refused or withdrawn funding for well-designed and important surveys because of pressure from conservative minorities.

In 1995, the Sexuality Research Assessment Project of the Social Science Research Council published a comprehensive sexuality research review entitled *Sexuality Research in the United States: An Assessment of the Social and Behavioral Sciences*. This report identified and described major information gaps that prevent understanding of how sexual behaviors develop in the context of society and culture and how sexual socialization occurs in families, schools, the media, and peer groups. Without that understanding, efforts to effectively address problems and projects in gender, HIV/AIDS, adolescent sexuality, sexual orientation, sexual coercion, and research methodology are crippled.

In the following selections, John Bancroft argues that the lack of federal, private sector, and academic funding for research prevents legislators, educators, and social service and health care professionals from dealing with serious problems in American families and society. Beverly R. Newman opposes any funding for sexuality research that supports the philosophy of Alfred Kinsey and the institute that carries his name. She maintains that all sex research in the United States has been contaminated by Kinsey, whom she says "blithely collected data obtained as results from massive sexual experimentation on babies and children."

YES ⬅

John Bancroft

The Medical Community Needs Kinsey's Research Now More Than Ever

The United States leads the industrialized world in a number of important ways, but they are not all positive. Our country heads the league tables for sex related problems—teenage pregnancies, sexually transmitted diseases and sexual assaults. We have our fair share of other problems as well, such as child sexual abuse and the common sexual dysfunctions that can undermine the stability of marriage. Yet, we remain ignorant or uncertain about many aspects of these problems. If scientists and policymakers are to tackle them effectively, they must better understand the problems.

Human sexuality is complex; sociocultural and biological determinants must be taken into account. For that reason, we need an ongoing tradition of interdisciplinary scholarship. The Kinsey Institute for Research in Sex, Gender and Reproduction, one of Indiana University's several research institutes, is unique not only in the United States but in the world in its established commitment to such interdisciplinary scholarship.

So why am I asked to defend state funding of the Kinsey Institute? Because there is an ongoing campaign by vocal and well-funded elements to close it down. Their principal target appears to be sex education. They misguidedly believe that by discrediting Alfred Kinsey, who died 42 years ago, they will undermine modern sex education. And what better way to discredit Kinsey than closing down the institute named for him?

In December 1995, the Family Research Council successfully lobbied to introduce a bill into Congress aimed at the institute's federal funding, but that House bill got nowhere. In January 1998, a resolution was passed by the Indiana House of Representatives urging the withdrawal of state funding for the Kinsey Institute; that effort was instigated by Concerned Women for America, or CWA. That measure also died quietly when the Legislature ended its session in February. Both efforts were anchored in a dislike of Kinsey and what he represented—as well as a considerable amount of misinformation.

I recently met with the sponsor of the Indiana resolution, and discovered that his case was based largely on the current campaign of misinformation from CWA. He had read nothing written by Kinsey himself; he knew nothing about the Kinsey Institute's work and mission today and apparently was not interested. He wanted its closure as a symbolic denigration of Kinsey by Indiana University.

The campaign of misinformation is extraordinary, with statement upon statement with no basis in fact. For example: According to some allegations, Kinsey believed that "all sex laws should be eliminated, including laws against rape"; that "there was no moral difference between one sexual outlet and any other"; that the consequences of such beliefs included a 526 percent increase in the number of rapes in the United States; and that Kinsey's "theories" produced a 560 percent increase in crime, a 300 percent increase in out-of-wedlock births, a 200 percent increase in divorce rates and a 200 percent increase in teen suicides. These allegations, and many others like them, are ridiculous.

Sex education today, we are told in this disingenuous campaign, is based on research Kinsey carried out with sexual criminals. Kinsey studied sexual criminals; the Kinsey Institute published a book on "sexual offenders" in 1965 based on this data, which has nothing to do with sex education. Kinsey reported observations of children's sexual responses made by a few of these sexual criminals; the evidence in the much-cited "Table 34" contains information from one such man. The nature of this information, which was made clear in the book, represents a small proportion of the evidence presented about childhood sexuality, a tiny proportion of his two published books, and it has nothing to do with sex education today or in the past. In fact, sex education today is not based on Kinsey's research in any respect. Insofar as sex education relies on research findings, it uses far more recent and relevant research.

Kinsey's research is discredited, we are told by opponents of the institute, because, having interviewed these sexual criminals, he then did not report them to the police.

At the time of Kinsey's research, virtually all forms of sexual activity outside marriage and several forms of sexual activity within marriage (not including raping one's wife) were illegal. He attached great importance to the confidentiality he guaranteed his subjects, and this was crucial to the success of his whole research endeavor.

Kinsey's mission, his detractors claim, was to undermine sexual morality as we know it. In his last book, the volume on the female, he was principally concerned about the lack of sexual understanding between men and women and how this undermined the stability of marriage. Ironically, considering how Kinsey so often has been accused to the contrary, the book underscores that he saw heterosexual marital sex as the norm. True, Kinsey is not beyond criticism. He made mistakes; with the benefit of 50 years of hindsight, one can say that he was naïve in several respects. But he was a pioneer who broke through the social taboos to carry out the first substantial survey of sexual behavior, which remains the largest and richest collection of data on sexual behavior ever collected and is used by researchers today.

What of the institute named for him? The Kinsey Institute fulfills its mission in a number of ways. It has uniquely rich collections of materials relevant to the understanding of human sexuality and how it has changed over time and across cultures. In addition to its extensive library of books and papers, the institute has major collections of photography, art, films and videos as well as archival papers and manuscripts. As we work to preserve these collections and make them more accessible to scholars, so we find a steady increase in demand for access from the academic community.

The institute organizes interdisciplinary meetings, bringing scholars together from around the world and producing publications from these events. The institute has a research program; we are studying the effects of steroidal contraceptives on the sexuality and well-being of women and the impact of such effects on the acceptability and continuation with these methods. This is research that should have been conducted several decades ago. We are exploring with Family Health International how this research methodology can be adapted to address the same questions in other countries in the developing world, tackling an issue of crucial importance to the effectiveness of familyplanning programs worldwide. We are investigating the impact of themenstrual cycle on the sexuality of women.

In the area of male sexuality, we have a novel research program studying the neuropsychology of male sexual response. This research not only may prove to be considerably relevant to understanding common problems of male sexual dysfunction but also may shed light on why some men persist in taking sexual risks, an issue crucial to the HIV/AIDS epidemic. We are collaborating with colleagues in the medical school to use brain-imaging techniques to investigate central mechanisms involved in the control of sexual response.

We have been fortunate to have two postdoctoral fellows funded by the Social Science Research Council's, or SSRC's new Sexuality Research Fellowship program. Last year, our SSRC fellow, a historian, used the institute's archives to further her study of the history of transsexualism in the United States between 1930 and 1970. This year and next, we have a fellow studying the relationship between childhood sexual play and adult sexual adjustment by asking young adults to recall their childhood experiences, as well as describing their sexual development during adolescence and since. This data will be compared with data obtained from Kinsey's original survey, permitting the parallel study of two data sets collected 50 years apart. The Kinsey Institute provides specialized clinical services to men and women who have sexual dysfunctions and women with menstrual-cycle-related problems. This form of clinical care, in which both psychological and physical aspects are given equal importance, is threatened by the current health-care system in the United States. Our clinics, and the training of health professionals associated with them, will help to keep these important clinical skills alive and available.

And finally, the institute is attaching increasing importance to its role as an "information service," provided through our World Wide Web site. I would urge anyone who wants to know more about the Kinsey Institute and its current activities to visit us at http://www.indiana.edu/~kinsey/.

We are legally restricted in how we can use many of the materials in our collections, and because of this we restrict access to scholars with bona fide research interests. However, we are progressively "coming out of the closet." For the last three years we have provided courses for the local community through the university's continuing-studies and mini-university programs. Last October, we had our first major public exhibit of items from our art and photography collections. The six-week-long exhibit, "The Art of Desire: Erotic Treasures From the Kinsey Institute," was held in the fine-arts gallery on the Bloomington campus. This effort celebrated the 50th anniversary of the founding of the institute and was a great success. We give tours for an increasing number of visitors to the institute and, following the recent political interest, we have invited state legislators to visit the institute to learn more about our activities. We are proud of the Kinsey Institute, and we believe its role will grow. In fact, the need for interdisciplinary research of this kind is so great today that, rather than closing us down, comparable institutes should be set up on other campuses around the country. Then there will be a reasonable chance that the need for an established tradition of interdisciplinary scholarship in human sexuality will be met.

As for sex education, the Kinsey Institute is not directly involved, but we recognize its importance. It is not a straightforward issue, however. There is need for vigorous debate as well as careful evaluation of the effects of different policies. And, of course, issues of sexual morality will be central to this debate as, I hope, will evidence derived from sound scientific research. But a productive debate only can flourish in a climate of honesty and respect for varying opinions, none of which are in the forecast of the anti-Kinsey movement.

NO ↵

Research That Mainstreams Sexual Perversity Does Not Serve the Public Good

Deep in America's heartland is the heart of one of history's biggest coverups. Hundreds, perhaps thousands, of sex crimes undoubtedly have been committed in the name of science, and yet a major state university continues to battle for the sake of protecting the name and the reputation of a callous, maniacal scientist who blithely collected data obtained as results from massive sexual experimentation on babies and children. Alfred C. Kinsey is the world's most famous sex researcher, who got unprecedented media attention after the publication of *Sexual Behavior in the Human Male* in 1948 and *Sexual Behavior in the Human Female* in 1953. Less well-known is the fact that he was a classic example of a sexual addict, who induced his own wife to commit adultery on films he made in the attic of their home in Bloomington, Ind.

In recent weeks Bloomington, home to the Kinsey Institute for Research in Sex, Gender and Reproduction, based at Indiana University, has witnessed a raging inferno of citizen anger that is spreading throughout the Hoosier State. While taxpayers foot the bill for the Kinsey Institute through annual appropriations of $750,000, the public is not welcome to use or view the Kinsey Institute, which is cloaked in secrecy. Callers are informed that there are VIP tours set up every so often, but even then a Kinsey representative must accompany the visitors at all times. State Sen. John Waterman made two unannounced visits to the institute last month—one during office hours on a weekday—but was unable even to take the elevator up to the third floor of Morrison Hall, where the institute is housed at public expense. Accompanied by an ex-Indiana University police officer, Waterman was told by the officer that he never had been permitted to have the keys to the third floor of Morrison Hall.

Recently, Waterman and another Indiana legislator, Rep. Woody Burton, led an unprecedented campaign to denounce and defund the institute. On Jan. 21 the Indiana House of Representatives passed Burton's House Concurrent Resolution No. 16, which excoriated the institute's founder and directed that, "No public funds should be used to operate or support institutions that further the claims made by Alfred Kinsey's research."

What are those controversial claims? The most far-reaching is that children naturally are given to initiating sexual acts and that virtually all forms of sexual behavior should be acknowledged as normal and tolerated. Kinsey's verbose prose is hardly quotable but nonetheless radical in its implications. Consider his condescending dismissal of sex between humans and animals: "There is probably no type of human sexual behavior which has been more severely condemned by that segment of the population which happens not to have had such experience, and which accepts the age-old judgment that animal intercourse must evidence a mental abnormality, as well as immorality." Translation: It's all good.

This and other malignant myths manufactured by the Kinsey Institute have metastasized during the last 50 years. Kinsey's books and the publications of the institute have created what I call the "Kinsey dogma," a body of unproven assumptions about sexual behavior which are often not normal, fruitful or truthful. It is built upon vile crimes against captive babies and children in the name of science. Wardell Pomeroy, a devoted fellow researcher of Kinsey, who worked at the Kinsey Institute for 13 years, still is spewing classic Kinsey dogma. According to Pomeroy in his book, *Boys and Sex:* "[F]or boys approaching or entering adolescence (p. 13) . . . Your sex life, like everybody else's, probably began before you were born (p. 32) . . . We know now that both male and female babies as young as four to six months have orgasm (p. 33) . . . Small boys often want to try intercourse with their girl playmates (p. 38)."

This elementary-level sex text then continues to instruct its young audience in homosexual "oral sex," which is portrayed as common oral behavior of young children. This sex text and its companion book, *Girls and Sex,* are found in the children's section of most libraries. The sex text repeatedly instructs girls about the benefits of early intercourse between a boy and a girl as a training ground for marriage. Pomeroy's main message to young girls is that "essentially nothing humans do sexually . . . can be called abnormal" since humans are mammals, and mammals "engage in practically every kind of sex."

Kinsey's pernicious and fallacious dogma, pervasive in our schools, courts and professions, is poison to children. Children who have been sexualized early in life are often easy to spot. They are the kids who manipulate themselves at school, experience rage and terrifying flashbacks, cannot control their fears and anger, run away from home, drop out of school with early and multiple pregnancies, make repeated suicide attempts throughout their lives and fight lifelong addictions and depression. This is the norm for young survivors, who have been sexualized by acts of incest, child molestation or pornography.

Expert opinion holds that children who are sexually violated, whether through incest, molestation or exposure to pornography, frequently and chronically suffer from post-traumatic stress disorder, dissociation and/or multiple personality disorder. According to the textbook *Psychology,* by John Santrock, "A summary of the research literature on multiple personality suggests that the most striking feature related to the disorder is an inordinately high rate of sexual or physical abuse during early childhood."

The sex-education programs in U.S. schools are the most catastrophic failure ever witnessed in American education, just in sheer numbers of sexual casualties through unwanted pregnancies, abortions, sexually transmitted diseases and sexual dysfunctions. What else could you expect from a program founded on the works of a man who promoted animal-human sex and, as noted by historian James Jones, Kinsey's biographer, "attempted to put child molesters in a benign light"?

It may be argued—and many psychologists do—that children are not born sexual. When children exhibit sexual or criminal behaviors, these have been learned through harmful acts inflicted upon them or in the presence of children by adults or much-older children. Sexual abuse, for instance, includes pornography or live sex acts displayed in front of children. According to the National Adoption Information Clearinghouse, the classic signs of sexually abused children, which are listed in school manuals and professional training materials throughout the United States, are exactly what Kinsey followers claim to be normal behavior, specifically advanced sexual knowledge and early sexual promiscuity. These are the key indicators of child molestation, not childhood sexuality. Classic Kinsey dogma—that all sex is natural, normal and acceptable—promotes exactly such behaviors by young children.

The Kinsey dogma, which American sex education has been founded upon, is lies built upon crimes. The infamous *Sexual Behavior in the Human Male* acknowledges the cooperation of numerous schools, orphanages and children's homes in which Kinsey or his assistants did "research." Beginning on page 175 of Kinsey's sexual manual are tables of experimental data about babies and children containing such tell-tale phrases as: "Based on actual observation[s]." Table 30 details the sexual responses of hundreds of babies and children, observed but not timed. Table 31 records observations of 317 males from age two months to 15 years old. Table 32 records "observations [of 188 boys] timed with second-hand or stop watch. Ages range from five months of age to adolescence." Table 33 details observed and sometimes timed responses of 182 young males timed by the second. Table 34 includes data from sexual experiments on infants as young as five months old and children, who were sexually tortured for up to 24 hours at a time.

Where did the nine adult males who observed these sexual responses, according to Kinsey, gain access to hundreds of babies and children to time their sexual responses for up to 24 hours at a time?

The enormity and the severity of these sexual crimes against children never have been denounced by the Kinsey Institute despite the data having required the sexual torture of infants and children. The matter that needs to be disclosed is the extent to which Kinsey and his colleagues actually facilitated such research by encouraging it, purchasing the data of sexual predators, training them accurately to time their captive subjects and/or personally conducting the experiments themselves. Somewhere in the history and secrecy of the Kinsey Institute are the answers to these questions.

No matter what good work in which the Kinsey Institute may claim to be engaged in today, its history is based upon criminal acts of the most heinous and vicious kind. Until now, they had not been denounced or even admitted by Indiana officials. Kinsey Institute staff continue to speak of Kinsey as a devoted husband, successful father and a very principled scientist, despite the brutal revelations contained in the recent biography of Kinsey written by Jones, a former member of the science advisory board of the Kinsey Institute. The continuing denial of Kinsey Institute staff in the face of the documented monstrous realities about Kinsey in *Alfred C. Kinsey: A Public/Private Life* speaks volumes about the institute's credibility. According to Jones, "Kinsey was having sex with other men and arranging for his wife, Clara, to be filmed having sex with [Kinsey Institute] staff members," and Kinsey was so sexually addicted that he escalated to performing acts of severe sadomasochism on himself on film. In 1954, says Jones, Kinsey threw a rope over the exposed ceiling pipes of his basement office at Indiana University, tied it to his genitals and jumped off a chair. The fact is, Kinsey delighted in homosexual sadomasochism and simply disregarded sex-crime laws that differed with his own obsessions and addictions to sex.

The citizens of Indiana are beginning to realize that Kinsey should never have been walking the streets freely, let alone administering a major university institution. Kinsey is a prime example of the awful realities of "sexual liberation." Like any sex addict, he could not get enough sex and misused sex. The man perceived to be the founder of sex education in American schools reduced sex to the primitive, mechanical level of plants and animals, and his namesake institute continues to attempt to normalize sexual aberrations in the name of science. The institute boasts of having the nation's best collections on the history of transsexuality and supports fellowships on homosexual parenting. The shameful Kinsey legacy continues to menace the lives of America's children.

POSTSCRIPT

Should Sexuality Research Receive Public Funding?

Childhood sexuality appears to be the pivotal issue in the debate over funding for sexuality research. Certainly, of all the areas of human sexual behavior, childhood sexuality remains the prime area that has been largely unexplored by researchers. Childhood is widely seen as a period of asexual innocence. Strong taboos continue concerning childhood eroticism, and childhood sexual expression and learning are still divisive social issues.

John Money, an international gender expert, summed up the question of funding for sexuality research in the United States in his book *The Lovemap Guidebook* (Continuum, 1999). He states that the politics of the forbidden restrict the content of the curriculum in sex education, the procedures for treating sexological maladies, and the scope of what gets approved, funded, and published in sexological research. Restrictions on research apply especially to childhood sexuality. Money believes that it would be the "kiss of death" to submit a grant application for the developmental investigation of childhood sexual rehearsal play or the developmental content of juvenile sexual ideation and imagery.

In trying to ascertain why it is nearly impossible to obtain funding for certain kinds of sexuality research, Patricia Koch and David Weis, coeditors of *Sexuality in America: Understanding Our Sexual Values and Behavior* (Continuum, 1999), believe it might be interesting to determine the extent to which American researchers accept the premise that scientific explorations of sexuality might be harmful to children. For example, the field of child development, a sizable branch of American psychology, has largely ignored the issue of sexuality. An examination of standard developmental texts or reviews of the child development research literature is striking for this omission.

In the selections by Bancroft and Newman, what are the background issues that underlie the surface arguments for and against the funding of sex research? How important do you think this kind of research is? Should it be in America's national priorities?

Suggested Readings

V. L. Bullough, *Science in the Bedroom: A History of Sex Research* (Basic Books, 1994).

P. B. Koch and D. L. Weis, eds., *Sexuality in America: Understanding Our Sexual Values and Behavior* (Continuum, 1999).

W. B. Pomeroy, *Dr. Kinsey and the Institute for Sex Research* (Harper & Row, 1972).

ISSUE 16

Do Schools Perpetuate
a Gender Bias?

YES: Janice Weinman, from "Girls Still Face Barriers in Schools That Prevent Them From Reaching Their Full Potential," *Insight on the News* (December 14, 1998)

NO: Judith Kleinfeld, from "In Fact, the Public Schools Are Biased Against Boys, Particularly Minority Males," *Insight on the News* (December 14, 1998)

ISSUE SUMMARY

YES: Janice Weinman, executive director of the American Association of University Women (AAUW), states that, while there has been some progress since the AAUW published its study entitled *How Schools Shortchange Girls* in 1991, its 1998 review of 1,000 research studies entitled *Gender Gaps: Where Schools Still Fail Our Children* found that girls still face a gender gap in math, science, and computer science.

NO: Psychologist and author Judith Kleinfeld argues that despite appearances, girls still have an advantage over boys in terms of their future plans, teachers' expectations, and everyday school experiences. Furthermore, minority males in particular are at a disadvantage educationally.

In every country there are more male architects than female architects. Why is this so? Why do females outnumber males in other careers? Are these gender differences due to teachers paying more attention to male students than to female students, taking more questions from males than females, and/or guiding males into certain courses and academic tracks and females into less challenging ones? Do female teachers favor female students over male students? Do male teachers tend not to refer male students for counseling or remedial courses when they really need this extra help? Are the gender differences we see in post-school career paths due to a social bias?

In 1970 women accounted for only 8 percent of all medical degrees, 5 percent of law degrees, and 1 percent of dental degrees. In 1990, women earned 36 percent of medical degrees, 40 percent of law degrees, and 32 percent of dental degrees. In 1999 more women than men attended college. The women also earned higher grades and graduated more often.

In an article entitled "Sex Differences in the Brain," *Scientific American* (September 1992), Doreen Kimura, a professor of psychology and neural research, probes beneath the surface of possible gender biases in American schools. She describes a wide range of differences in the way males and females learn and states that these differences are a reflection of differing hormonal influences on fetal brain development. Kimura maintains that this helps to explain differences in occupational interests and overall capabilities between the sexes.

On the other hand, social psychologist Carol Tavris concludes in *The Mismeasure of Women* (Peter Smith Publishers, 1998), that scientific efforts conducted over the past century have yielded enough conflicting views and distorted findings to invalidate the idea that gender differences are rooted in the brain. She maintains that although biology is not irrelevant to human behavior, it is not fully responsible. The notion of gender difference, in her opinion, has consistently been used to define women as fundamentally different from and inferior to men in body, psyche, and brain.

The question of whether women and men are essentially similar or different is often drowned in emotional responses, unspoken assumptions, and activist politics. This sometimes results in patriarchal biases that dogmatically stress gender differences as justification for "natural gender roles" and can lead to sex discrimination. But similar emotional responses, unspoken assumptions, and activist politics are just as likely to result in a different bias that dogmatically maintains that the only significant difference between men and women is in their sexual anatomy.

For 3,000 years many Western thinkers have viewed human development as the result to two separate, parallel, noninteracting influences. *Nature*—genes and hormones—was believed to be dominant before birth and irrelevant after birth. *Nurture*—the learning and social environment—was believed to be irrelevant during the nine months of pregnancy, but would dominate after birth.

As you read these two selections, see if you can detect any traces or undercurrents of the *Nature vs. Nurture* debate. If you find these undercurrents, do they influence your own appraisal of the arguments presented?

In the following selections, Janice Weinman cites an AAUW report in order to support her conviction that both the quantity and quality of education for females falls short of that for males. Judith Kleinfeld counters that males, particularly minority males, are at a disadvantage when it comes to educational opportunities. She asserts that the AAUW report is merely "junk science."

Janice Weinman

Girls Still Face Barriers in Schools That Prevent Them From Reaching Their Full Potential

T he American Association of University Women, or AAUW, has been a nonprofit, nonpartisan advocate for equal opportunities for women and girls for more than a century. Specifically, we work to improve education for girls.

The need for this is clear. AAUW's 1992 report, *How Schools Shortchange Girls*, reviewed more than 1,300 studies and documented disturbing evidence that girls receive an inequitable education, both in quality and quantity, in America's classrooms. In particular, we found girls faced a gender gap in math and science.

In October, the AAUW Educational Foundation released *Gender Gaps: Where Schools Still Fail Our Children*. Synthesizing 1,000 research studies, *Gender Gaps* measures schools' progress in providing a fair and equitable education since 1992. While girls have improved in some areas, such as math and science, they face an alarming new gap in technology that threatens to make women bystanders in the 21st-century economy.

Gender Gaps found that girls make up only a small percentage of students in computer-science classes. While boys are more likely to enroll in advanced computer-applications and graphics courses, girls take data-entry and clerical classes, the 1990s version of typing. Boys enter the classroom with more prior experience with computers and other technology than girls. Girls consistently rate themselves significantly lower than boys on computer ability, and boys exhibit higher self-confidence and a more positive attitude about computers than do girls.

Critics such as Professor Judith Kleinfeld have questioned why research should focus on the educational experiences of girls. They contend that girls are in fact doing quite well in school. The attention AAUW brings to girls and gender equity, they argue, leads to the neglect of boys.

AAUW believes that all students deserve a good education. To make sure that all students are performing to high academic standards, educators must address the learning needs of different groups of students—boys and girls, African-Americans and Hispanics, rich and poor. AAUW agrees that boys, like girls, face academic challenges. In fact, *Gender Gaps* clearly highlights the fact that boys still lag behind in communications skills. These gaps must be addressed by schools so that all children, boys and girls, have equal opportunity to develop to their full potential.

AAUW's work to eliminate gender bias in the classroom and address gender gaps in education benefits both boys and girls. Rather than pit one group against another, we believe this is a win-win scenario for all students. However, since Kleinfeld does make some specific charges against AAUW's research, allow me to address her claims.

First, Kleinfeld's report—commissioned by the conservative Women's Freedom Network—uses 1998 figures, which show girls improving in math and science, to critique our 1992 finding that there was a gender gap in math and science. That's like using today's lower crime rates to say a 6-year-old study on increasing crime rates created a false alarm. AAUW recognizes and applauds the gains girls have made during the last six years. In fact, *Gender Gaps* documents the improvements girls have made in math and science since AAUW brought national attention to the problem in 1992.

Even if you look at the most recent data, the way Kleinfeld does, there still are significant gender differences in schools that must be addressed, including grades and test scores, health and development risks and career development.

As both *How Schools Shortchange Girls* and *Gender Gaps* reported, girls earn better grades than boys. Despite this fact, boys continue to score higher than girls on high-stakes tests—the Preliminary Scholastic Assessment Tests, or PSAT, the Scholastic Assessment Tests, or SAT, the American College Test, or ACT—that determine college admissions and scholarship opportunities. Boys score higher on both the math and verbal sections on these exams, with the gender gaps being the widest for high-scoring students.

As both *Gender Gaps* and Kleinfeld point out, girls' enrollment in advanced placement, or AP, or honors courses is comparable to those of boys, except in AP physics and AP computer science. In fact, more girls take AP English, foreign language and biology. However, girls do not score as well as boys on the AP exams that can earn college credit, even in subjects such as English where girls earn top grades.

Girls' academic success also is affected by the tough issues facing students—pregnancy, violence and harassment—that rarely are discussed in school. AAUW believes that schools can play a key role in developing healthy and well-balanced students.

Although Kleinfeld tries to discredit AAUW's work by pointing to the large number of boys in special education, our 1992 report paid careful attention to the fact that boys outnumbered girls in these programs by startling percentages. It also cited studies on learning disabilities and attention-deficit disorders that indicated that they occurred almost equally in boys and girls.

Girls continue to be more vulnerable to some risks than boys. As *Gender Gaps* reports, one in five girls has been sexually or physically abused, one in four shows signs of depression and one in four doesn't get health care when she needs it. Schools limit gender equity when they fail to confront or discuss risk factors for students.

AAUW also is well-known for our research on self-esteem. In 1991, AAUW commissioned the first national scientific survey on self-esteem, *Short-changing Girls, Shortchanging America*. This survey was stratified by region, included an unprecedented number of children (3,000 children ages 9 to 15), and rigorously was reviewed by a team of academic advisers. The 1991 survey offered solid evidence of differences in self-esteem between girls and boys.

Although girls who were surveyed for *Shortchanging Girls, Shortchanging America* self-reported that teachers called on and gave more attention to girls, their self-esteem nevertheless declined. Despite girls' perceptions, the 1992 report, which looked at many other studies in addition to the AAUW survey, found that girls received significantly less attention than boys in the classroom. Contrary to what Kleinfeld asserts, neither AAUW's 1991 survey nor 1992 report drew a causal relationship between self-esteem and academic achievement. AAUW's research on self-esteem looked at multiple patterns across multiple indicators—including general self-esteem, family importance, academic self-esteem, isolation, voice, acceptance, friends and attention in classrooms—and used multiple methodologies. The repeated conclusion our research revealed is that girls face a dramatic drop in self-esteem as they get older that has devastating consequences on their aspirations and their futures. Kleinfeld's work looks at only two questions from our survey to draw her own conclusions.

Beyond K–12 public schools, Kleinfeld looks at college degrees to declare that women have achieved parity in the professional world. Although more women than men enter college, entry into higher education doesn't guarantee equitable conditions. That's why AAUW has worked to include key provisions in the reauthorization of the Higher Education Act to make sure women's needs are addressed on campus. For example, although women are three times as likely as men to be single parents while in college, campus-based child care still is hard to find and afford.

And women still are underrepresented in nontraditional fields such as math and science that lead to greater earning power upon graduation. There are disparities at the undergraduate, master's and doctorate levels in these fields, which have a profound effect on careers.

You only need to look outside of the classroom and into the boardroom to see that women are still a long way from equality. Women earn only 76 cents for every dollar that a man earns. In 1995, women represented 70 percent of all adults with incomes below the poverty level, and two out of three minimum-age earners are women. Out of the entire Fortune 500, there are only two female CEOs and a total of seven in the Fortune 1,000. And women only make up 11 percent of Congress.

No one wins in Kleinfeld's who's-worse-off debate. AAUW's work to eliminate gender bias in the classroom and address gender gaps in education benefits both boys and girls. Our research has resonated with parents, teachers and policymakers who have used our research as a catalyst for positive change in their public schools. Our 1,500 branches across the country conduct programs to empower and encourage young girls. Our fellowships help women succeed in school and advance into fields that historically have been off limits.

AAUW believes that all students deserve a good education and the opportunity to develop to their full potential. And we know from experience that we can help girls close the gender gap—we've seen them improve in math and science. Now we must do the same for technology to make sure all students have the technological skills to compete in the 21st century.

 **NO**

In Fact, the Public Schools Are Biased Against Boys, Particularly Minority Males

Think back to your own school days. Who got into more trouble in school—the boys or the girls? Who got the best grades—the boys or the girls? Who was the valedictorian in your high school—a boy or a girl?

Yes, school is just the same as you remember it.

Feminist-advocacy groups such as the American Association of University Women, or AAUW, have promoted a big lie: the idea that schools shortchange girls. The AAUW studies are advocacy research—junk science. In fact, their latest study is going to give me lots of examples for my research-methods class on how to lie with statistics. It's all there—graphs drawn to make a little gap look like a big one, percentages calculated with the wrong numerical base to show that girls score lower than boys on advanced placement, or AP, tests in English when the girls actually score higher. Such a gold mine of tricks!

Why the deception? The short answer is money. The long answer is money and career advancement. The idea that females are victims garners millions of dollars in federal and foundation funding for feminist-advocacy groups to launch special programs for girls. This idea also helps well-educated women gain special preferences in their battle for elite jobs at the top.

Who are the real victims? The losers are the students the schools really do shortchange—mostly minority males. Women's-advocacy groups have hijacked the moral capital of the civil-rights movement to promote the special interests of well-off, well-connected women. Along the way they have scared many parents, who are worrying about their daughters in the schools when they should be worrying about their sons.

When I told my own university students that the AAUW had just discovered a new gender gap—a computer gap—a great groan arose from the class. Puzzled and surprised, I asked each student how he or she used computers. Are women really going to be bystanders in the technological 21st century, as the AAUW would have us believe?

The students' answers laid bare the fallacy in the AAUW's latest headline-grabber. The women in the class, no less than the men, could use spreadsheets, databases and word-processing programs. The women could search the Internet. The women learned the computer programs they needed to use.

So what's all the hysteria about the computer gap? If you read the 1998 AAUW report, you will be in for a surprise. All this uproar comes down to a difference of 5 percent in the proportion of male high-school students (30 percent) compared to female high-school students (25 percent) who sign up for computer-science courses. These are the kinds of courses that teach computer-programming skills for students interested in computer-science careers.

Males indeed are more likely than females to choose computer science as a career. So what? Women aren't as interested as men in turning into Dilberts-in-a-cubicle. According to a report on women in mathematics and science from the National Center for Education Statistics, twice as many female college students (20 percent) compared to male college students (less than 10 percent) now seek prestigious professional careers.

The truth is that males and females have somewhat different interests and somewhat different areas of intellectual strength and weakness, and these differences show up in schools. Here are the facts:

Grades: Females are ahead.   If the schools were biased against girls, such bias should be easy to detect. After all, the schools give clear and measurable rewards: grades, class rank and honors. These rewards are valuable in getting into an elite college or getting a good job.

Every study, even the AAUW's own 1998 report, concedes that girls consistently earn higher grades than boys throughout their schooling. Girls get higher class rank and more academic honors in every field except mathematics and science (I'll discuss this difference later). Girls, not boys, are more apt to be chosen for gifted and talented programs, the gateway into a far higher-quality education. Girls drop out of school less often than boys and less often repeat a grade. Wherever the schools hand out the prizes, girls get more than their share.

Standardized achievement tests: Females do better in some subjects; males do better in others.   Even though girls get better grades, the schools still might be shortchanging girls if they actually aren't learning as much as boys. Grades, after all, have a lot to do with whether students are willing to play along with the school's demands for neatness and conformity.

On standardized tests, females surpass males by a mile on tests of writing ability. Females also surpass males in reading achievement and in study skills. Males surpass females on tests of science, mathematics and a few areas of social studies.

The gender gap in mathematics and science is closing, as the AAUW 1998 report admits. The gender-equity police take credit for it, but the real cause is higher graduation requirements in high school. Girls now take just as many high-school science and mathematics courses as boys do, with the exception of a small difference in physics.

In a nutshell, boys end up with lower grades than girls even in subjects where standardized tests show boys know more. So against which sex are schools biased?

High-stakes tests: What's really going on.   The AAUW makes much of the fact that males surpass females on high-stakes tests, such as the Scholastic Assessment Tests, or SAT. Here's what they don't tell you. More than 75,500 additional females take the SAT than males, and these "additional" females are less likely to have taken rigorous academic courses than other students, points out a 1998 College Board study on sex and the SAT.

Here is the way the trick works. Let's say you are comparing the top-10 male basketball players with the top 10 female players in the same high school. Assume that the males and the females have the same shooting ability. But then add to the female group five girls who try hard but aren't as good. Of course, the female shooting average will be lower than the males'.

The AAUW pulls a similar trick in comparing scores on AP tests, tough tests taken by the most advanced high-school students. The AAUW report admits that girls take AP tests in greater number than boys but pulls a fast one by saying that these girls earn lower scores even in areas of historic strength, such as English.

Take a look at the actual facts in the federal report, *The Condition of Education 1998*. Almost twice as many girls as boys took the AP English test. Among the girls, 46 per 1,000 12th-graders got a score of 3 or higher, qualifying them for college credit. Among the boys, 27 per 1,000 12th-graders got such a high score. What's the truth? Girls earn far higher scores than boys on the AP English test, the opposite of what the AAUW claims.

Males fall at the extremes—flaming failures and academic stars.   More boys do show up at the top in fields such as mathematics and science. But then more boys also show up at the bottom. Boys are twice as likely to be placed in special-education classes for the learning-disabled. Boys outnumber girls by 4–1 in neurological impairments such as autism or dyslexia.

This has less to do with bias than with biology. On many human characteristics, including intellectual abilities, males are just more variable than females. More males show up at the high end of the bell curve and more males show up at the low end of the bell curve. From the standpoint of natural selection, males are the more expendable sex. Nature takes more chances with males, producing more oddities of every kind, whether genius or insanity.

Women's advocacy groups push programs to equalize male and females in mathematics and science. Social engineering cannot make real differences go away, nor should it.

College success: Females now surpass males.   Many people don't realize that women have become the majority of college students. In 1996, women earned 55 percent of bachelor's degrees and 55 percent of all master's degrees, and African-American females are much further ahead.

Insofar as self-esteem is concerned, both girls and boys have rather high opinions of themselves. The best research, now accepted even by feminist-advocacy groups, shows no difference between teenage boys and girls in self-esteem. The latest AAUW report on gender gaps is strangely silent about the self-esteem gap they trumpeted a few years ago.

On the issue of whether girls get less class participation than boys, it is clear that teachers do not silence girls. Everyone agrees that teachers give boys more attention of the negative, disciplinary kind. Who gets more academic attention? This research is a confusing mess, with no clear patterns.

So, who are the public schools biased against? The right answer is boys. Many studies show that American schools, far from shortchanging girls, are biased against boys. In fact, the AAUW found the same thing but buried these results in unpublished tables. I had to badger the AAUW office for weeks to get a 1990 Greenberg-Lake survey and pay close to $100 for the photocopying. But you can see that the AAUW had good reason to hide these findings. According to the AAUW's hidden study, both boys and girls agree, sometimes by overwhelming margins, that teachers think girls are smarter, compliment girls more often and like to be around girls more.

The media doesn't often report studies which contradict the feminist party line. A good example is the 1997 report on gender issues published by the Met-Life Foundation, an organization with no political ax to grind. This study concludes:

1. Contrary to the commonly held view that boys are at an advantage over girls in school, girls appear to have an advantage over boys in terms of their future plans, teachers' expectations, everyday experiences at schools and interactions in the classroom;
2. Minority girls hold the most optimistic views of the future and are the group most likely to focus on education goals;
3. Minority boys are the most likely to feel discouraged about the future and the least interested in getting a good education; and
4. Teachers nationwide view girls as higher achievers and more likely to succeed than boys.

If anyone needs help in school, it is minority boys. They are the victims of the AAUW's junk science.

POSTSCRIPT

Do Schools Perpetuate a Gender Bias?

Jerome Kagan, a major researcher in the development of personality, asserts that many prefer to downplay nature and emphasize nurture when discussing the origin of phychological differences in males and females. This tendency, he says, owes much to the prevailing commitment Americans have to egalitarianism. If differences between individuals, between the genders, or between gender orientations are innate and biologically based, there is little that can be done about them. If, however, differences are due to inequities in the social environment, there may be a lot that can be done to reduce or eliminate these differences. But there is a third option. This option has three essential components. First is the belief that male and female brains and personalities are gender differentiated by hormones and genes as a fetus is developing in the womb and after birth. Second is the observation that parents, teachers, and society engage in biased gender scripting. Third is the conclusion that innate biological differences in the brain interact with gender-biased scripting at critical periods throughout our lives.

Alice Rossi, in her 1983 Presidential Address to the American Sociological Association, pointed out that attempts to explain human behavior and therapies that seek to change behavior "carry a high risk of eventual irrelevance [if they] neglect the fundamental biological and neural differences between the sexes [and] the mounting evidence of sexual dimorphism from the biological and neural sciences." Although Rossi seems to favor the belief that male and female brains are wired differently, she offers an important distinction. She carefully states that gender "diversity is a biological fact, while [gender] equality is a political, ethical, and social precept."

If the biological and neuropsychological evidence supports the existence of significant differences in male and female brains, then we have to be careful to view these differences as part of human diversity and not in terms of superior versus inferior or good versus bad. Human diversity does not necessarily deny or obstruct human equality, because human equality is a political, moral, and social issue. Too often human diversity is used to support the superiority of one group over another group.

On the other hand, educators of all grades may need to carefully examine the ways in which boys and girls are treated differently in their classrooms. Some researchers have observed a tendency for educators of preschool students to compliment boys on their *performance* (e.g., "Billy, you're such a good runner!") and girls on their *appearance* (e.g., "Karen, you look so pretty today!"). Furthermore, when an educator gives a simple instruction like, "I need a few strong boys to help me move some chairs," she or he may be completely unaware that the directions exclude girls from the possibility of helping. Educators who begin to recognize that the key skill needed for such an activity is *strength* and not *being a boy* will help their students make empowering strides toward life's opportunities.

Suggested Readings

N. Angier, "How Biology Affects Behavior and Vice Versa," *The New York Times* (May 30, 1995).

A. Fausto-Sterling, *Myths of Gender: Biological Theories About Women and Men,* 2d ed. (Basic Books, 1992).

C. Gorman, "Sizing Up the Sexes," *Time* (January 20, 1992).

D. Kimura, "Sex Differences in the Brain," *Scientific American* (September 1992).

R. Pool, *Eve's Rib: Searching for the Biological Roots of Sex Differences* (Crown Publishers, 1994).

C. Tavris, *The Mismeasure of Woman: Why Women Are Not the Better Sex, the Inferior Sex, or the Opposite Sex* (Simon & Schuster, 1992).

L. Wright, "Double Mystery," *The New Yorker* (August 7, 1995).

ISSUE 17

Should Society Support Cohabitation Before Marriage?

YES: Dorian Solot and Marshall Miller, from *Unmarried to Each Other: The Essential Guide to Living Together as an Unmarried Couple* (Marlowe & Company, 2002)

NO: David Popenoe and Barbara Dafoe Whitehead, from *Should We Live Together? What Young Adults Need to Know About Cohabitation Before Marriage: A Comprehensive Review of Research* (The National Marriage Project, 2001)

ISSUE SUMMARY

YES: Dorian Solot and Marshall Miller, founders of the Alternatives to Marriage Project (www.unmarried.org), describe some of the challenges faced by people who choose to live together without marrying, and offer practical advice for couples who face discrimination.

NO: David Popenoe and Barbara Dafoe Whitehead, directors of the National Marriage Project (marriage.rutgers.edu), contend that living together before marriage is not a good way to prepare for marriage or avoid divorce. They maintain that cohabitation weakens the institution of marriage and poses serious risks for women and children.

What do Americans think of sexual relationships and living together before marriage? Attitudes have changed dramatically during the past generation. In a 1969 Gallup poll of American adults, two-thirds said it was morally wrong for a man and a woman to have sexual relations before marriage. A more recent (2001) poll revealed that only 38 percent of American adults share this opinion today. These two surveys focus on the sexual behavior of young people before marriage. When the question is broadened to examine how today's Americans feel about couples "living together," or cohabiting, 52 percent approve.

In practice, more than one-half of Americans live together before marrying. Many cohabiting couples will live together for a relatively short period of time, with most couples either breaking up or marrying within about 1½ years, though couples with children are more likely to stay together. In addition, the 2000 U.S. Census indicates that there are almost 4 million opposite-sex, unmarried households in the United States. (These households include both couples who have been married previously and those who have never been married.) Forty-one percent of these households have at least one child under the age of 18.

Like their married counterparts, infidelity is not common among the majority of cohabiting couples, though rates are slightly different. According to the U.S. chapter of the *International Encyclopedia of Sexuality* (Continuum, 2004), about 94 percent of married persons had sex only with their spouse during the last year, compared with 75 percent of cohabiting persons.

Despite the growing acceptance of cohabitation, couples who live together without marrying often face pressure from family and loved ones to "tie the knot." For some, marriage may be in their future plans; others may be perfectly happy with their decision not to marry; still other couples may be legally restricted from marrying—as of 2004, only Massachusetts permits same-sex couples to legally marry. Recognizing the pressures and discrimination some cohabiting couples may face, the Alternatives to Marriage Project advocates for the "equality and fairness for unmarried people, including people who choose not to marry, cannot marry, or live together before marriage."

The first essay that follows is from a chapter of *Unmarried to Each Other: The Essential Guide to Living Together as an Unmarried Couple,* a guide written by the organization's cofounders, Dorian Solot and Marshall Miller.

On the other side of the debate is the National Marriage Project, which expresses concern about the growing trend toward greater acceptance of cohabitation. The National Marriage Project provides "research and analysis on the state of marriage in America and to educate the public on the social, economic and cultural conditions affecting marital success and child wellbeing." The second essay, written by the National Project's co-directors, David Popenoe and Barbara Dafoe Whitehead, provides commentary and analysis of existing literature on cohabitation. It warns young people, especially young women, of the dangers of cohabitation to them and their children.

 **YES**

When Others Disagree: Surviving Pressure and Discrimination

We wish living together were easy. We wish all parents welcomed the news of their child's cohabitation with cries of, "How wonderful, darling! I'll bring over a lasagna so you won't have to worry about dinner while you unpack." We wish friends threw celebratory bashes, ministers blessed the new level of love and commitment, wise neighbors shared their insights about getting through hard times, and landlords cheerfully added another name to the lease.

Unfortunately, that's not the world in which we live. While an unmarried couple moving to the block generally isn't worthy of backyard gossip anymore, it's not unusual for partners to run into snags along the way. For gay, lesbian, bisexual, and transgender (GLBT) people, homophobia is often a bigger problem than marital status discrimination, though the two are closely linked. This chapter offers insights on some common challenges from the outside, and suggests practical ways to deal with those who predict catastrophe for your relationship, those who nudge you down the aisle, and those who discriminate against you. Although we can't guarantee the naysayers will help load furniture into your U-Haul for the big move, if you're lucky they might give you a friendly wave as you pull away.

Pressure Not To Live Together

There's no question acceptance of cohabitation has come a long way quickly. In a span of a few decades the act of sharing a home without sharing a marriage license has been transformed from scandalous to normal. Today it's something most people do before they marry. But despite how common it's become, living together still draws frowns, wrinkled brows, and even outright condemnation from some people. Nicole describes her parents as "rigid Catholics" and says they frequently tell her she's "living in sin." Her father warns her of eternal damnation, saying, "Your life on earth is so short, but eternity is so long."

> *Every holiday it's a nightmare filled with anxiety when we have to get together with my family, because my mother makes it so uncomfortable for*

the two of us. Even though we've been together for nine years, and I don't rely on her financially or anything, she makes it very, very uncomfortable. About six months ago it all came to a head. She said that I wasn't welcome at her house, so I don't go to her house anymore except at holidays.

This intense disapproval isn't because cohabiting partners store their toothbrushes so close together, or because people believe that seeing your sweetheart's morning bedhead should be an experience only for married spouses. The real reason why there's opposition to unmarried people living together is this: cohabitors have sex. Of course, *lots* of unmarried people have sex, whether they live with their lovers or not. At least 70 percent of first-time brides and 83 percent of first-time grooms are not virgins on their wedding day—the percentages are even higher for younger generations—revealing exactly how much unmarried lovemaking is going on. Much of that sex involves far less love and commitment than is present in many cohabiting relationships. But the nose-wrinklers care about sex between cohabitors because there's no attempt to hide it, no polite, "We were just sitting here in the back room having a conversation. Really!" When romantically-involved unmarried people live together, everyone assumes they're having sex, and critics say they're flaunting it. That's where the arguments begin. . . .

MOM ALWAYS KNOWS

Have you heard the joke about the cohabiting guy whose mother came to dinner? His mom had long been suspicious of the relationship between her son, John, and his roommate, Julie. When they had her over for dinner one night, John read his mother's mind, and volunteered, "I know what you must be thinking, Mom, but I assure you, Julie and I are just roommates."

About a week later, Julie came to John and said, "Ever since your mother came to dinner, I haven't been able to find the beautiful silver gravy ladle. You don't suppose she took it, do you?" John said, "Well, I doubt it, but I'll write her a letter just to be sure." So he sat down and wrote a letter:

"Dear Mother, I'm not saying you did take a gravy ladle from my house, and I'm not saying you did not take a gravy ladle from my house, but the fact remains that one has been missing ever since you were here for dinner. Love, John."

Several days later, John received a letter from his mother:

"Dear Son, I'm not saying that you do sleep with Julie, and I'm not saying that you do not sleep with Julie, but the fact remains that if she were sleeping in her own bed, she would have found the gravy ladle by now. Love, Mother."

The Arguments

Whether you're already living together or just talking about it, odds are you've crossed paths with some of the common arguments against cohabitation. Maybe your relatives are the number one anti-cohabiting campaigners in your life, or perhaps you've encountered a sermon in church or read some disturbing statistics about living together in the newspaper. Whatever the source, almost every line of argument fits into one of these categories: Living in Sin Arguments, Pseudo-Scientific Arguments, or Mars and Venus Arguments. Each one emphasizes a different concern and warrants a different response. Below are explanations about the problems with each kind of argument, and tips for how to respond.

Living In Sin Arguments: The Moral View Against Cohabitation

These are the classic arguments, the meat and potatoes, of why you shouldn't live with your partner. You've probably heard, "Cohabitors are living in sin. It's wrong," or "The Bible says you shouldn't cohabit," or "People who shack up are undermining family values." Those are just the polite versions. At their most hostile, these sometimes bring dire warnings of hellfire and eternal doom.

Words like these can be deeply hurtful, particularly when respected people of faith aim them at people of their own religion. Some cohabitors feel forced to choose between their faith and their relationship, even when the relationship is a good one. Anita says:

> *I have been in so much turmoil about my perplexing situation. I am forty-nine-years-old and engaged to a wonderful man, but because of my past divorce I will lose all my medical benefits if I marry. I love this man with all my heart. I want to marry by my Christian beliefs, but I have a heart problem and limited funds, so I cannot afford to lose my health insurance. We live together, and we are happy. But I am so torn. I pray all the time for God to love me and not scorn me for what I am doing. I would love to have His blessing upon us without the legal marriage, and to know that we will still go to heaven.*

Jacquie says that the Bible's messages are the only things that trouble her about being in an unmarried relationship.

> *According to the scriptures, I'm in trouble. The book of Deuteronomy says that my former husband is my husband until the day they throw dirt on me. In the church's eyes, we are wrong. In the African-American community, that is one of the biggest things that we struggle with.*

Fortunately, there are many religious and ethical people who disagree with this moralistic view against cohabitation, and believe in supporting healthy, loving relationships regardless of marital status.

How To Respond to Living in Sin Arguments
Understand the Bible in today's context.   You might be surprised to realize that despite claims like, "Cohabitation is entirely contrary to God's law," there's

nothing in the Judeo-Christian Bible that explicitly says cohabitation is wrong. In fact, the Bible includes teachings about holy unmarried relationships that are valid alternatives to marriage, and poems in the Song of Songs that celebrate an unmarried relationship. Rabbi Arthur Waskow says of these, "I believe that the Song of Songs is our best guide from the ancient tradition as to how sexuality could express the joyful and pleasurable celebration of God."

While parts of the Bible do address "fornication," or sex between unmarried people, many religious leaders and scholars believe that some Biblical teachings are no longer applicable to today's world. Of the many mores mentioned and permitted in the Bible, most faith traditions—liberal, mainstream, fundamentalist, and evangelical alike—now condemn behaviors such as polygamy, slavery, and the treatment of women as property. Reverend Jim Maynard of American Baptists Concerned says, "Most hold that the Bible is inspired by God but written in the words of humans. It contains human perspectives and prejudice that reflect that time and place in which it was written. What is normal for one day and time is not always applicable to others." While the Bible can provide inspiration and guidance, many clergy agree that one need not interpret it literally to remain true to one's faith. It's the relationship between the two spouses (even legally unmarried ones) and God that ultimately matters, not the opinion of the minister or the cranky lady in the front pew.

Many Christian leaders have called for the church to stay focused on Jesus's message of love. For instance, in 2000 Dr. William Walsh, the Bishop of Killaloe in Ireland, publicly apologized for the Catholic Church's attitude towards cohabiting couples and said, "Christ did not condemn those who failed to meet the ideals of the church . . . We must not condemn. We must not question the nature of that love that may not meet with our ideals. We must celebrate family, and all that is possible in family; the love between married spouses and between parents and children; the love of the unmarried mother and unmarried father and their children, and the struggle that being an unmarried mother and father can be in our society."

Help others respect your decision.   If the person who accuses you of "living in sin" is close to home—a parent or relative, member of your faith community, or someone else with whom you'll have an ongoing relationship—you can work to help him better understand and respect your decision to live together. It helps to know exactly what concerns him. If the values underlying your relationship are his primary care, he may soften if he realizes you share his values of commitment, honesty, love, and integrity. It might help him to understand what your relationship means to you, how your shared values are central to your love, and why you aren't or can't be married. Witnessing you put these values into practice over a period of years can be the most powerful way to earn the respect of these doubters. Few would remain judgmental of Anita, the woman above with a heart problem, if they understood her situation and saw the Christian values woven into her daily life.

Other objectors' opposition to living together stems from a deeply held moral or religious belief that opposes all unmarried sex and rigidly upholds heterosexual marriage as the only acceptable form of family. A friendly conversation is unlikely to transform one of these types into someone who supports your relationship. It might be possible, though, to come to respect each other's points of view, mutually understand that you've made different choices, and agree to disagree. Marshall experienced this "hate the sin, love the sinner" approach firsthand:

> *Before his death at age ninety-one, my grandfather regularly attended Sunday services at his southern Virginia Baptist retirement home. One of his preacher's favorite pastimes was rallying against those who "live in sin." Although our living together had never seemed to concern my grandfather before he moved to the retirement home, over time this preacher's message caused him to decide that he no longer wanted to see or talk to Dorian and me because of the sin he felt we were committing. His silent treatment lasted for months, and while it hurt us, we were fortunate to have support from the rest of my family. After lots of conversations with my parents, he eventually came around, reaching out to us with the compromise, "I don't hate you, I just hate what you're doing." We were glad to have several months of positive re-connections before he passed away.*

It's not easy, and sometimes not even possible, to reach this point with every family member. But it can be worth trying.

Live the kind of "family values" that matter.   Pundits and politicians who lament "declining family values" are usually talking about a narrow view of family. In the real world, family ties aren't based on whether you're legally married, have children, or are heterosexual. Unmarried partners can be a family unit, and part of each other's extended families. Connect with each other's extended families by going to visit them (especially for important occasions like reunions, graduations, performances, and significant birthdays and anniversaries), spending holidays together, planning opportunities for each other's relatives to meet each other, signing greeting cards together, staying connected by phone and email, and finding common interests or hobbies to explore with "in-laws" (some unmarried people jokingly call theirs "out-laws"). Joan said this kind of positive family relationship earned her and her male partner, Fran, a respectful tolerator, if not a supporter:

> *Fran's dad is eighty-four and very opinionated. He's been a deacon in the Catholic Church. Considering how conventional and traditional his views are, it's amazed both of us that he has accepted me and accepted our relationship as well as he has. It's really been a pleasure. I think it's because he kind of likes me, and I like him. He's also very close to Fran, and I think it's really important to him to maintain Fran's love and goodwill and the closeness that they have. I think he would like it if Fran got married, but he doesn't make an issue of it.*

The more your relationship fits into your family's culture, the easier it becomes for people to choose to forget about how you are different. Finding ways for each other's relatives to meet and connect is one of the most powerful ways we've found to strengthen ties. Dorian describes one method we've used:

> Marshall and I each have sisters who are much younger than we are. When we were in college they'd sometimes visit us, so we decided to create an annual "Sister Convergence" weekend. Starting when the girls were six, seven, and eight, they'd come every spring with teddy bears and sleeping bags in tow, eat piles of peanut butter and jelly sandwiches, teach us the sing-song hand-clapping games they'd learned on the playground, make embroidery-thread friendship bracelets they'd sell to our housemates, and surprise us with stealth tickling attacks. The hiding of the peanut butter jar's top became part of the annual tradition; back home they'd talk to us on the phone, giggling with glee when they heard we'd finally discovered where they stowed it behind a sofa cushion or deep in a sock drawer. They grew up knowing each other and looking forward to their weekends together. Even though they're not related, I think they feel like each other's extended families.

Create your own family.   Unfortunately, being connecting to extended family isn't an option for everyone. Many who have been rejected from or need to separate themselves from their family of origin find tremendous strength by forming an intentional family. These kinds of families can include your partner, close friends, or other people who play a significant role in your life. You might choose to share holidays or important events with them, and see them as an place to turn for support during difficult times.

Find a supportive faith community.   If you're a religious person, you may not have to settle for a faith community that condemns your relationship. You can tell a lot about a given church's stance on diverse families by looking at its approach to gay and lesbian issues. Some denominations and many individual churches, synagogues, and clergy have affirmed their support for GLBT people, and these are more likely to welcome all kinds of "non-traditional" relationships. Unitarian Universalists, Quakers, Reform and Reconstructionist Jews, and the United Church of Christ are particularly known for welcoming all people, regardless of their sexual orientation or marital status. . . .

Pseudo-Scientific Arguments: The "Scientific" View Against Cohabitation

In the 1980s and 1990s, when arguments based on morality ceased to pack the punch they once did, anti-cohabitation campaigners donned crisp white lab coats, re-tooling their messages for today's science-trusting public. The new arguments sound like, "Living together before marriage increases the risk of divorce," "Cohabitors are less committed to each other than married couples," and "Cohabiting couples experience more domestic violence than married ones." Gwen heard them from her mother:

> I received a major backlash from both my parents in response to my choice to live with my boyfriend. My mother actually called and lectured to me extensively for forty minutes about the various kinds of research to substantiate her opinion that cohabiting relationships are very unhealthy.

Arguments like these can be confusing, since to many couples it makes intuitive sense to live together before tying the knot. The reality is, many of the statistics batted around in the media don't tell the whole story. It's not a coincidence the general public is becoming familiar with these semi-truths—some political groups have made them a central part of their anti-cohabitation campaigns. Yet most of the facts about cohabitation that are published in respected research journals and presented at academic conferences draw quite different conclusions.

How to Understand the Truth Behind Pseudo-Scientific Arguments

Understand the difference between "the average cohabitor" and your life.   You are not necessarily "average." With eleven million cohabitors in this country, it is nearly impossible to draw any meaningful conclusions about what we all have in common. Yet pseudo-scientific arguments do just that.

People live with a partner for incredibly varied reasons—if cohabitors were paint colors, we'd be a veritable rainbow. For sake of explanation, imagine that one kind of cohabitor, couples who live together as a step between dating and marriage, are red paint. Senior citizens who live together so they don't lose their pensions will be yellow paint, and unmarried couples of several decades' duration with no plans to marry are green. Low-income couples who would like to marry but want to be sure their future spouse can help them escape poverty are blue.

Anytime a researcher comes up with an average about cohabitors, she takes all the red, yellow, green, blue, and a bunch of other colors for all the other cohabitors, stirs them together, and come up with a oh-so-serious, scientifically accurate shade of—you guessed it—brown. As everyone focuses on this average number that's been produced—the muddy brown color—they forget that this average is utterly meaningless when it comes to understanding the red cohabitors, the yellow ones, or any of the others.

Cohabiting types that exist in large numbers affect the color of the whole pool when it's averaged. So since poor people, whom we colored blue, cohabit at higher rates than middle or upper-class ones, the average brown color will always have a blue tint. That means that certain characteristics about poor people, like the fact that they tend to have more health problems and higher rates of depression will make the average for *all* cohabitors look more depressed and unhealthy. But those tendencies aren't necessarily true for other cohabitors in the pool. Average cohabiting couples who plan to marry or are considering marriage have characteristics very similar to married people. Green cohabitors in very long-term relationships are statistically a small splash—their characteristics hardly show up in the average at all.

In short, because of the way some groups pull the average up or down, statistics about cohabitation often lead to distorted conclusions. Poor people who cohabit in large numbers make the average cohabitor income look low, but if you're making a good salary, that doesn't affect you. There are higher levels of alcoholism in the cohabitor population because people are less likely to marry partners with alcohol problems, but that doesn't mean that living together will drive you to drink. The quality of your relationship—not any statistical average—determines whether your union will be strong.

Realize there is no evidence that cohabitation causes divorce. It's true research finds that on average, cohabitors who later marry have a higher divorce rate than those who marry without living together first. But it's a misrepresentation to say that cohabitation *causes* divorce. Here's why. This research compares two groups of people, those who live together before they marry and those who don't. But people aren't randomly assigned to these different groups—they choose to live together or not because they're different kinds of people. Those who don't live together before marriage are a minority today, and they tend to be more conservative, with stronger religious beliefs and stronger opposition to divorce. Given this, it's no surprise that this group doesn't consider divorce an acceptable option. The difference between the two groups' divorce rates is likely attributable to the types of people in each group, not because the cohabitation ruins their relationships. As Sociologist Judith Seltzer writes, "Claims that individuals who cohabit before marriage hurt their chances of a good marriage pay too little attention to this evidence."

Given that many couples cohabit to test their compatibility before making a lifetime commitment to marriage, could cohabitation actually result in *lower* divorce rates? It's possible. The divorce rate has been falling slightly since its peak two decades ago. During that same time period, the cohabitation rate has skyrocketed. There's no way to know for certain how the changes in divorce and cohabitation affect each other—just because two things happen at the same time (correlation) doesn't prove that one caused the other (causation). Since some cohabitors live together to try out a relationship but then ultimately break up, it's likely these people successfully avoided a marriage that would have ended in divorce. Chances are good the divorce rate would be higher if not for cohabitation.

Cohabitation opponents make a lot of noise about divorce statistics because divorce is such a common fear. When you look at all the facts, whether you divorce ultimately may not have much to do with whether you live together. If you never marry, you don't need to worry about divorce, though the end of a long-term relationship has the same emotional impact. Chapter 4 is about what you can do to keep your relationship strong.

Know that commitment and marriage are not the same thing. As with most stereotypes, there's a grain of truth to the claim that cohabitors are less committed than married spouses. Dating couples are usually less committed than married ones, too. Since most people move through the stages from dating to living together to marriage, you'd expect average commitment levels to follow the same trends—lowest among dating couples, highest among married ones—and they do.

Of course there are some cohabitors who have no commitment to each other, just as there are married couples who aren't very committed and soon got divorced. Other cohabitors' levels of commitment easily match the most loving, stable married pairs. Some have plans to marry and just haven't done so yet, while others stay together for decades without a marriage license. In all murkiness of averages, there's no way to distinguish the couple who's owned a home togther for thirty years from one who moved in together last week when one partner got evicted. Sure, scientists can come up with an average number to indicate commitment among cohabitors. But it won't tell you anything about your own relationship.

It's worth pondering how those scientists even come up with a number that equals commitment. It's a slippery concept to pin down using a survey—imagine trying to compare your commitment to your relationship to your friend's commitment to his using a numerical scale. One oft-cited study of cohabitors and married couples found a difference of 1.3 points on a twenty point scale of "commitment," and a finding that small isn't unusual. So the pundits are telling the truth when they say cohabitors on average aren't as committed as married people—but it sure isn't the whole truth.

The best way to win the argument over commitment is to prove your relationship can stand the test of time. As the years tick by and you weather some tough times, outsiders will realize you're in it for the long haul. Calling yours a "committed relationship" or describing yourselves as "life partners" if that describes you can help people understand.

Understand the "accumulation factor."   Cohabitation opponents exaggerate every negative research conclusion about the subject while ignoring research that finds cohabitors are just like everyone else. One of the most alarming claims might be that cohabiting women are at higher risk of domestic violence than married ones. What's actually going on? First of all, there isn't much of a difference between married and cohabiting women on this characteristic. One British study that's often cited found that 2 percent of married women had experienced domestic assault in the previous year, compared with 3 percent of cohabiting women. Nonetheless, since any amount of domestic violence is unacceptable, even a 1 percent difference could be cause for concern.

A more recent study explores why that difference exists. It finds that if you track a group of new cohabitors over time, the ones with less violent relationships are more likely to marry. No surprise there. The couples still in the cohabitor pool after the non-violent couples marry—the ones who "accumulate"—are probably using excellent judgement by deciding not to make a lifetime commitment to a dangerous partner. But they affect the average for the whole pool, and make it look as if cohabitors have more abusive relationships. It's likely that a similar process clouds a great deal of the research that compares married to unmarried people.

Marriage isn't a shield that can protect anyone from abuse, and cohabitation isn't automatically a battleground. A non-violent partner is unlikely to turn aggressive because you've cohabited too long. An abusive partner is unlikely to be transformed if you get married, and in fact, marrying could put you at greater risk. Marital status is a poor way to predict whether any particular relationship will be safe.

Mars and Venus Arguments: The Gendered View Against Cohabitation

Mars and Venus Arguments assume that all men (from Mars) are looking for sex without responsibility, while all women (from Venus) are looking for husbands and babies soon after. Mars and Venus are believed to be in their own orbits, at risk for major problems when they interact or live together. Women are most often the targets of these kinds of arguments, but men aren't immune. Perhaps you've heard, "In cohabitation, men get to have sex without making a commitment," "Women are the ones who get hurt by living together," or, "He won't buy the cow if you give away the milk for free."

It's certainly possible to run into these kinds of problems if you and your partner haven't talked about what living together means to you. If one of you thinks it's a new level of commitment while the other thinks it's a way to split the rent check, you're headed for trouble. If one partner thinks you're practically engaged while the other sees the setup as a roommate "with benefits," there's conflict ahead. But if you're on the same page because you've had a few of those capital letter Relationship Talks, you're unlikely to be taken by surprise, whatever your gender. Don't be surprised if Mars is the one dreaming of hearth and home, while Venus is hesitant to get tied down—gender roles aren't what they used to be. Sebastian gets a kick out of reminding people of this:

> *My friends and acquaintances will say to me, "Oh, how long have you guys been together?" I'll say, "Almost eight years." They're in shock, and of course the next question is, "Why don't you get married?," as if they're asking, what's wrong with you? And of course they immediately assume that Janna wants to get married and I don't, because I want to go sow my wild oats, afraid of commitment, guy problem, or whatever. It's actually kind of fun to pop their bubble, to explain the decision that we've made together. I enjoy seeing them try to take that in.*

Despite all the stereotypes, many more women have serious hesitations about marrying than men. Among hundreds of long-term male-female unmarried couples we've talked to, it's nearly always the woman who feels strongly about not marrying. Women's preferences about marriage generally seem to "trump" their male partners, perhaps because they tend to have stronger feelings on the issue—if a woman wants to marry, she'll keep looking until she finds a man who consents, and Stacey is a typical example:

> *I've been with my partner for fifteen years and we've lived together ever since my pregnancy and the birth of our daughter, who is now ten. My father always wanted to know why we didn't get married. He pestered me about it, refusing to accept that I didn't wish to be married—after all, he thought, all women want to get married. One day he finally asked my partner straight out why he didn't marry me. When my partner said he was more than willing to get married, but that I was the one refusing, I think my father just gave up.*

How To Respond to Mars and Venus Arguments

Point out that it's a lot easier to have sex without commitment if you're not *living together.* If you're feeling bold, try, "We were making love long before we made the commitment to move in together." People who truly want sex without commitment don't cohabit—they just find a casual relationship or one-night-stand. By comparison, most partners who move in together are already in an intimate, sexual relationship and want to *increase* their level of connection and commitment. We don't know anyone who decided to cohabit because they wanted sex without commitment. As Mark told us, "My girlfriend and I intend to marry but do not want to rush into it before we are truly ready. We decided to live together because we were spending all our time together, anyway—why rent two apartments when we could rent one? We saw living together as a commitment to each other."

Point out that humans are not cattle. "Mom, I'm not a cow," ought to suffice. Many younger women have never even heard the warning that if they "give away the milk for free," their partner "won't buy the cow." The adage used to refer to women who "gave away" sex without holding out for marriage. The theory was that if the man could get sex without paying the price (marriage), he would never feel the need to say "I do." Women of older generations were probably surprised to read the recent discussion about the saying on the Alternatives to Marriage Project's online list:

> *Someone mentioned the old adage about the cow and men getting free milk. What is this supposed to mean? Isn't the woman getting "free milk," as well? After all, women do enjoy sex, too.*
>
> —Jessica

> *I've been saying that to my boyfriend for about fifteen years. I also told him that if he wanted to get married, he shouldn't have moved in with me. When I saw the phrase, I thought the woman was getting the free milk.*
>
> —Tori

Most women today recognize themselves as sexual beings with their own desires, who choose sexual relationships or not based on their own situation and values. It doesn't make sense to men today, either. More than eight in ten first-time grooms has had sex before he marries, yet there men stand at the altar, undeterred by all that "free milk."

Gendered double standards still exist. Women are still expected to guard sex, are labeled "sluts" if they're perceived to be having too much sex, and are targeted for warnings about "ruining their reputations." Men, on the other hand, are told they need to guard their money. Guys hear that if they're not careful, while he's busy enjoying sex with his live-in lover, she will max out his credit cards and expect a stream of expensive gifts until she finds the next guy to run off with. The best way to prevent being taken advantage of is to understand your partner throughly—whatever your gender or what you want to protect. Know whether each of you is responsible with money, what sex means to each partner, and what your expectations are about commitment and monogamy. If you're clear about what living together means for you, it'll be much easier to calm the fears provoked by Mars and Venus alarmists. . . .

NO ⬅

**David Popenoe and
Barbara Dafoe Whitehead**

Should We Live Together? What Young Adults Need to Know about Cohabitation Before Marriage: A Comprehensive Review of Recent Research

Executive Summary

Cohabitation is replacing marriage as the first living together experience for young men and women. When blushing brides walk down the aisle at the beginning of the new millennium, well over half have already lived together with a boyfriend.

For today's young adults, the first generation to come of age during the divorce revolution, living together seems like a good way to achieve some of the benefits of marriage and avoid the risk of divorce. Couples who live together can share expenses and learn more about each other. They can find out if their partner has what it takes to be married. If things don't work out, breaking up is easy to do. Cohabiting couples do not have to seek legal or religious permission to dissolve their union.

Not surprisingly, young adults favor cohabitation. According to surveys, most young people say it is a good idea to live with a person before marrying.

But a careful review of the available social science evidence suggests that living together is not a good way to prepare for marriage or to avoid divorce. What's more, it shows that the rise in cohabitation is not a positive family trend. Cohabiting unions tend to weaken the institution of marriage and pose special risks for women and children. Specifically, the research indicates that:

- Living together before marriage increases the risk of breaking up after marriage.
- Living together outside of marriage increases the risk of domestic violence for women, and the risk of physical and sexual abuse for children.

- Unmarried couples have lower levels of happiness and wellbeing than married couples.

Because this generation of young adults is so keenly aware of the fragility of marriage, it is especially important for them to know what contributes to marital success and what may threaten it. Yet many young people do not know the basic facts about cohabitation and its risks. Nor are parents, teachers, clergy and others who instruct the young in matters of sex, love and marriage well acquainted with the social science evidence. Therefore, one purpose of this paper is to report on the available research.

At the same time, we recognize the larger social and cultural trends that make cohabiting relationships attractive to many young adults today. Unmarried cohabitation is not likely to go away. Given this reality, the second purpose of this paper is to guide thinking on the question: "should we live together?" We offer four principles that may help. These principles may not be the last words on the subject but they are consistent with the available evidence and may help never-married young adults avoid painful losses in their love lives and achieve satisfying and long-lasting relationships and marriage.

1. **Consider not living together at all before marriage.** Cohabitation appears not to be helpful and may be harmful as a try-out for marriage. There is no evidence that if you decide to cohabit before marriage you will have a stronger marriage than those who don't live together, and some evidence to suggest that if you live together before marriage, you are more likely to break up after marriage. Cohabitation is probably least harmful (though not necessarily helpful) when it is prenuptial—when both partners are definitely planning to marry, have formally announced their engagement and have picked a wedding date.
2. **Do not make a habit of cohabiting.** Be aware of the dangers of multiple living together experiences, both for your own sense of wellbeing and for your chances of establishing a strong lifelong partnership. Contrary to popular wisdom, you do not learn to have better relationships from multiple failed cohabiting relationships. In fact, multiple cohabiting is a strong predictor of the failure of future relationships.
3. **Limit cohabitation to the shortest possible period of time.** The longer you live together with a partner, the more likely it is that the low-commitment ethic of cohabitation will take hold, the opposite of what is required for a successful marriage.
4. **Do not cohabit if children are involved.** Children need and should have parents who are committed to staying together over the long term. Cohabiting parents break up at a much higher rate than married parents and the effects of breakup can be devastating and often long lasting. Moreover, children living in cohabiting unions with stepfathers or mother's boyfriends are at higher risk of sexual abuse and physical violence, including lethal violence, than are children living with married biological parents.

Should We Live Together? What Young Adults Need to Know about Cohabitation Before Marriage: A Comprehensive Review of Recent Research

Living together before marriage is one of America's most significant and unexpected family trends. By simple definition, living together—or unmarried cohabitation—is the status of couples who are sexual partners, not married to each other, and sharing a household. By 2000, the total number of unmarried couples in America was almost four and three-quarters million, up from less than half a million in 1960.[1] It is estimated that about a quarter of unmarried women between the ages of 25 and 39 are currently living with a partner and about half have lived at some time with an unmarried partner (the data are typically reported for women but not for men). Over half of all first marriages are now preceded by cohabitation, compared to virtually none earlier in the century.[2]

What makes cohabitation so significant is not only its prevalence but also its widespread popular acceptance. In recent representative national surveys nearly 66% of high school senior boys and 61% of the girls indicated that they "agreed" or "mostly agreed" with the statement "it is usually a good idea for a couple to live together before getting married in order to find out whether they really get along." And three quarters of the students stated that "a man and a woman who live together without being married" are either "experimenting with a worthwhile alternative lifestyle" or "doing their own thing and not affecting anyone else."[3]

Unlike divorce or unwed childbearing, the trend toward cohabitation has inspired virtually no public comment or criticism. It is hard to believe that across America, only thirty years ago, living together for unmarried, heterosexual couples was against the law.[4] And it was considered immoral—living in sin—or at the very least highly improper. Women who provided sexual and housekeeping services to a man without the benefits of marriage were regarded as fools at best and morally loose at worst. A double standard existed, but cohabiting men were certainly not regarded with approbation.

Today, the old view of cohabitation seems yet another example of the repressive Victorian norms. The new view is that cohabitation represents a more progressive approach to intimate relationships. How much healthier women are to be free of social pressure to marry and stigma when they don't. How much better off people are today to be able to exercise choice in their sexual and domestic arrangements. How much better off marriage can be, and how many divorces can be avoided, when sexual relationships start with a trial period.

Surprisingly, much of the accumulating social science research suggests otherwise. What most cohabiting couples don't know, and what in fact few people know, are the conclusions of many recent studies on unmarried cohabitation and its implications for young people and for society. Living together before marriage may seem like a harmless or even a progressive family trend until one takes a careful look at the evidence.

How Living Together Before Marriage May Contribute to Marital Failure

The vast majority of young people today want to marry and have children. And many if not most see cohabitation as a way to test marital compatibility and improve the chances of long-lasting marriage. Their reasoning is as follows: Given the high levels of divorce, why be in a hurry to marry? Why not test marital compatibility by sharing a bed and a bathroom for a year or even longer? If it doesn't work out, one can simply move out. According to this reasoning, cohabitation weeds out unsuitable partners through a process of natural de-selection. Over time, perhaps after several living-together relationships, a person will eventually find a marriageable mate.

The social science evidence challenges the popular idea that cohabiting ensures greater marital compatibility and thereby promotes stronger and more enduring marriages. Cohabitation does not reduce the likelihood of eventual divorce; in fact, it is associated with a higher divorce risk. Although the association was stronger a decade or two ago and has diminished in the younger generations, virtually all research on the topic has determined that the chances of divorce ending a marriage preceded by cohabitation are significantly greater than for a marriage not preceded by cohabitation. A 1992 study of 3,300 cases, for example, based on the 1987 National Survey of Families and Households, found that in their marriages prior cohabitors "are estimated to have a hazard of dissolution that is about 46% higher than for noncohabitors." The authors of this study concluded, after reviewing all previous studies, that the enhanced risk of marital disruption following cohabitation "is beginning to take on the status of an empirical generalization."[5]

More in question within the research community is why the striking statistical association between cohabitation and divorce should exist. Perhaps the most obvious explanation is that those people willing to cohabit are more unconventional than others and less committed to the institution of marriage. These are the same people, then, who more easily will leave a marriage if it becomes troublesome. By this explanation, cohabitation doesn't cause divorce but is merely associated with it because the same types of people are involved in both phenomena.

There is substantial empirical support for this position. Yet, in most studies, even when this "selection effect" is carefully controlled statistically, a negative effect of cohabitation on later marriage stability still remains. And no positive contribution of cohabitation to marriage has been ever been found.[6]

The reasons for a negative "cohabitation effect" are not fully understood. One may be that while marriages are held together largely by a strong ethic of commitment, cohabiting relationships by their very nature tend to undercut this ethic. Although cohabiting relationships are like marriages in many ways—shared dwelling, economic union (at least in part), sexual intimacy, often even children—they typically differ in the levels of commitment and autonomy involved. According to recent studies, cohabitants tend not to be as committed as married couples in their dedication to the continuation of the relationship and reluctance to terminate it, and they are more oriented toward their own personal autonomy.[7] It is reasonable to speculate, based on these studies, that once this low-commitment, high-autonomy pattern of relating is learned, it becomes hard to unlearn. One study found, for example, that "living with a romantic partner prior to marriage was associated with more negative and less positive problem solving support and behavior during marriage." A reason for this, the authors suggest, is that because long-term commitment is less certain in cohabitation, "there may be less motivation for cohabiting partners to develop their conflict resolution and support skills."[8]

The results of several studies suggest that cohabitation may change partners' attitudes toward the institution of marriage, contributing to either making marriage less likely, or if marriage takes place, less successful. A 1997 longitudinal study conducted by demographers at Pennsylvania State University concluded, for example, "cohabitation increased young people's acceptance of divorce, but other independent living experiences did not." And "the more months of exposure to cohabitation that young people experienced, the less enthusiastic they were toward marriage and childbearing."[9]

Particularly problematic is serial cohabitation. One study determined that the effect of cohabitation on later marital instability is found only when one or both partners had previously cohabited with someone other than their spouse.[10] A reason for this could be that the experience of dissolving one cohabiting relationship generates a greater willingness to dissolve later relationships. People's tolerance for unhappiness is diminished, and they will scrap a marriage that might otherwise be salvaged. This may be similar to the attitudinal effects of divorce; going through a divorce makes one more tolerant of divorce.

If the conclusions of these studies hold up under further investigation, they may contain the answer to the question of why premarital cohabitation should effect the stability of a later marriage. The act of cohabitation generates changes in people's attitudes toward marriage that make the stability of marriage less likely. Society wide, therefore, the growth of cohabitation will tend to further weaken marriage as an institution.

An important caveat must be inserted here. There is a growing understanding among researchers that different types and life-patterns of cohabitation must be distinguished clearly from each other. Cohabitation that is an immediate prelude to marriage, or prenuptial cohabitation—both partners plan to marry each other in the near future—is different from other forms. There is some evidence to support the proposition that living together for a short period of time with the person one intends to marry has no adverse effects on the subsequent marriage. Cohabitation in this case appears to be very similar to marriage; it merely takes place during the engagement period.[11] This proposition would appear to be less true, however, when one or both of the partners has had prior experience with cohabitation, or brings children into the relationship.

Percentage of High School Seniors Who "Agreed" or "Mostly Agreed" with the Statement That "It Is Usually a Good Idea for a Couple to Live Together before Getting Married in Order to Find Out Whether They Really Get Along," by Period, United States

	Boys	Girls
1976–1980	44.9	32.3
1981–1985	47.4	36.5
1986–1990	57.8	45.2
1991–1995	60.5	51.3
1996–2000	66.0	61.3

Source: *Monitoring the Future 2000,* and earlier surveys conducted by the Survey Research Center at the University of Michigan

Cohabitation as an Alternative to Marriage

According to the latest information available, 46% of all cohabitations in a given year can be classified as precursors to marriage.[12] Most of the remainder can be considered some form of alternative to marriage, including trial marriages, and their number is increasing. This should be of great national concern, not only for what the growth of cohabitation is doing to the institution of marriage but for what it is doing, or not doing, for the participants involved. In general, cohabiting relationships tend in many ways to be less satisfactory than marriage relationships.

Except perhaps for the short term prenuptial type of cohabitation, and probably also for the post-marriage cohabiting relationships of seniors and retired people who typically cohabit rather than marry for economic reasons,[13] cohabitation and marriage relationships are qualitatively different. Cohabiting couples report lower levels of happiness, lower levels of sexual exclusivity and sexual satisfaction, and poorer relationships with their parents.[14] One reason is that, as several sociologists not surprisingly concluded after a careful analysis, in unmarried cohabitation "levels of certainty about the relationship are lower than in marriage."[15]

It is easy to understand, therefore, why cohabiting is inherently much less stable than marriage and why, especially in view of the fact that it is easier to terminate, the break-up rate of cohabitors is far higher than for married partners. After 5 to 7 years, 39% of all cohabiting couples have broken their relationship, 40% have married (although the marriage might not have lasted), and only 21% are still cohabiting.[16]

Still not fully known by the public at large is the fact that married couples have substantial benefits over the unmarried in labor force productivity, physical and mental health, general happiness, and longevity.[17] There is evidence that these benefits are diluted for couples who are not married but merely cohabiting.[18] Among the probable reasons for the benefits of marriage, as summarized by University of Chicago demographer Linda Waite,[19] are:

- *The long-term contract implicit in marriage.* This facilitates emotional investment in the relationship, including the close monitoring of each other's behavior. The longer time horizon also makes specialization more likely; working as a couple, individuals can develop those skills in which they excel, leaving others to their partner.
- *The greater sharing of economic and social resources by married couples.* In addition to economies of scale, this enables couples to act as a small insurance pool against life uncertainties, reducing each person's need to protect themselves from unexpected events.
- *The better connection of married couples to the larger community.* This includes other individuals and groups (such as in-laws) as well as social institutions such as churches and synagogues. These can be important sources of social and emotional support and material benefits.

In addition to missing out on many of the benefits of marriage, cohabitors may face more serious difficulties. Annual rates of depression among cohabiting couples are more than three times what they are among married couples.[20] And women in cohabiting relationships are more likely than married women to suffer physical and sexual abuse. Some research has shown that aggression is at least twice as common among cohabitors as it is among married partners.[21] Two studies, one in Canada and the other in the United States, found that women in cohabiting relationships are about nine times more likely to be killed by their partner than are women in marital relationships.[22]

Again, the selection factor is undoubtedly strong in findings such as these. But the most careful statistical probing suggests that selection is not the only factor at work; the intrinsic nature of the cohabiting relationship also plays a role. As one scholar summed up the relevant research, "regardless of methodology. . . .cohabitors engage in more violence than spouses."[23]

Why Cohabitation Is Harmful for Children

Of all the types of cohabitation, that involving children is by far the most problematic. In 2000, 41% of all unmarried-couple households included a child under eighteen, up from only 21% in 1987.[24] For unmarried couples in the 25–34 age group the percentage with children is higher still, approaching half of all such households.[25] By one recent estimate nearly half of all children today will spend some time in a cohabiting family before age 16.[26]

One of the greatest problems for children living with a cohabiting couple is the high risk that the couple will break up.[27] Fully three quarters of children born to cohabiting parents will see their parents split up before they reach age sixteen, whereas only about a third of children born to married parents face a similar fate. One reason is that marriage rates for cohabiting couples have been plummeting. In the last decade, the proportion of cohabiting mothers who go on to eventually marry the child's father declined from 57% to 44%.[28]

Parental break up, as is now widely known, almost always entails a myriad of personal and social difficulties for children, some of which can be long lasting.

For the children of a cohabiting couple these may come on top of a plethora of already existing problems. Several studies have found that children currently living with a mother and her unmarried partner have significantly more behavior problems and lower academic performance than children in intact families.[29]

It is important to note that the great majority of children in unmarried-couple households were born not in the present union but in a previous union of one of the adult partners, usually the mother.[30] This means that they are living with an unmarried "stepfather" or mother's boyfriend, with whom the economic and social relationships are often tenuous. For example, unlike children in stepfamilies, these children have few legal claims to child support or other sources of family income should the couple separate.

Child abuse has become a major national problem and has increased dramatically in recent years, by more than 10% a year according to one estimate.[31] In the opinion of most researchers, this increase is related strongly to changing family forms. Surprisingly, the available American data do not enable us to distinguish the abuse that takes place in married-couple households from that in cohabiting-couple households. We do have abuse-prevalence studies that look at stepparent families (both married and unmarried) and mother's boyfriends (both cohabiting and dating). Both show far higher levels of child abuse than is found in intact families.[32] In general, the evidence suggests that the most unsafe of all family environments for children is that in which the mother is living with someone other than the child's biological father. This is the environment for the majority of children in cohabiting couple households.[33]

Part of the differences indicated above are due to differing income levels of the families involved. But this points up one of the other problems of cohabiting couples—their lower incomes. It is well known that children of single parents fare poorly economically when compared to the children of married parents. Not so well known is that cohabiting couples are economically more like single parents than like married couples. While the 1996 poverty rate for children living in married couple households was about 6%, it was 31% for children living in cohabiting households, much closer to the rate of 45% for children living in families headed by single mothers.[34]

One of the most important social science findings of recent years is that marriage is a wealth enhancing institution. According to one study, childrearing, cohabiting couples have only about two-thirds of the income of married couples with children, mainly due to the fact that the average income of male cohabiting partners is only about half that of male married partners.[35] The selection effect is surely at work here, with less well-off men and their partners choosing cohabitation over marriage. But it also is the case that men when they marry, especially those who then go on to have children, tend to become more responsible and productive.[36] They earn more than their unmarried counterparts. An additional factor not to be overlooked is the private transfer of wealth among extended family members, which is considerably lower for cohabiting couples than for married couples.[37] It is clear that family members are more willing to transfer wealth to "in-laws" than to mere boyfriends or girlfriends.

Who Cohabits and Why

Why has unmarried cohabitation become such a widespread practice throughout the modern world in such a short period of time? Demographic factors are surely involved. Puberty begins at an earlier age, as does the onset of sexual activity, and marriages take place at older ages mainly because of the longer time period spent getting educated and establishing careers. Thus there is an extended period of sexually active singlehood before first marriage. Also, our sustained material affluence enables many young people to live on their own for an extended time, apart from their parents. During those years of young adulthood, nonmarital cohabitation can be a cost-saver, a source of companionship, and an assurance of relatively safe sexual practice. For some, cohabitation is a prelude to marriage, for some, an alternative to it, and for yet others, simply an alternative to living alone.[38]

More broadly, the rise of cohabitation in the advanced nations has been attributed to the sexual revolution, which has virtually revoked the stigma against cohabitation.[39] In the past thirty years, with the advent of effective contraceptive technologies and widespread sexual permissiveness promoted by advertising and the organized entertainment industry, premarital sex has become widely accepted. In large segments of the population cohabitation no longer is associated with sin or social impropriety or pathology, nor are cohabiting couples subject to much, if any, disapproval.

Another important reason for cohabitation's growth is that the institution of marriage has changed dramatically, leading to an erosion of confidence in its stability. From a tradition strongly buttressed by economics, religion, and the law, marriage has become a more personalized relationship, what one wag has referred to as a mere "notarized date." People used to marry not just for love but also for family and economic considerations, and if love died during the course of a marriage, this was not considered sufficient reason to break up an established union. A divorce was legally difficult if not impossible to get, and people who divorced faced enormous social stigma.

In today's marriages love is all, and it is a love tied to self-fulfillment. Divorce is available to everyone, with little stigma attached. If either love or a sense of self-fulfillment disappear, the marriage is considered to be over and divorce is the logical outcome.

Fully aware of this new fragility of marriage, people are taking cautionary actions. The attitude is either try it out first and make sure that it will work, or try to minimize the damage of breakup by settling for a weaker form of union, one that avoids a marriage license and, if need be, an eventual divorce.

The growth of cohabitation is also associated with the rise of feminism. Traditional marriage, both in law and in practice, typically involved male leadership. For some women, cohabitation seemingly avoids the legacy of patriarchy and at the same time provides more personal autonomy and equality in the relationship. Moreover, women's shift into the labor force and their growing economic independence make marriage less necessary and, for some, less desirable.

Underlying all of these trends is the broad cultural shift from a more religious society where marriage was considered the bedrock of civilization and people were imbued with a strong sense of social conformity and tradition, to a more secular society focused on individual autonomy and self invention. This cultural rejection of traditional institutional and moral authority, evident in all of the advanced, Western societies, often has had "freedom of choice" as its theme and the acceptance of "alternative lifestyles" as its message.

In general, cohabitation is a phenomenon that began among the young in the lower classes and then moved up to the middle classes.[40] Cohabitation in America—especially cohabitation as an alternative to marriage—is more common among Blacks, Puerto Ricans, and disadvantaged white women.[41] One reason for this is that male income and employment are lower among minorities and the lower classes, and male economic status remains an important determinant as to whether or not a man feels ready to marry, and a woman wants to marry him.[42] Cohabitation is also more common among those who are less religious than their peers. Indeed, some evidence suggests that the act of cohabitation actually diminishes religious participation, whereas marriage tends to increase it.[43]

People who cohabit are much more likely to come from broken homes. Among young adults, those who experienced parental divorce, fatherlessness, or high levels of marital discord during childhood are more likely to form cohabiting unions than children who grew up in families with married parents who got along. They are also more likely to enter living-together relationships at younger ages.[44] For young people who have already suffered the losses associated with parental divorce, cohabitation may provide an early escape from family turmoil, although unfortunately it increases the likelihood of new losses and turmoil. For these people, cohabitation often recapitulates the childhood experience of coming together and splitting apart with the additional possibility of more violent conflict. Finally, cohabitation is a much more likely experience for those who themselves have been divorced.

Conclusion

Despite its widespread acceptance by the young, the remarkable growth of unmarried cohabitation in recent years does not appear to be in children's or the society's best interest. The evidence suggests that it has weakened marriage and the intact, two-parent family and thereby damaged our social wellbeing, especially that of women and children. We can not go back in history, but it seems time to establish some guidelines for the practice of cohabitation and to seriously question the further institutionalization of this new family form.

In place of institutionalizing cohabitation, in our opinion, we should be trying to revitalize marriage—not along classic male-dominant lines but along modern egalitarian lines. Particularly helpful in this regard would be educating young people about marriage from the early school years onward, getting them to make the wisest choices in their lifetime mates, and stressing the importance of long-term commitment to marriages. Such an educational venture could build on the fact that a huge majority of our nation's young people still express the strong desire to be in a long-term monogamous marriage.

These ideas are offered to the American public and especially to society's leaders in the spirit of generating a discussion. Our conclusions are tentative, and certainly not the last word on the subject. There is an obvious need for more research on cohabitation, and the findings of new research, of course, could alter our thinking. What is most important now, in our view, is a national debate on a topic that heretofore has been overlooked. Indeed, few issues seem more critical for the future of marriage and for generations to come.

Notes

1. U. S. Census Bureau. *Statistical Abstract of the United States: 2000* (Washington, DC: GPO, 2001): 52.

2. Larry Bumpass and Hsien-Hen Lu. "Trends in Cohabitation and Implications for Children's Family Contexts in the U.S.," *Population Studies* 54 (2000) 29–41. The most likely to cohabit are people aged 20 to 24.

3. J. G. Bachman, L. D. Johnston and P. M. O'Malley, *Monitoring the Future: Questionnaire Responses from the Nation's High School Seniors, 2000.* (Ann Arbor, MI: Institute for Social Research, University of Michigan: 2001).

4. The state statutes prohibiting "adultery" and "fornication," which included cohabitation, were not often enforced.

5. Alfred DeMaris and K. Vaninadha Rao, "Premarital Cohabitation and Subsequent Marital Stability in the United States: A Reassessment," *Journal of Marriage and the Family* 54 (1992): 178–190. A Canadian study found that premarital cohabitation may double the risk of subsequent marital disruption. Zheng Wu, *Cohabitation* (New York: Oxford University Press, 2000), 149.

6. The relationship between cohabitation and marital instability is discussed in the following articles: Alfred DeMaris and William MacDonald, "Premarital Cohabitation and Marital Instability: A Test of the Unconventional Hypothesis." *Journal of Marriage and the Family* 55 (1993): 399–407; William J. Axinn and Arland Thornton, "The Relationship Between Cohabitation and Divorce: Selectivity or Causal Influence," *Demography* 29-3 (1992): 357–374; Robert Schoen "First Unions and the Stability of First Marriages," *Journal of Marriage and the Family* 54 (1992): 281–284; Elizabeth Thomson and Ugo Colella, "Cohabitation and Marital Stability: Quality or Commitment?" *Journal of Marriage and the Family* 54–9 (1992): 259–267; Lee A Lillard, Michael J. Brien, and Linda J. Waite, "Premarital Cohabitation and Subsequent Marital Dissolution: A Matter of Self-Selection?" *Demography*, 32-3 (1995): 437–457; David R. Hall and John Z. Zhao, "Cohabitation and Divorce in Canada: Testing the Selectivity Hypothesis," *Journal of Marriage and the Family* 57 (1995): 421–427; Marin Clarkberg, Ross M. Stolzenberg, and Linda Waite, "Attitudes, Values, and Entrance into Cohabitational versus Marital Unions," *Social Forces* 74-2 (1995): 609–634; Stephen L. Nock, "Spouse Preferences of Never-Married, Divorced, and Cohabiting Americans," *Journal of Divorce and Remarriage* 24–3/4 (1995): 91–108.

7. Stephen L. Nock, "A Comparison of Marriages and Cohabiting Relationships," *Journal of Family Issues* 16–1 (1995): 53–76. See also: Robert Schoen and Robin M. Weinick, "Partner Choice in Marriages and Cohabitations," *Journal of Marriage and the Family* 55 (1993): 408–414; and Scott M. Stanley, Sarah W. Whitton and Howard Markman, "Maybe I Do: Interpersonal Commitment and Premarital and Non-Marital Cohabitation," unpublished manuscript, University of Denver, 2000.

8. Catherine L. Cohan and Stacey Kleinbaum, "Toward A Greater Understanding of the Cohabitation Effect: Premarital Cohabitation and Marital Communication," *Journal of Marriage and the Family*, 64 (2002): 180–192.

9. William G. Axinn and Jennifer S. Barber, "Living Arrangements and Family Formation Attitudes in Early Adulthood," *Journal of Marriage and the Family* 59 (1997): 595–611. See also Marin Clarkberg, "Family Formation Experiences and Changing Values: The Effects of Cohabitation and Marriage on the Important Things in Life," in Ron Lesthaeghe, ed., *Meaning and Choice: Value Orientations and Life Course Decisions*, NIDI Monograph 38, (The Hague: Netherlands, Netherlands Interdisciplinary Demographic Institute, forthcoming). Axinn and Thornton, 1992, op. cit., and Elizabeth Thomson and Ugo Colella, 1992, op. cit.

10. DeMaris and McDonald, 1993, op. cit.; Jan E. Stets, "The Link Between Past and Present Intimate Relationships." *Journal of Family Issues* 14–2 (1993): 236–260.

11. Susan L. Brown and Alan Booth, "Cohabitation Versus Marriage: A Comparison of Relationship Quality," *Journal of Marriage and the Family* 58 (1996): 668–678.

12. Lynne N. Casper and Suzanne M. Bianchi, *Continuity and Change in the American Family* (Thousand Oaks, CA: Sage Publications, 2002) Ch. 2. Suprisingly, only 52% of those classified as "precursors to marriage" had actually married after five to even years and 31% had split up!

13. Albert Chevan, "As Cheaply as One: Cohabitation in the Older Population," *Journal of Marriage and the Family* 58 (1996): 656–666. According to calculations by Chevan, the percentage of noninstitutionalized, unmarried cohabiting persons 60 years of age and over increased from virtually zero in 1960 to 2.4 in 1990, p. 659. See also R. G. Hatch, *Aging and Cohabitation.* (New York: Garland, 1995).

14. Nock, 1995; Brown and Booth, 1996; Linda J. Waite and Kara Joyner, "Emotional and Physical Satisfaction with Sex in Married, Cohabiting, and Dating Sexual Unions: Do Men and Women Differ?" Edward O. Laumann and Robert T. Michaels, eds., *Sex, Love, and Health in America* (Chicago: University of Chicago Press, 2001) 239–269; Judith Treas and Deirdre Giesen, "Sexual Infidelity Among Married and Cohabiting Americans" *Journal of Marriage and the Family* 62 (2000): 48–60; Renate Forste and Koray Tanfer, "Sexual Exclusivity Among Dating, Cohabiting, and Married Women," *Journal of Marriage the Family* 58 (1996): 33–47; Paul R. Amato and Alan Booth, *A Generation at Risk.* (Cambridge, MA: Harvard University Press, 1997) Table 4–2, p. 258.

15. Larry L. Bumpass, James A. Sweet, and Andrew Cherlin, "The Role of Cohabitation in Declining Rate of Marriage," *Journal of Marriage the Family* 53 (1991): 913–927.

16. Casper and Bianchi, 2002, op. cit.

17. Lee A. Lillard and Linda J. Waite, "Till Death Do Us Part: Marital Disruption and Mortality," *American Journal of Sociology* 100 (1995): 1131–1156; R. Jay Turner and Franco Marino, "Social Support and Social Structure: A Descriptive Epidemiology," *Journal of Health and Social Behavior* 35 (1994): 193–212; Linda J. Waite, "Does Marriage Matter?" *Demography* 32–4 (1995): 483–507; Sanders Korenman and David Neumark "Does Marriage Really Make Men More Productive?" *The Journal of Human Resources* 26–2 (1990): 282–307; George A. Akerlof "Men Without Children." *The Economic Journal* 108 (1998): 287–309.

18. Allan V. Horwitz and Helene Raskin White, "The Relationship of Cohabitation and Mental Health: A Study of a Young Adult Cohort," *Journal of Marriage and the Family* 60 (1998): 505–514; Waite, 1995.

19. Linda J. Waite, "Social Science Finds: 'Marriage Matters,'" *The Responsive Community* (Summer 1996): 26–35 See also: Linda J. Waite and Maggie Gallagher, *The Case for Marriage* (New York: Doubleday, 2000).

20. Lee Robins and Darrel Reiger, *Psychiatric Disorders in America*. (New York: Free Press, 1990) 72. See also: Susan L. Brown, "The Effect of Union Type on Psychological Well-Being: Depression among Cohabitors versus Marrieds," *Journal of Health and Social Behavior* 41–3 (2000).

21. Jan E. Stets, "Cohabiting and Marital Aggression: The Role of Social Isolation," *Journal of Marriage and the Family* 53 (1991): 669–680. Margo I. Wilson and Martin Daly, "Who Kills Whom in Spouse Killings? On the Exceptional Sex Ratio of Spousal Homicides in the United States," *Criminology* 30–2 (1992): 189–215. One study found that, of the violence toward women that is committed by intimates and relatives, 42% involves a close friend or partner whereas only 29% involves a current spouse. Ronet Bachman, "Violence Against Women." (Washington, DC: Bureau of Justice Statistics. 1994) p. 6 A New Zealand study compared violence in dating and cohabiting relationships, finding that cohabitors were twice as likely to be physically abusive toward their partners after controlling statistically for selection factors. Lynn Magdol, T.E. Moffitt, A. Caspi, and P.A. Silva: "Hitting Without a License," *Journal of Marriage and the Family* 60–1 (1998): 41–55.

22. Todd K. Shackelford, "Cohabitation, Marriage and Murder," *Aggressive Behavior* 27 (2001): 284–291; Margo Wilson, M. Daly and C. Wright, "Uxoricide in Canada: Demographic Risk Patterns," *Canadian Journal of Criminology* 35 (1993): 263–291.

23. Nicky Ali Jackson, "Observational Experiences of Intrapersonal Conflict and Teenage Victimization: A Comparative Study among Spouses and Cohabitors," *Journal of Family Violence* 11 (1996): 191–203.

24. U. S. Census Bureau. Current Population Survey, March 2000.

25. Wendy D. Manning and Daniel T. Lichter, "Parental Cohabitation and Children's Economic Well-Being," *Journal of Marriage and the Family* 58 (1996): 998–1010.

26. Bumpass and Lu, 2000, op.cit. Using a different data set, however, Deborah R. Graefe and Daniel T. Lichter conclude that only about one in four children will live in a family headed by a cohabiting couple sometime during childhood. "Life Course Transitions of American Children: Parental Cohabitation, Marriage, and Single Motherhood," *Demography* 36–2 (1999): 205–217.

27. Research on the instability of cohabiting couples with children is discussed in Wendy D. Manning, "The Implications of Cohabitation for Children's Well-Being," in Alan Booth and Ann C. Crouter, eds., *Just Living Together: Implications for Children, Families, and Public Policy* (Hillsdale, NJ: Lawrence Erlbaum Associates, 2002) It seems to be the case, however, that—just as with married couples—cohabiting couples with children are less likely to break up than childless couples. Zheng Wu, "The Stability of Cohabitation Relationships: The Role of Children," *Journal of Marriage and the Family* 57 (1995): 231–236.

28. Bumpass and Lu, 2000, op.cit.

29. Elizabeth Thompson, T. L. Hanson and S. S. McLanahan, "Family Structure and Child Well-Being: Economic Resources versus Parental Behaviors," *Social Forces* 73–1 (1994): 221–242; Rachel Dunifon and Lori Kowaleski-Jones, "Who's in the House? Effects of Family Structure on Children's Home Environments and Cognitive Outcomes," *Child Development*, forthcoming; and Susan L. Brown, "Parental Cohabitation and Child Well-Being," unpublished manuscript, Department of Sociology, Bowling Green State University, Bowling Green, OH.

30. By one estimate, 63%. Deborah R. Graefe and Daniel Lichter, 1999, op.cit.

31. Andrea J. Sedlak and Diane Broadhurst, *The Third National Incidence Study of Child Abuse and Neglect* (Washington, DC: HHS-National Center on Child Abuse and Neglect, 1996).

32. See, for example, Margo Wilson and Martin Daly, "Risk of Maltreatment of Children Living with Stepparents," in R. Gelles and J. Lancaster, eds. *Child Abuse and Neglect: Biosocial Dimensions,* (New York: Aldine de Gruyter, 1987); Leslie Margolin "Child Abuse by Mothers' Boyfriends: Why the Overrepresentation?" *Child Abuse and Neglect* 16 (1992): 541–551. Martin Daly and Margo Wilson have stated: "stepparenthood per se remains the single most powerful risk factor for child abuse that has yet been identified." *Homicide* (New York: Aldine de Gruyter, 1988) p. 87–88.

33. One study in Great Britain did look at the relationship between child abuse and the family structure and marital background of parents and, although the sample was very small, the results are disturbing. It was found that, compared to children living with married biological parents, children living with cohabiting but unmarried biological parents are 20 times more likely to be subject to child abuse, and those living with a mother and a cohabiting boyfriend who is not the father face an increased risk of 33 times. In contrast, the rate of abuse is 14 times higher if the child lives with a biological mother who lives alone. Robert Whelan, *Broken Homes and Battered Children: A Study of the Relationship Between Child Abuse and Family Type,* (London: Family Education Trust, 1993). See especially Table 12, p. 29. (Data are from the 1980s.) See also Patrick F. Fagan and Dorothy B. Hanks, *The Child Abuse Crisis: The Disintegration of Marriage, Family and The American Community.* (Washington, DC: The Heritage Foundation, 1997).

34. Wendy D. Manning and Daniel T. Lichter "Parental Cohabitation and Children's Economic Well-Being," *Journal of Marriage and the Family* 58 (1996): 998–1010.

35. Wendy D. Manning and Daniel T. Lichter, 1996.

36. Sanders Korenman and David Neumark, "Does Marriage Really Make Men More Productive?" *The Journal of Human Resources* 26–2 (1990): 282–307; George A. Akerlof "Men Without Children," *The Economic Journal* 108 (1998): 287–309; Steven L. Nock, *Marriage in Men's Lives* (New York: Oxford University Press, 1998).

37. Lingxin Hao, "Family Structure, Private Transfers, and the Economic Well-Being of Families with Children," *Social Forces* 75–1 (1996): 269–292.

38. R. Rindfuss and A. VanDenHeuvel, "Cohabitation: A Precursor to Marriage or an Alternative to Being Single?" *Population and Development Review* 16 (1990): 703–726; Wendy D. Manning, "Marriage and Cohabitation Following Premarital Conception," *Journal of Marriage and the Family* 55 (1993): 839–850.

39. Larry L. Bumpass, "What's Happening to the Family?" *Demography* 27–4 1990): 483–498.

40. Arland Thornton, William G. Axinn and Jay D. Treachman, "The Influence of School Enrollment and Accumulation on Cohabitation and Marriage in Early Adulthood," *American Sociological Review* 60–5 (1995): 762–774; Larry L. Bumpass, James A. Sweet, and Andrew Cherlin, "The Role of Cohabitation in Declining Rates of Marriage," *Journal of Marriage and the Family* 53 (1991): 913–927.

41. Wendy D. Manning and Pamela J. Smock, "Why Marry? Race and the Transition to Marriage among Cohabitors," *Demography* 32–4 (1995): 509–520; Wendy D. Manning and Nancy S. Landale, "Racial and Ethnic Differences in the Role of Cohabitation in Premarital Childbearing," *Journal of Marriage and the Family* 58 (1996): 63–77; Laura Spencer Loomis and Nancy S. Landale, "Nonmarital Cohabitation and Childbearing Among Black and White American Women," *Journal of Marriage and the Family* 56 (1994): 949–962; Robert Schoen and Dawn Owens "A Further Look at First Unions and First Marriages," in S. J. South and Stewart E. Tolnay, eds., *The Changing American Family* (Boulder, CO: Westview Press, 1992) 109–117.

42. Daniel T. Lichter, Diane K. McLaughlin, George Kephart, and David J. Landry, "Race and the Retreat from Marriage: A Shortage of Marriageable Men?" *American Sociological Review* 57–6 (1992): 781–789; Pamela J. Smock and Wendy D. Manning, "Cohabiting Partners' Economic Circumstances and Marriage," *Demography* 34–3 (1997): 331–341; Valerie K. Oppenheimer, Matthijs Kalmijn and Nelson Lim, "Men's Career Development and Marriage Timing During a Period of Rising Inequality," *Demography* 34–3 (1997): 311–330.

43. Arland Thornton, W. G. Axinn and D. H. Hill, "Reciprocal Effects of Religiosity, Cohabitation and Marriage," *American Journal of Sociology* 98–3 (1992): 628–651.

44. Arland Thornton, "Influence of the Marital History of Parents on the Marital and Cohabitational Experiences of Children," *American Journal of Sociology* 96–4 (1991): 868–894; Kathleen E. Kiernan, "The Impact of Family Disruption in Childhood on Transitions Made in Young Adult Life," *Population Studies* 46 (1992): 213–234; Andrew J. Cherlin, Kathleen E. Kiernan, and P. Lindsay Chase-Lansdale, "Parental Divorce in Childhood and Demographic Outcomes in Young Adulthood," *Demography* 32–3 (1995): 299–318.

45. Monica A. Seff, "Cohabitation and the Law," *Marriage and Family Review* 21–3/4 (1995): 141–165, 149.

46. Marvin vs. Marvin (Calif. Supreme Court, 1976).

47. Toni Ihara and Ralph Warner, *The Living Together Kit: A Guide for Unmarried Couples* (Berkeley, CA: Nolo Press, 8th edition, 1997). These contracts are not yet upheld by all states, and their enforceability is often in question.

48. Richard F. Tomasson "Modern Sweden: The Declining Importance of Marriage," *Scandinavian Review* (1998): 83–89. The marriage rate in the United States is two and a half times the Swedish rate.

49. This is one of the messages in the runaway bestseller *The Rules*, by Ellen Fein and Sherrie Schneider (New York: Warner Books, 1995), plus other popular books of recent vintage on dating, mate selection and marriage.

POSTSCRIPT

Should Society Support Cohabitation Before Marriage?

There is a common misperception that premarital sex is a cultural phenomenon that was introduced to American society during the sexual revolution of the 1960s and 1970s. Sexologist Robert T. Francoeur dispels this myth by commenting on the prevalence of premarital sex dating back to colonial American times. As an example, Francoeur describes the courtship ritual of "bundling," which helped frontier farmers know that a bride-to-be was fertile and could produce children to work the farm: A courting couple was permitted to sleep together, fully dressed, in a small bed in the corner of a small, often single-room log cabin or sod house. A bundling board between the couple or a bundling bag for the woman was not an insurmountable obstacle to sexual intercourse. When the prospective bride became pregnant, the marriage was announced. This is but one example of historically positive and functional attitudes toward premarital sexual intercourse in the United States.

Other countries have experienced growing trends in relationship patterns that contrast with the U.S., rise in cohabitation. In Sweden and other Scandinavian countries, for example, a concept called "LAT" (living alone together) has become increasingly popular. Adult couples who "LAT" maintain a committed interpersonal relationship but also maintain separate households. In Italy, mammoni (literally, "mama's boys") are adult men who continue to live at home with their parents. While calling a man a "mama's boy" may be an insult in American culture, it is not so in Italy, where more and more men are avoiding marriage into their later adult years, regardless of whether or not they are involved in a committed relationship. Not surprisingly, this growing trend has resulted in a drastic lowering of the Italian birth rate.

In the United States, why would a couple want to choose cohabitation before marriage, or as a relationship option instead of marriage? The following reasons have been identified:

- Some couples are not legally allowed to marry because they are members of the same sex, and some heterosexual couples avoid marriage in objection to an institution that is not legally available to all.
- Some couples believe that one's intimate relationship does not require the endorsement of government or religion.
- Some people are troubled by the divorce rate, or have experienced a divorce themselves, and wish to avoid the risk (or stigma) of divorce.
- Some people believe that a relationship does not need to be a lifelong commitment.

- Some people are not sure if their current partner is the one they would select for a lifetime commitment. They might try cohabitation as a precursor to marriage.
- Some people feel their relationship is working fine without marriage.
- Some people might lose financial benefits if they decide to marry (such as from the pension of a prior spouse).
- Some people are uncomfortable with marriage's historical view toward women as property.

Some opponents of cohabitation before marriage are concerned primarily about the sexual aspect of these relationships; namely, they believe that sexual intercourse before marriage is impermissible. However, sexual and marital trends indicate that most young people begin having intercourse in their mid-to-late teens, about *seven to nine* years before they marry. Is it better for young people to begin having sex later, or consider marrying earlier? Are the main issues the timing of sex and the marital decision, or the health and happiness of the couple?

Suggested Readings

R. T. Francoeur, "Challenging Common Religious/Social Myths of Sex, Marriage, and Family," *Journal of Sex Education and Therapy* (vol. 26, no. 4, 2001).

T. Ihara, R. Warner, and F. Hertz, *Living Together: A Legal Guide for Unmarried Couples* (Nolo Press, 2001).

L. M. Latham, "Southern Governors Declare War on Divorce," http://www.salon.com (January 24, 2000).

K. S. Peterson, "Changing the Shape of the American Family," *USA Today* (April 18, 2000).

K. S. Peterson, "Wedded to Relationship but Not to Marriage," *USA Today* (April 18, 2000).

D. Popenoe and B. Dafoe Whitehead, *Ten Important Research Findings on Marriage and Choosing a Marriage Partner: Helpful Facts for Young Adults* (National Marriage Project, Rutgers University, 2004).

R. Schoen, "The Ties That Bind: Perspectives on Marriage and Cohabitation," *Journal of Marriage and Family* (August 1, 2001).

P. J. Smock, "Cohabitation in the United States: An Appraisal of Research, Themes, Findings, and Implications," *Annual Review of Sociology* (2000).

D. Solot and M. Miller, "Ten Problems (Plus One Bonus Problem) with the National Marriage Project's Cohabitation Report," *A Report of the Alternatives to Marriage Project* (2001).

Human Rights Campaign

The Human Rights Campaign is America's largest gay and lesbian organization. It seeks to increase public understanding through innovative education and communication strategies.

http://www.hrc.org

Alliance for Marriage

Alliance for Marriage is a non-profit research and education organization dedicated to promoting marriage and addressing the epidemic of fatherless families in the United States. It educates the public, the media, elected officials, and civil society leaders on the benefits of marriage for children, adults, and society.

http://www.allianceformarriage.org

American Civil Liberties Union (ACLU)

The ACLU works to defend and preserve the individual rights and liberties guaranteed to every person in this country by the Constitution and laws of the United States.

http://www.aclu.org

Sex Worker Outreach Project (SWOP)

SWOP is a Web site that focuses on safety, dignity, diversity, and the changing needs of sex industry workers, to foster an environment that enables and affirms individual choices and occupational rights.

http://www.swop-usa.org

PART 3

Legal Issues

*T*he democratic ideal holds that government should make only those laws that are absolutely necessary to preserve the common good. Unless government can demonstrate a "compelling need," it should not infringe on the privacy and personal rights of individual citizens. This principle raises some perplexing questions when applied to the rights of individuals to engage in sexually intimate relationships. This section examines three such questions involving interpersonal relationships, prostitution, and the liability of schools in cases of sexual harassment.

- Should Same-Sex Marriage Be Legal?

- Should Prostitution Be Legal?

- Should Schools Pay Damages for Student-on-Student Sexual Harassment?

ISSUE 18

Should Same-Sex Marriage Be Legal?

YES: Human Rights Campaign, from *Answers to Questions about Marriage Equality* (Human Rights Campaign, 2004)

NO: John Cornyn, from "In Defense of Marriage," *National Review* (July 2004)

ISSUE SUMMARY

YES: The Human Rights Campaign (HRC), America's largest gay and lesbian organization, explains why same-sex couples should be afforded the same legal right to marry as heterosexual couples.

NO: John Cornyn, U.S. Senator from Texas, says a constitutional amendment is needed to define marriage as permissible only between a man and a woman. Senator Cornyn contends that the traditional institution of marriage needs to be protected from activist courts that would seek to redefine it.

On May 17, 2004, Massachusetts became the first state in the United States to grant marriage licenses to same-sex couples. The state acted under the direction of its supreme court, which had found that withholding marriage licenses from lesbian and gay couples violated the state constitution. More than 600 same-sex couples applied for marriage licenses that first day alone. The first same-sex couple to be issued marriage licenses was Marcia Kadish and Tanya McClosky. That couple had waited over 18 years for the day to arrive. Since then, over 3,000 same-sex marriages have been performed in Massachusetts.

After the Massachusetts ruling, gay and lesbian couples across the country sought marriage licenses from their municipalities. Many were denied, while others found loopholes in laws that allowed them to file for licenses. In Oregon, for example, the law stated that marriage is a "civil contract entered into in person by males at least 17 years of age and females at least 17 years of age." Since the law did not state that males had to marry females, gay and lesbian marriages were never technically against the law. Marriage licenses were also issued in counties in California, New Jersey, New York, and Washington. In San Francisco, Mayor Gavin Newsom challenged state law and allowed city officials to wed same-sex couples. Ultimately, the gay and lesbian marriages and marriage licenses in all states other than Massachusetts were ruled illegal and invalid.

The court ruling that paved the way for same-sex marriage in Massachusetts opened a firestorm of controversy. Supporters heralded the decision as a step toward equality for all Americans. Opponents of gay and lesbian nuptials spoke out against the redefinition and destruction of traditional marriage. President George W. Bush endorsed a constitutional amendment that would define marriage as being between a man and a woman saying that "the sacred institution of marriage should not be redefined by a few activist judges."

Several years earlier, President Bill Clinton signed the Defense of Marriage Act (DOMA), which said that states were not required to recognize same-sex marriages performed in other states. Nevertheless, supporters of the constitutional amendment believe DOMA is not enough to keep courts from redefining traditional marriage. Gay rights supporters oppose the amendment, which they feel unjustly writes discrimination into the Constitution. Even many conservatives oppose the amendment because they believe it to be too strong of a federal intrusion into the rights of states. The issue was pressed to the forefront of the 2004 presidential election when Vice President Dick Cheney's lesbian daughter Lynn (who supported President Bush) was referenced by both John Edwards and John Kerry during the vice presidential and presidential debates when questions concerning gay and lesbian marriage were asked. On election day that year, 11 states (including Oregon) voted on measures that would define marriage in their state as being between a man and a woman, thus banning same-sex marriage in those states. All 11 of those measures passed.

In the following essays, the Human Rights Campaign (HRC) answers common questions about same-sex marriage and the law, religion, and family. HRC also reviews the benefits that same-sex marriages could potentially have for gay and lesbian couples and society. Senator John Cornyn argues that the traditional definition of marriage is threatened by activist judges who seek to redefine the most fundamental union the world has ever known. Cornyn states that protecting marriage is about ensuring that relationships consisting of husband and wife will remain the "gold standard" for raising children.

Answers to Questions About Marriage Equality

10 Facts

1. Same-sex couples live in 99.3 percent of all counties nationwide.
2. There are an estimated 3.1 million people living together in same-sex relationships in the United States.
3. Fifteen percent of these same-sex couples live in rural settings.
4. One out of three lesbian couples is raising children. One out of five gay male couples is raising children.
5. Between 1 million and 9 million children are being raised by gay, lesbian and bisexual parents in the United States today.
6. At least one same-sex couple is raising children in 96 percent of all counties nationwide.
7. The highest percentages of same-sex couples raising children live in the South.
8. Nearly one in four same-sex couples includes a partner 55 years old or older, and nearly one in five same-sex couples is composed of two people 55 or older.
9. More than one in 10 same-sex couples include a partner 65 years old or older, and nearly one in 10 same-sex couples is composed of two people 65 or older.
10. The states with the highest numbers of same-sex senior couples are also the most popular for heterosexual senior couples: California, New York and Florida.

Why Same-Sex Couples Want to Marry

Many same-sex couples want the right to legally marry because they are in love—either they just met the love of their lives, or more likely, they have spent the last 10, 20 or 50 years with that person—and they want to honor their relationship in the greatest way our society has to offer, by making a

---

These facts are based on analyses of the 2000 Census conducted by the Urban Institute and the Human Rights Campaign. The estimated number of people in same-sex relationships has been adjusted by 62 percent to compensate for the widely-reported undercount in the Census. (See "Gay and Lesbian Families in the United States: Same-Sex Unmarried Partner Households" on www.hrc.org.)

public commitment to stand together in good times and bad, through all the joys and challenges family life brings.

Many parents want the right to marry because they know it offers children a vital safety net and guarantees protections that unmarried parents cannot provide.

And still other people—both gay and straight—are fighting for the right of same-sex couples to marry because they recognize that it is simply not fair to deny some families the protections all other families are eligible to enjoy.

Currently in the United States, same-sex couples in long-term, committed relationships pay higher taxes and are denied basic protections and rights granted to married heterosexual couples. Among them:

- **Hospital visitation.** Married couples have the automatic right to visit each other in the hospital and make medical decisions. Same-sex couples can be denied the right to visit a sick or injured loved one in the hospital.
- **Social Security benefits.** Married people receive Social Security payments upon the death of a spouse. Despite paying payroll taxes, gay and lesbian partners receive no Social Security survivor benefits—resulting in an average annual income loss of $5,528 upon the death of a partner.
- **Immigration.** Americans in binational relationships are not permitted to petition for their same-sex partners to immigrate. As a result, they are often forced to separate or move to another country.
- **Health insurance.** Many public and private employers provide medical coverage to the spouses of their employees, but most employers do not provide coverage to the life partners of gay and lesbian employees. Gay employees who do receive health coverage for their partners must pay federal income taxes on the value of the insurance.
- **Estate taxes.** A married person automatically inherits all the property of his or her deceased spouse without paying estate taxes. A gay or lesbian taxpayer is forced to pay estate taxes on property inherited from a deceased partner.
- **Retirement savings.** While a married person can roll a deceased spouse's 401(k) funds into an IRA without paying taxes, a gay or lesbian American who inherits a 401(k) can end up paying up to 70 percent of it in taxes and penalties.
- **Family leave.** Married workers are legally entitled to unpaid leave from their jobs to care for an ill spouse. Gay and lesbian workers are not entitled to family leave to care for their partners.
- **Nursing homes.** Married couples have a legal right to live together in nursing homes. Because they are not legal spouses, elderly gay or lesbian couples do not have the right to spend their last days living together in nursing homes.
- **Home protection.** Laws protect married seniors from being forced to sell their homes to pay high nursing home bills; gay and lesbian seniors have no such protection.
- **Pensions.** After the death of a worker, most pension plans pay survivor benefits only to a legal spouse of the participant. Gay and lesbian partners are excluded from such pension benefits.

Why Civil Unions Aren't Enough

Comparing marriage to civil unions is a bit like comparing diamonds to rhinestones. One is, quite simply, the real deal; the other is not. Consider:

- Couples eligible to marry may have their marriage performed in any state and have it recognized in every other state in the nation and every country in the world.
- Couples who are joined in a civil union in Vermont (the only state that offers civil unions) have no guarantee that its protections will even travel with them to neighboring New York or New Hampshire—let alone California or any other state.

Moreover, even couples who have a civil union and remain in Vermont receive only second-class protections in comparison to their married friends and neighbors. While they receive state-level protections, they do not receive any of the *more than 1,100 federal benefits and protections of marriage.*

In short, civil unions are not separate but equal—they are separate *and* unequal. And our society has tried separate before. It just doesn't work.

Marriage:	Civil unions:
• State grants marriage licenses to couples.	• State would grant civil union licenses to couples.
• Couples receive legal protections and rights under state and federal law.	• Couples receive legal protections and rights under state law only.
• Couples are recognized as being married by the federal government and all state governments.	• Civil unions are not recognized by other states or the federal government.
• Religious institutions are not required to perform marriage ceremonies.	• Religious institutions are not required to perform civil union ceremonies.

"I Believe God Meant Marriage for Men and Women. How Can I Support Marriage for Same-Sex Couples?"

Many people who believe in God—and fairness and justice for all—ask this question. They feel a tension between religious beliefs and democratic values that has been experienced in many different ways throughout our nation's history. That is why the framers of our Constitution established the principle of separation of church and state. That principle applies no less to the marriage issue than it does to any other.

Indeed, the answer to the apparent dilemma between religious beliefs and support for equal protections for all families lies in recognizing that marriage has a significant religious meaning for many people, but that it is also a legal contract. And it is strictly the legal—not the religious—dimension of marriage that is being debated now.

Granting marriage rights to same-sex couples would *not* require Christianity, Judaism, Islam or any other religion to perform these marriages. It would not require religious institutions to permit these ceremonies to be held on their grounds. It would not even require that religious communities discuss the issue. People of faith would remain free to make their own judgments about what makes a marriage in the eyes of God—just as they are today.

Consider, for example, the difference in how the Catholic Church and the U.S. government view couples who have divorced and remarried. Because church tenets do not sanction divorce, the second marriage is not valid in the church's view. The government, however, recognizes the marriage by extending to the remarried couple the same rights and protections as those granted to every other married couple in America. In this situation—as would be the case in marriage for same-sex couples—the church remains free to establish its own teachings on the religious dimension of marriage while the government upholds equality under law.

It should also be noted that there are a growing number of religious communities that have decided to bless same-sex unions. Among them are Reform Judaism, the Unitarian Universalist Association and the Metropolitan Community Church. The Presbyterian Church (USA) also allows ceremonies to be performed, although they are not considered the same as marriage. The Episcopal Church and United Church of Christ allow individual churches to set their own policies on same-sex unions.

"This Is Different from Interracial Marriage. Sexual Orientation Is a Choice"

"We cannot keep turning our backs on gay and lesbian Americans. I have fought too hard and too long against discrimination based on race and color not to stand up against discrimination based on sexual orientation. I've heard the reasons for opposing civil marriage for same-sex couples. Cut through the distractions, and they stink of the same fear, hatred, and intolerance I have known in racism and in bigotry."

— Rep. John Lewis, D-Ga., a leader of the black civil rights movement, writing in *The Boston Globe*, Nov. 25, 2003

Decades of research all point to the fact that sexual orientation is not a choice, and that a person's sexual orientation cannot be changed. Who one is drawn to is a fundamental aspect of who we are.

In this way, the struggle for marriage equality for same-sex couples is just as basic as the fight for interracial marriage was. It recognizes that Americans should not be coerced into false and unhappy marriages but should be free to marry the person they love—thereby building marriage on a true and stable foundation.

"Won't This Create a Free-for-All and Make the Whole Idea of Marriage Meaningless?"

Many people share this concern because opponents of gay and lesbian people have used this argument as a scare tactic. But it is not true. Granting same-sex couples the right to marry would in no way change the number of people who could enter into a marriage (or eliminate restrictions on the age or familial relationships of those who may marry). Marriage would continue to recognize the highest possible commitment that can be made between two adults, plain and simple.

Organizations That Support Same-Sex Parenting

American Academy of Pediatrics

American Academy of Family Physicians

Child Welfare League of America

National Association of Social Workers

North American Council on Adoptable Children

American Bar Association

American Psychological Association

American Psychiatric Association

American Psychoanalytic Association

"I Strongly Believe Children Need a Mother and a Father"

Many of us grew up believing that everyone needs a mother and father, regardless of whether we ourselves happened to have two parents, or two *good* parents.

But as families have grown more diverse in recent decades, and researchers have studied how these different family relationships affect children, it has become clear that the *quality* of a family's relationship is more important than the particular *structure* of families that exist today. In other words, the qualities that help children grow into good and responsible adults—learning how to learn, to have compassion for others, to contribute to society and be respectful of others and their differences—do not depend on the sexual orientation of their parents but on their parents' ability to provide a loving, stable and happy home, something no class of Americans has an exclusive hold on.

That is why research studies have consistently shown that children raised by gay and lesbian parents do just as well on all conventional measures of child development, such as academic achievement, psychological well-being and social abilities, as children raised by heterosexual parents.

That is also why the nation's leading child welfare organizations, including the American Academy of Pediatrics, the American Academy of Family Physicians and others, have issued statements that dismiss assertions that only heterosexual couples can be good parents—and declare that the focus should now be on providing greater protections for the 1 million to 9 million children being raised by gay and lesbian parents in the United States today.

"What Would Be Wrong with a Constitutional Amendment to Define Marriage as a Union of a Man and Woman?"

In more than 200 years of American history, the U.S. Constitution has been amended only 17 times since the Bill of Rights—and in each instance (except for Prohibition, which was repealed), it was to extend rights and liberties to the American people, not restrict them. For example, our Constitution was amended to end our nation's tragic history of slavery. It was also amended to guarantee people of color, young people and women the right to vote.

The amendment currently under consideration (called the Federal Marriage Amendment) would be the only one that would single out one class of Americans for discrimination by ensuring that same-sex couples would not be granted the equal protections that marriage brings to American families.

Moreover, the amendment could go even further by stripping same-sex couples of some of the more limited protections they now have, such as access to health insurance for domestic partners and their children.

Neither enshrining discrimination in our Constitution nor stripping millions of families of basic protections would serve our nation's best interest. The Constitution is supposed to protect and ensure equal treatment for *all* people. It should not be used to single out a group of people for different treatment.

TEXT OF PROPOSED FEDERAL MARRIAGE AMENDMENT:

"Marriage in the United States shall consist only of the union of a man and a woman.

Neither this [C]onstitution [n]or the constitution of any state, nor state or federal law, shall be construed to require that marital status or the legal incidents thereof be conferred upon unmarried couples or groups."

— H.J. Resolution 56, introduced by Rep. Marilyn Musgrave, R-Colo., in May 2003. It has more than 100 co-sponsors. A similar bill was introduced in the U.S. Senate in November 2003. In February 2004, President Bush said that he would support a constitutional amendment to define marriage as between only a man and a woman.

"How Could Marriage for Same-Sex Couples Possibly Be Good for the American Family—or Our Country?"

"We shouldn't just allow gay marriage. We should insist on gay marriage. We should regard it as scandalous that two people could claim to love each other and not want to sanctify their love with marriage and fidelity."

— Conservative Columnist David Brooks, writing in
The New York Times, Nov. 22, 2003.

The prospect of a significant change in our laws and customs has often caused people to worry more about dire consequences that could result than about the potential positive outcomes. In fact, precisely the same anxiety arose when some people fought to overturn the laws prohibiting marriage between people of different races in the 1950s and 1960s. (One Virginia judge even declared that "God intended to separate the races.")

But in reality, opening marriage to couples who are so willing to fight for it could only strengthen the institution for all. It would open the doors to more supporters, not opponents. And it would help keep the age-old institution alive.

As history has repeatedly proven, institutions that fail to take account of the changing needs of the population are those that grow weak; those that recognize and accommodate changing needs grow strong. For example, the U.S. military, like American colleges and universities, grew stronger after permitting African Americans and women to join its ranks.

Similarly, granting same-sex couples the right to marry would strengthen the institution of marriage by allowing it to better meet the needs of the true diversity of family structures in America today.

"Can't Same-Sex Couples Go to a Lawyer to Secure All the Rights They Need?"

Not by a long shot. When a gay or lesbian person gets seriously ill, there is no legal document that can make their partner eligible to take leave from work under the federal Family and Medical Leave Act to provide care—because that law applies only to married couples.

When gay or lesbian people grow old and in need of nursing home care, there is no legal document that can give them the right to Medicaid coverage without potentially causing their partner to be forced from their home— because the federal Medicaid law only permits married spouses to keep their home without becoming ineligible for benefits.

And when a gay or lesbian person dies, there is no legal document that can extend Social Security survivor benefits or the right to inherit a retirement plan without severe tax burdens that stem from being "unmarried" in the eyes of the law.

These are only a few examples of the critical protections that are granted through more than 1,100 federal laws that protect only married couples. In the absence of the right to marry, same-sex couples can only put in place a handful of the most basic arrangements, such as naming each other in a will or a power of attorney. And even these documents remain vulnerable to challenges in court by disgruntled family members.

"Won't This Cost Taxpayers too Much Money?"

No, it wouldn't necessarily cost much at all. In fact, treating same-sex couples as families under law could even save taxpayers money because marriage would require them to assume legal responsibility for their joint living expenses and reduce their dependence on public assistance programs, such as Medicaid, Temporary Assistance to Needy Families, Supplemental Security Income disability payments and food stamps.

Put another way, the money it would cost to extend benefits to same-sex couples could be outweighed by the money that would be saved as these families rely more fully on each other instead of state or federal government assistance.

For example, two studies conducted in 2003 by professors at the University of Massachusetts, Amherst, and the University of California, Los Angeles, found that extending domestic partner benefits to same-sex couples in California and New Jersey would save taxpayers millions of dollars a year.

Specifically, the studies projected that the California state budget would save an estimated $8.1 million to $10.6 million each year by enacting the most comprehensive domestic partner law in the nation. In New Jersey, which passed a new domestic partner law in 2004, the savings were projected to be even higher—more than $61 million each year.

(Sources: "Equal Rights, Fiscal Responsibility: The Impact of A.B. 205 on California's Budget," by M. V. Lee Badgett, Ph.D., IGLSS, Department of Economics, University of Massachusetts, and R. Bradley Sears, J.D., Williams Project, UCLA School of Law, University of California, Los Angeles, May 2003, and "Supporting Families, Saving Funds: A Fiscal Analysis of New Jersey's Domestic Partnership Act," by Badgett and Sears with Suzanne Goldberg, J.D., Rutgers School of Law-Newark, December 2003.)

"Where Can Same-Sex Couples Marry Today?"

In 2001, the Netherlands became the first country to extend marriage rights to same-sex couples. Belgium passed a similar law two years later. The laws in both of these countries, however, have strict citizenship or residency requirements that do not permit American couples to take advantage of the protections provided.

In June 2003, Ontario became the first Canadian province to grant marriage to same-sex couples, and in July 2003, British Columbia followed suit—becoming the first places that American same-sex couples could go to get married.

In November 2003, the Massachusetts Supreme Judicial Court recognized the right of same-sex couples to marry—giving the state six months to begin issuing marriage licenses to same-sex couples. It began issuing licenses May 17, 2004.

In February 2004, the city of San Francisco began issuing marriage licenses to same-sex couples after the mayor declared that the state constitution forbade him to discriminate. The issue is being addressed by California courts, and a number of other cities have either taken or are considering taking steps in the same direction.

Follow the latest developments in California, Oregon, New Jersey, New Mexico, New York and in other communities across the country on the HRC Marriage Center (www.hrc.org/marriage).

Other nations have also taken steps toward extending equal protections to all couples, though the protections they provide are more limited than marriage. Canada, Denmark, Finland, France, Germany, Iceland, Norway, Portugal and Sweden all have nationwide laws that grant same-sex partners a range of important rights, protections and obligations.

For example, in France, registered same-sex (and opposite-sex) couples can be joined in a civil "solidarity pact" that grants them the right to file joint tax returns, extend social security coverage to each other and receive the same health, employment and welfare benefits as legal spouses. It also commits the couple to assume jo- responsibility for household debts.

Other countries, including Switzerland, Scotland and the Czech Republic, also have considered legislation that would legally recognize same-sex unions.

"What Protections Other Than Marriage Are Available to Same-Sex Couples?"

At the federal level, there are no protections at all available to same-sex couples. In fact, a federal law called the "Defense of Marriage Act" says that the federal government will discriminate against same-sex couples who marry by refusing to recognize their marriages or providing them with the federal protections of marriage. Some members of Congress are trying to go even further by attempting to pass a Federal Marriage Amendment that would write discrimination against same-sex couples into the U.S. Constitution.

At the state level, only Vermont offers civil unions, which provide important state benefits but no federal protections, such as Social Security survivor benefits. There is also no guarantee that civil unions will be recognized outside Vermont. Thirty-nine states also have "defense of marriage" laws explicitly prohibiting the recognition of marriages between same-sex partners.

Domestic partner laws have been enacted in California, Connecticut, New Jersey, Hawaii and the District of Columbia. The benefits conferred by these laws vary; some offer access to family health insurance, others confer co-parenting rights. These benefits are limited to residents of the state. A family that moves out of these states immediately loses the protections.

10 Things You Can Do

Every Family Deserves Equal Protections. How Can I Help?

1. Urge your members of Congress to oppose the Federal Marriage Amendment, or any constitutional amendment to ban marriage for same-sex couples. Make a personal visit if you can. HRC's field team can help you. Or fax a message through HRC's Action Network. Visit www.hrc.org and click on "Take Action."
2. Sign the Million for Marriage petition at www.millionformarriage.org and ask 10 friends and family to do the same.

3. Talk to your friends and family members about the importance of marriage for same-sex couples and their children. Recent polls of the GLBT community show that many people have not yet talked to parents, siblings or other family members about the discrimination they face. Nothing moves the hearts and minds of potential straight allies more than hearing the stories of someone they know who is gay, lesbian, bisexual or transgender. For more information, download "Talking about Marriage Equality" from HRC's Online Action Center.
4. Write a letter to the editor of your local newspaper saying why you support marriage for same-sex couples and why a constitutional amendment against it is a bad idea.
5. Next time you hear someone say marriage is only meant for heterosexual couples, speak up. If you hear this on a radio program, call in. If you hear it on television, call or send an e-mail. If it comes up in conversation, set the record straight.
6. Host a house party to educate your friends and family about marriage equality. Invite a diverse group and inspire them to write letters to Congress and your state government at your house party. Visit www.hrc.org to receive a house party kit.
7. Meet with clergy and other opinion leaders in your community and ask them to join you in speaking out in support of marriage equality and against the Federal Marriage Amendment. Let HRC know the results. E-mail field@hrc.org.
8. Share your story about why marriage equality matters to you and send it to HRC's family project at familynet@hrc.org. Personal stories are what move hearts and minds.
9. Become a member of HRC and support our work on behalf of marriage equality. Visit www.hrc.org.
10. Register to vote and support fair-minded candidates. (Go to www.hrc.org and click on "Take Action.")

Additional National Resources

Human Rights Campaign: www.hrc.org

HRC is the nation's largest national organization working to advance equality based on sexual orientation and gender expression and identity to ensure that gay, lesbian, bisexual and transgender Americans can be open, honest and safe at home, at work and in their communities. Of particular interest to people following the marriage issue:

The Human Rights Campaign Foundation's FamilyNet

Project (www.hrc.org/familynet) offers the most comprehensive resources about GLBT families, covering marriage, parenting, aging and more. HRC's Action Center (www.hrc.org/actioncenter), offers important updates about what's happening in legislatures nationwide and the latest online grassroots advocacy tools.

Other important resources include:

American Civil Liberties Union: www.aclu.org

ACLU works in courts, legislatures and communities throughout the country to defend and preserve the individual rights and liberties guaranteed by the Constitution and laws of the United States.

Freedom to Marry Collaborative: www.freedomtomarry.org

A gay and non-gay partnership working to win marriage equality.

Children of Lesbians and Gays Everywhere (COLAGE): www.colage.org

Fosters the growth of daughters and sons of GLBT parents by providing education, support and community, advocating for their rights and rights of their families.

Dignity USA: www.dignityusa.org

Works for respect and justice for all GLBT persons in the Catholic Church and the world through education, advocacy and support.

Family Pride Coalition: www.familypride.org

A national education and civil rights organization that advances the well-being of GLBT parents and their families through mutual support, community collaboration and public understanding.

Federation of Statewide LGBT Advocacy Organizations: www.federationlgbt.org

The GLBT advocacy network of state/territory organizations committed to working with each other and with national and local groups to strengthen statewide advocacy organizing and secure full civil rights in every U.S. state and territory.

Gay & Lesbian Advocates & Defenders: www.glad.org

The GLBT legal organization that successfully brought the case that led to the civil union law in Vermont and the recognition of marriage equality in Massachusetts.

Gay & Lesbian Victory Fund: www.victoryfund.org

Committed to increasing the number of openly gay and lesbian public officials at federal, state and local levels of government.

Lambda Legal: www.lambdalegal.org

A national legal group committed to achieving full recognition of the civil rights of, and combating the discrimination against, the GLBT community and people with HIV/AIDS, through impact litigation, education and public policy work.

Log Cabin Republicans: www.lcr.org

Operates within the Republican Party for the equal rights of all Americans, including gay men and women, according to the principles of limited government, individual liberty, individual responsibility, free markets and a strong national defense.

Marriage Equality USA: www.marriageequality.org

Works to secure the freedom and the right of same-sex couples to engage in civil marriage through a program of education, media campaigns and community partnerships.

National Center for Lesbian Rights: www.nclrights.org

A national legal resource center devoted to advancing the rights and safety of lesbians and their families through a program of litigation, public policy advocacy, free legal advice and counseling and public education.

National Black Justice Coalition: www.nbjcoalition.org

An ad hoc coalition of black GLBT leaders who have come together to fight against discrimination in our communities, to build black support for marriage equality and to educate the community on the dangers of the proposal to amend the U.S. Constitution to discriminate against GLBT people.

National Gay & Lesbian Task Force: www.ngltf.org

Dedicated to building a national civil rights movement of GLBT people through the empowerment and training of state and local leaders, and research and development of national policy.

National Latina/o Lesbian, Gay, Bisexual & Transgender Organization (LLEGÓ): www.llego.org

Develops solutions to social, health and political disparities that exist due to discrimination based on ethnicity, sexual orientation and gender identity affecting the lives and well-being of Latina/o GLBT people and their families.

Parents, Families & Friends of Lesbians & Gays (PFLAG): www.pflag.org

Promotes the health and well-being of GLBT people, their families and friends, through support, education and advocacy with the intention of ending discrimination and securing equal civil rights.

Soulforce: www.soulforce.org

An interfaith movement committed to ending spiritual violence perpetuated by religious policies and teachings against GLBT people through the application of the principles of non-violence.

Universal Fellowship of Metropolitan Community Churches: www.mcchurch.org

A worldwide fellowship of Christian churches with a special outreach to the world's GLBT communities.

NO ↵

John Cornyn

In Defense of Marriage: The Amendment That Will Protect a Fundamental Institution

In 1996, three fourths of the House and Senate joined President Bill Clinton in a strong bipartisan effort to defend the traditional institution of marriage, by enacting the federal Defense of Marriage Act (DOMA). That act defined, as a matter of federal law, the institution of marriage as the union of one man and one woman—reflecting the views of the vast majority of Americans across the country. Today, as it debates a constitutional amendment to defend marriage, the Senate will revisit precisely the same question: Should the institution of marriage continue to be defined as the union of one man and one woman—as it has been defined for thousands of years?

Since the 1996 vote, two things have changed. First, activist courts have so dramatically altered the meaning of the Constitution, that traditional marriage laws are now under serious threat of being invalidated by judicial fiat nationwide—indeed, the process has already begun in numerous states across the country. Second, the broad bipartisan consensus behind marriage that was exhibited in 1996 has begun to fracture. Some who supported DOMA just a few years ago are, for partisan reasons, unwilling to defend marriage today. Although the defense of marriage should continue to be a bipartisan endeavor—and kept out of the hands of activist lawyers and judges—there is no question that both the legal and the political landscapes have changed dramatically in recent years.

Commitment to Marriage

One thing has never changed, however: Throughout our nation's history, across diverse cultures, communities, and political affiliations, Americans of all stripes have remained committed to the traditional institution of marriage. Most Americans strongly and instinctively support the following two fundamental propositions: Every human being is worthy of respect, and the traditional institution of marriage is worthy of protection. In communities across America, adults form caring relationships of all kinds, while children are raised through the heroic efforts of parents of all kinds—including single parents, foster parents, and adoptive parents. We admire, honor, and respect those relationships and those efforts.

At the same time, most Americans believe that children are best raised by their mother and father. Mankind has known no stronger human bond than that between a child and the two adults who have brought that child into the world together. For that reason, family and marriage experts have referred to the traditional institution of marriage as the "gold standard" for raising children. Social science simply confirms common sense. Social science also confirms that, when society stops privileging the traditional institution of marriage (as we have witnessed in a few European nations in recent years), the gold standard is diluted, and the ideal for raising children is threatened.

There are a number of important issues facing our nation—and the raising and nurturing of our next generation is one of them. Nearly 120 years ago, in the case of *Murphy* v. *Ramsey*, the U.S. Supreme Court unanimously concluded that "no legislation can be supposed more wholesome and necessary in the founding of a free, self-governing commonwealth" than "the idea of the family, as consisting in and springing from *the union for life of one man and one woman in the holy estate of matrimony*" (emphasis added). That union is "the sure foundation of all that is stable and noble in our civilization; the best guaranty of that reverent morality which is the source of all beneficent progress in social and political improvement." Moreover, that same Court unanimously praised efforts to shield the traditional institution of marriage from the winds of political change, by upholding a law "which endeavors to withdraw all political influence from those who are practically hostile to its attainment."

False Arguments

Today, however, the consensus behind marriage appears to be unraveling. Of course, those who no longer support traditional marriage laws do not say so outright. Instead, they resort to legalistic and procedural arguments for opposing a marriage amendment. They hope to confuse the issue in the minds of well-meaning Americans and to distract them from the importance of defending marriage, by unleashing a barrage of false arguments.

For example:

- *Why do we need a federal constitutional amendment, when we already have DOMA?*

The need for a federal constitutional amendment is simple: The traditional institution of marriage is under constitutional attack. It is now a national problem that requires a national solution. Legal experts and constitutional scholars across the political spectrum recognize and predict that the *only way* to preserve the status quo—the *only way* to preserve the traditional institution of marriage—is a constitutional amendment.

Immediately after the U.S. Supreme Court announced its decision in *Lawrence* v. *Texas* in June 2003, legal experts and commentators predicted that, under *Lawrence*, courts would begin to strike down traditional marriage laws around the country.

In *Lawrence*, the Court explicitly and unequivocally listed "marriage" as one of the "constitutional" rights that, absent a constitutional amendment, must be granted to same-sex couples and opposite-sex couples alike. Specifically, the Court stated that "our laws and tradition afford constitutional protection to personal decisions relating to *marriage*, procreation, contraception, family relationships, child rearing, and education. . . . Persons in a homosexual relationship may seek autonomy for these purposes, just as heterosexual persons do" (emphasis added). The *Lawrence* majority thus adopted the view endorsed decades ago by one of its members—Justice Ruth Bader Ginsburg. While serving as general counsel of the American Civil Liberties Union, she wrote that traditional marriage laws, such as anti-bigamy laws, are unconstitutional and must be struck down by courts.

It does not take a Supreme Court expert to understand the meaning of these words. And Supreme Court experts agree in any event. Legal scholars are a notoriously argumentative bunch. So it is particularly remarkable that the nation's most recognized constitutional experts—including several liberal legal scholars, like Laurence Tribe, Cass Sunstein, Erwin Chemerinsky, and William Eskridge—are in remarkable harmony on this issue. They predict that, like it or not, DOMA or other traditional marriage laws across the country will be struck down as unconstitutional by courts across the country.

Indeed, the process of invalidating and eradicating traditional marriage laws nationwide has already begun. Most notably, four justices of the Massachusetts Supreme Judicial Court invalidated that state's marriage law in its *Goodridge* decision issued last November, which it reaffirmed in February.

Those decisions were breathtaking, not just in their ultimate conclusion, but in their rhetoric as well. The court concluded that the "deep-seated religious, moral, and ethical convictions" that underlie traditional marriage are "no rational reason" for the institution's continued existence. It argued that traditional marriage is a "stain" on our laws that must be "eradicated." It contended that traditional marriage is "rooted in persistent prejudices" and "invidious discrimination," rather than in the best interest of children. Amazingly, it even suggested abolishing the institution of marriage outright, stating that "if the Legislature were to jettison the term 'marriage' altogether, it might well be rational and permissible." And for good measure, the court went out of its way to characterize DOMA itself as unconstitutionally discriminatory.

Without a federal constitutional amendment, activist courts, and judges will only continue striking down traditional marriage laws across the country—including DOMA itself. Lawsuits challenging traditional marriage laws are now pending in courtrooms across America—including four lawsuits in federal court.

In 2000, Nebraska voters ratified a state constitutional amendment protecting marriage in that state. Yet that state constitutional amendment has been challenged in federal district court as violating federal constitutional law. As Nebraska's attorney general, Jon Bruning, testified last March, the state expects the federal district judge to strike down its constitutional amendment. A federal lawsuit has also been filed in Florida to strike down DOMA as unconstitutional under *Lawrence*. Lawyers are similarly claiming that DOMA is unconstitutional in a pending federal bankruptcy case in Washington state. And in Utah, lawyers have filed suit arguing that traditional marriage laws, such as that state's anti-polygamy law, must be struck down under *Lawrence*. And that just covers lawsuits in federal court—in addition, dozens of suits have been filed in state courts around the country.

A representative of the Lambda Legal organization—a champion of the ongoing nationwide litigation campaign to abolish traditional marriage laws across the country—recently stated: "We won't stop until we have [same-sex] marriage nationwide." This nationwide litigation campaign also enjoys the tacit, if not explicit, support of leading Democrats—including Sens. John Kerry and Ted Kennedy, Rep. Jerrold Nadler, and former presidential candidates Howard Dean and Carol Moseley Braun. All of them have attacked DOMA as unconstitutional, and thus presumably *want* DOMA to be invalidated by the courts—and without a constitutional amendment, their wishes may very well come true. The only way to stop the lawsuits, and to ensure the protection of marriage, is a constitutional amendment.

- *Why do we need an amendment now?*

Last September, the Senate subcommittee on the Constitution, Civil Rights and Property Rights examined the threat posed to the traditional institution of marriage by the *Lawrence* decision.

Detractors of the hearing scoffed that the threat was a pure fabrication, motivated by partisan politics. But then, just two months later, the Massachusetts *Goodridge* decision, relying specifically on *Lawrence*, struck down that state's traditional marriage law—precisely as predicted at the hearing.

Detractors then scoffed that the *Goodridge* decision would not stick. They argued that the state's own constitutional amendment process would be sufficient to control their courts. But then, the Massachusetts court reaffirmed its decision in February. The court even refused to bend after the Massachusetts legislature formally approved a state constitutional amendment—an amendment that can only take effect, if ever, no earlier than 2006.

Detractors then scoffed that DOMA had not been challenged, so there was no reason to take constitutional action at the federal level. But then, lawyers began to challenge DOMA. Cases are now pending in federal courts in Florida and Washington. Additional challenges are, of course, inevitable.

The truth is that, for these detractors, there will never be a good time to protect the traditional institution of marriage—because they don't want to protect the traditional institution of marriage. The constitutional amendment to protect marriage is not a "preemptive strike" on the Constitution, as detractors allege—it's a precautionary solution. Parents take responsible precautions to protect their children. Spouses take responsible precautions to protect their marriage. Likewise, government has the responsibility to take precautions to protect the institution of marriage.

• *Why can't the states handle this? After all, isn't marriage traditionally a state issue?*

This argument borders on the fraudulent. There is nothing that a state can do to fully protect itself against federal courts hostile to its laws except a federal constitutional amendment. Nebraska has already done everything it can, on its own, to defend marriage—up to and including a state constitutional amendment. Yet its amendment has already been challenged in federal court, where it is expected to be struck down. As state and local officials across the country have repeatedly urged, when it comes to defending marriage, the real threat to states' rights is judicial activism—not Congress, and certainly not the democratic process.

Moreover, the Constitution cannot be amended without the consent of three-fourths of the state legislatures. States can protect marriage against judicial activism—but only if Congress provides them the opportunity to consider a federal constitutional amendment protecting marriage.

• *Isn't our Constitution too sacred for such a political issue as defending marriage?*

No one is suggesting that the Constitution should be amended lightly. But the defense of marriage should not be ridiculed as a political issue. Nor should we disparage the most democratic process established under our Constitution by our Founding Fathers.

Our Founding Fathers specifically insisted on including an amendment process in the Constitution, because they humbly believed that no man-made document could ever be perfect. The constitutional amendment process was deliberatively considered and wisely crafted, and we have no reason to fear it.

We have amended the Constitution no fewer than 27 times—most recently in 1992 to regulate Congressional pay increases. The sky will not fall if Americans exercise their democratic rights to amend it again. Surely, the protection of marriage is at least as important to our nation as the regulation of Congressional pay, the specific manner in which we coin our money, or the countless other matters that can be found in our nation's charter.

Moreover, there is a robust tradition of constitutional amendments to reverse constitutional decisions by the courts with which the American people disagree—including the 11th, 14th, 16th, 19th, 24th, and 26th Amendments.

Opponents of the marriage amendment apparently have no objection to the courts amending the Constitution. Yet the power to amend the Constitution belongs to the American people, through the democratic process—not the courts. The courts alter the Constitution—under the guise of interpretation—far more often than the people have. Because of *Lawrence*, it is inevitable that the Constitution will be amended on the issue of marriage—the only question is how, and by whom. Legal scholars across the political spectrum agree that a constitutional amendment by the people is the only way to fully protect marriage against the courts.

- *Why would we ever want to write discrimination into the Constitution? Why would we ever want to roll back the Bill of Rights?*

This argument is offensive, pernicious—and revealing.

Marriage is not about discrimination—it is about children. It is offensive to characterize the vast majorities of Americans who support traditional marriage—individuals like Reverend Ray Hammond of the Bethel African Methodist Episcopal Church in Boston, Reverend Richard Richardson of the St. Paul African Methodist Episcopal Church in Boston, and Pastor Daniel de Leon, Sr., of Alianza de Ministerios Evangélicos Nacionales (AMEN) and Templo Calvario in Santa Ana, California—as bigots. It is offensive to characterize the laws, precedents, and customs of all fifty states as discriminatory. And it is offensive to slander the 85 senators who voted for DOMA as hateful.

Moreover, it is *precisely because* some activists believe that traditional marriage is about discrimination, and not about children, that they believe that all traditional marriage laws are unconstitutional and therefore must be abolished by the courts. These activists leave the American people with no middle ground. They accuse others of writing discrimination into the Constitution—yet they are the ones writing the American people out of our constitutional democracy.

Just last week, representatives of Sens. John Kerry and John Edwards said that the marriage amendment would "roll back rights." If you believe that traditional marriage is only about discrimination and about violating the rights of adults—as Sens. Kerry and Edwards apparently believe—then you have no choice but to oppose all traditional marriage laws. Any other position is incoherent at best—and deceptive at worst.

Marriage Protection

So the issue has been joined—precisely as it was in 1996. Despite typical Washington Beltway tricks to overcomplicate and confuse matters, the question remains a simple one: Should marriage, defined as the union of one man and one woman, be protected against judicial activism and the will of legal and political elites? If you believe that the answer is yes—as vast majorities of Americans do—then you have no legal option but to support a federal constitutional amendment protecting marriage.

The American people believe that every human being deserves respect, and the traditional institution of marriage deserves protection. As members of Congress continue to debate this issue, we should also remember what else the American people deserve: honesty.

The Honorable John Cornyn is a United States. senator from Texas and chairman of the Senate Judiciary subcommittee on the Constitution, Civil Rights and Property Rights. He is a former state-supreme-court justice and state attorney general. Since September 2003, he has chaired three hearings to examine the legal threat to the traditional institution of marriage.

POSTSCRIPT

Should Same-Sex Marriage Be Legal?

While the United States considers a constitutional amendment that would prohibit same-sex marriage, several European countries have given legal status to same-sex couples, including Denmark, France, Germany, the Netherlands, Sweden, Iceland, Belgium, and Norway. In 2003, Canada removed language from its laws that confined marriage to a man and a woman.

In the United States, attitudes remain divided. According to a Gallup poll conducted in July 2004, 62 percent of Americans believed that same-sex marriages should not be recognized. However, only 48 percent of those polled supported a constitutional amendment that would define marriage as being between a man and a woman.

Support is stronger for civil unions—a concept intended as a legal equivalent to marriage, in all but name. 54 percent of Americans support civil unions. One state, Vermont, has enacted legislation permitting civil unions, permitting spousal rights to same-sex couples within that state only. Four other states—California, Hawaii, Maine, and New Jersey—have laws that provide spousal-like rights to unmarried couples. While some regard civil unions as an acceptable compromise to this divisive debate, others regard such arrangements with memories of the "separate but equal" days of segregation.

Opponents of same-sex marriage frequently rely on biblical references to condemn the practice. They cite passages that describe marriage as between man and woman (1 Cor 7:2), and others that denounce homosexuality in general (Lev 18:22; Cor 6:9; 1 Tim 1:9–11). Yet, if the Bible is to be relied upon for enacting marital legislation, other biblical passages may give legislators pause, such as those that endorse polygamy (Gen 29:17–28; 2 Sam 3:2–5) and a man's right to have concubines (2 Sam 5:13; 1 Kings 11:3; 2 Chron 11:21), or those that prohibit divorce (Deut 22:19; Mark 10:9) or mandate female virginity in order for a marriage to be valid (if a wife is not a virgin, she can be executed, the Bible says) (Deut 22:13–21).

Biblical references and implications notwithstanding, the Human Rights Campaign says that fully recognized same-sex marriages are essential to ensuring the same legal protections and benefits that are available to heterosexual married couples. Do you agree? Do you believe civil unions are a just substitution? Why or why not?

Cornyn argues that while the efforts of single, foster, and adoptive parents are heroic, the relationship between a child and his or her biological mother and father are the "gold standard." Do you believe that single-parent families, adoptive families, and gay and lesbian families cause that gold standard to be "diluted," as Cornyn states?

How do you view the argument to amend the U.S. Constitution? What potential benefits or difficulties do you foresee resulting from this action? Finally, what do you believe is the *purpose* of marriage? Is marriage primarily about love? Rights? Children and family? Monogamy? Other considerations? Do you regard it as primarily a religious institution or a legal institution? Is there any *single, predominant* purpose of marriage, or are there many purposes worthy of consideration?

Suggested Readings

R.H. Bork, "Stop Courts from Imposing Gay Marriage," *Wall Street Journal* (August 7, 2001).

M. Bronski, "Over the Rainbow," *Boston Phoenix* (August 1–August 7, 2003).

S. Feldhan and D. Glass, "Why Is Reality TV Marriage OK When Gay Marriage Is Not?" *Atlanta Journal-Constitution* (December 2003).

R. Goldstein, "The Radical Case for Gay Marriage: Why Progressives Must Join this Fight," *The Village Voice* (September 3–9, 2003).

J. Jacoby, "The Timeless Meaning of Marriage," *Boston Globe* (November 2003).

B. Knickerbocker, "A Drubbing for Same Sex Marriage," *Christian Science Monitor* (November 2004).

K. Mantilla, "Gay Marriage: Destroying the Family to Save the Children," *Off Our Backs* (vol. 34, no. 5–6, May–June 2004).

J. Rauch, "Leave Gay Marriage to the States," *The Wall Street Journal* (July 27, 2001).

ISSUE 19

Should Prostitution Be Legal?

YES: James Bovard, from "Safeguard Public Health: Legalize Contractual Sex," *Insight on the News* (February 27, 1995)

NO: Anastasia Volkonsky, from "Legalizing the 'Profession' Would Sanction the Abuse," *Insight on the News* (February 27, 1995)

ISSUE SUMMARY

YES: Author James Bovard asserts that legalizing sex work would help stem the spread of AIDS and free up the police to focus on controlling violent crime.

NO: Anastasia Volkonsky, founding director of PROMISE, an organization dedicated to combating sexual exploitation, maintains that decriminalizing prostitution would only cause more social harm, particularly to women.

Prior to the Civil War, prostitution was tolerated in the United States to a limited extent, even though it was socially frowned upon. Few states had specific laws making prostitution a crime. After the Civil War, however, some states passed laws to segregate and license prostitutes operating in "red light districts." In 1910 Congress tried to eliminate the importation of young women from Asia and South America for purposes of prostitution by passing the Mann Act, which prohibited any male from accompanying a female across a state border for the purpose of prostitution, debauchery, or any other immoral purpose. During World War I concern for the morals and health of U.S. soldiers led the U.S. Surgeon General to close down all houses of prostitution near military training camps, especially the famous whorehouses of the French Quarter and Storyville, New Orleans. By 1925 every state had enacted an antiprostitution law.

The effectiveness and the social and economic costs of criminalizing prostitution have been continually questioned. The sexual revolution and the women's movement have added new controversies to the debate. Some advocates of women's rights and equality condemn prostitution as male exploitation of women and their bodies. Others champion the rights of women to control their own bodies, including the right to exchange sexual favors for money. This new attitude is reflected in the term *sex worker*, which has recently begun to replace *prostitute*. New social problems confuse the issue further: the growing concern over drug abuse, the risk of human immunodeficiency virus (HIV) infection among street prostitutes, and the exploitation of teenage girls and boys.

European countries have taken different approaches to prostitution. In Germany, where prostitution is legal and regulated, there are efficient and convenient drive-in motels—often owned and run by women—where customers can arrange a pleasant, safe encounter with a sex worker. Italy and France, long-time bastions of regulated prostitution, have abandoned this approach because of organized efforts of women to abolish it and evidence that other approaches to prostitution could reduce the spread of venereal disease more effectively than legalization and regulation. Since 1959 solicitation on the streets of Great Britain has been a crime, but prostitution per se is no longer against the law. The British authorities have concluded that prostitution cannot be controlled simply by making it a crime. However, they do have laws prohibiting sex workers from advertising their services by posting their business cards in public phone booths. In the Soviet Union in the 1920s, the government provided job training, employment, housing, and health care for former prostitutes. In the 1930s the government's attitude changed to intolerance when it became apparent that working women were turning to prostitution as a way of achieving a higher standard of living than they would otherwise be able to maintain. After the collapse of the Soviet Union, sex work in Russia and abroad became an acceptable career choice for many young women.

In the following selections, James Bovard advocates legalizing sex work to help stem the spread of AIDS and to allow police to focus their time and energy on violent crimes. Anastasia Volkonsky argues that decriminalizing sex work would hurt society in general and allow males to continue exploiting women, particularly those who are poor and vulnerable.

YES ↰

James Bovard

Safeguard Public Health: Legalize Contractual Sex

The call to legalize prostitution once again is becoming a hot issue. Columnists have been complaining about the conviction of Heidi Fleiss, the "Holly wood madam," saying it is unfair that the law punishes her but not her clients. San Francisco has appointed a task force to analyze the issue of legalizing prostitution. (A similar task force in Atlanta recommended legalization in 1986, but the city has not changed its policies.)

As more people fear the spread of AIDS, the legalization of prostitution offers one of the easiest means of limiting the spread of the disease and of improving the quality of law enforcement in this country.

Prostitution long has been illegal in all but one state. Unfortunately, laws against it often bring out the worst among the nation's law-enforcement agencies. Since neither prostitutes nor their customers routinely run to the police to complain about the other's conduct, police rely on trickery and deceit to arrest people.

In 1983, for example, police in Albuquerque, N.M., placed a classified advertisement in a local paper for men to work as paid escorts—and then arrested 50 men who responded for violating laws against prostitution. In 1985, Honolulu police paid private citizens to pick up prostitutes in their cars, have sex with them and then drive them to nearby police cars for arrest. (One convicted prostitute's lawyer complained: "You can now serve your community by fornicating. Once the word gets out there will be no shortage of volunteers.") In San Francisco, the police have wired rooms in the city's leading hotels to make videotapes of prostitutes servicing their customers. But given the minimal control over the videotaping operation, there was little to stop local police from watching and videotaping other hotel guests in bed.

Many prostitution-related entrapment operations make doubtful contributions to preserving public safety. In 1985, eight Fairfax County, Va., police officers rented two $88-a-night Holiday Inn rooms, purchased an ample supply of liquor and then phoned across the Potomac River to Washington to hire a professional stripper for a bachelor party. The stripper came, stripped and was busted for indecent exposure. She faced fines of up to $1,000 and 12 months in jail. Fairfax County police justified the sting operation by claiming it was necessary to fight prostitution. But the department had made only 11 arrests on prostitution charges in the previous year—all with similar sting operations.

In 1992, police in Des Moines, Wash., hired a convicted rapist to have sex with masseuses. The local police explained that they hired the felon after plainclothes police officers could not persuade women at the local Body Care Center to have intercourse. Martin Pratt, police chief in the Seattle suburb, claimed that the ex-rapist was uniquely qualified for the job and, when asked why the police instructed the felon to consummate the acts with the alleged prostitutes, Pratt explained that stopping short "wouldn't have been appropriate."

A New York sting operation [in 1994] indirectly could have helped out the New York Mets: Two San Diego Padres baseball players were arrested after speaking to a female undercover officer. A Seattle journalist who also was busted described the police procedure to *Newsday:* "He said that he was stuck in traffic when he discovered that a miniskirted woman in a low-cut blouse was causing the jam, approaching the cars that were stopped. 'She came up to the windows, kind of swaggering,' he said. He said that she offered him sex, he made a suggestive reply, and the next thing he knew he was surrounded by police officers who dragged him out of his car and arrested him."

Many police appear to prefer chasing naked women than pursuing dangerous felons. As Lt. Bill Young of the Las Vegas Metro Police told Canada's *Vancouver Sun,* "You get up in a penthouse at Caesar's Palace with six naked women frolicking in the room and then say: 'Hey, baby, you're busted!' That's fun." (Las Vegas arrests between 300 to 400 prostitutes a month.) In August 1993, Charles County, Md., police were embarrassed by reports that an undercover officer visiting a strip joint had had intercourse while receiving a "personal lap dance."

In some cities, laws against prostitution are transforming local police officers into de facto car thieves. Female officers masquerade as prostitutes; when a customer stops to negotiate, other police rush out and confiscate the person's car under local asset-forfeiture laws. Such programs are operating in Detroit, Washington, New York and Portland, Ore. The female officers who masquerade as prostitutes are, in some ways, worse than the prostitutes—since, at least, the hookers will exchange services for payment, while the police simply intend to shake down would-be customers.

Shortly after the Washington police began their car-grabbing program in 1992, one driver sped off after a plainclothes officer tried to force his way into the car after the driver spoke to an undercover female officer. One officer's foot was slightly injured, and police fired six shots into the rear of the car. The police volley could have killed two or three people—but apparently the Washington police consider the possibility of killing citizens a small price to pay for slightly and temporarily decreasing the rate of prostitution in one selected neighborhood.

The same tired, failed antiprostitution tactics tend to be repeated ad nauseam around the country. Aurora, Colo., recently announced plans to buy newspaper ads showing pictures of accused johns. The plan hit a rough spot when the *Denver Post* refused to publish the ads, choosing not to be an arm of the criminal-justice system. One Aurora councilman told local radio host

Mike Rosen that the city wanted to publish the pictures of the accused (and not wait until after convictions) because some of them might be found not guilty "because of some legal technicality."

In recent years, the Washington police force has tried one trick after another to suppress prostitution—including passing out tens of thousands of tickets to drivers for making right turns onto selected streets known to be venues of solicitation. (Didn't they see the tiny print on the street sign saying that right turns are illegal between 5 p.m. and 2 a.m.?) Yet, at the same time, the murder rate in Washington has skyrocketed and the city's arrest and conviction rates for murders have fallen by more than 50 percent.

The futile fight against prostitution is a major drain on local lawenforcement resources. A study published in the *Hastings Law Journal* in 1987 is perhaps the most reliable estimate of the cost to major cities. Author Julie Pearl observed: "This study focuses on sixteen of the nation's largest cities, in which only 28 percent of reported violent crimes result in arrest. On average, police in these cities made as many arrests for prostitution as for all violent offenses.

Last year, police in Boston, Cleveland, and Houston arrested twice as many people for prostitution as they did for all homicides, rapes, robberies, and assaults combined, while perpetrators evaded arrest for 90 percent of these violent crimes. Cleveland officers spent eighteen hours—the equivalent of two workdays—on prostitution duty for every violent offense failing to yield an arrest." The average cost per bust was almost $2,000 and "the average big-city police department spent 213 man-hours a day enforcing prostitution laws." Pearl estimated that 16 large American cities spent more than $120 million to suppress prostitution in 1985. In 1993, one Los Angeles official estimated that prostitution enforcement was costing the city more than $100 million a year.

Locking up prostitutes and their customers is especially irrational at a time when more than 35 states are under court orders to reduce prison overcrowding. Gerald Arenberg, executive director of the National Association of the Chiefs of Police, has come out in favor of legalizing prostitution. Dennis Martin, president of the same association, declared that prostitution law enforcement is "much too time-consuming, and police forces are short-staffed." Maryland Judge Darryl Russell observed: "We have to explore other alternatives to solving this problem because this eats up a lot of manpower of the police. We're just putting out brush fires while the forest is blazing." National surveys have shown that 94 percent of citizens believe that police do not respond quickly enough to calls for help, and the endless pursuit of prostitution is one factor that slows down many police departments from responding to other crimes.

Another good reason for reforming prostitution laws is to safeguard public health: Regulated prostitutes tend to be cleaner prostitutes. HIV-infection rates tend to be stratospheric among the nation's streetwalkers. In Newark, 57 percent of prostitutes were found to be HIV positive, according to a *Congressional Quarterly* report. In New York City, 35 percent of prostitutes were HIV-positive; in Washington, almost half.

In contrast, brothels, which are legal in 12 rural Nevada counties, tend to be comparative paragons of public safety. The University of California at Berkeley School of Public Health studied the health of legal Nevada brothel workers compared with that of jailed Nevada streetwalkers. None of the brothel workers had AIDS, while 6 percent of the unregulated streetwalkers did. Brothel owners had a strong incentive to police the health of their employees, since they could face liability if an infection were passed to a customer.

Prostitution is legal in several countries in Western Europe. In Hamburg, Germany, which some believe has a model program of legalized prostitution, streetwalkers are sanctioned in certain well-defined areas and prostitutes must undergo frequent health checks. Women with contagious diseases are strictly prohibited from plying their trade. (While some consider Amsterdam a model for legalization, the system there actually has serious problems. A spokesman for the association of Dutch brothels recently told the Associated Press: "The prostitutes these days are not so professional any more. In the past, prostitutes had more skills and they offered better services. Most of them now work only one or two evenings per week, and that's not enough time for them to become good.")

Bans on prostitution actually generate public disorder—streetwalkers, police chases, pervasive disrespect for the law and condoms littering lawns. As long as people have both money and sexual frustration, some will continue paying others to gratify their desires. The issue is not whether prostitution is immoral, but whether police suppression of prostitution will make society a safer place. The ultimate question to ask about a crackdown on prostitution is: How many murders are occurring while police are chasing after people who only want to spend a few bucks for pleasure?

In 1858, San Francisco Police Chief Martin Burke complained: "It is impossible to suppress prostitution altogether, yet it can, and ought to be regulated so as to limit the injury done to society, as much as possible." Vices are not crimes. Despite centuries of attempts to suppress prostitution, the profession continues to flourish. Simply because prostitution may be immoral is no reason for police to waste their time in a futile effort to suppress the oldest profession.

NO ↩

Anastasia Volkonsky

Legalizing the "Profession" Would Sanction the Abuse

Prostitution commonly is referred to as "the world's oldest profession." It's an emblematic statement about the status of women, for whom being sexually available and submissive to men is the oldest form of survival.

As the "world's oldest," prostitution is presented as an accepted fact of history, something that will always be with us that we cannot eradicate. As a "profession," selling access to one's body is being promoted as a viable choice for women. In an era in which the human-rights movement is taking on some of history's most deeply rooted oppressions and an era in which women have made unprecedented strides in politics and the professions, this soft-selling of prostitution is especially intolerable.

Calls for legalization and decriminalization of prostitution put forth by civil libertarians are not forward-thinking reforms. They represent acceptance and normalization of the traffic in human beings. Moreover, the civil-libertarian portrayal of the prostitute as a sexually free, consenting adult hides the vast network of traffickers, organized-crime syndicates, pimps, procurers and brothel keepers, as well as the customer demand that ultimately controls the trade.

In studies replicated in major cities throughout the United States, the conditions of this "profession" are revealed to be extreme sexual, physical and psychological abuse. Approximately 70 percent of prostitutes are raped repeatedly by their customers—an average of 31 times per year, according to a study in a 1993 issue of the *Cardozo Women's Law Journal*. In addition, 65 percent are physically assaulted repeatedly by customers and more by pimps. A majority (65 percent and higher) are drug addicts. Increasingly, prostituted women are HIV positive. Survivors testify to severe violence, torture and attempted murders. The mortality rate for prostitutes, according to Justice Department statistics from 1982, is 40 times the national average.

What can be said of a "profession" with such a job description? How can it be said that women freely choose sexual assault, harassment, abuse and the risk of death as a profession? Such a term might be appealing for women who are trapped in the life, as a last-ditch effort to regain some self-respect and identify with the promises of excitement and glamor that may have lured them into prostitution in the first place. A substantial portion of street-walkers are homeless or living below the poverty line. Even most women who work in outcall or escort services have no control over their income because they are at the mercy of a pimp or pusher. Most will leave prostitution without savings.

Prostitution is not a profession selected from among other options by today's career women. It comes as no surprise that the ranks of prostitutes both in the United States and globally are filled with society's most vulnerable members, those least able to resist recruitment. They are those most displaced and disadvantaged in the job market: women, especially the poor; the working class; racial and ethnic minorities; mothers with young children to support; battered women fleeing abuse; refugees; and illegal immigrants. Women are brought to the United States from Asia and Eastern Europe for prostitution. In a foreign country, with no contacts or language skills and fearing arrest or deportation, they are at the mercy of pimps and crime syndicates.

Most tellingly, the largest group of recruits to prostitution are children. The average age of entry into prostitution in the United States is approximately 14, sociologists Mimi Silbert and Ayala Pines found in a study performed for the Delancey Foundation in San Francisco. More than 65 percent of these child prostitutes are runaways. Most have experienced a major trauma: incest, domestic violence, rape or parental abandonment. At an age widely considered too young to handle activities such as voting, drinking alcohol, driving or holding down a job, these children survive by selling their bodies to strangers. These formative years will leave them with deep scars—should they survive to adulthood.

⌘

Sensing this contradiction between the reality of prostitution and the rhetoric of sexual freedom and consensual crime, some proposals to decriminalize prostitution attempt to draw a distinction between "forced" prostitution and "free" prostitution. A June 1993 *Time* article about the international sex industry notes that "faced with the difficulty of sorting out which women are prostitutes by choice and which are coerced, many officials shrug off the problem," implying that when one enters prostitution, it is a free choice. The distinction between force and freedom ends in assigning blame to an already victimized woman for "choosing" to accept prostitution in her circumstances.

"People take acceptance of the money as her consent to be violated," says Susan Hunter, executive director of the Council for Prostitution Alternatives, a Portland, Ore.-based social-service agency that has helped hundreds of women from around the country recover from the effects of prostitution. She likens prostituted women to battered women. When battered women live with their batterer or repeatedly go back to the batterer, we do not take this as a legal consent to battering. A woman's acceptance of money in prostitution should not be taken as her agreement to prostitution. She may take the money because she must survive, because it is the only recompense she will get for the harm that has been done to her and because she has been socialized to believe that this is her role in life. Just as battered women's actions now are understood in light of the effects of trauma and battered woman syndrome, prostituted women suffer psychologically in the aftermath of repeated physical and sexual assaults.

To make an informed choice about prostitution, says Hunter, women need to recover their safety, sobriety and self-esteem and learn about their options. The women in her program leave prostitution, she asserts, "not because we offer them high salaries, but because we offer them hope. . . . Women are not voluntarily returning to prostitution."

Proponents of a "consensual crime" approach hold that the dangers associated with prostitution are a result of its illegality. Legal prostitution will be safe, clean and professional, they argue; the related crimes will disappear.

Yet wherever there is regulated prostitution, it is matched by a flourishing black market. Despite the fact that prostitution is legal in 12 Nevada counties, prostitutes continue to work illegally in casinos to avoid the isolation and control of the legal brothels. Even the legal brothels maintain a business link with the illegal pimping circuit by paying a finder's fee to pimps for bringing in new women.

Ironically, legalization, which frequently is touted as an alternative to spending money on police vice squads, creates its own set of regulations to be monitored. To get prostitutes and pimps to comply with licensing rules, the penalties must be heightened and policing increased—adding to law-enforcement costs.

Behind the facade of a regulated industry, brothel prostitutes in Nevada are captive in conditions analogous to slavery. Women often are procured for the brothels from other areas by pimps who dump them at the house in order to collect the referral fee. Women report working in shifts commonly as long as 12 hours, even when ill, menstruating or pregnant, with no right to refuse a customer who has requested them or to refuse the sexual act for which he has paid. The dozen or so prostitutes I interviewed said they are expected to pay the brothel room and board and a percentage of their earnings—sometimes up to 50 percent. They also must pay for mandatory extras such as medical exams, assigned clothing and fines incurred for breaking house rules. And, contrary to the common claim that the brothel will protect women from the dangerous, crazy clients on the streets, rapes and assaults by customers are covered up by the management.

Local ordinances of questionable constitutionality restrict the women's activities even outside the brothel. They may be confined to certain sections of town and permitted out only on certain days, according to Barbara Hobson, author of *Uneasy Virtue*. Ordinances require that brothels must be located in uninhabited areas at least five miles from any city, town, mobile-home park or residential area. Physically isolated in remote areas, their behavior monitored by brothel managers, without ties to the community and with little money or resources of their own, the Nevada prostitutes often are virtual prisoners. Local legal codes describe the women as "inmates."

Merely decriminalizing prostitution would not remove its stigma and liberate women in the trade. Rather, the fiction that prostitution is freely chosen would become encoded into the law's approach to prostitution. Decriminalization would render prostitution an invisible crime without a name. "The exchange of money [in prostitution] somehow makes the crime of rape invisible" to society, says Hunter.

Amy Fries, director of the National Organization For Women's International Women's Rights Task Force, speaks from experience in studying and combating the sex trade both internationally and in the Washington area. Decriminalization, she says, does not address the market forces at work in prostitution: "[Prostitution] is based on supply and demand. As the demand goes way up, [the pimps] have to meet it with a supply by bringing in more girls."

Ultimately, changing the laws will benefit the customer, not the prostitute. Legalization advocates identify the arrest as the most obvious example of the abuse of prostitutes. But, surprisingly, former prostitutes and prostitutes' advocates say the threat of jail is not a top concern. Considering the absence of any other refuge or shelter, jail provides a temporary safe haven, at the very least providing a bunk, a square meal and a brief respite from johns, pimps and drugs. This is not to make light of abuses of state and police power or the seriousness of jail—the fact that for many women jail is an improvement speaks volumes about their lives on the streets.

It is the customers who have the most to lose from arrest, who fear jail, the stigma of the arrest record and the loss of their anonymity. The argument that prostitution laws invade the privacy of consenting adults is geared toward protecting customers. Prostitutes, working on the streets or in brothels controlled by pimps, have little to no privacy. Furthermore, decriminalization of prostitution is a gateway to decriminalizing pandering, pimping and patronizing—together, decriminalizing many forms of sexual and economic exploitation of women. A 1986 proposal advocated by the New York Bar Association included repeal of such associated laws and the lowering of the age of consent for "voluntary" prostitution. Despite the assertion that prostitutes actively support decriminalization, many women who have escaped prostitution testify that their pimps coerced them into signing such petitions.

Of the many interests contributing to the power of the sex industry—the pimps, the panderers and the patrons—the acts of individual prostitutes are the least influential. Yet, unfortunately, there are incentives for law enforcement to target prostitutes for arrest, rather than aggressively enforcing laws against pimps, johns and traffickers. It is quicker and less costly to round up the women than to pursue pimps and traffickers in elaborate sting operations. The prostitutes are relatively powerless to fight arrest; it is the pimps and johns who can afford private attorneys. And, sadly, it is easier to get a public outcry and convictions against prostitutes, who are marginalized women, than against the wealthier males who are the majority of pimps and johns.

Prostitution is big business. Right now, economics provide an incentive for procuring and pimping women. In all the debates about prostitution, the factor most ignored is the demand. But it is the customers—who have jobs, money, status in the community, clean arrest records and anonymity—who have the most to lose. New legal reforms are beginning to recognize that. An increasing number of communities across the country, from Portland to Baltimore, are adopting car-seizure laws, which allow police to impound the automobiles of those who drive around soliciting prostitutes. This approach recognizes that johns degrade not only women who are prostitutes, but also others by assuming that any females in a given area are for sale. Other towns have instituted, legally or as community efforts, measures designed to publicize and shame would-be johns by publishing their names or pictures and stepping up arrests.

Globally, a pending U.N. Convention Against All Forms of Sexual Exploitation would address the modern forms of prostitution with mechanisms that target pimps and johns and that hold governments accountable for their policies.

Hunter supports the use of civil as well as criminal sanctions against johns, modeled after sexual harassment lawsuits. "People will change their behavior because of economics," she points out, using recent changes in governmental and corporate policy toward sexual harassment as an example of how the fear of lawsuits and financial loss can create social change.

At the heart of the matter, prostitution is buying the right to use a woman's body. The "profession" of prostitution means bearing the infliction of repeated, unwanted sexual acts in order to keep one's "job." It is forced sex as a condition of employment, the very definition of rape and sexual harassment. Cecilie Hoigard and Liv Finstad, who authored the 1992 book *Backstreets,* chronicling 15 years of research on prostitution survivors, stress that it is not any individual act, but the buildup of sexual and emotional violation as a daily occurrence, that determines the trauma of prostitution.

Cleaning up the surrounding conditions won't mask the ugliness of a trade in human beings.

POSTSCRIPT

Should Prostitution Be Legal?

There are a number of ways in which lawmakers could deal with the "world's oldest profession":

- Outlaw prostitution entirely. Enforcing such a law would run the risk of draining a community's resources.
- Outlaw some behavior associated with prostitution, such as street solicitation or loitering, but this can raise difficult distinctions. When, for instance, does casual flirtation and overt come-ons to a stranger become illegal solicitation?
- Legalize sex work and control it by licensing "body work therapists," requiring regular medical checkups, and setting aside specific areas where sex workers can ply their trade.
- Decriminalize all sexual activities between consenting adults, whether or not money changes hands. Advertising and solicitation could be limited by social propriety, and minors could be protected against recruitment and exploitation by the laws regulating child abuse and age of consent. (Note that age of consent laws vary greatly state to state, from 14 in Hawaii to 18 in several states, with additional restrictions that depend on the age differences between partners.)

What is your opinion on this issue now that you have thought about the reasons proposed by Bovard and Volkonsky? What alternative solutions not mentioned here would you propose?

Suggested Readings

N. J. Almodovar, "Prostitution and the Criminal Justice System," *The Truth Seeker* (Summer 1990).

S. Bell, *Reading, Writing, and Rewriting the Prostitute Body* (Indiana University Press, 1994).

V. Bullough and B. Bullough, *Women and Prostitution: A Social History* (Prometheus Press, 1987).

H. Moody and A. Carmen, *Working Women: The Subterranean World of Street Prostitution* (Little, Brown, 1995).

L. Primoratz, "What's Wrong With Prostitution?" *Philosophy* (1993).

L. Shrage, "Prostitution and the Case for Decriminalization," *Dissent* (Spring 1996).

ISSUE 20

Should Schools Pay Damages for Student-on-Student Sexual Harassment?

YES: Bernice Sandler, from "Without Lawsuits, Schools Will Tolerate Serious Misbehavior That Hurts All Students," *Insight on the News* (August 9, 1999)

NO: Sarah J. McCarthy, from "Don't Bankrupt Our School Systems With the Quick-Fix Solution of Punitive Damages," *Insight on the News* (August 9, 1999)

ISSUE SUMMARY

YES: Bernice Sandler, a senior scholar at the National Association for Women in Education, maintains that schools should pay damages for student-on-student sexual harassment. She cites several cases in which school authorities ignored blatant and pervasive sexual harassment of students by other students until the parents of the harassed students forced action by filing lawsuits seeking compensation for damages.

NO: Author Sarah J. McCarthy objects to schools paying damages for student-on-student sexual harassment, stating that Congress and lawmakers often jump to legislation as a quick-fix solution. She asserts that new laws authorizing the filing of lawsuits would empty taxpayers' pockets, bankrupt school districts, and lead to centralized thought control, an Americanized version of Chairman Mao's cultural revolution in China.

In the fall of 1991 stories of sexual harassment suddenly became very hot news in newspaper headlines, popular magazines, and television news broadcasts. The issue emerged with law professor Anita Hill's charge that Judge Clarence Thomas had sexually harassed her while he served as chair of the Equal Employment Opportunity Commission. The allegation came close to derailing Thomas's nomination to the United States Supreme Court. In the sports world, three members of the New England Patriots football team (and the team itself) were fined nearly $50,000 for lewd gestures and remarks to *Boston Herald* reporter Lisa Olson in their locker room.

Sexual harassment charges were also leveled at America's political leaders.The majority leader of Florida's House of Representatives lost his position for allowing an "offensive, degrading and inappropriate" atmosphere of sexual innuendo amongst his staff. The 18-year career of U.S. senator Brock Adams, a recognized leader on women's issues, ended with charges that he had sexually harassed and even raped eight women who worked with him. U.S. senator Robert Packwood also faced attack, as a congressional ethics committee investigated charges that he had regularly sexually harassed female colleagues. As a result, Packwood was forced to resign from the Senate in September 1995.

In late 1991 and throughout most of 1992, the infamous Tailhook Association convention of Navy and Marine Corps pilots made national news. After interviewing more than 1,500 officers and civilians, investigators implicated more than 70 officers in sexual harassment and assaults against at least 26 women and several men. Charged with participating in or covering up the affair, the officers were referred for disciplinary review and possible dismissal from the service. Top admirals were charged with tacitly approving this activity for years, and major promotions for two admirals were lost because of questions of sexual harassment.

In 1993 the American Association of University Women Education Foundation polled 1,632 teenagers in grades 8 to 11 in 79 schools on sexual harassment. They found that 76 percent of the girls and 56 percent of the boys reported being on the receiving end of unwanted sexual comments or looks. Two-thirds of the girls and 42 percent of the boys said they were touched, grabbed, or pinched in a sexual way. Some researchers questioned whether or not all the behaviors included in the survey should be legitimately considered sexual harassment. Christina Hoff Sommers at Clark University in Massachusetts stated, "They're committed to finding gender bias everywhere, behind every door, in every hallway, and they find it. What this is going to invite is we're going to begin litigating high-school flirtation. In order to find gender bias against girls, they had to ask questions so broad that they invited complaints from boys." Countering this criticism, Maryka Biaggio at Pacific University in Oregon defended the broad, inclusive nature of the questions. "We know that people in general tend to underreport or minimize occurrences of sexual harassment, so in order to get a good sense of an individual's experience, you have to put forth a fairly inclusive definition."

Billie Wright Dziech, coauthor of *The Lecherous Professor: Sexual Harassment on Campus* (Beacon Press, 1984) and an opponent of student-professor sexual relationships, says, "We need clear definitions. We need to recognize that they are not hard and fast. They will differ for different individuals. This is slippery terminology." Dziech suggests distinguishing between what is considered normal flirting and "horseplay between men and women," a "sexual hassle," and "sexual harassment." But even that distinction will differ with different people and with the same person in different situations.

In the following selections, Bernice Sandler asserts that schools should pay damages for student-on-student sexual harassment as a way to curb serious student misbehavior. Sarah J. McCarthy counters that punishment should be focused on the wrongdoers, not the school district as a whole.

YES ↵

Bernice Sandler

Without Lawsuits, Schools Will Tolerate Serious Misbehavior That Hurts All Students

In May the Supreme Court decided a case involving a fifth-grade girl who continually had been asked for sexual intercourse by a classmate who sat next to her. The court ruled in *Davis vs. Monroe County Board of Education* that schools could be required to pay punitive damages for sexual harassment of students by other students. For five months the boy continually tried to touch his classmate's breasts and genitals, saying he wanted to have sex with her. He rubbed up against her in the classroom and hallways of the elementary school they attended. Although the girl's mother complained to the school after each incident, the school would not even reassign the girl's seat. The girl's grades dropped, and her father found a suicide note. Finally, when it became clear that the school would do nothing, the mother filed a criminal complaint against the boy, who pleaded guilty.

The court confirmed that student-to-student harassment is prohibited by Title IX, the law that prohibits sex discrimination in schools receiving federal dollars. Schools must respond to sexual harassment by students or face the possible loss of federal funds and/or a lawsuit and damages.

Many people are not aware of the extent to which student-to-student sexual harassment is common in many educational institutions. Growing up always has been a difficult time but, in recent years, for whatever reasons, behaviors even among kindergartners and throughout high schools and colleges are worse than ever, and bad behavior occurs more often. Many more youngsters are the victims of behaviors which are far more aggressive, obscene, more insistent and invasive than the behaviors many of us remember when we were in our teens or younger.

There are verbal slurs—8-year-olds are called "whores," "sluts" and worse. There is a lot of sexual touching and grabbing. One 6-year-old girl continually was told by fourth-grade boys on the school bus to have oral sex with her father (in far less polite terms); a 13-year-old girl faced a daily gauntlet of 15 to 20 boys, who would stare at her large breasts and together call her a "cow" and follow her around as they "mooed" at her; one boy had a girl put her hand down his pants; some boys and girls continually are asked for sexual activity; and there are children of all ages who have had their crotches grabbed. There are schools in which boys and girls will not wear pants with elastic waists because other children pull them down, often along with underwear. And crotch-grabbing is not a rarity in many schools. One teenager in a magnet school in one the richest counties in the country said that she "hated it when the guys would grab your genitals as you walk up the stairs. You never know who it is because the stairways are crowded."

These behaviors are a blight in all kinds of schools, public and private, and in the best and worst neighborhoods. School buses, outdoor playgrounds, stairways and cafeterias often are hotbeds of sexual harassment, since supervision either is lax or missing.

At one prestigious, small, liberal-arts college, two first-year male students worked in pairs: One would block a female from going forward while the other grabbed her crotch from behind. When the two men were brought before the dean, they said they could not understand what the fuss was about, stating, "But everybody does this in high school!"

If you have children or access to them, don't ask if these things happen to them or if they do any of these things. Instead, tell the child something such as, "Boys [or children] used to do a lot of teasing when I was in school. What kinds of things do they do in your school?" You may be surprised at what they tell you.

Sexual harassment is not simply boys-will-be-boys behavior. It is a form of sexual bullying, using sexuality as a form of power to dominate or terrorize another person. Just as we no longer allow bosses or coworkers to put pressure on employees for sex, whether it is a pat on the rear or a breast being grabbed, schools should not allow their students to suffer the same behaviors that are illegal in the workplace and often rise to the level of sexual abuse. The Supreme Court has ruled that such behaviors no longer can be tolerated in our schools.

In a study of nearly 2,000 students in Texas public schools in grades seven through 12, nearly six in 10 girls reported that they were harassed every other day, and a large number reported they were harassed on average once a week. Boys were responsible for 70 percent of the incidents reported by all children. When the results for boys and girls were combined, 89 percent of the students experienced some form of sexual harassment. Few reported it to their parents or teachers. Of those who reported an incident to a teacher, two-thirds said that nothing happened to the harasser.

The impact of sexual harassment is substantial. Children exposed to such severe and pervasive student-to-student behaviors often find it difficult to concentrate on learning. They may avoid certain areas of the school or cut classes if they are older. Grades may drop. Many of the severely harassed children become depressed. Some children, especially girls, even contemplate suicide. Boys are more likely to turn their anger out toward others, often in violent behavior. Harassment is upsetting—even more so when children ask for help and their teachers, counselors and principals ignore their pleas to stop such behaviors. Kids need to be able to trust the adults in their world.

Students of all ages have a right to feel safe in school, safe from sexual intrusions, safe from unwanted and inappropriate behaviors. Teachers often don't intervene when bad behaviors occur, erroneously believing that kids need to "learn" to handle this kind of behavior "on their own." Why should we expect children to be able to handle abusive behaviors which even adults find challenging?

Understandably, some people are worried that as a result of the Supreme Court's decision, schools will be sued for the slightest infractions such as the usual teasing between boys and girls. We remember the 6-year-old North Carolina boy who kissed a girl and then was suspended for the day—a case of overkill, to be sure. This is not what the Supreme Court has in mind. Its concern is about behavior that is "severe, pervasive and objectively offensive," behaviors that interfere with students' ability to learn or receive the benefits of their education. The court added that "damages are not available for simple acts and teasing and name-calling among school children, however, even when these comments target differences in gender." Additionally, for a school to be liable for money damages, it must have been "deliberately indifferent to known acts of student-to-student sexual harassment and the harasser is under the school's disciplinary authority."

Good schools don't need the specter of a lawsuit to respond quickly and adequately to sexual-harassment complaints, but not all schools are good.

Will some schools be sued when children sexually harass each other? Most schools never will face a lawsuit because they will act to stop sexual harassment when it occurs. Most schools will initiate some sort of training for teachers and students addressing appropriate and inappropriate behavior in school and ways teachers and other employees (such as bus drivers and cafeteria workers) should respond.

What we have learned from the workplace, colleges and schools is that the vast majority of people do not want to sue. Also, with few exceptions, almost all complaints can be handled informally either by various kinds of intervention by school personnel or by helping the student who is harassed to deal with the harassment. For example, in some elementary schools children have written letters to the children who have harassed them, asking that the behavior stop. The letter then is delivered and read to the harassing child by an adult.

A high tolerance for sexual bullying certainly can lead to lawsuits. Certainly, some schools will be sued, however—not because a student sexually harasses another but only because a school has allowed the harassment to continue and ignored children who were hurting and needed help.

Schools that handle sexual harassment like other behavior problems are not likely to be sued at all. For example, schools rarely, if ever, are sued because students hit each other—teachers usually intervene to stop that kind of behavior. Similarly, schools in which adults intervene to stop sexually harassing behaviors are not likely to be sued.

Will it be hard to distinguish between "simple teasing" and "severe, pervasive and offensive behavior?" It may not be hard most of the time, but even if the behavior does not rise to the legal level, as in the case of a one-time sexual joke, a single comment about another teenager's breast or penis or an act of mean-spirited name-calling, schools should not look the other way. They need to teach students how to grow up respecting other people and that some behaviors simply are not appropriate in school. Ignoring any kind of bad behavior implies that either the behavior is acceptable or that the teacher is weak and unable to deal with it. Ignoring such behaviors almost always leads to more behaviors of the same kind.

As a result of the Supreme Court's decision, most schools will take more seriously all kinds of bad behaviors, including other forms of harassment and bullying, and school personnel will have to learn how to intervene to stop them. It is not unrealistic to teach children that hurtful behaviors are not tolerated in schools or to encourage children to respect each other. Of course, good schools have been doing that for a long time. Now others can catch up.

Remember the old nursery rhyme, "Georgie Porgie, pudding and pie, kissed the girls and made them cry"? Georgie Porgie is in big trouble these days. He is recognized as a sexual harasser because he made girls miserable to the point of tears. Georgie Porgie had better watch out.

NO ↩

Don't Bankrupt Our School Systems With the Quick-Fix Solution of Punitive Damages

Now that Congress has inserted the ghost of Anita Hill into every adult male-female interaction, the Supreme Court has decided it's time to go after the kids. Though school officials say that student sexual harassment is a delicate issue, given the raging hormones that cause teens to perform acts of super-human stupidity, the court is blurring the line between adolescent bungling and criminal behavior by making school districts liable for punitive damages if anyone crosses the line. Parents and teachers have been trying to stop teen-age stupidity since the beginning of time, but Justice Sandra Day O'Connor and four other members of the divided Supreme Court think they have found the cure—punitive damages, which is their usual standby and the legal profession's Johnny-One-Note-Magic-Bullet-Cure for everything: Sue for $2 million and call me in the morning.

In May the court ruled in *Davis vs. Monroe County Board of Education* that a fifth-grade girl could proceed with a lawsuit seeking damages against her school district for ignoring sexual battery by a fifth-grade boy who had been found guilty in juvenile court. The court ruled that the school district must have been informed of the harassment and indifferent to it before they could be liable. (By contrast, private businesses are liable even if they have no idea that harassment is occurring in the workplace under the legal standard that they "should have known" about it.) Certainly schools have an obligation to protect students from criminal activity. But it's not clear why, unlike physical assault or bullying among same-sex students, unwanted sexual advances should be treated as a federal civil-rights matter rather than a question of school discipline.

Following classmates in the halls, riding past their houses, boys chasing girls and pony-tail pulling once were signs of teenagers in love. The smooth operators in my high school used to snap off girls' plastic pop-it beads and try for slam-dunks by tossing them down the girls' blouses. Today, any male peacock strutting his stuff by cruising past a girl's house risks being turned in as a stalker.

Back in the days before we knew these guys were stalkers and harassers, we thought their escapades were funny—even romantic. We used to thrill to

From Sarah J. McCarthy, "Don't Bankrupt Our School Systems With the Quick-Fix Solution of Punitive Damages," *Insight on the News* (August 9, 1999). Copyright © 1999 by News World Communications, Inc. Reprinted by permission of *Insight on the News*.

songs like "Born to Run," about "dying on Highway 9 in an everlasting kiss," and "Leader of the Pack." These are real American memories like the things that happened in the movie *American Graffiti* —memories we never could have had in a place like China, where government killjoys at the time were outlawing public hand-holding. Who would've thought it could've happened here?

The best-kept secret in America is that being sexually harassed can be one of the peak experiences of our lives. When I was 16, my boyfriend Harry and his gang, the Mad Mechanics, who had low-slung cars that made a lot of noise, had heard on the school grapevine that I was going to a party at the home of a guy in my neighborhood. The Mad Mechanics drove by the party house in a male-dominance display much like the chest-pounding behaviors they inherited from the great apes. The neighborhood guys turned out the lights and hid under the furniture at the first roar of the engines, but in reality, no one was too scared. The party guys used the darkened house as a chance to kiss the girls while the Mad Mechanics roared by.

Sexual harassment? Maybe, but it was the only time I felt like Natalie Wood in *West Side Story* in the middle of a rumble between the Jets and the Sharks. For Harry, who went on to fly hundreds of bombing missions in Vietnam, I'm glad he could go onto adulthood with his career untarnished by his teenage capers. Harry and I broke up a few months later when, upon arriving at our school picnic, I discovered he'd been riding the Tilt-A-Whirl with some girl he'd probably convinced she was the star of *West Side Story.*

In his *Newsday* column "Lunatic Feminists Arise on the Right," Robert Reno, an ardent supporter of the Supreme Court's ruling to protect girls from sexist language and hostile environments, rails against what he calls the new conservative "female TV gas bags"—women he says who are "fetching, wall-to-wall right wing and blond to their roots, like Laura Ingraham and Monica Crowley," women he designates as "silly," "lunatic," "dumb" and "deeply snide." (You have to wonder what would happen to American womanhood without chivalrous defenders such as Reno.)

But these women, bad as they are, are just "irrelevant distractions" compared with the objects of Reno's real wrath—Boston-based attorney and Independent Women's Forum, or IWF, member Jennifer Braceras, who wrote a *Wall Street Journal* article saying that for kids "a kiss on the cheek, a sexually suggestive remark, the persistent pursuit of a romantic relationship with someone who is not interested, even unwanted sexual touching, all may be normal parts of growing up when the individuals are peers."

"Who raised this woman?" Reno howls. "You'd never hear Phyllis Schlafly come out for kissing or touching in the classroom. She'd cane the whole lot of them."

"What a mouthful," he roars on, surmising that the IWF is a group of right-wing female renegades defending the rights of third-grade harassers. Her article, says Reno, "savages the Supreme Court decision that prohibits boorish little schoolboys from making repulsive pests of themselves by being sexually obnoxious to the girls in their class." The court decision "seems the least we can do for the girls who are going to grow up to run this country," he wails, "the way they have run more socially advanced nations." Reno glosses over the fact that these future presidents someday will have to compete with male candidates who have been toughened in wars such as in Vietnam and the Persian Gulf.

What Reno and other punitive-damage aficionados miss is that those of us who argue against lawsuits as the magic bullet for undesirable behaviors are not in favor of harassment but are concerned about the collateral damage caused by these penalties. The threat of financial annihilation via lawsuits is not the best environment in which freedom can thrive. Schools that could have their budget wiped out by a single child-against-child or employee-against-employee lawsuit would be pushed to go overboard in trying to control speech or behavior that could appear actionable to a creative trial lawyer.

"This is already the normal state of affairs in the workplace," says columnist John Leo. "Sexual-harassment law has given employers a powerful incentive to act in a defensive manner, warning workers against comments, gestures, office chitchat about the latest joke on a sitcom." Many schools already ban hand-holding, passing romantic notes and chasing members of the opposite sex during recess. One teacher's manual says that a child's comment of "You look nice" could be sexual harassment, depending on the "tone of voice" and "who else is around." ("You look nice" as sexual harassment! So much for the Land of the Free.) "Next year, kids will be suspended for behavior nobody's ever been suspended for," said Bruce Hunter of the American Association of School Administrators.

Beyond concerns about emptying taxpayers' pockets and bankrupting school districts, we have to wonder what effect this centralized behavior control will have on the kids. Squelching spontaneous behaviors such as teasing, joking and chasing members of the opposite sex is an outrageous thing to do to an entire nation of schoolchildren because a few have gone out of bounds. Instead, third-graders who create a hostile environment can be punished with suspensions without involving the entire school population of the United States in an Americanized version of Mao's Cultural Revolution.

The nonchalance with which Congress passes sexual-harassment laws, combined with an impassioned preference for overblown fines, is frightening. Laws are passed with a casualness about the definitions of the acts they are criminalizing and with drifting definitions such as the broadening of sexual assault to mean any unwanted touching. How can someone be sure a touch or a kiss is unwanted before it occurs?

In an article, "Could You Be the Next Monica?" by Nurith Aizenman in the July 1999 *New Woman* magazine, GOP former representative Susan Molinari of New York says she didn't "set out to make Monica Lewinsky's life miserable" when she pushed through ground-breaking sexual-assault legislation five years ago. Molinari only wanted to give a woman accusing a man of sexual assault the chance to bolster her case by showing that he also had attacked other women. Sensible enough—but the law defined sexual assault so broadly (essentially any attempt at unwanted touching) that it allowed lawyers in the Paula Jones case to probe President Clinton's past for other violations. That investigation, in turn, set an unexpected precedent: Now any woman who's had a consensual relationship with a man accused of harassment could find herself subpoenaed just as Lewinsky was. Molinari was astonished to learn that her law was behind Lewinsky's interrogation. "The law was supposed to target sexual assault," Molinari says.

And consider, if you can, the import of this revealing admission by Democratic former representative Patricia Schroeder of Colorado: "It was so much more fun to legislate than oversee. You could find many reasons to put more regulations on. We didn't feel accountable as much as we should have to make sure regulations were being applied reasonably."

It would be an oversimplification to claim that most school harassment is like the madcap adventures in *American Graffiti* or that high-school harassers are harmless. There are serious cases of harassment that need to be remedied.

In Pittsburgh, fraternity brothers at a university held "Pig Parties," inviting the ugliest dates they could find. The guy with the ugliest date would win. The girls soon realized why they were invited and would flee the party in tears. In cases such as these, the punishment should be placed at the door of the offending students rather than with the school or with the student body at large in the form of higher tuition payments to cover lawsuit expenses.

How can justice be achieved for victims of pig parties and sexual assault without trampling freedoms for everyone else? Penalties that focus punishments on the wrongdoers and minimize them for others would be the optimal solution. Current penalties do exactly the opposite. It would be a good start for the Supreme Court and American law schools to explore alternatives to threats of financial annihilation as a wholesale method of behavioral control. At least when the Mad Mechanics showed up, they had more than one tool in their box.

POSTSCRIPT

Should Schools Pay Damages for Student-on-Student Sexual Harassment?

The high cost of fighting sexual harassment often makes suffering in silence more appealing for women. "Many strong, successful professional women have made conscious decisions to ignore sexual harassment in their offices," maintains feminist Naomi Wolf, "because they know that as soon as they complained, there would be 50 other [women] waiting to take their jobs." Camille Paglia, author of *Sexual Personae: Art and Decadence from Nefertiti to Emily Dickenson* (Yale University Press, 1990), counters, "Women allow themselves to become victims when they don't take responsibility. If getting the guy to stop means putting a heel into his crotch, then just do it. Don't complain about it 10 years later." Yet, as Deborah Tannen, author of *You Just Don't Understand: Women and Men in Conversation* (Morrow, 1990), asserts, "Women have learned that confrontation is to be avoided and they don't have the verbal tools to attack this kind of problem head-on as a man would."

This issue continues to return time and again to the American conscience in television series episodes, such as *Law & Order, Ally McBeal, The Practice,* and *Sex and the City* because American society is still trying to deal with the conflicting issues posed by a recently awakened awareness of sex harassment. The issue is having a chilling effect on everyday male-female relations, on dating and courtship, in the workplace, on college campuses, and even in elementary and high schools. Anthropologist Lionel Tiger predicts a "return to a kind of Victorian period" in which men will be reluctant to try developing a relationship with any woman who initially seems aloof.

The Tailhook incident, which made headlines around the world, seems to have had some global influence. The Belgian and Dutch governments have launched public information campaigns on sexual harassment, and the Spanish and French governments have recently passed laws making sexual harassment a crime. The European Commission, the administrative arm of the 12-nation European Community, has issued a code defining sexual harassment.

Sexual harassment is fast becoming a global issue that will continue to have reverberations in the ways women and men relate to each other for years to come. The selections by Sandler and McCarthy are particularly challenging because they focus attention on examples of sexual harassment of young children by their peers in elementary, intermediate, and high schools. To what extent should schools and school administrators be held responsible for monitoring and working to eliminate student-on-student sexual harassment and punishing it when it occurs? When these questions are answered, American parents and other adults will need to find the most effective ways to educate youth about the differences between healthy flirtation and unwanted and unacceptable sexual harassment.

Suggested Readings

J. B. Brandenburg, *Confronting Sexual Harassment: What Schools and Colleges Can Do* (Teachers College Press, 1997).

L. Greenhouse, "Court Rules Schools Can Be Liable for Unchecked Sexual Harassment," *The New York Times* (May 25, 1999).

L. Greenhouse, "In Coming Term, High Court Will Add to Sex Harassment Rulings," *The New York Times* (September 30, 1998).

L. Greenhouse, "School Districts Are Given a Shield in Sex Harassment," *The New York Times* (June 23, 1998).

L. Greenhouse, "Schools May Be Sued for Student-On-Student Harassment, Divided Court Rules," *The New York Times* (May 24, 1999).

J. Larkin, *Sexual Harassment: High School Girls Speak Out* (Second Story Press, 1994).

L. McMillen, "Misleading Studies Seen on Sexual Harassment," *Chronicle of Higher Education* (September 27, 1996).

R. J. Shoop and D. Edwards, *How to Stop Sexual Harassment in Our Schools: A Handbook and Curriculum Guide for Administrators and Teachers* (Allyn & Bacon, 1994).

Contributors to This Volume

EDITOR

WILLIAM J. TAVERNER, M.A., is the editor of the *American Journal of Sexuality Education* and is director of The Center for Family Life Education, the acclaimed education department of Planned Parenthood of Greater Northern New Jersey. He is also an adjunct professor of human sexuality at Fairleigh Dickinson University, and trains sexuality educators nation-wide on a wide range of human sexuality topics. Taverner has served as editor or coeditor for five editions of *Taking Sides: Clashing Views on Controversial Issues in Human Sexuality,* and as an associate editor for the *International Encyclopedia of Sexuality.* He has coauthored several popular sexuality education manuals, including *All Together Now: Teaching about Contraception and Safer Sex; Making Sense of Abstinence, Educating about Abor-tion; Positive Images: Teaching Abstinence, Contraception, and Sexual Health;* and *Streetwise to Sex-Wise: Sexuality Education for High-Risk Youth.* He is also the author of *Sexuality and Substance Abuse.* Taverner earned a master's degree in human sexuality from New York University. He can be reached at billtaverner@earthlink.net.

STAFF

Larry Loeppke	Managing Editor
Jill Peter	Senior Developmental Editor
Nichole Altman	Developmental Editor
Beth Kundert	Production Manager
Jane Mohr	Project Manager
Tara McDermott	Design Coordinator
Bonnie Coakley	Editorial Assistant
Lori Church	Permissions

AUTHORS

DIANE D. ARONSON is executive director of RESOLVE: The National Infertility Association, a nonprofit consumer advocacy and patient support organization in Somerville, Massachusetts.

JOHN BANCROFT is the director of the Kinsey Institute, and was trained in medicine at the University of Cambridge and served in Oxford University's psychiatry department.

JAMES BOVARD is the author of several books, including *Shakedown: How Government Screws You from A to Z* and *Lost Rights: The Destruction of American Liberty.*

STEPHEN G. BREYER is an associate justice of the United States Supreme Court, appointed by President Bill Clinton in 1994.

JANE E. BRODY is the personal health columnist for the *New York Times,* and author of several best-selling books on health and nutrition.

GEORGE W. BUSH is the 43rd president of the United States and was formerly the governor of Texas.

RHONDA CHITTENDEN is a regional educator for Planned Parenthood of Greater Iowa, and is a regular columnist for *Sexing the Political,* an online journal of Gen X feminists on sexuality.

JOHN CORNYN, U.S. Senator from Texas, chairs the Senate Judiciary subcommittee on the Constitution, Civil Rights and Property Rights. He is a former state supreme court justice and state attorney general.

ELIZABETH CRAMER is an author who writes about the abuse of women.

EDWIN J. DELATTRE is a professor of philosophy and education, and dean emeritus for the School of Education at Boston University.

DON FEDER is a nationally syndicated author and former opinion writer for the *Boston Herald.* He is the author of *Who's Afraid of the Religious Right?* and *A Jewish Conservative Looks at Pagan America.*

NORA GELPERIN is the director of training and education for the Network for Family Life Education at Rutgers University and has presented workshops at local, state, and national conferences.

SALLY GUTTMACHER is an associate professor in the department of health studies at New York University. Her research interests include policy and prevention of chronic and infectious diseases, poverty and public health, and women's health.

TERENCE M. HINES is a professor of psychology at Pace University in Pleasantville, New York.

PAUL JOANNIDES is a research psychoanalyst. He is the author of *The Guide To Getting It On!* which has won four awards and has been translated into 14 languages.

IVER JUSTER is a family physician and medical informaticist involved in design, execution, and analysis of studies of clinical information tools designed to empower physicians and patients in making evidence-based health care decisions.

ANTHONY M. KENNEDY is an associate justice of the United States Supreme Court, appointed by President Ronald Reagan in 1988.

JUDITH KLEINFELD is a professor of psychology at the University of Alaska at Fairbanks and author of *Gender Tales: Tensions in the Schools.*

LORETTA M. KOPELMAN is a professor and chair of the department of medical humanities in the School of Medicine at East Carolina University. She is coeditor of *Children and Health Care: Moral and Social Issues.*

JUDITH LEVINE is the author of *Harmful to Minors: The Perils of Protecting Children from Sex,* which won the 2002 Los Angeles Times Book Prize.

MERRILL MATTHEWS, JR., is a medical ethicist and a vice president of domestic policy at the National Center for Policy Analysis, a nonpartisan, nonprofit research institute in Dallas, Texas.

SARAH J. McCARTHY is the coauthor, with Ralph R. Reiland, of *Mom & Pop vs. the Dreambusters: The Small Business Revolt Against Big Government* and often writes on lawsuit abuse.

MARSHALL MILLER is the co-founder of the Alternatives to Marriage Project (www.unmarried.org) and co-author of *Unmarried to Each Other: The Essential Guide to Living Together as an Unmarried Couple.*

DOUGLAS F. MUNCH is founder and president of DFM, Ltd., a strategic management consulting firm specializing in the health care industry. He has more than 20 years of senior health care experience encompassing pharmaceuticals, medical products, and diagnostics.

P. MASILA MUTISYA is an assistant professor in the department of curriculum and instruction in the School of Education at Fayetteville State University in North Carolina. He teaches courses on foundations of education, human development, and multicultural education.

BEVERLY R. NEWMAN teaches at Ivy Tech College in Indianapolis, Indiana, counsels survivors of sexual abuse, and has testified before the Indiana Legislature about children's issues.

DAVID POPENOE is co-director of the National Marriage Project and a professor of sociology at Rutgers University. He is the author of several books, including *Life Without Father: Compelling New Evidence that Fatherhood and Marriage are Indispensable for the Good of Children and Society.*

DAVID L. RIEGEL is the author of *Understanding Loved Boys and Boylovers* and *Beyond Hysteria: Boy Erotica on the Internet.* He has also published articles in *Archives of Sexual Behavior,* the *Journal of Psychology and Human Sexuality* and *Sexuality and Culture.*

STEPHANIE ANN SANDERS is an associate director and associate scientist for the Kinsey Institute for Research in Sex, Gender, and Reproduction at Indiana University.

BERNICE SANDLER, a senior scholar at the National Association for Women in Education, consults with educational institutions on gender, including sexual harassment.

DAVID SATCHER was the 16th Surgeon General of the United States, serving two presidential administrations from 1998 to 2002.

LAURA SCHLESSINGER is the host of the radio talk show "The Dr. Laura Schlessinger Show." She is also the author of *The Ten Commandments: The Significance of God's Laws in Everyday Life.*

GARY SCHUBACH is a sex educator, lecturer, writer, and an associate professor for the Institute for the Advanced Study of Human Sexuality in San Francisco. He moderates the Web site www.DoctorG.com.

DORIAN SOLOT is the executive director of the Alternatives to Marriage Project (www.unmarried.org) and co-author of *Unmarried to Each Other: The Essential Guide to Living Together as an Unmarried Couple.*

NADINE STROSSEN is a professor in the School of Law at New York University in New York City and a general counsel for the American Civil Liberties Union.

CAROLYN SUSMAN is a reporter for the *Palm Beach Post.*

PATRICIA TAYLOR is the author of *Expanded Orgasm*; producer of the video, *Expand Her Orgasm Tonight*; and moderator of www.ExpandedLovemaking.com. She also teaches and has a private practice in Sausalito, California.

ANASTASIA VOLKONSKY is a writer and researcher based in San Francisco, California, and a founding director of PROMISE, an organization dedicated to combating sexual exploitation.

JANICE WEINMAN is the executive director of the American Association of University Women.

BARBARA DAFOE WHITEHEAD is co-director of the National Marriage Project, and author of numerous publications, including *Why There Are No Good Men Left: The Romantic Plight of the New Single Woman.*

Index